SCHOLARS' GUIDE
TO WASHINGTON, D.C.
FOR
RUSSIAN/SOVIET STUDIES

СЦРАВОЧНИК ДЛЯ
ИССЛЕДОВАТЕЛЬСКОЙ РАБОТЫ
ПО ВОПРОСАМ
РОССИИ И СОВЕТСКОГО СОЮЗА
В ВАШИНГТОНЕ

THE WILSON CENTER

W

KENNAN INSTITUTE
FOR
ADVANCED
RUSSIAN STUDIES

SCHOLARS' GUIDE

TO WASHINGTON, D.C.

FOR

RUSSIAN/SOVIET STUDIES

THE BALTIC STATES, BYELORUSSIA, CENTRAL ASIA, MOLDAVIA,
RUSSIA, TRANSCAUCASIA, THE UKRAINE

STEVEN A. GRANT

Second Edition Revised by

BRADFORD P. JOHNSON
MARK H. TEETER

Series Editor
ZDENĚK V. DAVID

KENNAN INSTITUTE
FOR ADVANCED RUSSIAN STUDIES

OF THE

WOODROW WILSON INTERNATIONAL CENTER FOR SCHOLARS

SMITHSONIAN INSTITUTION PRESS
WASHINGTON, D.C.
1983

Scholars' Guide to Washington, D.C., no. 1, revised

The original publication of this work was assisted by a grant from the Morris and Gwendolyn Cafritz Foundation, Washington, D.C.

Library of Congress Cataloging in Publication Data

Grant, Steven A.
Scholar's guide to Washington, D.C., for Russian/Soviet studies.

(Scholar's guide to Washington, D.C.; no. 1)
Bibliography: p.
Includes indexes.

1. Soviet Union—Library resources—Washington (D.C.) I. Johnson, Bradford P. II. Teeter, Mark H. III. Title. IV. Series
Z2491.G67 1983 [DK17]   026.947   83-600231
ISBN 0-87474-490-3
ISBN 0-87474-489-X (pbk.)

Designed by Elizabeth Dixon

CONTENTS

FOREWORD

This guide is sponsored by the Woodrow Wilson International Center for Scholars, the nation's "living memorial" to its twenty-eighth president. It is the first revised edition of the first volume in a reference series describing the scholarly resources of the Washington, D.C., area. Begun in 1977, these guides were inspired, in part, by the accumulated lore about scholarly materials that was developing among fellows in the Wilson Center.

The Soviet Union has emerged since World War II as the area of most vital concern to the national interest of the United States. The *Guide* covers not only general Soviet affairs and the (Great) Russian society but also the other national components of the Soviet Union that have attracted increasing attention in the last decade, including the Baltic states, Byelorussia, Central Asia, Moldavia, Transcaucasia, and the Ukraine. The Wilson Center has long supported research on the Soviet Union and its components, particularly through its Kennan Institute for Advanced Russian Studies, established in 1975.

Taken as a whole, the series of guides exemplifies the Wilson Center's "switchboard function" of facilitating connections between the vast resources of the nation's capital and those who have scholarly or practical needs—or simple curiosity. These guides—like the center's annual fellowship program—are designed to serve the national and international scholarly communities. At least 20,000 visiting scholars come each year to Washington from elsewhere in America and abroad to pursue serious research. The guides are designed to inform scholars, many of them outside the major university research centers in the United States, about possibilities for engaging in research on particular topics in Washington. The guides cover the metropolitan area of Washington, but they are not merely of local importance. In the city's libraries, archives, and data banks, in its universities and research centers, and especially in the federal agencies and international organizations concentrated here, Washington holds resources of national—indeed of worldwide—significance.

The series of guides is under the general editorship of Wilson Center Librarian Zdeněk V. David, who has devised the basic format. Elizabeth Dixon is largely responsible for the design and publication arrangements. The original preparation of this particular *Guide* owed much to S. Frederick Starr, the energetic first secretary of the Kennan Institute. The author, Steven A. Grant, is now senior Soviet analyst, Office of Research, U.S. Information Agency. The late Sergius Yakobson, former chief of the Slavic and Central European Division, Library of Congress (1951–71), was consultant. The revision of the text for the second edition was undertaken by Bradford P. Johnson and Mark H. Teeter, associates of the Kennan Institute, with the advice of Steven A. Grant. Wilson Center staff members providing advice and assistance were Prosser Gifford, John Glad, Abbott Gleason, and George Liston Seay.

The center has now prepared guides for scholars in the fields of Latin American and Caribbean (1979), East Asian (1979), African (1980), Central and East European (1980), Middle Eastern (1981), South Asian (1981), and Southeast Asian (1983) studies, as well as a guide covering film and video collections (1980). All were published by the Smithsonian Institution Press (P.O. Box 1579, Washington, D.C. 20013). Forthcoming volumes will survey resources in the Washington area for scholars interested in Northwest and Southwest Europe. A guide to audio resources (musical and other sound recordings) is also under preparation.

Washington, D.C.   James H. Billington, Director
October 26, 1982   Woodrow Wilson International Center for Scholars

INTRODUCTION

Purpose. This volume is intended to serve as a basic reference aid for scholars interested in utilizing the diverse and often unique resources of the nation's capital for research in the field of Russian/Soviet studies. Although the *Guide* is intended for the serious researcher, those with a more casual interest in Russia/USSR will also find much of value within its pages.

Washington is unsurpassed as a resource for research on American policy toward the Soviet Union. The scholars, diplomats, technocrats, bureaucrats, journalists, politicians, and political activists who populate the nation's capital all play a role in affecting U.S. policy toward the USSR. Additionally, various interest groups vie for the U.S. Government's attention and a multitude of consultants compete for its research grants. The vehicles for this purpose are often the organizations described in this *Guide.* Washington, however, is more than just a political arena. Its massive library collections not only contain some of the largest holdings in Russian and other languages of the Soviet Union but also boast specialized collections of maps, sound recordings, and films, as well as those on modern medicine and agriculture. The city also contains one of the largest and most comprehensive museum systems in the country: the Smithsonian Institution. In Washington a scholar can study modern Soviet economic policy or Byzantine political philosophy, Caucasian rugs or medieval Armenian manuscripts. Here history is both made and preserved. The goal of this *Guide* is to indicate the research possibilities of Washington, D.C., in the field of Russian/ Soviet studies by exploring and describing the many collections and organizations available in this capital city.

Scope. The geographic scope of this *Guide* embraces the present-day Soviet Union of Soviet Socialist Republics, formerly known as the Russian Empire. Thus it covers not only (Great) Russia and its peoples but also the Baltic states (Estonia, Latvia, Lithuania), Byelorussia, Central Asia (Kazakhstan, Kirghizstan, Tadzhikistan, Tukmenistan, Uzbekistan), Moldavia (i.e., the Moldavian Soviet Socialist Republic), Transcaucasia (Armenia, Azerbaidzhan, Georgia), and the Ukraine. The terms "Russia/Russian/Russianist," used in this volume, should be understood to refer to the Russian Empire and to its successor, the Soviet Union, a political entity that includes numerous non-Russian nationalities in addition to the Russians. Conversely, only a few Polish and Finnish resources are noted in the *Guide* and those concern the pre-1917 period, because these peoples are now primarily outside the USSR. The Washington, D.C., area resources for research on Poland and Finland receive a systematic coverage in this series respectively in the *Guide* for Central and East European studies (1980) and in the forthcoming *Guide* for Northwest European studies. Because of the close historical ties of the Russian Empire and the Soviet Union to neighboring areas the reader's attention is called also to the guides for East Asian (1979), Middle Eastern (1981), South Asian (1981), and Southeast Asian (1983) studies.

The Guide's subject coverage concentrates on the disciplines of the social sciences and humanities traditionally considered under the rubric Russian/Soviet-area studies, although the fields of science and technology have been included where relevant.

Contents. More than 500 collections, organizations, and agencies have been surveyed as part of the preparation for this volume. Although it provides such basic directory information as names, addresses, telephone numbers, and details about individual collections, the *Guide* is primarily a descriptive and evaluative survey of Washington's research resources. The main body of the work is divided into two parts. The first part examines Washington-area resource *collections*: libraries; archives and manuscripts depositories; art, map, music, and film collections; and data banks. Each entry describes the size, content, and organizational format of a particular collection's Russian/Soviet holdings and quantitatively evaluates subject/nationality strengths and unique materials within those holdings. The second part is comprised of Washington-based *organizations*, public and private, which deal with the Soviet Union and/or its nationality components and are potential sources of information or assistance to researchers. Included are research centers and information offices; academic programs at local universities; U.S., Soviet, international and other government agencies; private academic, professional, and cultural associations; cultural-exchange organizations; churches and religious bodies; and publishing media and groups. Each entry describes the organization's functions bearing on the USSR and/or its nationality components; delineates its pertinent research activities, materials, and products (published and unpublished, classified and unclassified); and discusses the restrictions on scholarly access to unpublished and classified materials. Brief introductions highlight special features of each section and provide related supplemental information. For example, these introductory paragraphs explain the library survey techniques (section A), and Freedom of Information Act procedures (section K). At the back of the book, readers will find a series of appendixes (listing U.S.-USSR bilateral agreements, Washington-area meetings, library collections by size of Russian/Soviet holdings, bookstores, housing and transportation information, federal government holidays, and standard entry formats), a bibliography, and indexes (personal papers collections, library subject-strengths, subjects, and names of organizations and collections).

Methodology. Preparation of this work began with the compilation of a list of all Washington-area collections and organizations thought to be potential sources of information or assistance for scholarly research on the Soviet Union and/or its nationality components. The bibliography at the end of this volume contains the reference sources consulted in the compilation of this list. Each pertinent collection and organization was then investigated in person and/or by telephone. Information was gleaned from on-site examinations, printed materials, and discussions with staff members. The measurements of library collections were conducted in mid-1976; all other information was updated for this revised second edition during the summer and fall of 1982. For possible future revisions of this *Guide*, suggestions by readers for additions, alterations, and improvements will be greatly appreciated. Please notify the Librarian, Wilson Center, Smithsonian Institution Building, 1000 Jefferson Drive, SW, Washington, D.C. 20560.

Acknowledgments. Appreciation is extended to Zdeněk V. David, librarian of the Wilson Center Library, for his patience and valuable advice. The revision and updating of the section on archival and manuscript resources (section B) was significantly facilitated by the researches of Steven A. Grant and John H. Brown for the compilation of *The Russian Empire and Soviet Union: A Guide to Manuscripts and Archival Materials in the United States* (Boston: G. K. Hall, 1981). More generally, the process of revision and updating benefitted from the accumulated experience and findings of the authors of the other guides in this series: Michael Grow, Hong N. Kim, Purnima M. Bhatt, Bonnie G. Rowan, Kenneth J. Dillon, Steven R. Dorr, Enayetur Rahim, Patrick M. Mayerchak, James R. Heintze, and Louis A. Pitschmann. Eleanor S. Adams served as the chief assistant for the project; Vladimir Dubinsky, Rostyslav Serafimovych, and Cherie Settle also provided research assistance. Ms. Adams, in addition, efficiently typed most of the manuscript. Finally, as in the first edition of the *Guide*, grateful appreciation is again extended to the hundreds of men and women on the staffs of the institutions here described who contributed their time and knowledge to this project. Many, but by no means all, of these individuals are mentioned in the pages that follow.

HOW TO USE THIS GUIDE

The following comments are made to facilitate the use of this reference work. For additional explanations concerning particular types of collections and organizations (libraries, U.S. Government agencies, embassies, etc.) see the Introductory Note to each section.

Format. The main body of the volume is divided into seven collection sections (A–G) and eight organization sections (H–Q). Within each section, entries are arranged alphabetically by the name of the individual collection or organization. In the section containing U.S. Government agencies (K), functional descriptors precede the generic name (e.g., State Department rather than Department of State).

Standard Entry Format. A brief introductory paragraph to each section is preceded by a standard entry format (see also Appendix VII), which outlines the categories and sequence of information contained within each entry. The numbers of the entry format correspond to the numerical arrangement of each entry. If a particular number does not appear in an entry, that category of information was either not applicable or not available. If a single institution or organization has more than one entry in the *Guide*, references to all entries are gathered under the main entry and also in the Name Index.

Indexes. Four indexes provide access to information in the text from several perspectives. The Personal Papers Index includes the names of individuals whose papers and manuscripts are located in libraries and other depositories in the Washington, D.C., area. The Library Subject-Strength Index ranks the major library collections in the area by subject and by nationality group. The scale of evaluation used to rank these libraries is explained in the introduction to the library section (A) and preceding the index. (See also Appendix III for size estimates of the major Russian/Soviet library collections.) The Subject Index covers rather broad categories and includes nationality headings. The Name Index includes the names of all organizations and institutions covered in the *Guide*; subdivisions of highly differentiated agencies are grouped under the main entry in the index. Names of individuals are not included in this index.

Names, Addresses, and Telephone Numbers. This information is subject to frequent changes, particularly for U.S. Government agencies and highly differentiated organizations where reorganization and personnel changes occur often. All telephone numbers include area codes (202 for the District of Columbia, 301 for the Maryland suburbs, and 703 for the Virginia suburbs) to assist those placing telephone calls from outside the Washington area. When dialing from within the Washington metropolitan area, the above-mentioned area codes should be ignored since these would all be local calls.

Transliteration. The transliteration system used in this book is essentially that of the Library of Congress. Certain seeming inconsistencies are due to the authors' attempt—for ease of retrieval—to spell names as they appear in the catalogs or other materials of the collection being described. Similarly, some organizations appear under names of their own transliteration.

Abbreviations. Most abbreviations used in these pages are self-explanatory. The following brief list includes those that may not be.

FBIS   Foreign Broadcast Information Service (see entry Q7)
GPO   Government Printing Office (see entry Q9)
JPRS   Joint Publications Research Service (see entry Q10)
LC   Library of Congress (see entry A37)
NARS   National Archives and Records Service (see entry B6)
NTIS   National Technical Information Service (see entry Q13)
OCLC   Online Computer Library Center (see entries A22, E2)

COLLECTIONS

A Libraries

Library Entry Format (A)

1. General Information
   a. *address; telephone number(s)*
   b. hours of service
   c. conditions of access (including availability of interlibrary loan service and photocopying facilities)
   d. name/title of director and heads of relevant divisions

2. Size of Collection

3. Description and Evaluation of Collection
   a. narrative assessment of Russia/USSR holdings—subject and area strengths/weaknesses
   b. tabular evaluation of subject strength:

Subject Category	Number of Titles	Rating (A–D) *
Philosophy and Religion		
History		
Geography and Ethnography		
Economics		
Sociology		
Politics and Government		
Foreign Relations		
Law		
Education		
Fine Arts		
Language		
Literature		
Military Affairs		
Bibliography and Reference		
Ukrainians		
Byelorussians		
Baltic Nationalities		
Caucasian Nationalities		
Central Asian Nationalities		
Siberian Nationalities		

4. Special Collections (periodicals, newspapers, government documents, maps, films, tapes)

5. Noteworthy Holdings

6. Bibliographic Aids Facilitating Use of Collection

---

*A—comprehensive collection of primary and secondary sources (Library of Congress collection to serve as a standard of evaluation)

B—substantial collection of primary and secondary sources; sufficient for some original research (holdings of roughly one-tenth those of the Library of Congress)

C—substantial collection of secondary and primary sources, many in Russian; sufficient to support graduate instruction (holdings of roughly one-half those of B collection)

D—collection of secondary and primary sources, some in Russian; sufficient to support undergraduate instruction (holdings of roughly one-half those of C collection)

Introductory Note

Of the libraries examined for the *Guide,* the Library of Congress (entry A37) is unquestionably the most important source of printed material in virtually every subject and category. Two good general collections—which necessarily pale in comparison with the Library of Congress—are the libraries of the University of Maryland (entry A39) and the State Department (entry A57). A number of specialized government agency libraries complement these with invaluable collections in selected topic areas: the National Library of Medicine (entry A48), for example, offers the greatest collection of Russian medical literature outside the Soviet Union (along with a wealth of material on related social sciences); the Commerce Department's Foreign Demographic Analysis Division Library (entry A14) and Patent Office Scientific Library (entry A54) represent specialized collections that are major resources in their respective fields for the Russianist. Scholars with an interest in Byzantine influences on Russian civilization will find the Dumbarton Oaks Research Library (entry A17) of great value. Briefly put, both the major and minor collections available to the Russianist in the Washington area merit attention—and will reward the scholar handsomely for time spent in them.

Most large and general collections, plus some smaller or more specialized ones, are evaluated on a scale of A to D. These rankings are based on quantity and quality of holdings for twenty subject categories. The Library of Congress was taken as a standard for A collections: comprehensive collections of primary and secondary sources. The B collection was defined as a substantial collection (roughly one-tenth the size of the Library of Congress's) of primary and secondary sources, sufficient for original research. A substantial collection of secondary and primary sources (about one-half the size of a B collection), many in Russian, sufficient for graduate instruction, was considered a C collection. Finally, a D collection was taken to be one of secondary and primary sources (about one-half of a C collection, but not less than 100 titles in major subjects), some in Russian, sufficient to support undergraduate teaching.

The totals given for library holdings and other collections of materials are derived mostly from measurements of shelflists. The number of book or other titles was calculated on the basis of 100 index cards per inch and 85 titles per 100 cards (unless otherwise noted). Libraries other than the Library of Congress were measured for fewer call numbers on the assumption that they would be unlikely to have materials if the Library of Congress did not have a significant number of titles. All these remarks mean that the size of collections tends to be understated rather than overstated. Furthermore, the numbers given are not reflective of the continually changing, growing, and improving condition of most of the collections examined (measurements were made in mid-1976).

It was too difficult to measure law holdings for certain general library collections because of the lack of a developed Library of Congress classification schedule. In such instances the word "unmeasured" appears in the subject category listings.

Interlibrary loan service usually means (a) most of the materials, except periodicals, will be loaned to most outside institutions but not to individuals and (b) the library will borrow materials for its own institutional community.

Advanced International Studies Institute   See entry H1

A1   Air Force Department—Office of Air Force History Library

1 a. *Headquarters USAF/CHO*
Bolling Air Force Base, Building 5681
Washington, D.C. 20332
(202) 767-5088/5089

  b. 7:15 A.M. 4:00 P.M., Monday–Friday

  c. Open to researchers, by appointment. Many holdings are classified or otherwise restricted. Interlibrary loan service is not available; limited photocopying facilities are available. Copies of microfilm holdings may be purchased from the Albert F. Simpson Historical Research Center, Maxwell Air Force Base, Alabama 36112, which holds the originals of almost all of this microfilm collection.

  d. Dr. Richard H. Kohn, Chief
Colonel John Schlight, Deputy Chief
William Heimdahl, Chief, Reference

2–3. The library contains government documents and personal papers of air force personnel, the majority on microfilm. Several hundred items pertain to the Soviet Union directly, many more relate to the USSR generally or indirectly. Most relevant material dates from the period of World War II and after. Included are air force intelligence and policy documents, unit histories, and histories of specific wars. Among the collections of personal papers related to the Soviet Union are those of Generals John K. Cannon and Thomas D. White, and Major Generals Elmer E. Adler and William H. Blanchard.

6. The office has a useful index to the microfilm holdings. Two publications of value for helping Russianists locate pertinent material are *United States Air Force History. A Guide to Documentary Sources,* comp. Lawrence J. Paszek (1973), and *An Aerospace Bibliography,* comp. Samuel Duncan Miller (1978).

A2   Alexander Graham Bell Association for the Deaf—Volta Bureau Library

1 a. *3417 Volta Place, NW*
      Washington, D.C. 20007
      (202) 337-5220

 b. 9:00 A.M.–4:30 P.M., Monday–Friday

 c. Open to the public, by appointment. Interlibrary loan service and photocopying facilities are available.

 d. Suzanne Neel, Manager, Information Services, and Director, Volta Bureau Library

2.   The library contains more than 25,000 volumes, documents, and periodical titles, which deal with the subjects of speech, hearing, and deafness. Approximately 235 books and pamphlets—all in Russian—are on Russian/Soviet aspects of these problems.

3.   For such a highly specialized collection, the subject categories are not germane. For this one aspect of the sociology category, the holdings certainly rate a B.

4.   The library currently receives two Soviet periodicals: *Defektologiia* (since 1970) and *Chtenie s gub.*

5.   The library has a box with about ten items of great interest, including pamphlets, correspondence (some translated), photos, and periodical clippings. Almost all of this material was written and/or sent to the bureau by N. and F. Rau, apparently the driving forces behind pre- and postrevolution Russian studies of the deaf and mute. Most items date from the late 1920s or early 1930s. It should be noted that many of the library's books were penned by N. and F. Rau or their offspring.

6.   There are no published materials to facilitate access to the collection. All Russian materials, except the two current periodicals, however, are kept together on one shelf.
   In the reading room, besides a card catalog arranged by author, title, and subject, is a very useful index to *Volta Review,* the bureau's own publication. It is also arranged by author, title, and subject; under "Russia" are at least eighteen articles, dating from 1922 to 1957.

A3   American Federation of Labor and Congress of Industrial Organizations Library (AFL-CIO Library)

1 a. *815 Sixteenth Street, NW, Room 102*
      Washington, D.C. 20006
      (202) 637-5297

 b. 9:00 A.M.–4:30 P.M., Monday–Friday

 c. Open to the public for on-site use. Photocopying facilities are available.

 d. Dora Kelenson, Librarian

2. The vertical-file drawers have several folders of interest.

3. File material—including pamphlets, articles, and clippings—may be found mainly in two drawers under "Communism" (and "Communism-Labor Unions") and "USSR." Items are arranged by date of publication and subject. The majority of pieces are not about trade unions or even economics but are more general; they also appear to be all in English. Nevertheless, some material, especially that from the 1920s to 1940s, might prove valuable. Some items are propaganda pieces printed in the Soviet Union and may be rare.

It should be noted that the AFL-CIO is currently in the process of establishing an archive. The goal is to consolidate, locate, and organize AFL-CIO materials worldwide. Obviously, there would be much of interest to the Russianist in such an archive. The scheduled completion date is 1985; scholars should contact Archivist Katharine Vogel (202/637-5331) for up-to-date information on the archive's status.

American Gas Association Library   See entry M8

A4   American Institute of Architects Library

1 a. *1735 New York Avenue, NW*
Washington, D.C. 20006
(202) 626-7493

b. 8:30 A.M.–5:00 P.M.,   Monday–Friday

c. Open to the public for on-site use. Limited interlibrary loan service and photocopying facilities are available.

d. Stephanie Byrnes, Librarian

2. The total collection numbers about 22,000 volumes on architecture, construction, urban planning, and related subjects. The library is an extremely valuable facility for research on architecture in general. Russian/Soviet-area specialists will thus find it significant, even though at present holdings in their field represent a small proportion of the collection.

3–4. The library has a small collection of books on Russian/Soviet architecture. A number of books on urban planning and urban affairs relating to the USSR are also available. Other pertinent volumes are on such topics as art and travel.

A slim vertical-file folder holds some correspondence and newspaper clippings relating to the Soviet Union.

Currently the library receives three periodicals from the USSR: *Stroitel'stvo i arkhitektura Moskvy* (from 1956), *Stroitel'stvo i arkhitektura Leningrada* (from 1967), and *Arkhitektura SSSR* (irregularly).

A5 The American Legion—National Security-Foreign Relations Functional Library

1 a. *1608 K Street, NW*
Washington, D.C. 20006
(202) 861-2730

b. 8:00 A.M.–4:30 P.M., Monday–Friday

c. Open to researchers. Limited photocopying facilities are available.

d. Spence Leopard, Research Analyst

5. The library has one full drawer of vertical-file material on the USSR in general (arranged chronologically), U.S.-USSR relations, USSR-China relations, and similar topics. Material is from the *Christian Science Monitor, Congressional Record, New York Times,* and *Washington Post.*

American Psychiatric Association Library   See entry M14

American Red Cross Library   See entry B1

A6 American University Library

1 a. *Massachusetts and Nebraska avenues, NW*
Washington, D.C. 20016
(202) 686-2320

b. Academic year:
8:00 A.M.–Midnight, Monday–Thursday
8:00 A.M.–10:00 P.M., Friday
9:00 A.M.–9:00 P.M., Saturday
11:00 A.M.–Midnight, Sunday
Summer hours are set annually.

c. Open to the public for on-site use; only members of the university may borrow books. Interlibrary loan service and photocopying facilities are available.

d. Donald D. Dennis, Director

2. Approximately 350,000 volumes are in the collections.

3 b. Subject categories and evaluations:

Subject	Number of Titles	Rating
Philosophy and Religion	95	D
History	1,660	C/D
Geography and Ethnography	40	D
Economics	310	D
Sociology	110	D
Politics and Government	175	D
Foreign Relations	280	B/C
Law	Unmeasured	
Education	30	D
Fine Arts	140	D
Language	235	C
Literature	1,200	C
Military Affairs,	40	D
Bibliography, and Reference	Unmeasured	
Ukrainians	25	D or below
Byelorussians	2	Below D
Baltic Nationalities	25	D or below
Caucasian Nationalities	55	D/C
Central Asian Nationalities	75	D/C
Siberian Nationalities	75	D/C

5.   There are at least two noteworthy holdings. In the mid-1970s, Dr. Boris Filippov gave the university a small part of his private library of Russian-related materials, consisting of some 2,000 Russian-language books and journals. A considerable number are translations into Russian of Soviet books originally written in the languages of other Soviet nationalities. These works are of great value to researchers who are without knowledge of languages other than Russian and are studying minority/nationality questions in the USSR. The library also possesses a complete set in twenty-two volumes of *Sobranie dokumentov samizdata*—xerox copies kept in loose pages of holdings of Radio Liberty from the dissident movement in the Soviet Union. The work comprises about 2,000 documents.

6.   The library follows the Library of Congress classification system. Card catalogs are divided into two parts: author/title and subject. A serials list provides holding records of all periodicals and newspapers held by the library. A printed *Library Guide* and several useful reference guides are available.

NOTE: The library also receives some 150–200 Soviet books annually through an exchange arrangement (in which Stanford University and the University of Chicago also take part) with the USSR Academy of Science's Institute for Scientific Information in the Social Sciences. These books are largely in social science fields, with a special concentration on economics. Russianists should contact Professor Linda Lubrano (202/686-3865) of the university's Russian Studies program (see entry J1) for further information.

Armenian Assembly Charitable Trust Library   See entry M21

A7   Arms Control and Disarmament Agency (ACDA) Library

1 a.   *ACDA, State Department*
320 Twenty-first Street, NW
Washington, D.C. 20451
(202) 632-5971

b.   9:00 A.M.–4:30 P.M.,   Monday–Friday

c.   Researchers must have an ACDA library card to use this library. Applications by mail normally take one week to ten days to process. Interlibrary loan service and photocopying facilities are available, the latter for a fee and for ACDA materials only.

d.   Diane Ferguson, Librarian

2–3.   The collection totals some 3,500 books on most aspects of arms control and political, military, and economic matters. Roughly 500 titles relate directly to the USSR, but much more material here will be pertinent. For research on the topics of disarmament and arms control the library should prove to be a valuable resource.

4.   Most Soviet periodicals and newspapers are held not by the library but by individual staff members of the agency (who are located in the State Department building). The agency currently receives about ten such titles, almost all in Russian (for example, *Izvestiia, Krasnaia Zvezda, Novoe vremia, Pravda, Voennoistoricheskii zhurnal,* and *Zarubezhom*).
   The library holds approximately 250 unclassified reports from different government agencies and some private organizations on questions of arms control.

5.   Clippings from about ten U.S. newspapers, on the subject of arms control, are maintained in a vertical-file collection. There are currently some five drawers of material. Soviet periodicals are not clipped. (Note: This collection should not be confused with the much larger collection of vertical-file material held in the agency's Public Affairs Office, for which see entry K3.)

NOTE: A substantial portion of the holdings of the ACDA Library are located in the Special Collections Division of the George Washington University Library (entry A24). These holdings are, however, accessible through the ACDA Library.

A8 Army Library (Army Department)

1 a. *The Pentagon, Room 1A518*
Washington, D.C. 20310
(202) 697-4301

b. 9:00 A.M.–4:00 P.M., Monday–Friday

c. Entrance to the Pentagon, where the library is housed, requires a building pass. Interlibrary loan service is available.

d. Mary L. Shaffer, Director

2. Approximately one million volumes are in the library, which subscribes to about 2,000 periodicals.

3. Holdings pertaining to Russia/USSR total roughly 2,000 volumes and government documents. The strength of the collection lies in military affairs, international relations, and history. For these subjects, the library falls into category C.

4. The library has some seventy-five Soviet journals and newspapers in the original language or translation. Roughly one-third of these titles are concerned with military affairs; another substantial amount are scientific.
    The Army Studies section of the library has computer terminals with access to the Defense Technical Information Center data base (see entry G4). One of the two terminals is for classified material, the other is for unclassified material. The library has several commercial data bases for clients but does not conduct searches for outsiders.

6. The Army Library publishes a monthly acquisition list, selected special bibliographies of interest to the Defense Department, and (irregularly) a periodical holdings list.

NOTE: The Army Department also maintains a Reference Library, in room 5A486 of the Pentagon (202/697-2806). The Reference Library has about 300–500 still photographs of Soviet-related subjects. Most photos are of captured World War II Soviet military equipment and of Soviet military operations in that war. See entry K4 for a description of the Army Department, generally.

A9 Association of American Railroads—Economics and Finance Department Library

1 a. *1920 L Street, NW, Room 523*
Washington, D.C. 20036
(202) 835-9100

b. 9:00 A.M.–4:00 P.M., Monday–Friday

c. Open to the public, except the stacks. Interlibrary loan service and photocopying facilities are available.

d. Helene M. Rowland, Supervisor, Library Service

2–3.   The collection is rather small, with material on many different aspects of transportation, and is particularly strong on railroading and related subjects. Some books are on Russia and Siberia, in the English language.

6.   The microfiche and card catalogs are a significant resource for researchers. The microfiche catalog is arranged by author, title,. and subject and includes periodical articles and books. Material not held in the library is also recorded. Entries are most comprehensive for earlier years, beginning from 1910.

Sample measurements from this catalog: railroads, Russia—approximately 950 entries; railroads, Siberia—approximately 70 entries; transportation, Russia—approximately 40 entries.

The catalog should be a basic research tool for locating English-language works on Russian/Soviet railroads and transportation.

B'nai Brith International Headquarters Library   See entry M27

Brookings Institution Library   See entry H7

A10   Catholic University of America—Mullen Library

1 a.   *620 Michigan Avenue, NE*
Washington, D.C. 20064
(202) 635-5070/5074

b.   Hours vary considerably during the academic year and in summer; call (202) 635-5077 for the current schedule.

c.   Open to the public; borrowing privileges are restricted. Visiting researchers should inquire at the Circulation Division (202/635-5060) about temporary borrowing arrangements. Interlibrary loan service and photocopying facilities are available.

d.   John G. Lorenz, Interim Director
Anthony Zito, Archivist (202/635-5065)

2.   The total collection contains approximately 1,500,000 volumes.

3 b.   Subject categories and evaluations:

Subject	Number of Titles	Rating
Philosophy and Religion	240	C
History	855	D
Geography and Ethnography	20	Below D
Economics	140	D or below
Sociology	130	D
Politics and Government	120	D

Subject	Number of Titles	Rating
Foreign Relations	150	C
Law	Unmeasured	
Education	20	D or below
Fine Arts	65	Below D
Language	120	D/C
Literature	255	D
Military Affairs	15	Below D
Bibliography and Reference	25	Below D
Ukrainians	40	D
Byelorussians	1	Below D
Baltic Nationalities	40	D
Caucasian Nationalities	50	D/C
Central Asian Nationalities	50	D
Siberian Nationalities	30	D

5.   The Department of Archives and Manuscripts of the library holds the following pertinent collections:

Archive of the Committee on Special War Activities of the National Catholic War Council. One folder in this collection contains correspondence on the Siberian War Prisoners Repatriation Fund, January 1920–July 1923.

John Brophy Papers. A labor leader and union organizer, Brophy visited the USSR in 1927 as part of a trade union delegation that observed Soviet labor conditions. The papers include Brophy's correspondence about the trip and numerous postcards covering aspects of the contemporary Soviet scene.

Joseph D. Keenan Papers. Keenan was, among other things, involved in the War Production Board and in labor unionization for post-World War II Germany. Included here are his 1945–47 correspondence and an oral history account (prepared later) dealing with labor issues in Germany during those years and Soviet attitudes toward them.

Aloysius Cardinal Muench Papers. Materials of this papal emissary to Germany immediately after World War II are in 203 boxes; they include his official correspondence and shed light on matters relating to Soviet policy toward Germany (e.g., refugees in Germany, German labor unions).

Terence Powderly Papers. Powderly was U.S. commissioner-general of immigration, 1896–1912.

6.   The main Mullen collection is served by a subject-title/author card catalog.

A11   Census Bureau Library (Commerce Department)

1 a.   *Federal Office Building 3, Room 2451*
Suitland, Maryland 20233
Mail Stop 396
(301) 763-5042 (Reference)

b.   8:00 A.M.–5:00 P.M.,   Monday–Friday

c. Open to the public. Interlibrary loan service and photocopying facilities for both printed material and microfiche are available.

d. Betty Baxtresser, Chief, Library and Information Services Branch

2. Holdings total approximately 250,000 items. Subjects include demography, population studies, economic statistics, and certain social sciences. The library currently receives more than 3,000 periodical titles.

3 a. Much of the Russian-area holdings are on permanent loan to the Bureau's Foreign Demographic Analysis Division (see entries A14 and K8). Remaining in this library are some 315 bound volumes and three periodical titles (sixty-three items). These materials include censuses, yearbooks, and statistical publications.

6. The dictionary card catalog is divided into three sections, one covering acquisitions up to February 1976; the second, March 1976 to June 1980; and the third, since July 1980. The pre-1976 materials are listed in *Catalogs of the Bureau of the Census Library,* 20 vols. (Boston: G. K. Hall, 1976), and first supplement, 5 vols. (1979).
A monthly list of acquisitions and current periodicals is available.

Center for Defense Information Library See entry H8

Center for Naval Analyses Library See entry H11

A12 Commerce Department—Assistant Secretary for International Economic Policy—USSR Affairs Division Collection

1 a. *Fourteenth Street between Constitution Avenue and*
E Street, NW, Room 3414
Washington, D.C. 20230
(202) 377-4655

b. 8:30 A.M.–5:00 P.M., Monday–Friday

c. Open to researchers, by appointment. Interlibrary loan service is not available. Photocopies of trade agreements, active and inactive, are available. Other material may be photocopied in the main Commerce Department Library.

d. Val Zabijaka, Librarian

2–3. There are at least 500 books on the Soviet economy, especially trade. Materials are in both Russian and English. The library receives a handful of newspapers, five journals, and three East-West trade newsletters, most of which the staff clips and then discards. The clippings go into a substantial vertical file collection. Taken altogether, the holdings represent a C or B level for the economics category only.

5. The large vertical-file collection is noteworthy. Some five drawers are full of Soviet-area unclassified materials. A couple of cabinets contain classified items. The files are arranged by subject—i.e., by industrial or economic activity.

A13 Commerce Department Library

1 a. *Fourteenth Street between Constitution Avenue and
E Street, NW, Room 7046
Washington, D.C. 20230
(202) 377-5511*

  b. 8:30 A.M.–4:45 P.M., Monday–Friday

  c. Open to the public for on-site use. Interlibrary loan service is not available.
Photocopying facilities are available.

  d. Stanley J. Bougas, Director

2. Holdings total nearly 350,000 volumes. Subjects covered include economics and
related fields, particularly trade. The library receives more than 1,400 current periodicals.

3 a. The library, disconcertingly, has been weeding out its collection for some time,
generally of pre-1940 material—without at the same time pulling the appropriate cards
from its shelflist. Not only is the resultant loss of titles saddening, but effective meas-
uring of the shelflist is almost impossible.
  From visual inspection of the shelves as well as shelflist measurement, it appears
that the library has substantial holdings for Russianists only in the economics category.
The estimated number of titles in this field is about 250–300 books plus a few periodicals. Some of the material is in Russian. The rating for this category is thus a D.

6. *Commerce Library Bulletin,* issued irregularly, contains a brief guide to the library
and a list of selected recent acquisitions.

A14 Commerce Department—Foreign Demographic Analysis Division
Library

1 a. *Location:
4235 Twenty-eighth Avenue
Marlow Heights, Maryland 20031
(301) 763-4020*

  *Mail:
Scuderi Building, Room 707
Bureau of the Census
Washington, D.C. 20233*

  b. 8:00 A.M.–4:30 P.M., Monday–Friday

  c. Open to researchers, by appointment. Limited interlibrary loan service and
photocopying facilities are available.

  d. Stephen Rapawy, Chief, USSR Population, Employment, and R&D Branch

2. The collection contains approximately 25,000 books, many filing cabinets of vertical-file material, and some 63,000 research cards. This is a major resource for Soviet-
area specialists.

3 a.   A vast majority of the holdings cover Russia/USSR; much of the material is in Russian. The strength of the collection is in the categories of economics (all aspects), sociology (in part), and in those other subjects that relate to manpower, population studies, research and development, and statistics.

b.   Subject categories and evaluations:

Subject	Rating
Philosophy and Religion	Below D
History	D
Geography and Ethnography	C
Economics	A
Sociology	A
Politics and Government	C
Foreign Relations	B
Law	C/D
Education	B
Fine Arts	Below D
Language	Below D
Literature	Below D
Military Affairs	B
Bibliography and Reference	D
(Nationalities)	Not applicable

4.   The library currently receives from the Soviet Union about 125 periodicals and more than twenty newspapers. It also has a substantial number of U.S. Government publications and documents that deal with the USSR, including Joint Publication Research Service translations.

5.   The most noteworthy holdings are the extensive vertical-file collection and the manual data-retrieval system of research cards. These cards contain translations and abstracts of articles and books arranged by title, name, and date. The system is cross-referenced, so that although there are only about 63,000 original entry cards, the total number of cards is roughly 250,000. Information in the system dates from September 1961.

The vertical files contain reports of travel to the USSR, newspaper and magazine clippings, and many other papers and reports. The files and cards represent an enormous potential gold mine for researchers.

6.   The library produces accession lists of its Soviet periodicals. There is also a classification scheme (photocopy) available to guide researchers in using the sui generis shelving system.

NOTE: Many items in this collection are on permanent loan from the Commerce Department's Bureau of the Census Library (entry A11).

A15   Congressional Quarterly, Inc.—Editorial Reports Library

1 a.   *1414 Twenty-second Street, NW*
Washington, D.C. 20037
(202) 887-8569 (Circulation)
(202) 887-8570 (Librarian)
(202) 887-8600 (Research)

b. 9:00 A.M.–5:30 P.M.,   Monday–Friday

c. Closed to the public. Researchers, however, may receive permission from the librarian to use the collection. Limited interlibrary loan service and photocopying facilities are available.

d. Edna M. Frazier-Cromwell, Librarian

2. The library contains more than 6,000 bound volumes and 500 microforms. Current events, international relations, and politics are the major subjects covered.

3–4. This library will be a joy for researchers who want to follow U.S. Government attitudes and policies toward the USSR. Congressional hearings and voting records, other government documents and reports, and the *Congressional Quarterly* provide the Soviet-area specialist a wealth of information with which to work.

5. The extensive vertical-file collection will also interest Soviet-area specialists. There are numerous folders here on the USSR (three inches thick), U.S.-Soviet relations, bilateral agreements, Soviet relations with other countries, summit meetings, the SALT talks, foreign trade, and other subjects.

A16 Defense Mapping Agency Hydrographic/Topographic Center (Defense Department)—Map Library

1 a. *Erskine Hall, Room 171*
6500 Brookes Lane, NW
Washington, D.C. 20315
(202) 227-2114

b. 7:30 A.M.–4:00 P.M.,   Monday–Friday

c. Open to researchers with prior permission from the director. Interlibrary loan service and photocopying facilities are available.

d. Captain Wallace C. Palmer, Director
Claude Marshall, Technical Information Specialist

2. The library holds about 500,000 documents, approximately 380,000 aerial photographs, and several thousand items in microform. The material covers virtually all aspects of geodesy and surveying.

3 a. On Russia/USSR there are nearly 2,000 volumes, almost all pertaining to surveying and geographic exploration. For this part of the geography and ethnography subject categories, the collection ranks at the B level.

4–5. The library holds *Zapiski* (Transactions) of the topographic section of the Russian/Soviet general staff from 1837 to 1941 and hydrographic section of the Russian and Soviet Navy from 1851 to 1941.

6. The quarterly *Geodetic Abstracts,* which ceased publication in 1975, had abstracts from foreign periodicals. In 1968 the Army Department published *The Department of Defense Geodetic Library,* a brief guide to the collection. For information on the library's map collection, see entry E1.

Dibner Room (Smithsonian Institution Libraries—Special Collections Branch)   See entry K31

A17   Dumbarton Oaks Research Library (Trustees for Harvard University)

1 a. *1703 Thirty-second Street, NW*
Washington, D.C. 20007
(202) 342-3240

  b. 9:00 A.M.–5:00 P.M.,   Monday–Friday

  c. Open to researchers for on-site use with prior permission from the librarian. Photocopying facilities are available.

  d. Irene Vaslef, Librarian

2. The holdings focus on Byzantine civilization and related periods and cultures. There are more than 85,000 volumes in the collection, and the library has subscriptions to nearly 900 current periodicals. The librarian estimates that about eleven percent of total holdings are Slavic.

3a–b. Because the library has its own classification scheme and relevant holdings are limited, the usual categories are not germane here.

Subject	*Area*		*Number of Titles*
Art and Archaeology	Russia		550
	Caucasus		195
	Russia in Asia		45
	Mongolia		4
	Other		6
		Total	800
Documents	Russia		50
	Caucasus		6
	Ukraine		6
	Other		3
		Total	65
Language	Caucasus		10
	Russia		7
	Church Slavic		6
	Other		2
		Total	25
History	Russia		425
	Caucasus		105
	Ukraine and Black Sea		45
	Slavic coins		35
		Total	610

Subject	Area		Number of Titles
Laws	Russia		31
	Caucasus		4
		Total	35
Church	Russia		130
	Slavic Church		120
	Caucasus		15
	Karaite Jews		2
		Total	267
Reference	Russia		35
	Caucasus		35
		Total	70
Philology	unmeasured amount of some interest		

There are sufficient primary and secondary sources here, many in Russian, for the scholar to conduct original research in certain subjects.

4. See Dumbarton Oaks, Center for Byzantine Studies, in the Film Collections (entry F2) and Research Centers (entry H13) sections.

The library currently receives about twenty-five periodicals in Russian (or other languages of the USSR). Most concern art and architecture; others are on history and religion.

6. A catalog for this collection has been published: *Dictionary Catalogue of the Byzantine Collection of the Dumbarton Oaks Research Library,* 12 vols. (Boston: G. K. Hall and Co., 1975). A major bibliographic undertaking of immense value to researchers, currently being published in London by Mansell, is Dumbarton Oaks Bibliographies, series 1: *Literature on Byzantine Art, 1892–1967,* ed. Jelisaveta S. Allen, based on *Byzantinische Zeitschrift.* Volume 1, published in 1973 in two parts, is topographically arranged, first by continent and then by country. The second volume is presently in press.

Dwight D. Eisenhower Institute for Historical Research (Smithsonian Institution) Collection   See entry K31

A18   Energy Library (Energy Department)

1 a.   *Energy Department (DOE)*
Routes 270 and 118
Germantown, Maryland 20545

Library Branch (D.C.):
James Forrestal Building
1000 Independence Avenue, SW
Washington, D.C. 20585

Federal Energy Regulation Commission (FERC)
825 North Capitol Street, NE
Washington, D.C. 20426

(Daily shuttle service is available among the three DOE facilities.)

b. 8:30 A.M.–5:00 P.M., Monday–Friday

c. Open to the public for on-site use. Initially, researchers should call in advance. Interlibrary loan service and photocopying facilities are available.

d. C. Neil Sherman, Director (301/353-4301)
Denise B. Diggin, Chief, Library Branch (Germantown) (301/353-2855)
Maria Vignone, Chief, Library Branch (D.C.) (202/252-9534)
Robert F. Kimberlin, Chief, Library Branch (FERC) (202/357-5479)

2–3. The Energy library is divided into three major branches, as indicated above. In all it contains more than 24,000 cataloged titles, some five percent of which concern Soviet energy industries. The library also subscribes to more than 2,500 professional journals. Computer terminals in each facility access more than 100 different data bases but may be used only by DOE and other government agency personnel. The holdings of the branch facilities are designed to complement each other. The Germantown headquarters handles the bulk of the technical material, some economics literature, and the cataloging operations. The D.C. branch houses the statistics collection, including the journals. The D.C. staff also performs literature searches and provides interlibrary loan and photocopying services. The FERC branch houses most current congressional materials. Basic reference material is available at each branch. Smaller library facilities are maintained in various DOE offices.

4. The library's special collections include more than 650,000 uncataloged technical reports, 20,000 reels of microfilmed congressional hearings from the eighty-second to the eighty-sixth congresses, and microfiche holdings of all reports and documents from the sixty-ninth through the ninety-fourth congresses, more than 2,600 items. The library has in paper copy selected hearings held before 1970 and on microfiche all hearings held after 1970.

6. A complete listing of cataloged books, annually updated and in print form, is available for on-site use at each branch.

Environmental Protection Agency Library   See entry K15

A19   European Community Information Service Library

1 a. *2100 M Street, NW, Suite 707*
Washington, D.C. 20037
(202) 862-9500

b. 9:00 A.M.–5:00 P.M., Monday–Friday

c. Open to the public. Photocopying facilities are available.

d. Ella Krucoff, Chief, Reference, and Documentation/Information Specialist

2. The library contains at least 18,000 titles and more than 1,000 vertical-file folders.

3 a. This facility is a minor resource for Russianists. It groups together all holdings for Eastern Europe and the Soviet Union. On the subjects of East-West trade, economics, politics, and legal affairs it has a small collection of books.

4–5. Five vertical files contain articles, pamphlets, documents, and other papers of some value to the Russian/Soviet-area scholar.

Librarians can help researchers locate information on the interests and dealings on all levels of the European Communities—European Economic Community, European Coal and Steel Community, and European Atomic Energy Community—with Eastern Europe and the USSR. The library is particularly strong in its collections of trade statistics.

6. A number of unpublished card catalogs assists the researcher in using the library; one catalog is arranged by country and/or region.

A20 Export-Import Bank Library

1 a. *811 Vermont Avenue, NW*
Washington, D.C. 20571
(202) 566-8320

b. 8:15 A.M.–4:30 P.M., Monday–Friday

c. Open to the public. Interlibrary loan service is available.

d. Theodora McGill, Librarian

2–4. The library holds more than 15,000 books and about 1,000 periodical titles. While only a small fraction of the book collection concerns the Soviet Union (about thirty books), the library does receive the noteworthy Soviet business periodical *Economic Bulletin,* published in English by the Soviet International Bank for Economic Cooperation. The library also subscribes to the Economist Intelligence Unit, Ltd., *USSR Quarterly Economic Review.*

6. A periodicals list is available upon request. The library maintains a card catalog. The functions of the Export-Import Bank are described in entry K16.

Federal Reserve System Library   See entry K17

Folger Shakespeare Library   See entry F4

Freer Gallery of Art Library (Smithsonian Institution)   See entry B3

A21 Gallaudet College Library

1 a. *Seventh Street and Florida Avenue, NE*
Washington, D.C. 20002
(202) 651-5566

b. 8:00 A.M.–11:00 P.M., Monday–Friday
9:00 A.M.–8:00 P.M., Saturday
1:00 P.M.–11:00 P.M., Sunday

c. Photocopying facilities are available.

d. Fern Edwards, Head Librarian
Jeanne Conway, Public Relations Librarian

2–5. Of the 170,000 volumes in this library, approximately 300 pertain to the USSR (in English). Some twenty-five concern the schooling and education of the deaf in the Soviet Union.

General Accounting Office Library   See entry K18

A22   Geological Survey Library (Interior Department)

1 a. *12201 Sunrise Valley Drive*
Mail Stop 950
Reston, Virginia 22092
(703) 860-6671/6672 (Reference)
(703) 860-6679 (Maps)

b. 7:15A.M.–4:15 P.M., Monday–Friday

c. Open to the public. Interlibrary loan and photocopying facilities are available.

d. George H. Goodwin, Jr., Chief Librarian
Barbara A. Chappell, Chief, Reference and Circulation Section

2. This main library of the Geological Survey contains approximately 500,000 bound and unbound monographs, 300,000 pamphlets and reprints, and several thousand doctoral dissertations and technical reports in microform. Currently the library receives more than 10,000 periodical and serial titles. The library's large map collection is described in entry E2.

3 a. The holdings are most comprehensive in the earth sciences, although the other natural sciences are also represented. There are materials on such topics as the environment, marine geology, resource conservation, and space satellites. The library attempts not to duplicate the holdings of the Interior Department's Natural Resources Library (entry A31); the two should be considered complementary.

The library has its own classification system, which is simple and effective to use. Basically a decimal system, the scheme has a geographic breakdown for general and specific subjects. For most subject categories, except science, the collection seems to fall below the D level. Holdings in science, or at least certain aspects of it, deserve an A rating. Some items in the sciences, however, relate to other subject categories. For example, agriculture, forestry, horticulture, and soils are classed under biology in this scheme, but the *Guide* has tended to treat such subjects as part of the economics category. Readers should keep this overlap in mind for some of the measurements that follow.

Subject	Russia/ USSR	Baltic	Siberia	Central Asia
Mineralogy				
Petrology	185 titles	—	95 titles	25 titles
General				
Structural				
Dynamic Geology	135	14	255	70
Historical				
Geology	290	8	140	37
Economic				
Geology				
Mineral Resources	900	19	340	75
Geography				
Physical Geography	470	24	200	45
Paleontology	90	—	40	10
Mathematics				
Astronomy				
Engineering				
Surveying	155	—	25	12
Biology				
(including Botany				
and Zoology)	70	70	12	

In addition, the library has a section of publications of official geological bodies from most nations of the world. These materials are grouped by country (or area): Russia/ USSR, 300 titles; Siberia, 40 titles; Central Asia, 15 titles. These measurements do not include figures for the map collection, which appear elsewhere, or serials, which are given under point 4.

4. The extensive serials collection is divided into three groups of materials.

	Russia/USSR	Baltic	Siberia	Central Asia
Nonofficial geological	475 titles	25 titles	30 titles	25 titles
Official nongeological	35	4	—	—
Other sciences	850	35	70	50

A statistical table for maps is given in entry E2.

6. The Reference and Circulation Section of the library maintains a translation file with over 1,500 translations of articles on geology and related subjects; the bulk of the translations are from Russian.

The library's catalog has been published: *Catalog of the United States Geological Survey Library,* 25 vols. (Boston: G. K. Hall, 1964), with periodic supplements.

The brief guide *U.S. Geological Survey Library* (1975) is available without charge.

NOTE: The Geological Survey has three branch libraries located elsewhere in the country. Their holdings supplement those of the main library in many cases. A rapid interlibrary loan system makes the collections of the branch libraries readily accessible to scholars in the capital.

A23 Georgetown University—Lauinger Library

1 a. *Thirty-seventh and O streets, NW*
Washington, D.C. 20057
(202) 625-4095 (Office)
(202) 625-4173 (Reference)

b. Academic year:
8:30 A.M.–Midnight, Monday–Thursday
8:30 A.M.–10:00 P.M., Friday
10:00 A.M.–10:00 P.M., Saturday
11:00 A.M.–Midnight, Sunday

During the summer hours are curtailed. For information regarding library hours, call (202) 625-3300.

c. Open to researchers. Interlibrary loan service and photocopying facilities are available.

d. Joseph E. Jeffs, Librarian

2. The holdings for all of the university's libraries total 1,284,000 volumes; the main campus library (Lauinger) holds 983,000 volumes.

3 b. Subject categories and evaluations:

Subject	*Number of Titles*	*Rating*
Philosophy and Religion	290	C
History	2,530	C
Geography and Ethnography	50	D
Economics	455	D
Sociology	115	D
Politics and Government	330	D/C
Foreign Relations	110	C
Law	45	D
Education	40	D
Fine Arts	160	D
Language	520	B
Literature	2,270	C
Military Affairs	70	D
Bibliography and Reference	130	D
Ukrainians	80	D
Byelorussians	10	D
Baltic Nationalites	80	D
Caucasian Nationalities	20	D
Central Asian Nationalities	70	D/C
Siberian Nationalities	70	D/C

4. There are no major special collections. The library receives approximately twelve periodicals and five newspapers from the Soviet Union and is a depository for selected U.S. Government documents. The audiovisual department holds some recordings of

Russian music and also three short films of minor interest (on Chekhov, Lenin, Trotskii, and Stanislavskii).

5.   The library has two major microform holdings: *Recueil de traites . . . (1761-1944)*, by G. F. Martens, and *Russian Historical Sources*, 1st and 2d series, 48 vols. (New York: Readex Microfilm Corporation of New York), which includes source material in Russian libraries, archives, and museums.

The Division of Special Collections (also called the Archives, Manuscripts, and Rare Books Division) has a number of items of interest. The Reverend Edmund A. Walsh, S.J., Papers (about three shelf feet) contain information about the Papal Relief Mission to Russia in the early 1920s and the extension of diplomatic recognition to the USSR. Father Walsh was the founder of the Georgetown Foreign Service School, which is named after him. The Fulton Oursler Memorial Collection papers include his correspondence with Upton Sinclair concerning the unfinished film "Qué Viva Mexico" that Sinclair worked on with Sergei Eisenstein. The Victor M. Baydalakoff Papers (1932–65) concern the founding and administration of the National Workers Alliance in Germany and the subsequent founding of the Russian National Workers Alliance in America, 1956. The William R. Downs Papers (1927–77, twelve feet) include Down's reports on the Battle of Stalingrad, the Berlin airlift, and the Korean War. The Robert F. Kelly Papers (1915–75) describe Soviet domestic affairs, U.S.-USSR relations, and the founding of Radio Liberty. The Sophie A. Nordhoff-Jung Papers include fifteen letters, 1901–2, written to her from Moscow by the noted African explorer Paul Du Chaillu. The Arthur Ransome Papers (three inches) of the Frank Kurt Cylke Collection include manuscript translations of Russian fairy tales. In the rare books section is an incomplete run of the proceedings of the Russian Academy of Sciences in French (1.5 shelves), a 1719 volume on Russian military law, and a couple of art books—on icons and paintings—from the early twentieth century. Direct inquiries about these materials to Special Collections Librarian George M. Barringer; University Archivist Jon Reynolds; or Manuscript Curator Nicolas B. Scheetz (202/625-3230/4160).

6.   There are no published catalogs for the library. Of some help might be a brief listing entitled *Georgetown University Library Microform Holdings* (1972) and the more recent and substantial, but limited, *Major Titles/Sets in Microform in the Libraries of the Consortium of Universities of Washington, D.C.*, ed. Sally J. Roof and George D. Arnold (1974).

NOTE: The Fred O. Dennis Law Library of the Georgetown University Law Center has a small (uncataloged) collection of pertinent books in its Foreign Law Section. Among these volumes are works on Soviet legislation and law codes, and USSR constitutions, statutes, and treatises. The Law Center is off-campus, at 600 New Jersey Avenue, NW, Washington, D.C. 20001. For information regarding law library hours, call (202) 624-8260.

The 163,000-volume Woodstock Theological Center Library, located in the lower level of Lauinger Library, has strong holdings on ecclesiastical history and law, religious studies, and theology. Its collection of Jesuitica is believed to be as strong as any in the U.S. Library Director Father Henry Bertels, S.J., estimates that ten percent of the holdings pertain to Russia/ USSR (the Orthodox Church and aspects of religion in the USSR). The library receives *Journal of the Moscow Patriarchate*, in English translation.

A24 George Washington University—Gelman Library

1 a. *2130 H Street, NW*
   Washington, D.C. 20052
   (202) 676-6558

   b. For most of the academic year:
   8:30 A.M.–Midnight, Monday–Friday
   10:00 A.M.–Midnight, Saturday and Sunday

   Hours vary during exam periods, summer sessions, and at other times. For information regarding library hours, call (202) 676-6845.

   c. Open to the public for on-site use. Interlibrary loan service and photocopying facilities are available.

   d. James B. Alsip, Librarian

2. The total library collection, excluding the medical and law libraries, numbers more than 800,000 volumes. The library currently receives about 8,800 serials and 45 newspapers.

3 b. Subject categories and evaluations:

Subject	Number of Titles	Rating
Philosophy and Religion	125	D
History	1,440	C/D
Geography and Ethnography	40	D
Economics	400	D
Sociology	105	D
Politics and Government	300	D/C
Foreign Relations	135	C
Law	Unmeasured	
Education	40	D
Fine Arts	100	D
Language	525	B
Literature	1,930	C
Military Affairs	50	D
Bibliography and Reference	70	D or below
Ukrainians	40	D
Byelorussians	10	D
Baltic Nationalities	70	D
Caucasian Nationalities	15	D
Central Asian Nationalities	60	D/C
Siberian Nationalities	55	D

NOTE: Some titles in the library of the Institute for Sino-Soviet Studies (ISSS) not held in the main library are included in these figures. The ISSS facility is further described in entry H15.

5. The Special Collections Division (202/676-7497) has one item of note: the papers of Frederick R. Kuh, an American journalist. The materials, covering the years 1924–

67, include his diaries (1938–44), personal correspondence, travel notes, clippings, scrapbooks, and other items. Among Kuh's sources was Ivan Maiskii, Soviet ambassador to Great Britain, 1932–43. The papers shed light on Soviet and U.S. foreign policy. Kuh knew Secretary of State John Foster Dulles in the 1950s. A finding aid and partial bibliographic index for the papers are available.

6.   Irene Lettrich in the cataloging department would be of help to researchers seeking Slavic materials.

NOTE: The Jacob Burns Law Library of the university has a small collection of books on Russian/Soviet law, international law and foreign relations, and related subjects. It is located on campus, at 716 Twentieth Street, NW (202/676-6646).

George Washington University—Institute for Sino-Soviet Studies Library   See entry H15

George Washington University—Slavic Languages and Literature Department Library   See entry J5

A25   Goddard Space Flight Center Library (National Aeronautics and Space Administration)

1 a.   *Goddard Space Flight Center, Building 21*
Greenbelt, Maryland 20771
(301) 344-7218

   b.   8:00 A.M.–4:30 P.M.,   Monday–Friday

   c.   Closed to the public. Researchers, however, may receive permission from the librarian to use the collection.

   d.   Adelaide A. Del Frate, Librarian

2.   The collections include approximately 50,000 books and more than 30,000 serial titles covering the subjects of astronautics, astronomy, mathematics, physics, and space sciences and technology. Russian-related materials are not concentrated and thus difficult to quantify; they are, however, substantial and deserve scholars' attention.

4.   The library currently receives more than 170 periodicals relating to the USSR—eighty in Russian and ninety-three in English translation.

6.   There are no card catalogs, but a series of computerized catalogs is printed each month. These catalogs are organized by author, title, and subject; thus, Russian-related materials are relatively easy to find.

In the monthly *Goddard Library New Books Listing* are translations of the tables of contents of selected Russian-language journals received by the library. Most of these journals included at present are in the field of astronomy.

Contact Wanda Korwin (301/344-6930), on the reference staff, for further information about specific holdings.

NOTE: The Headquarters Library of the National Aeronautics and Space Administration is described in entry K25.

A26 Health and Human Services Department Library (HHS)

1 a. *330 Independence Avenue, SW*
Washington, D.C. 20201
(202) 245-6791 (Reference)

b. 9:00 A.M.–5:30 P.M., Monday–Friday

c. Open to the public for on-site use. Interlibrary loan service and limited photocopying facilities are available.

d. John Boyle, Acting Director

2. The library contains approximately 850,000 volumes and receives some 5,000 periodicals and serials. The social sciences, especially those related to the department's purview, are well represented in the collection.

3 a. Currently the library is a minor resource for the Soviet-area specialist. The library contains materials, not in large numbers, on economics, sociology, and other subjects.

4. Approximately thirteen Russian-language and a few English-language periodicals pertaining to Russia/USSR are received by the library.

6. The library's catalog has been published: the *U.S. Department of Health, Education, and Welfare Author/Title Catalog of the Department Library,* 29 vols. (Boston: G. K. Hall, 1965), with a seven-volume supplement (1973).

NOTE: Most or all of the library's Russian-related education holdings were moved to the library of the National Institute of Education (NIE) when the latter was established in the mid-1970s. NIE's Education Research Library is described in entry A47. For health materials, see the National Library of Medicine (entry A48).

A27 Hillwood Museum Library and Archives

1 a. *4155 Linnean Avenue, NW*
Washington, D.C. 20008
(202) 686-5807

b–c. The library and archives are not presently accessible to the public. No services are available.

d. Katrina V. H. Taylor, Assistant Curator

2.   The collection contains about 2,000 books and pamphlets, plus approximately 100 photographs (in two albums and in separate frames) and many other documents, letters, and memorabilia.

3 a.   The library is, in some respects, a highly specialized one. Although it contains many general works of history and biography, in English and Russian, its great strength lies in its works on art. Many titles are rare and unusual and may be unique in the area. Without parallel are the large numbers of sale catalogs and other materials from museums and galleries in the USSR (or elsewhere) describing Russian/Soviet items offered for sale and at auction. These alone make the collection a major resource for art historians and other specialists.

Among the library's other assets are a multivolume set of prints of the Russian nobility, histories of Russian military units, lavish histories of Russian art, and many art books in large or expensive format. Several items were gifts to Mrs. Marjorie Merriweather Post from Soviet émigrés.

It is difficult to describe more fully the holdings or to evaluate them because at present there is no complete catalog for the library (see point 6). The collection, however, must rate at least a B for some aspects of the fine arts category. Valuable primary research can certainly be conducted here.

4–5.   Two photo albums are kept in the library. The first contains some 50–100 photos of barracks scenes and officers of the Preobrazhensky Guards, plus the family and estates of Colonel Serge Sheremet'ev. The second has photographs from 1887–88 of Moscow monuments, women in native costumes, Saint Petersburg architectural monuments, Tsarskoe Selo, Peterhof, and people of the capital (a total of about twenty-eight photos, some hand-colored). An additional dozen photos, mostly of the imperial family, are framed and on display in the museum proper.

Another album in the library contains letters from and about the Russian imperial family, historical documents, and miscellanea, such as a handkerchief of the Grand Duchess Olga.

Other articles on exhibit in the museum itself include documents granting the title of nobility signed by Elizabeth I, Nicholas I, and Alexander III, as well as a letter of Catherine II from 1770 bearing her signature (the museum proper is described in entry C3).

6.   Although there is no catalog for the library, there are two card files for the materials. The first lists books by author, in alphabetical order. The second lists catalogs, arranged by the location of the museum or gallery in which the subject exhibition was held.

A28   House of Representatives Library

1 a.   *Cannon House Office Building, B-18*
New Jersey and Independence avenues, SE
Washington, D.C. 20515
(202) 225-0462/0463

b.   9:00 A.M.–5:30 P.M.,   Monday–Friday

c.   Open to the public, for on-site use. It is advisable to call in advance. Interlibrary loan service and photocopying facilities are not available.

d.   Dr. Emanuel R. Lewis, Librarian

2. The library holds some 200,000 volumes.

4. This library should be of value to scholars studying the U.S. Government's re-lations with Russia/USSR. It has complete sets of House and Senate reports, the *Congressional Record,* published House and joint committee hearings, statutes-at-large, and many more congressional documents. Indications are that it would be easier, faster, and more efficient to use such materials here rather than, say, at the Library of Congress.

A29 Housing and Urban Development Department (HUD) Library

1 a. *451 Seventh Street, SW, Room 8141*
Washington, D.C. 20410
(202) 755-6370

b. 8:30 A.M.–5:15 P.M., Monday–Friday

c. Open to the public. Interlibrary loan service and photocopying facilities are available.

d. Elsa S. Freeman, Director

2. The library contains nearly 500,000 items, including some 1,800 current periodical titles. About 200 titles pertain to Russia/USSR.

3 a. About ten to fifteen percent of the Soviet-area titles are in the Russian language. The materials cover architecture, city growth and planning, construction, housing, and land use in the USSR. The reference staff can be of significant help in locating some holdings with geographic subject matter. The collection rates a B or C for certain aspects of the economics, sociology, and fine arts categories.

6. The library's catalog has been published: *Dictionary Catalog of the United States Department of Housing and Urban Development,* 19 vols. (Boston: G. K. Hall, 1972), with two two-volume supplements.
   Housing and Planning References is a bimonthly bibliographic tool that lists (and occasionally annotates) articles, books, and documents appearing worldwide. One would find frequent references here under the USSR and Siberia.

NOTE: Most foreign materials that come into HUD go not to the library but to Susan Judd in the Technology and Documentations Division of the department's Office of International Affairs. See HUD entry K20.

A30 Howard University—The Founders Library (and others)

1 a. *500 Howard Place*
Washington, D.C. 20059
(202) 636-7250 (Circulation)
(202) 636-7252/7253 (Reference)

b. Academic year:
8:00 A.M.–Midnight, Monday–Friday
8:00 A.M.–5:00 P.M., Saturday
Noon–Midnight, Sunday
Certain collections and summer semester have different hours; call for more information.

c. Open to researchers for on-site use. Interlibrary loan service and photocopying facilities are available.

d. Binford H. Conley, Director of Libraries

2. The entire library system—comprising Founders and some eight other libraries—contains nearly 900,000 volumes.

3. Subject categories and evaluations (shelflist measurements for all libraries except medical and law, which have insignificant Russian/USSR holdings):

Subject Categories	Number of Titles	Rating
Philosophy and Religion	40	Below D
History	605	D or below
Geography and Ethnography	6	Below D
Economics	130	D or below
Sociology	45	Below D
Politics and Government	85	D or below
Foreign Relations	75	D
Law	Unmeasured	
Education	25	D
Fine Arts	30	Below D
Language	65	D
Literature	510	D
Military Affairs	10	Below D
Bibliography and Reference	10	Below D
Ukrainians	4	Below D
Byelorussians	1	Below D
Baltic Nationalities	6	Below D
Caucasian Nationalities	3	Below D
Central Asian Nationalities	11	D or below
Siberian Nationalities	11	D or below

4. The manuscript division of the Moorland-Spingarn Research Center, located in Room 109 of the Founders Library, contains two small collections of possible interest to the Russianist: the Paul Robeson Papers, which include a number of letters to Robeson from a Soviet delegation, and a set of eighty slides of Pushkin.

Institute for Defense Analysis Library   See entry H20

A31 Interior Department—Natural Resources Library

1 a. *C Street, between Eighteenth and Nineteenth streets, NW*
Washington, D.C. 20240
(202) 343-5821
(202) 343-5815 (Reference)

b. 7:45 A.M.–5:00 P.M.,   Monday–Friday

c. Open to the public for on-site use; only departmental employees may borrow books. Interlibrary loan service and photocopying facilities are available.

d. Phillip Haymond, Director

2. The library holds more than 800,000 volumes and currently receives 4,500 periodical and 10,000 serial titles annually. Subjects covered include the use and conservation of natural resources, in all forms, and animal life. The library attempts not to duplicate the holdings of the Geological Survey Library (entry A22); the two should be considered complementary.

3 a. Although the library has a handful of titles in most subject categories, these holdings are not of much significance. Only in the categories of science and technology does the library have much to offer the Russianist. Many of these titles will bear on the subjects of economics, history, sociology, and others. A selection of subject measurements includes: agriculture, fish culture: 85 titles; agriculture, soils: 20 titles; geology, mineralogy, paleontology, petrology: 110 titles; hydraulic engineering: 25 titles; metallurgy, mining engineering: 180 titles; conservation, natural history: 15 titles; zoology: 105 titles.

These measurements represent only the tip of the iceberg and conceal more than they reveal of the wealth of Russian-area materials of the library. The best estimate of the collection's rank for the fields of its concentration is an A.

4. Carl Messick, of the Gifts and Exchanges Section, who works closely with the library's Slavic materials, estimates that the library currently receives about one hundred Russian periodicals.

5. A translation file is maintained in the library. Russian holdings total between 500 and 725 items. Most pieces are typewritten or printed papers and articles, not books. Therefore, only a part of the translation file material appears in the measurements given under point 3. Physically, the translations occupy three full five-drawer file cabinets located in the stacks.

6. The library's catalog has been published: *Dictionary Catalog of the Departmental Library,* 37 vols. (Boston: G. K. Hall, 1967), with five supplements, the last of which covers through 1974.

The library publishes a Bibliography Series (thirty-eight titles to date). Two items are of interest: No. 6, *Reindeer in Russia and the Scandinavian Countries,* by Ludmilla Floss (1967); and No. 9, *Natural Resources in Foreign Countries: A Contribution toward a Bibliography of Bibliographies,* by Mary Anglemyer (1968); both available from National Technical Information Service. (Other titles may also be helpful.)

The staff has issued these guides: *Abstracting and Indexing Services Received in the Departmental Library* (1968) and *Abstracting and Indexing Services in the Office of Library Services,* rev. ed. (1970).

The 1980 edition of the department's *Libraries and Information Services Directory* has recently appeared. The small brochure *Using Your Departmental Library* (1976), a guide to library holdings and services, is available without charge.

NOTE: The Interior Department has a number of branch libraries located throughout the country, and many have holdings not duplicated in the main library in Washington. A rapid interlibrary loan system makes the collections of the branch libraries readily accessible to scholars in the capital.

A32 International Labor Office (ILO) (International Labor Organization)—Washington Branch Library

1 a. *1750 New York Avenue, NW, Room 330*
Washington, D.C. 20006
(202) 376-2315

b. 8:30 A.M.–5:00 P.M., Monday–Friday

c. Open to the public. Interlibrary loan service and photocopying facilities are available.

d. Patricia S. Hord, Librarian

2. The library holds about 13,250 volumes plus 3,600 ILO documents for a total of 16,850 items.

3 a. The subject categories are not particularly germane. Of most importance to the researcher is the fact that the library contains almost all publications of ILO. Holdings fall for the most part in the categories of economics, law, and sociology and cover the following subjects: broad areas of national economies (e.g., agriculture and industry); conditions, hours, and wages of labor; employment and unemployment; health, safety, and welfare; labor legislation; labor statistics; maritime questions; social policy and economic development; specific industries, such as aviation, coal mining, forestry; standards of living; and trade unions.

There is no way to quantify materials here of interest to the Russianist. The USSR has been a member of ILO between 1934 and 1940 and since 1954. The Ukrainian and Byelorussian SSRs have also been members since 1954. Therefore, information about the Soviet Union will appear in a great number of ILO publications not specifically concerned with the USSR. Aids to finding this information in ILO publications and elsewhere are noted in point 6. The library also has a handful of non-ILO works directly on the USSR, including R. Hislop's bound thesis "The United States and the Soviet Union in the ILO" (University of Colorado, 1961).

4. There is a set of several eight-by-ten-inch black-and-white photographs of Soviet working women in the library's still-photo collection. They were illustrations for a story in an ILO journal.

5. The ILO publication *Legislative Series* is a compilation of the most important laws and regulations of various nations on labor and social security, translated into English, since 1919. The Washington branch library has pulled material from this series and collected it geographically; thus, it has a vertical-file folder for all these laws of the USSR.

6. Guides of use for this library and more generally are *International Labour Documentation: Cumulative Edition, 1965–69*, 8 vols.; *Cumulative Edition, 1970–71*, 2 vols.; and *Cumulative Edition, 1972–76*, 5 vols. These are cumulations of the monthly publication *International Labour Documentation* (ILD), for which more than 1,000 journals are scanned and, when appropriate, abstracted, and in which appear all new books cataloged by the ILO library in Geneva, major new ILO publications, and other technical documents. Each issue contains approximately 250 short abstracts recorded in machine-readable form for computer processing. The cumulations supersede issues of the *ILD* only for the years indicated. There is a geographic index for the earlier cumulation but none for the more recent one. The staff of the Washington

branch library can help researchers use these guides most effectively, especially for the library's own holdings (i.e., ILO publications). A new cumulation is expected soon.

Subject Guide to Publications of the International Labour Office, 1919–64 (Geneva, 1967) and *ILO Catalogue of Publications in Print, 1982* (Geneva) are of interest because of the nature of the library's holdings. The first has a section on bibliographic contributions with a supplementary geographic index.

Legislative Series: Chronological Index of Legislation, 1919–78 (Geneva, 1980) is of value for this ILO publication. Each year an annual supplement is published entitled "Indexes and Chronological List of Labour Legislation," which contains a subject index and is arranged alphabetically by country. Also of help is *Legislative Series: General Subject Index, 1919–59* (Geneva, 1961) and *The Consolidated Index to the ILO Legislative Series, 1919–70* (INIFO, 1975). *Cumulative Index of Laws* (Geneva, 1977) published in the Legislative Series Part 1: 1919–45 and Part 2: 1946–75 contain a List of Texts Irrespective of Repeals, arranged in alphabetical order by originating country.

Because the Washington branch library can borrow materials from Geneva, the *ILO Photo Library: Catalogue* (Geneva, 1973), arranged by subject, region, and country, might also be of interest to the researcher.

A final tool to note is the chart entitled "Chart of Ratifications of International Labour Conventions" (1982), which shows at which sessions of the ILO's annual conferences 156 different conventions were adopted and whether they have been ratified by various member nations. For subjects of interest covered by these conventions, the researcher can then explore the ILO publications of proceedings and meetings for the years indicated in the chart.

A33 International Trade Commission (ITC) Library

1 a. *701 E Street, NW, Room 301*
       Washington, D.C. 20436
       (202) 523-0013

  b. 8:45 A.M.–5:15 P.M., Monday–Friday

  c. Open to the public. Interlibrary loan service and photocopying facilities are available.

  d. Dorothy J. Berkowitz, Chief, Library Division

2–3 The ITC Library holds approximately 80,000 volumes and 2,200 serial titles. The amount of Russian/Soviet material here probably does not exceed five percent of the total holdings. The library receives the quarterly *East-West Trade Report* (published by ITC), which is of interest to Russianists. A portion of the library's periodical holdings has been transferred to microform, and the serials may also be microfilmed in the future.

6. The author/subject/title dictionary card catalog contains geographic entries. The library also publishes a monthly acquisitions list entitled *Our Library Presents*.

A34 Joint Bank-Fund Library (Library of the International Bank for Reconstruction and Development *and* International Monetary Fund)

1 a. *700 Nineteenth Street, NW*
Washington, D.C. 20431
(202) 477-3125 (Librarian)
(202) 477-3167 (Reference)

b. 9:00 A.M.–5:00 P.M., Monday–Friday

c. Open to researchers, by appointment, for on-site use. Interlibrary loan service and photocopying facilities are available.

d. Maureen M. Moore, Librarian

2. The total collection consists of more than 150,000 volumes and nearly 4,000 periodical titles. The Russian/Soviet holdings number approximately 1,200 titles, of which some 20 are serial publications.

3 a. The subject category of interest here is economics. Among topics with a high concentration of holdings are: economic development, financial economics, and international commerce. There are also books on budget and central public administration, labor economics, land economics, macroeconomics, public finance, and statistics. For this category the collection rates a B.

Because the Soviet Union is not a member of the bank or fund, the library does not attempt to collect material on the USSR in a comprehensive fashion. Nevertheless, researchers would find this collection a substantial resource for the study of Russian/Soviet economics.

6. This library has a unique geographic catalog. This catalog and a detailed classification system make it easy to locate materials in the library.

Economics and Finance: Index to Periodical Articles, 4 vols. (Boston: G. K. Hall, 1972) is an excellent reference tool for both this and other libraries. Volume 4 contains a most useful geographic index. The index has been updated by two supplements, the first covering articles indexed 1972–74, the second covering articles indexed 1975–77.

The library also publishes a monthly *List of Recent Periodical Articles* (publication noted just above) and a monthly list of recent additions of books and monographs. Both lists are arranged by subject, geographic area, and country.

One brochure available without charge at the library containing broad but useful information is *Guide to the Joint Bank-Fund Library.*

Joint Publications Research Service—Reading Room   See entry Q10

A35 Kennan Institute for Advanced Russian Studies (Woodrow Wilson International Center for Scholars)—Library

1 a. *Smithsonian Institution Building*
1000 Jefferson Drive, SW
Washington, D.C. 20560
(202) 357-2567

b. 8:45 A.M.–5:15 P.M., Monday–Friday

c. Open to researchers with prior permission from the librarian or secretary of the Kennan Institute (202/357-2415). Interlibrary loan service and photocopying facilities are available. The librarian is a professional Slavic bibliographer, and the institute employs qualified assistants to perform bibliographic searches for its members. As part of a national presidential memorial (the Woodrow Wilson International Center for Scholars, see entry H31), the library has special access to the collections of the Library of Congress and other government libraries. In the field of Russian/Soviet studies it is virtually the only scholarly library in Washington to enjoy this status.

d. Dr. Zdeněk V. David, Librarian

2. The library contains more than 5,000 volumes (books and periodicals).

3 a. In the Washington area, this new and growing library (established in 1975) promises to develop one of the most significant collections, focused specifically on the support of fundamental scholarly research on Russia/USSR in the fields of the social sciences and the humanities. It is designed to assist primarily the work of the fellows of the Kennan Institute (entry H23), which is a part of the Woodrow Wilson International Center for Scholars. The bibliographic holdings and other reference materials, such as dictionaries, encyclopedias, guides, handbooks, and indexes, are particularly strong. Among others, they include the Brokgauz-Efron *Entsiklopedicheskii slovar'*, all three editions of *Bol'shaia sovetskaia entsiklopediia, Slovar' sovremennogo russkogo literaturnogo iazyka,* and *Cyrillic Union Catalog* (on microprint cards). The library also maintains regular contacts with other centers of bibliographic information in this area, especially the European Division of the Library of Congress.

The holdings include collections of documents on foreign policy (for instance, *Dokumenty vneshnei politiki SSSR*) and collected works of major writers (e.g. Chekhov, Dostoevskii, Pushkin, Tolstoi), historians (e.g. Karamzin, Kliuchevskii, Solov'ev), and public figures (e.g., Lenin, Stalin), as well as *Sobranie dokumentov samizdata.* In general, the library is strong in history (thirty-five percent of volumes held), law and politics (twenty percent), economics and sociology (fifteen percent), and theory, history, and criticism of literature (fifteen percent). Within these subject categories, especially history, is a substantial representation of works dealing with the individual nationalities of the USSR, particularly Byelorussians, Ukrainians, and the nations of the Baltic area, Central Asia, Siberia, and Transcaucasia. Local history of Great Russia (provinces and towns) is also well represented.

4. The library subscribes to Soviet newspapers as well as the leading American, British, French, German, and Soviet scholarly periodicals in the field of Russian/ Soviet studies, especially economics, history, literature, and politics. It also receives regularly *Daily Reports—Soviet Union,* issued by the Foreign Broadcast Information Service, and *Current Digest of the Soviet Press.*

A36 Labor Department Library

1 a. *200 Constitution Avenue, NW, Room N2439*
Washington, D.C. 20210
(202) 523-6992 (Reference)

b. 8:15 A.M.–4:45 P.M., Monday–Friday

c. Open to the public for on-site use. Limited interlibrary loan service and photocopying facilities are available.

d. Andre C. Whisenton, Library Director

2. The library contains more than 500,000 items and receives some 3,200 periodicals. The collection is very strong on labor and economics in general.

3 a. For all subject categories except economics, the library has holdings that rank below the D level; for example, there are about eighty titles in history.

In economics, much of the library's wealth went unmeasured from shelflist calculations. Researchers can pick up many of these titles in the subject headings of the card catalog (e.g., "Labor productivity—Russia" or "Wages—Russia"). The findings, approximately 850 titles in economics, warrant a C rating.

4. The library has about ten periodical titles relating to labor/economics in the USSR.

There is a substantial collection of International Labor Organization publications and many government reports on labor and statistics.

6. The library's catalog has been published: *U.S. Department of Labor Library Catalog*, 38 vols. (Boston: by G. K. Hall, 1975). *Periodicals Currently Received by the U.S. Department of Labor Library* (1980) pertains to the Periodicals Branch of the library. The accessions list entitled *Labor Literature* might also prove to be of interest.

Latvian Evangelical Lutheran Church   See entry P5

A37 Library of Congress (LC)

NOTE: Because of the size and diversity of holdings of LC—by every measurement the greatest resource in the Washington area for Russianists—the format of this entry is a modification of the standard one. Points 2 and 3 pertain almost exclusively to the main collections in the regular stack areas. Holdings that are physically separate or are worthy of more individual treatment and those materials that fall under the purview of one of LC's own divisions are described under point 4. Under point 6 the reader will find those publications and materials that pertain to the entire library. Other publications and research aids issued by or relating to the individual divisions are noted under those branches.

1 a. *Thomas Jefferson Building*
10 First Street, SE
(between Independence Avenue and East Capitol Street)

John Adams Building
110 Independence Avenue, SE
(between Second and Third streets)

James Madison Memorial Building
101 Independence Avenue, SE
(between First and Second streets)

Mail:
10 First Street, SE
Washington, D.C. 20540
(202) 287-5000 (LC Switchboard)

NOTE: Various LC divisions and sections are presently scheduled for relocation. Scholars are therefore advised to confirm the location of offices before visiting them. Should the telephone numbers supplied below be changed, the LC switchboard will be able to provide new listings.

   b. General Reading Rooms (Thomas Jefferson and John Adams buildings):
8:30 A.M.–9:30 P.M. (stack service to 8:30 P.M.), Monday–Friday
8:30 A.M.–5:00 P.M. (stack service to 4:00 P.M.), Saturday and working holidays
1:00–5:00 P.M. (stack service to 4:00 P.M.), Sunday
Closed on all holidays except Washington's Birthday, Columbus Day, and Veterans' Day. Division hours are noted below.

   c. For on-site use LC's facilities and staff are available to the public. There is a very good interlibrary loan service (exclusive of periodicals and newspapers), although the process often requires some waiting due to the volume of requests received. Photocopying facilities are available; and the library also has a Photoduplication Division.

   d. Daniel J. Boorstin, Librarian of Congress
Division chiefs are listed below.

2. Total LC holdings number more than 78 million items. The European Division estimates that all Slavic holdings exceed 800,000 items, of which some 500,000–600,000 are monographs and the rest are bound periodicals, issues of newspapers, and pamphlets. A breakdown for some of these holdings appears in point 3. Currently the division receives approximately 20,000 titles per year from the Soviet Union and some 3,500 active periodicals and serials (and another 1,000 irregularly) plus 125 newspapers. Other divisions—particularly the Asian Division and the African and Middle Eastern Division—also receive materials from the USSR, including some 600 monographs and issues of 300 periodicals and serials.

3 a–b. The reader is reminded of the remarks in the Introductory Note to the Libraries (A) section concerning what shelflist measurements can and cannot reveal. The following figures may cover approximately one-fourth of total Slavic holdings; at best they should reflect relative subject strengths.

Subject Category	*Number of Titles*
Philosophy and Religion	4,925
History	39,160
Geography and Ethnography (excl. atlases and maps)	2,670
Economics	24,150
Sociology	5,950
Politics and Government	8,410
Foreign Relations	1,770
Law (see under point 4)	12,590
Education	2,040
Fine Arts (excl. music)	6,885

Subject Category	Number of Titles
Language (Russian and Finno-Ugrian only)	5,205
Literature (Russian and Finno-Ugrian only; based on LC 1975 count)	37,130
Military Affairs	2,670
Bibliography, Reference, General	7,585
Ukrainians	7,550
Byelorussians	1,410
Baltic Nationalities	6,875
Caucasian Nationalities	4,400
Central Asian Nationalities	8,140
Siberian Nationalities	2,155
Science	3,910
Technology	5,985

NOTE: Atlases and maps of the Geography and Maps Division are described separately in entry E4. Music materials are detailed under point 4 and in entries D3 and D4. Figures for the nationalities subject categories in part duplicate totals for the history, geography, and law categories. On the basis of size and quality, LC's Russian/Soviet collections rate an A for every subject category.

Additional measurements of interest:

Subject Category	Number of Titles
Moldavian/Bessarabians	
History, geography, law	215
Poland	
History	5,205
Geography	1,020
Law	3,790
Language and Literature	7,635
Finland	
History	1,970
Geography	240
Law	1,070
Language and Literature	3,155

4.   Divisions of the Library of Congress

EUROPEAN DIVISION
John Adams Building, Fifth Floor
(202) 287-5417

Clara Maria Lovett, Chief (202/287-6520)
David H. Kraus, Assistant Chief (202/287-5414/5413)
Robert V. Allen, Area Specialist for Russia/Soviet Union (202/287-5415)

8:30 A.M.–4:30 P.M.,   Monday–Friday (but see European Reading Room hours, following)

This division should be the first point of contact for the Russian/Soviet-area specialist who wants to find out what Slavic materials LC has and how best to make use of them. Staff members would be of most help to researchers in supplying bibliographic references and offering assistance in the use of catalogs.

The European Reading Room (Thomas Jefferson Building, Room G-147, 202/287-5858) is a part of the division. A public reading room, the European Reading Room provides reference materials and services to researchers. Its reference collection numbers some 4,500 volumes of direct interest to Russianists, with total holdings about twice that size. Among its valuable materials are numerous dictionaries and encyclopedias, recent telephone directories for the capitals and major cities of the USSR, notebooks full of Russian-related clippings from the *New York Times,* and *samizdat* (self-published) material bound and in boxes. The room is open from 8:30 A.M. to 5:00 P.M., Monday through Saturday, and 1:00 to 5:00 P.M. on Sunday. On weekdays researchers can, however, arrange ahead of time for materials to be transferred to the Science Reading Room for evening use.

It is important to note that the European Reading Room receives, keeps, and services current Slavic Cyrillic newspapers and periodicals, excluding those received in the Law Library and Music Division but including those on science and technology. Thus, Russianists should not go to the Newspapers and Current Periodicals Room (in the James Madison Building) for these items.

Although a section of the General Reading Rooms Division shares in the control of the various union catalogs, the European Division staff can be of great help to researchers who use the Cyrillic and the Slavic-Cyrillic Union catalogs. The Cyrillic Union Catalog is available in microprint in the division. It provides, in three separate series, author, subject, and title listings of pre-1956 imprints. The Slavic-Cyrillic Union Catalog, available in the division in microfiche, provides (by main entry only) information on additional locations and some additional titles of pre-1956 items.

For post-1956 imprints, the current National Union Catalog covers U.S. and Canadian repositories and includes Slavic holdings. It should be noted that the *National Union Catalog, pre-1956 Imprints,* published in England by Mansell, includes only LC printed cards for Cyrillic materials. Thus it does not necessarily show such materials located in other libraries. Again, the Slavic-Cyrillic Union Catalog is perhaps the researchers best guide for pre-1956 items.

Readers familiar with the European Division will be pleased to learn that a considerable part of two large Slavic collections—the uncataloged Yudin and the "Cyrillic 4" materials—long accessible only through the European Reading Room has been fully processed and integrated into LC's regular collections. The bulk of the Yudin collection has been fully cataloged; thus access to it is through the normal procedures of the Main and General Reading rooms in the Jefferson and Adams buildings. The remaining incompletely cataloged material, largely "Cyrillic 4" items (but also including about 4,300 Yudin items), is shelved in the Northwest Attic of the Thomas Jefferson Building. This room holds some 14,000 monographs; 11,000 unbound issues of periodicals; and 7,000–8,000 pamphlets, which are boxed together by classification letters; only the last have recently been surveyed with a view to having them microfilmed.

Ukrainian-area specialists should note that the division office holds a useful unpublished guide entitled *Ukrainica in the Library of Congress: A Preliminary Survey* (1956), with a 1979 update. Researchers may consult these guides in the European Division office.

A number of the division's publications are of great value to Russianists: *Eighteenth-Century Russian Publications in the Library of Congress: A Catalog,* comp. T. Fessenko (1961), out of print; *Estonia: A Selected Bibliography,* comp. Salme Kuri (1958), out of print; *Index to Russian and Ukrainian Periodicals Available on Microfilm from the Library of Congress Photoduplication Service,* by Paul L. Horecky with John P. Balys and Robert G. Carlton (1968), out of print; *Newspapers of the Soviet Union in the Library of Congress (Slavic, 1954–1960; Non-Slavic, 1917–1960)* (1962), out of print; *Russian, Ukrainian, and Belorussian Newspapers, 1917-1953: A Union List,* comp. Paul Horecky (1953), out of print; *The USSR and East Central and Southeastern Europe; Periodicals in Western Languages,* comp. Paul L. Horecky and Robert G. Carlton, 4th rev. ed., comp. Janina Hoskins (1979).

LC publications not from but pertaining to the functions of this division include: *Glossary of Russian Abbreviations and Acronyms* (1967); *Guide to Soviet Bibliographies: A Selected List of References,* comp. J. Dorosh (1950); *Half a Century of Soviet Serials, 1917–1968: A Bibliography and Union List of Serials Published in the USSR,* 2 vols., comp. R. Smits (1968); *Latin America in Soviet Writings: A Bibliography,* 2 vols., comp. L. Okinshevich (Baltimore: Johns Hopkins University Press for Library of Congress, 1966). This title supersedes a 1959 bibliography by L. Okinshevich and C. Gorokhoff.

One further reference work, not an LC publication, deserves mention here: *List of the Serial Publications of Foreign Governments, 1815–1931,* ed. Winifred Gregory (New York: H. W. Wilson Co., 1932). A bound excerpt of the section on Russia/ USSR, prepared and annotated by V. Gsovski, is kept in the division by Robert Allen.

Published descriptions and guides to the division have been numerous over the years. The most recent is "The Slavic Collections of the U.S. Library of Congress," by David Kraus in *UNESCO Journal of Information Science, Librarianship, and Archives Administration* 1, no. 3 (1979). Still of interest is "The Library of Congress, Its Russian Program and Activities," by Sergius Yakobson in *The American Review on the Soviet Union* (August 1946). A one-page flyer, available without charge from the division, lists its publications in and out of print. The staff is currently preparing a brochure that will describe the facilities, services, holdings, and publications of the division; it should be available in the near future.

LAW LIBRARY
James Madison Memorial Building, Room 240
(202) 287-5079

Carleton W. Kenyon, Law Librarian (202/287-5065)
Ivan Sipkov, Chief, European Law Division
Tadeusz Sadowski, Senior Legal Specialist

8:30 A.M.–4:15 P.M.,   Monday–Friday
By prior arrangement, nonrare materials may be used on reserve in the reading room of the Law Library in the evening and on weekends: 8:30 A.M.–9:30 P.M., Monday–Friday; 8:30 A.M.–5:00 P.M., Saturday; 1:00–5:00 P.M., Sunday

The Law Library presently contains more than 1.7 million volumes, the European Law Division accounting for perhaps one-fourth of this total. The Law Library has its own public catalog and shelflists. Tadeusz Sadowski, the Russian/Soviet-area specialist, estimates that current Soviet acquisitions come to about 50 items per month or 600 per year. He puts total Russian/Soviet holdings at about 30,000 volumes, with 13,000 volumes from the imperial period and 17,000 from the Soviet; this is surely one of the largest, if not the largest, collections of Russian legal material outside the Soviet Union. The breakdown of this material (based on the shelflist measurements for the first edition of this guide) is as follows:

Call Number	Subject Category	Number of Titles
KR 1–1999	*Imperial Russia*	
1–85	Constitutional Law	205
89–91	History of Law, General	110
92–134	History of Law, by Period	220
203–278	General Collections of Laws	365
279–283	Comprehensive Works	50
285–418	Judiciary	460
440–499	Administrative Law, Local Gov't	155
500–625	Military Law and Court Martial, Naval Law	145
630–670	Education	45
680–683	Press	40
690–730	Public Health	45
740–790	Finance and Economics, Taxes	130
798–860	Civil Law, General and Specific	435
870–968	Commercial Law	340
970–996	Civil Procedure	100
998–1115	Criminal Law and Procedure	470
1200–1210	Ecclesiastical Law	135
1240–1466	Laws—Individual Classes/Local	240
1500–1536	Civil War Governments	25
1910–1981	Material in Russian of General Significance	390
KR 2000–	*USSR and RSFSR* and Other Republics*	
2000–2085	Constitutional Law	595
2101–2110	General Collections of Laws	75
2111–2123	Comprehensive Works	580
2151–2198	Judiciary, Courts, Trials	605
2200–2220	Administrative Law, Local Gov't	205
2225–2298	Special Topics	535
2300–2365	Civil and Commercial Law	1,540
2370–2374	International Law	100
2380–2396	Civil Procedure	195
2400–2475	Criminal Law and Procedure, Penology	960
2478–2481	Martial Law	35
2500–2577	Labor Law	875
2599–2622	Land Tenure	415
2640–2651	Forestry and Waters, Natural Resources	70
2700–2707	Housing	155
2710–2765	Ukraine (prerevolutionary and Soviet)	325
2766	Moldavia	45
2770–2799	Byelorussia (prerevolutionary and Soviet)	110
2800	Provincial and City Ordinances	25

* Russian Soviet Federated Socialist Republic

Call Number	Subject Category	Number of Titles
2801–2845	Caucasus (incl. Armenia, Azerbaidjan, Georgia)	180
2846–2882	Central Asia: Kazakstan, Tadjik, Turcoman, Turkestan, Uzbek	265
2890–2895	Kirghiz, Outer Mongolia, Siberia (Buriat, Yakut)	85
2883–2884, 2897	Estonia and Latvia, Lithuania	305
2885–2889	Crimea, German Volga, Karelo-Finnish, Shuvash, Tatar SSR	60
2898–2899	Other Caucasus, Central Asia	50
2900	Ostgebiete (Nazi-occupied areas in World War II)	5
3000	Periodicals	100

In addition to this cataloged material, some uncataloged holdings are kept in special cases. Relatively few in number, these items include some manuscripts and a large number of photographs. Staff members can assist researchers in using this uncataloged material.

The treasures to be found in these collections are many. A small portion of the imperial library of the tsars ("Winter Palace Collection") has been transferred from the Rare Books Division to the Law Library. About 128 titles, all but a handful with Alexander II's bookplate, deal exclusively with non-Russian law. The library also has three eighteenth-century editions of the Kievan *Russkaia Pravda,* the earliest-known Russian legal code. A copy of the rare 1819 publication of the 1497 *Sudebnik,* by Ivan III, is also here.

The library holds a 1649 edition of the *Ulozhenie,* by Tsar Aleksei Mikhailovich, the first printed Russian law code, along with an annotated manuscript copy and a German translation of it; the extremely rare 1650 printing of the *Kormchaia Kniga* (the Byzantine *Nomokanon);* and two English translations of the *Nakaz* (The Instruction), of Catherine the Great, one printed and the other manuscript, dating from the 1760s. As might be expected, the major law collections are here: *Polnoe sobranie zakonov, Svod zakonov Rossiiskoi Imperii, Svod voennykh postanovlenii,* and *Svod morskikh postanovlenii* and the decrees of the Ruling Senate.

Manuscript items include forty-six scrolls from the seventeenth and eighteenth centuries; the original *Ukazy* of Empress Anna Ivanovna (1730s), some with her autograph; the draft of a law code prepared for Alexander I by the State Council in 1813–14; reports and material relating to the White government at Omsk in the Civil War; material on the murder of Nicholas II and the imperial family; and, among the A. N. Iakhontov Papers, handwritten minutes of meetings of the Council of Ministers in 1914.

Some other printed sources of note: the work of the 1850s committees that prepared the 1861 emancipation of the serfs, a complete set of the *Sobranie uzakonenii* from 1863, and the Iakhontov *Zhurnaly Soveta Ministrov* of 1914.

From the Soviet period, the Law Library has equally impressive holdings. Constitutions for the USSR and its constituent republics, in various editions; law codes and regulations on virtually every subject; textbooks and treatises—all these and more are here. Although one cannot point out as many rare and valuable holdings among the Soviet items, it is their very comprehensiveness that makes the library a unique resource for Russianists.

The collections also include Polish materials totaling about 3,790 titles (KR 3001–3565) and Finnish sources measured at roughly 1,070 titles (KR 5000–5790).

Nonlegal scholars might note that many other social sciences, particularly history and political science, are extremely well represented here. In fact, at one time the Law Library appears to have had funds available for acquisitions when other LC divisions had less money at their disposal. The Soviet-area specialists in the library, as a consequence, bought up Russian sources even remotely related to law, and this broad range of books still remains here.

There is currently no published catalog available specifically for this collection. Indeed, LC does not even have a complete classification schedule for most foreign law materials. In any event, the Law Library has published a useful booklet describing many of its holdings: *The Law Library of the Library of Congress: Its History, Collections, and Services* (1978). The excellent section on Russian/Soviet materials in this publication, written by Tadeusz Sadowski, was used extensively in compiling the above account.

Further information about some of these Slavic acquisitions can be found in various issues of *Annual Report of the Librarian of Congress*; the supplementary *Library of Congress Quarterly Journal of Current Acquisitions*, from 1943 to 1964; and *Quarterly Journal of the Library of Congress*, from 1964 until recently, when the Law Library has not reported as actively as in the past. It is important to note that since 1964, not only current acquisitions but also earlier ones of current interest are described. Particularly valuable should be annual reports from the late 1920s and early 1930s, when the library's Russian holdings were expanding rapidly. Finally, in the August 1960 issue of *Quarterly Journal* appears Kazimierz Grzybowski's brief article describing the history and importance of the Iakhontov Papers.

MUSIC DIVISION
Thomas Jefferson Building, Room G-146
(202) 287-5507

Donald Leavitt, Chief

8:30 A.M.–5:00 P.M.,   Monday–Saturday

The collections of music and music literature assembled in LC are remarkably diverse and comprehensive. International in scope and spanning many centuries, the holdings include some 30,000 books, periodicals, and pamphlets; about 700,000 sound recordings; and more than 4 million pieces of music, including scores, sheet music, librettos, and miscellaneous items (including autography pieces, holographs, original manuscripts, and rare materials). Nontextual materials are described in entries D3 and D4.

Most holdings are not listed in the main public catalog. The reading room of the Music Division, however, has many tools to aid researchers. Materials can be located by type of music (the class[ified] catalog), by title or by name, and by author/title/subject. The class catalog is like a shelflist in that it is arranged by classification numbers; with a classification schedule in hand, the class catalog user has very nearly a subject and geographic index for some material. More important, the class catalog is unusual in that it includes cross-references. Titles with different call numbers are brought together in one place in the catalog. The name catalog has cards only for scores and sheet music (M classification). Other catalogs cover music literature (ML) and music theory (MT). Still another catalog (author/title only) is just for librettos (M, ML). There are some cross-references in these catalogs also.

Measurement of these various catalogs and/or the shelflist is a poor way to ascertain the division's holdings—so little of the material is arranged geographically. For whatever value they have, shelflist figures for M and ML listings totaled only 3,045 items.

By comparison, class catalog figures for the same call numbers came to more than 1,000 additional items. But the only true method of gauging the collections would have been to measure the reading room catalogs for individual composers. Instead of such a time-consuming undertaking, a survey of a few names was made. The results, in inches, for Tchaikovskii: 14.3, 2.8, 1, and 0.4 in the M, ML, MT, and libretto catalogs respectively—about 1,575 titles; Prokof'ev: 6.3, 0.7, 0.4, and 0.3—655 titles; Shostakovich: 4.3, 0.4, 0.2, and 8 titles—425 titles; Glinka: 1.8, 1, 0.1, and 6 titles—255 titles; Glazunov: 2.3, 0.2, 5 titles, and 1 title—220 titles; Dargomyzhskii: 0.5, 0.2, 1 title, and 2 titles—65 titles; and under Russia/Russian (various languages): 0.6, 5.4, and 0.2—525 titles.

But the real points to make about the holdings of the division are that LC attempts to collect the complete works of almost all major Russian/Soviet composers and, perhaps uniquely, of most minor composers as well; and that it has the original scores of music by a large number of the most important figures in the history of Russian music. Beyond these core items, the division holds such rare and valuable material as the Rachmaninoff Archives and Collection (about twenty-four shelf feet), the N. K. Medtner Collection (about four shelf feet), the Nicolas Slonimsky Papers from 1895–1969 (some twenty-four feet), letters of Milii Balakirev on music from the 1860s to 1880s, and a large collection of Stravinskii's music. The researcher would do well to consult two publications as guides to this wealth of material: *A Census of Autograph Manuscripts of European Composers in American Libraries,* by Otto Albrecht (Philadelphia: University of Pennsylvania Press, 1953) and the relevant section (pp. 137–46) of *The Russian Empire and Soviet Union: A Guide to Manuscripts and Archival Materials in the United States,* by Steven A. Grant and John A. Brown (Boston: G. K. Hall, 1981). The latter contains detailed descriptions of seventy-one separate collections of original and facsimile manuscripts among the division's Russian-related holdings.

A comprehensive printed bibliography of the cataloged resources of the division is an LC cumulative publication, *Music, Books on Music and Sound Recordings,* and its predecessor, *Library of Congress Catalog: Music and Phonorecordings: A Cumulative List of Works Represented by Library of Congress Printed Cards.* Both titles are available as volumes of the *National Union Catalog.* A free leaflet prepared by the division, *The Music Division: A Guide to Its Collections and Services,* provides useful assistance to visitors. Photocopying facilities and microfilm readers are available in the reading room area. With few exceptions, the collection circulates on interlibrary loan.

ASIAN DIVISION
Chinese and Korean Section
John Adams Building, Room A-1008
(202) 287-5423

Chi Wang, Head

8:30 A.M.–5:00 P.M., Monday–Friday
8:30 A.M.–5:00 P.M., Saturday

The Chinese and Korean Section holds some materials from the Soviet Union, both in Mongolian and in Russian. Some items from China in Mongolian are also here. Any materials in Siberian languages such as Buriat and Yakut could come to this section as well, although at present there appear to be none. The Mongolian holdings are almost entirely uncataloged and number no more than a few hundred items. Materials include several periodicals; what appear to be scholarly publications on folklore and economics; dictionaries; plus novels and other literary works. In addition, there are three manuscripts and seventy-seven xylographs—valuable examples of Mongolian block-print literature, on a variety of religious and other subjects—kept locked in the section's rare book room. See "A Description of Mongolian Manuscripts and Xylographs in Washington, D.C.," by David M. Farquhar in *Central Asiatic Journal* 1, no. 3 (n.d.). No published guides, descriptions, or lists of publications of this section would appear to be of interest for Russianists.

AFRICAN AND MIDDLE EASTERN DIVISION
Near East Section
John Adams Building, Room 1005
(202) 287-5421

George N. Atiyeh, Head
Abraham Bodurgil, Turkish and Armenian Area Specialist
Ibrahim Pourhadi, Persian and Central Asian Specialist

8:30 A.M.–5:00 P.M., Monday–Friday
8:30 A.M.–12:30 P.M., Saturday

The Near East Section currently receives some 4,000-5,000 items per year from the Soviet Union (about 600 monographs and issues of 300 periodicals, newspapers, and serials). Titles in twenty-one languages, including Armenian, Georgian, Kurdish, Persian, Turkic, and Turkish languages of Central Asia, are accessioned. Many holdings remain uncataloged, particularly Central Asian and Georgian materials, for which no catalogers are presently on the library staff. Armenian specialists should note that the section's holdings include a number of rare Armenian religious manuscripts from the fourteenth to the eighteenth centuries.

A 1982 survey of section collections produced the following figures:

	Armenian Titles/Volumes	Central Asian Titles/Volumes	Turkish (partially Soviet) Titles/Volumes	Persian (partially Soviet) Titles/Volumes
Cataloged monographs	9,000/11,500	5,000/7,000	13,000/17,000	10,000/14,000
Uncataloged monographs	—	6,000/7,000	—	8,500/11,000
Cataloged periodicals	10/160	—	242/1,000	—
Uncataloged periodicals	250/800	140/3,000	140/950	—
Microfilm newspapers	385 reels	37 reels	558 reels	—
Other microforms	7	11	37	—

Public catalogs and union catalogs for the Near East collections are located in the section room, accessible only during the hours stated above.

RARE BOOK AND SPECIAL COLLECTIONS DIVISION
Thomas Jefferson Building, Room 256
(202) 287-5434

William Matheson, Chief

These collections contain more than 300,000 volumes, 64,000 pamphlets, 36,000 broadsides, and 54,000 title pages filed for copyright purposes from 1790–1870. These figures do not include 6,000 recently acquired pieces of ephemera of movements on the political left, largely American in origin but with a strong international flavor in such areas as anarchism and communism.

A fascinating resource of the division for Russianists is the magnificent Russian Imperial Collection or Tsars' Library (sometimes called the "Winter Palace Collection" but actually assembled from several palaces). This ensemble of more than 2,400 volumes came to LC in the early 1930s from a New York bookseller. The handsome bindings are the first thing to strike the user of the library. The collection is largely made up of regimental histories, religious and inspirational works, and volumes presented by friends and authors to the Russian tsars. One half of the Russian Imperial Collection has been fully accessioned, given original cataloging when there are no other copies in the library's collections, and shelved by call number. Information on these books is available through the library's main catalog. Cards for some titles have been filed in alphabetical order and by call number in the division's special card file for the Russian Imperial Collection. Work on the collection will accelerate as staff members familiar with Russian are added to the division's staff. Reference staff can make available a file folder with information concerning the collection. The most important item in this folder is a typed history and description of the collection written by David Rose in November 1972.

The general collections of the division hold numerous items of extreme value. The two earliest pieces of interest are from the fifteenth century: John, Exarch of Bulgaria, "The Six Days of Creation," in Old Slavonic, printed on one leaf of paper—a copy of a tenth-century original; and a Glagolitic Missal, printed on paper in Venice or the Balkans in 1483. Among the sixteenth- and seventeenth-century treasures, first place must go to the division's copy of the *Deianiia Apostol'skie* (Acts of the Apostles), produced by Ivan Fedorov in 1564—the first book printed in Russia. The first Ukrainian printed book, a 1583 Bible, is also here. Other items include a first edition of *Slovo o polku Igoreve* (1800), two facsimiles of eleventh-century works, a number of significant Ukrainian works—e.g., *Trebnyk*, by Petro Mohila (1646), *Hrammatyka*, by Bishop Meletii Smotrytskyj (1648), and a liturgical manuscript of the sixteenth century from a western Ukrainian monastery. Perhaps as many as 300–400 items from before (and after) the eighteenth century are here, a large number taken from the Yudin Collection.

Next in significance is the division's special collection of Russian eighteenth-century publications. Almost all 1,300 volumes in this collection came from the great library of Gennadii Yudin. Volumes dated up to 1801 are included; all are fully cataloged. A catalog for these items has been published: *Eighteenth-Century Russian Publications in the Library of Congress: A Catalog*, by Tatiana Fessenko (1961). The collection includes dictionaries, histories (e.g., Ivan Boltin's famous *Kriticheskie zametki*), literary works (including translations), and much more. Especially rare is a copy of the first edition of Aleksandr Radishchev's famous *Puteshestvie iz Peterburga v Moskvu* (1789). In the broadsides collection are also some Russian materials. Portfolio 307 contains almost all these items. The portfolio holds about twenty different items and sets, with duplicates of some. These include appeals from both sides in the Russian Civil War, Lenin's decree on the land, and other propagandistic or polemical pieces. Many came from the papers of Edmund Charles Genet or John Reed; Genet's papers are deposited in the LC Manuscripts Division (see entry B4). Portfolio 318 also holds one item of potential interest from Riga (no. 3).

A catalog for this collection has been published: *Catalog of Broadsides in the Rare Book Division*, 4 vols. (Boston: G. K. Hall, 1972). Volume 1 is the *Geographic Shelflist Catalog*, wherein Russian materials appear on pp. 784–85.

For the division as a whole, two publications facilitate access to the holdings: *The Rare Book Division: A Guide to Its Collections and Services*, rev. ed. (1965), and *Some Guides to Special Collections in the Rare Book Division* (1974). Both are available without charge.

SCIENCE AND TECHNOLOGY DIVISION
John Adams Building, Fifth Floor, Science Reading Room
(202) 287-5639 (Reference)

Joseph W. Price, Chief (202/287-5664)

This division supervises LC's collections in science and technology, manages the Science Reading Room, and provides a variety of reference and bibliographic services. With the exception of technical agriculture and clinical medicine, the division attempts to collect in all aspects of science and technology. LC's holdings in these fields are vast indeed; as of 1981, the collections numbered some 3 million monographs, 60,000 journals, and 3 million technical reports. Russian-language materials abound throughout.

Reference services usually are provided without charge to users in person, by telephone, and by correspondence; inquiries by mail should be addressed to the Library of Congress, Science and Technology Division, Washington, D.C. 20540. On-site researchers should note the presence of computer terminals in the Science Reading Room. The division issues a series of bibliographic guides on a variety of subjects (e.g., alcohol fuels, solar energy) under the title *LC Science Tracer Bullet*; individual guides, as well as a master list of the series, are available without charge. Also available is a brief general guide: *Science and Technology Division* (1981). More substantial publications of potential interest to Russian/Soviet scholars are the ongoing multivolume works entitled *Antarctic Bibliography* (monthly and cumulative) and *Bibliography on Cold Regions Science and Technology* (annual).

NATIONAL REFERRAL CENTER
John Adams Building, Fifth floor
(202) 287-5670

Edward MacConomy, Chief (202) 287-5657

8:30 A.M.–4:30 P.M., Monday–Friday

The National Referral Center provides a unique and invaluable intermediary service. This data base is a subject-indexed inventory, continuously updated by staff analysts, containing descriptions of some 13,000 "information resources" (organizations, institutions, groups, and individuals) having specialized knowledge in virtually all fields. For anyone seeking advice on where to obtain information on a specific topic, the center provides a single place to obtain help without charge. The center itself does not furnish answers to inquiries—or bibliographic references that might do so—but acts as a liaison between those with questions and organizations or individuals with expertise on the subject of inquiry. All kinds of information resources are utilized: in government, industry, academics, and the professions. Even informal citizens' groups are now included. Inquiries may be made in person, by telephone, or by mail, and are generally handled within five days. No special forms are required to obtain referral service, but the center is most effective if inquiries include a specific, clear, and precise statement of the desired information; a list of what resources have already been checked; and any special qualifications of the inquirer which might facilitate access to resources otherwise not open. Requests on a single topic are most rapidly filled. The center's reply (usually in the form of a computer print-out) lists the names, addresses, and phone numbers of information resources which will provide information, and states what kind of information they may give. The center encourages organizations or individuals who have, or are aware of, specialized information capabilities to register themselves for the data base.

Telephone inquiries should be directed as follows: (202) 287-5670 for referral service or to schedule visits, (202) 287-5680 for registration of information resources, (202) 287-5683 for information about the center's publications or data base developments.

Correspondence should be addressed to: Library of Congress, National Referral Center, Washington, D.C. 20540.

The Center distributes without charge, upon request, a useful 1981 folder entitled *National Referral Center,* with more details about its operation and its publications. Among the latter are: *A Directory of Information Resources in the United States,* which is a general title for a series of broad selections from the data base occasionally compiled and issued by the center. The most recent of these directories is *Geosciences and Oceanography* (1981). The subtitles of some earlier volumes, all now out of date and some out of print, indicate the scope of the series: *Federal Government,* rev. ed. (1974); *Social Sciences,* rev. ed. (1973); *Biological Sciences* (1972); *Physical Sciences, Engineering* (1971). Similar to these is the *Directory of Federally Supported Information Analysis Centers,* 4th ed. (1979), available through the Superintendent of Documents, U.S. Government Printing Office, Washington, D.C. 20402.

Under the title *Who Knows?,* the center issues informal lists of resources on specific topics, such as environmental education, hazardous materials, or population. The lists are available without charge from the center. They must be requested individually by topic (a list of titles is available).

GENERAL READING ROOMS DIVISION
Thomas Jefferson Building, First Floor
(202) 287-5530

Ellen Z. Hahn, Chief

This division maintains four general reading rooms: the Main Reading Room, located on the first floor of the Thomas Jefferson Building (202/287-5520); Thomas Jefferson Reading Room, located on the fifth floor of the John Adams Building (202/287-5538); Local History and Genealogy Reading Room, located on the second floor of the Thomas Jefferson Building (202/287-5537); and the Microform Reading Room (202/287-5471), described in a following section. The division's reference librarians are on duty in all reading rooms; they attend to reference and bibliographic questions and, as necessary, direct inquiries to appropriate divisions or collections. The division's Telephone Reference, Correspondence, and Bibliography Section (Room 140E in the Thomas Jefferson Building; 202/287-5522) handles complex reference problems and provides bibliographic reference assistance by telephone or in response to written inquiries.

The spacious and lavishly decorated Main Reading Room houses a reference collection of some 50,000 volumes including atlases and maps, directories, government publications, indexes, statistical abstracts, and a few periodicals. An author/title dictionary catalog and a shelflist of the reference collection may be consulted in the reading room. In addition, a computer-generated Classed Catalog (shelflist) and a Subject Catalog of the Main Reading Room Reference Collection are available.

Information for Readers and *Tips for Students* provide useful information for researchers intending to visit the library. Researchers with time constraints may find it convenient to note that, if requested, the division will furnish names of free-lance researchers whose services may be hired. The division's pamphlet *Special Facilities for Research in the Library of Congress* contains other useful information.

CHILDREN'S LITERATURE CENTER
Thomas Jefferson Building, Room 140-H
(202) 287-5535

Margaret Coughlan, Acting Chief

8:30 A.M.–4:30 P.M., Monday–Friday

Researchers interested in children's literature and related topics should definitely make use of this section. In addition to a sizable collection of Russian fairy tales, picture books, stories, and the like (in Russian and in translation), there are also in the center reference materials not in the general collection. The card catalog is arranged by author and, for foreign publications, by country; the catalog is all the more useful because fiction and nonfiction items are filed together. The center publishes the quinquennial *Children's Literature: A Guide to Reference Sources* (1966; 3d suppl., 1982), which has a country breakdown and an international section.

PHOTODUPLICATION SERVICE
John Adams Building, Basement Level, Room G-1009
(202) 287-5640

Norman J. Shaffer, Chief (202/287-5654)

8:30 A.M.–4:25 P.M., Monday–Friday (doors close 4:15 P.M.)

The service provides photoreproductions of LC's holdings, as the law permits, for individuals and institutions. The service can furnish microfilm, photographs, photostats, slides, and many other forms of reproductions. Fees are charged according to the work required in fulfilling requests. The service receives, duplicates, and sells materials from other government agencies—for example, all unclassified CIA reports. The service has filmed many Russian and Soviet titles as part of the library's Preservation Program. The service maintains the LC Master Negative Microfilm Collection of more than 260,000 reels, which includes important manuscript collections, government documents of this and other countries, presidential papers, and many periodicals from around the world.

Information about titles available from the service may be found in the following publications (the first three titles are available from the Library of Congress Cataloging Distribution Service): *National Register of Microform Masters,* a six-volume cumulated edition includes all reports received between 1965–1975. Since 1975 the publication has been issued annually on a noncumulative basis; *Newspapers in Microform: Foreign Countries, 1948–1972* (1973), which, with *Newspapers in Microform: United States, 1948–1972,* supersedes the earlier *Newspapers in Microfilm*; *Newspapers in Microform,* an annual supplement to the two preceding titles. The annual volumes of this publication appearing between 1973 and 1977 have been cumulated in two volumes, one for U.S. newspapers and one for foreign newspapers; *Guide to Microforms in Print,* an annual publication of Microform Review, Inc., 520 Riverside Avenue, P.O. Box 405, Saugatuck Station, Westport, Connecticut 06880, includes selected and significant microfilm files available from the Library of Congress; *Micropublishers' Trade List Annual,* also available from Microform Review, includes copies of all circulars issued by the Photoduplication Service; *Library of Congress Photoduplication Service Circular Series,* available without charge. Circulars in this series frequently describe significant Russian and Soviet materials available on microfilm.

MICROFORM READING ROOM SECTION
Thomas Jefferson Building, First Floor, Room 140-B
(202) 287-5471

Robert V. Gross, Head

8:30 A.M.–9:30 P.M., Monday–Friday (stack service to 9:00 P.M.)
8:30 A.M.–5:00 P.M., Saturday
1:00–5:00 P.M., Sunday

The Microform Reading Room Section currently manages a collection in excess of two million pieces. The reading room is equipped with microform readers and reader-printers. Materials not commercially available or otherwise restricted may be obtained on interlibrary loan through the LC Loan Division (202/287-5441).

Generally, the items in commercially issued collections are not included in the Main Card Catalog or computerized catalog but are accessed through specialized guides and indexes, prepared by the micropublishers, and through the assistance of the reference staff of the section. For single titles, researchers should also consult the author/title card catalog located in the reading room and the reference guide *Selected Microform Collections in the Microform Reading Room,* comp. Lois Korzendorfer (1981), which lists major collections held by the section under entries designed to present the user with a basic idea of the scope and format of each collection. There is also another card file in the reading room for periodical holdings in microfilm.

Among the section's Russian collections are rare items from the Helsinki University Library (an imperial Russian depository from 1828 to 1917); the Russian revolutionary literature collection from Harvard University's Houghton Library; and large portions of the Slavica materials issued by the Inter Documentation Company in Zug, Switzerland. Other items of interest include doctoral dissertations, publications since 1975 of the Foreign Broadcast Information Service and Joint Publications Research Service, League of Nations and United Nations documents, and extensive portions of the Russia file from the British Foreign Office.

SERIAL AND GOVERNMENT PUBLICATIONS DIVISION
Newspaper and Current Periodical Room
James Madison Memorial Building, First Floor, Room LM-133
(202) 287-5690

Donald F. Wisdom, Chief

8:30 A.M.–9:30 P.M., Monday–Friday
8:30 A.M.–5:00 P.M., Saturday
1:00–5:00 P.M., Sunday

The Serial and Government Publications Division receives and services, through its Newspaper and Current Periodical Room, current unbound serials, official and non-official, and newspapers in Western languages relating to Russian/Soviet studies consistent with approved acquisition policies. All current unbound serials and newspapers in Cyrillic languages are received and serviced in the European Reading Room of the European Division, as noted above.

In addition, the Newspaper and Current Periodical Room provides reader and reference service for all noncurrent newspapers on microfilm or in bound volumes, including those in Cyrillic. As bound newspaper volumes are housed in a storage area away from the main buildings, one to two days' notice is required for their retrieval.

A small explanatory brochure, *Newspaper and Current Periodical Room,* is issued without charge by the division. The mimeographed pamphlet *How to Find Newspapers and Periodicals in the Library of Congress* (1979) also has some useful advice.

COLLECTIONS MANAGEMENT DIVISION
Thomas Jefferson Building, Room G-104-F
(202) 287-7400

Steven J. Herman, Chief

This division services the general book collections of LC, including both monographs and serials in the Slavic languages (except current editions of newspapers and periodicals, which are in the custody of the European Division). Researchers needing to use unique materials or materials not readily available on previous visits to LC may make advance arrangements for access by telephoning the division's Special Search Section (202/287-7488) or by writing this section in care of the Collections Management Division, Library of Congress, Washington, D.C. 20540.

5. Some noteworthy LC holdings on special subjects have been noted and described under the appropriate divisions above. The entire collection of the library is noteworthy for three main reasons: (1) size—this collection of Russian/Soviet-related materials is the most extensive in the world outside of the USSR; (2) all-inclusive nature—the comprehensiveness, breadth, and depth of the collection are outstanding; among the very few lacunae are provincial publications and titles on technical aspects of agriculture, health, medicine, the last three of which are in the National Agricultural Library and National Library of Medicine respectively; (3) continuity of effort—LC has been acquiring Russian-related materials for more than seventy years, with a minor gap in the years 1917-33.

6. The reader is reminded of the publications and other tools listed under the appropriate divisions above. The publications that follow are of a more general nature, of use not only to Russianists but to all scholars who come to LC or otherwise employ its services.

Unless contrary indication is given, these publications are for sale by the Superintendent of Documents, U.S. Government Printing Office, Washington, D.C. 20402 or by LC itself.

Major LC catalog publications:

The National Union Catalog, Pre–1956 Imprints. Published by the Mansell Company in England in 754 vols., this catalog supersedes the following two titles.

A Catalog of Books Represented by Library of Congress Printed Cards Issued (August 1898–July 1942), 167 vols. Suppl.: cards issued August 1, 1942–December 31, 1947, 42 vols.

The Library of Congress Author Catalog: A Cumulative List of Works Represented by Library of Congress Cards, 1948–52, 24 vols.

The National Union Catalog, A Cumulative Author List Representing Library of Congress Printed Cards and Titles Reported by Other American Libraries. Cumulation for 1953–57, 28 vols., available in reprint from Rowman and Littlefield; cumulation for 1958–62, 54 vols., out of print; cumulation for 1963–67, 72 vols., available from J. W. Edwards; cumulation for 1956–67, 125 vols., available from Rowman and Littlefield; cumulation for 1968–72, 119 vols., available from J. W. Edwards; cumulation for 1973–77, 135 vols., available from Rowman and Littlefield; cumulations for recent years available from LC Cataloging Distribution Service. Currently in nine monthly, three quarterly issues, and an annual cumulation, the catalog covers some 1,100 U.S. and Canadian libraries.

Monographic Series, an aid to locating works published as a series but with various titles. Published in three quarterly issues and an annual cumulation.

Library of Congress Catalog—Books: Subjects, A Cumulative List of Works Rep-

resented by Library of Congress Printed Cards, for 1945 and later imprints, arranged alphabetically by LC subject headings and by author under subject headings. Cumulation for 1950–54, 20 vols., available in reprint from Rowman and Littlefield; cumulation for 1955–59, 22 vols., available from Rowman and Littlefield; cumulations for 1960–64, 25 vols., and for 1965–69, 42 vols., available from J. W. Edwards; cumulation for 1970–74, 100 vols. published by Rowman and Littlefield; and cumulations for recent years available from LC Cataloging Distribution Service. From 1975 this catalog is no longer being published under the title above but is continued by the following title.

Subject Catalog continues the preceding work, published in three quarterly issues and an annual cumulation.

National Register of Microform Masters, annual, 1969 and later years available from LC Cataloging Distribution Service.

Other major publications, both LC and non-LC:

New Serial Titles: A Union List of Serials Commencing Publication After December 31, 1949, based on reports from some 800 U.S. and Canadian libraries; cumulation for 1950–70, four vols., available from R. R. Bowker Co.; cumulations for 1971–75 and 1976–80 available from LC Cataloging Distribution Service. Currently published in eight monthly and four quarterly issues with an annual cumulation (annuals cumulate up to five- or ten-year periods). This work is a supplement to *Union List of Serials in Libraries of the United States and Canada,* ed. Edna B. Titus, five vols., 3d. ed. (1965).

Combined Indexes to the Library of Congress Classification Schedules, comp. Nancy Olson, 15 vols., (Washington, D.C.: U.S. Historical Documents Institute, 1974–.) An aid to locating call numbers for materials by authors, names, geographic areas, subjects, and keywords.

Library of Congress Publications in Print, biennial. Available without charge from LC Cataloging Distribution Service.

Annual Report of the Librarian of Congress.

Quarterly Journal of the Library of Congress, particularly useful for the description of acquisitions of the various divisions.

Library of Congress Information Bulletin, weekly.

Monthly Index of Russian Accessions, published from 1948 to 1969, with no cumulations, but now ceased. Invaluable for its subject index to Soviet materials received by U.S. libraries, it also included translated tables of contents for journals.

Minor LC publications:

Information on the MARC System, 4th ed. (1974). Available without charge from LC Central Services Division.

Information for Readers in the Library of Congress, rev. ed. (1981). Available without charge from LC Central Services Division.

Special Facilities for Research [in the Library of Congress] (1973). Available without charge from LC Central Services Division.

National Preservation Report, triennial (formerly *Foreign Newspaper and Gazette Report*), available to libraries and institutions.

Special Collections in the Library of Congress: A Selective Guide (1980). For sale by Superintendent of Documents, U.S. Government Printing Office, Washington, D.C. 20402.

Digest of Public General Bills and Resolutions, published by LC Congressional Research Service in cumulations and supplements for current sessions of Congress.

Aeronautical Sciences and Aviation in the Soviet Union: A Bibliography, comp.

Bertha Kucherov (1955). Reprint available from University Microfilms, Ann Arbor, Michigan.

Checklist of Manuscripts in the Libraries of the Greek and Armenian Patriarchates in Jerusalem, microfilmed for LC, 1949–50, and prepared under direction of Kenneth W. Clark (1953). Available from LC Photoduplication Service.

National Censuses and Vital Statistics in Europe, 1918–1939: An Annotated Bibliography, by Henry J. Dubester (1948). 1940–48 suppl. Also published in 1948. Reprints available commercially.

Weather Modification in the Soviet Union, 1946–1966: A Selected Annotated Bibliography, by Nikolay T. Zikeev and George A. Doumani (1967). Available without charge from LC Central Services Division.

Scientific and Technical Serial Publications of the Soviet Union, 1945–1960 (1963). Electrostatic print available from University Microfilms, Ann Arbor, Michigan.

The Law of Marital Property in Czechoslovakia and the Soviet Union (1981). Available without charge from LC Law Library.

Unpublished Bibliographical Tools in Certain Archives and Libraries of Europe: A Partial List, comp. Lester K. Born (1952). Available to libraries and institutions from LC and also in reprint from University Microfilms, Ann Arbor, Michigan.

Soviet Geography: A Bibliography, ed. Nicholas Rodionoff (1951). Reprint (1969) available from Greenwood Press, Westport, Connecticut.

Calendar of Events in the Library of Congress, monthly. Available without charge from LC Central Services Division.

A note on the LC computer systems: Automation promises to revolutionize many aspects of scholarly research. While LC has, since the 1960s, applied automation to more of its operations, the most important computerized tool for researchers to be aware of is LOCIS (Library of Congress Information System), which consists of two parts: MUMS (Multiple Use MARC [Machine Readable Cataloging] System) and SCORPIO (Subject-Content-Oriented-Retriever-for-Processing-Information-Online). These tools do not make obsolete such traditional aids as bibliographies, card catalogs, and indexes, but they certainly supplement them in invaluable ways. Already the systems have proven to be of tremendous use for Russian/Soviet studies.

While a lengthy description of all LC computer systems is beyond the scope of this note, a few salient features can be indicated. For some bibliographic searches, MUMS and SCORPIO can save scholars vast amounts of time and effort. The information desired can appear on a computer-terminal screen for note-taking or be printed out by the user for study elsewhere. Individuals can perform many searches for themselves on terminals located off the Main Reading Room and in other reading rooms. The staff will show researchers how to use the computer terminals and will assist users during a search. Available for online searching and display to Russianists are English-language books cataloged from 1968, most Western European-language books printed or cataloged since the mid-1970s, and books in some other languages—including Estonian—printed or cataloged from 1976 (all dates here are not precise but approximate). Cyrillic materials have been available through MUMS and SCORPIO, in romanized form, since 1979. Searches can be performed by author, title, main entry, call number, subject, or added entries. Some examples of searches made in the past: books in translation published after 1969; discographies; pre-1901 maps; and translations of books in Class P (except juvenalia) published in 1974–75. For subject bibliographies, several subject headings and/or LC class numbers can be combined in a single search.

In addition, several other data files can be tapped. These include legislation in the U.S. Congress since 1973; research organizations willing to answer questions from the public; and selected articles and government publications on public-policy topics.

Literature and detailed information about MUMS and SCORPIO can be obtained in the Main Reading Room.

NOTE: See also entries B4, D3, D4, E4, F5, and F6.

A38 Martin Luther King, Jr., Memorial Library (District of Columbia Library)

1 a. *901 G Street, NW*
Washington, D.C. 20001
(202) 727-1111

   b. 9:00 A.M.–9:00 P.M., Monday–Thursday
   9:00 A.M.–5:30 P.M., Friday–Saturday
   Hours vary during the summer.

   c. Open to the public. Interlibrary loan service and photocopying facilities are available.

   d. Kathleen Wood, Central Librarian

2. The total library collection exceeds two million bound volumes, including books and periodicals. Russian/Soviet-related holdings number approximately 3,000 items.

3 a. In the total collection, only the history holdings (about one-third of the Russian/Soviet collection) rise to the level of a C rating. The Literature Division has about 300 titles of Russian and Soviet literature in translation. The Foreign Language Division has approximately 600 titles in Russian.

4. The library presently receives some 300 periodical titles and maintains specialized collections of art reproductions, films, records, slides, and tapes.
   Each division of the library maintains its own vertical-file collection. Russianists will find scattered materials of interest throughout. The Audio-Visual Division (Room 226) has a half dozen films on the Soviet Union.

6. The library maintains a card catalog that combines title, subject, and author listings. The library uses the Dewey Decimal cataloging system. Brochures describing special library programs and events are available without charge.

A39 Maryland University Libraries

1 a. *College Park, Maryland 20742*

   McKeldin Library (Main Library)
   (301) 454-5704

   Architecture Library
   (301) 454-4316

   Art Library
   (301) 454-2065

   b. McKeldin Library, fall and spring semesters and summer sessions:
   8:00 A.M.–11:00 P.M., Monday–Thursday

8:00 A.M.–6:00 P.M.,   Friday
10:00 A.M.–6:00 P.M.,   Saturday
Noon–11:00 P.M.,   Sunday
For other schedules, call the above telephone numbers.

c.   Open to the public; only university members may check out material. Interlibrary loan services and photocopying facilities (including microfilm and microfiche copiers) are available.

d.   Dr. Joanne Harrar, Director of Libraries

2.   Campus libraries hold about 1,500,000 volumes, 1,560,000 microform units, 250,000 U.S. and foreign documents, and 60,000 other items (including cassettes and films) for a total of more than 3,000,000 pieces. The libraries subscribe to approximately 16,500 serials.

3 b.   Subject categories and evaluations:

Subject Category	Number of Titles	Rating
Philosophy and Religion	480	B
History	4,470	B
Geography and Ethnography	155	C
Economics	1,620	B
Sociology	235	C
Politics and Government	750	B
Foreign Relations	125	C/B
Law	225	C
Education	130	C/B
Fine Arts	850	B
Language	1,330	B/A
Literature	5,965	B
Military Affairs	125	C/D
Bibliography and Reference	535	C/B
Ukrainians	240	C
Byelorussians	60	C/B
Baltic Nationalities	135	D/C
Caucasian Nationalities	70	D/C
Central Asian and Siberian Nationalities	385	C

This is a very good collection, probably ranking after LC's as the second-best general Russian collection in the Washington area.

4.   The university subscribes to a fairly large number of Russian-language periodicals; the researcher can count with some assurance that the library will have many basic journals in such subjects as economics, history, political science, and statistics. McKeldin Library receives only three newspapers from the USSR: *Izvestiia, Pravda,* and the English-language *Moscow News.* The library is a repository for many U.S., UN, and International Labor Organization documents; it also receives a large number of Rand Corporation publications.

In the Hornbake Library (undergraduate library) is an extensive audiovisual facility. A quick survey of materials there revealed at least half a dozen short documentary-type films on the Soviet Union (part of a televised series) and a cassette-tape collection with a good indexing guide showing many items involving the USSR.

5. Two large microform holdings are noteworthy. McKeldin Library's Periodicals/Microforms Room has, on microfiche, all three series of the *Polnoe sobranie zakonov Rossiiskoi imperii* and a substantial portion of the Inter Documentation Company (IDC) series of *zemstvo* (provincial self-government) publications. Of the latter, Maryland has seventy-six boxes of fiche, with publications from twenty-seven provinces and three non-*zemstvo* regions. Not all the publications of any single *zemstvo* are here. An annotated copy of IDC listings in the reference stacks serves as a handy catalog for this material.

The library's Archives and Manuscripts Department (301/454-2318) contains a number of collections of possible interest to the Russianist: the Joseph Irwin France Papers include scrapbooks with clippings pertaining to Russia; the Romeo Mansueti Papers contain one box of clippings on Russian science; and the Millard Tydings Papers include items on Finland in 1940 and Lithuania in the period 1945–49. The department is also in charge of an extensive collection of biographical data on prominent Soviet citizens gathered by the Munich Institute for the Study of the USSR; this material is currently unavailable to researchers and inquiries cannot be answered.

6. There are no published catalogs or descriptions of the libraries. Available without charge are brief printed guides to University of Maryland, College Park, libraries, McKeldin Library, and Hornbake Library. Also available are one-page flyers describing specific resources and policies of this library system.

NOTE: The Music Educators National Conference Historical Center, located in the Hornbake Library, serves as both the official archives of the Music Educators National Conference and a special reference collection devoted to the general history of music education. Among the center's holdings are some twenty to thirty miscellaneous Russian and Soviet textbooks and songbooks.

National Aeronautics and Space Administration—Goddard Space Flight Center Library   See entry A25

National Aeronautics and Space Administration—Headquarters Library   See entry K25

A40   National Agricultural Library (NAL)

1 a.   *Main Library* :
U.S. Route 1 and Interstate 95
Beltsville, Maryland 20705
(301) 344-3778 (Educational Resources Division)
(301) 344-3755 (Reference)

D.C. Branch :
South Building, Room 1052
Fourteenth Street and Independence Avenue, SW
Washington, D.C. 20250
(202) 447-3434

b.   8:00 A.M.–4:30 P.M.,   Monday–Friday (Main)
10:00 A.M.–2:30 P.M.,   Monday–Friday (Reference and Lending Services)
8:30 A.M.–5:00 P.M.,   Monday–Friday (D.C. Branch)

c. Open to the public. Interlibrary loan service and photocopying facilities are available. All photocopying requests should be sent to: National Agricultural Library, Room 303, attn: Photocopying Service, Beltsville, Maryland 20705.

d. Richard A. Farley, Director, NAL
Tatiana Tontarski, Russian-area Specialist (202/344-3704)

2. NAL holds more than 1.7 million volumes (monographs and serials) and 128,370 microforms and receives 16,000 periodicals. Library holdings principally cover technical agricultural subjects and related topics of botany, chemistry, economics, entomology, farming, forestry, food and nutrition, law, rural society, soil sciences, and water resources as they pertain to agriculture.

3 a. NAL is a major resource for Russian/Soviet-area scholars in the economics subject category. Because the library has two completely different cataloging sytems, one now inactive (see point 6), two tables of holdings follow. The first uses LC classification subject headings (modified), the second uses NAL's older, more detailed subject listings for agriculture and related topics. Combined figures and evaluations are given under point 4.

Subject Category	Number of Titles
Geography	95*
Economics	
HA-HG	930
S-SH	1,470

All other LC classification subject categories were below the D level; for example, total history holdings (in LC and NAL classification catalogs) come to only about sixty titles.   .

Subject Category	Number of Titles
Agriculture	1,070
Soil	220
Crops	20
Horticulture	45
Pomology	255
Forestry	77
Agricultural Colleges/ Experimental Stations	495
Entomology	25
Botany	320
Statistics	350
Economic History	20
General Literature (Travels)	25 (some nineteenth century)
Reference Books	155

Economics holdings thus total approximately 4,100 titles, the majority directly related to agriculture; this subject category accordingly rates an A, although the uneven nature of the collection must be kept in mind. Reference, bibliography, general works, and the geography category rank at the D level.

*Calculated at eighty titles per inch because these shelflist cards were thick and many titles went over one card.

4. NAL's collection of active and inactive Russian-area periodicals numbers some 920 titles. The library receives a copy of virtually all Agriculture Department publications as well as reports of department-funded research.

6. A most significant feature of NAL is its computerized information retrieval system, AGRICOLA. The AGRICOLA system currently indexes approximately 5,000 journals worldwide; the total number of book and journal article entries now available on the data base is approximately 1,750,000. AGRICOLA contains all items cataloged and indexed by the library since 1970. Current annual growth rate of the data base is approximately twenty percent. One can search the system using title words, author's name, subject headings, geographic codes, language, and many other approaches.

NAL staff searched by language and found the following total AGRICOLA items:

Language	Total Items	from Monographs	from Serials
Russian	63,973	4,498	245
Ukrainian	4,574	98	21
Byelorussian	706	6	1
Armenian	48	3	0
Azerbaidzhan	133	3	2
Estonian	149	34	9
Latvian	259	26	1
Lithuanian	20	16	3
Georgian	197	9	1
Polish	16,385	577	41
Finnish	1,023	223	20

The library also has access to other online systems: MEDLINE of the National Library of Medicine (entry A48), OCLC (entry E2), and more than 100 files available from commercial vendors.

A note about the card catalogs: two distinct catalogs plus a Translations File are located in NAL. The Dictionary Catalog contains all cards cataloged by the library from 1862 through 1965; author, title, and subject cards are interfiled. This catalog has been inactive since 1965. The Current Catalog is divided into a Name Catalog (entries by and about personal authors and corporate bodies and for titles) and Subject Catalog. The Translations File contains entries for translations of individual articles in periodicals, chapters and extracts from single books, and similar material. Only one entry appears for each translation, under the first author's name.

The library's catalog has been published: *Dictionary Catalog of the National Agricultural Library, 1862–1965,* 73 vols. (Totowa, N.J.: Rowman and Littlefield, 1967–70). Two monthly publications of great value to researchers are: *The National Agricultural Library Catalog,* begun in 1966, and *Bibliography of Agriculture.* Both have annual cumulations with author and subject indexes. The first reproduces LC printed cards, the second, AGRICOLA citations, which are often more detailed than the LC cards.

Two brief flyers of use to library patrons are *The National Agricultural Library: A Guide to Services,* rev. ed. (scheduled for publication in 1983), and a pamphlet describing AGRICOLA (formerly called CAIN-ONLINE).

A41 National Air and Space Museum Library (Smithsonian Institution)

1 a. *Seventh Street and Independence Avenue, SW*
Washington, D.C. 20560
(202) 357-3133

b. 10:00 A.M.–5:15 P.M., Monday–Friday

c. Open to researchers, by appointment.

d. Frank A. Pietropaoli, Librarian

2. The library holds a large number of items of value to Russian/Soviet-area scholars, primarily in its vertical-file and archival holdings.

3 a. The collection consists of approximately 22,000 books and 4,600 bound periodicals. Some material is from the USSR and/or in Russian. There is a small number of books by and about Soviet cosmonauts, on Soviet rocketry or space science, and on the Soviet space program. The books are in English (original or National Aeronautics and Space Administration [NASA] translation) almost exclusively. There are also some fifty to seventy-five books on Russian aeronautics, astronautics, and rocketry before 1917.

4–5. The subject and biographic files should be of great value to Soviet-area specialists. In the biographic files especially there are noteworthy holdings, including information—more or less extensive—on all Soviet cosmonauts and photographic portraits of most of them. The library also has several loose-leaf notebook-albums full of photos on the Soviet space program and the people involved in it.

Perhaps even more intriguing are the materials and photographs relating to the history of nineteenth-century Russian war rockets, such as devised by the pioneer scientists Aleksandr Zasiadko and Konstantin Konstantinov. Also available are photographs of flying machines and astronautical concepts of Nikolai Kibalchich, Konstantin Tsiolkovskii, and others. There are accompanying documents for these photos in the subject and biographic files, all copies of published, secondary sources.

For aeronautics, there are materials in the files for Russian aviation pioneers like Aleksandr Mozhaiskii, Igor Sikorsky, and Nikolai Zhukovskii. Twentieth-century aircraft designer/manufacturer Andrei Tupolev and a few of his colleagues have folders in the aeronautical subject files also.

In general, this library collection is the more valuable in that it attempts not to duplicate but to complement holdings in the NASA library, located nearby (see entry K25).

In using the vertical files, researchers should be aware that in the subject files for historical materials, there is both a chronological and a country breakdown.

6. A descriptive brochure, *NASM Library,* is available without charge.

A42 National Arboretum Library

1 a. *Twenty-fourth and R streets, NE*
Washington, D.C. 20002
(202) 472-9264

b. 8:00 A.M.–4:30 P.M., Monday–Friday

c. Open to the public. Interlibrary loan service and photocopying facilities are not available.

d. Dr. Henry Cathey, Director

2–3. The library holds approximately 5,000 volumes. In the herbarium of the arboretum, there are several thousand photographs of trees and plant specimens in Russia from the turn of the century up to the 1930s. The photos were taken by Agriculture Department plant explorers, particularly Frank Meyer, 1906–17, and H. L. Westover and C. R. Enlow, 1934. In 1963 John L. Creech and Donald H. Scott collected photographs of fruit and ornamental trees in Siberia. The staff requests advance notice from those wishing to use the collection.

A43 National Broadcasting Company Network News Library

1 a. *4001 Nebraska Avenue, NW*
   Washington, D.C. 20016
   (202) 686-4493

b. 9:00 A.M.–7:00 P.M., Monday–Friday

c. Access is granted on an individual basis.

d. Margot Dunlap, Librarian

5. The library maintains a substantial vertical-file collection. Clippings on political, economic, and other subjects relating to the USSR, among other nations, are taken from more than fifteen of the most important U.S. newspapers and journals. Materials are discarded after four years. Russianists will find here a rather broad sampling of U.S. reporting on Soviet affairs.

A44 National Bureau of Standards Library (Commerce Department)

1 a. *Location:*
   Route 70-S
   Gaithersburg, Maryland 20760
   (301) 921-3451

   Mail:
   Library Division
   National Bureau of Standards
   Commerce Department
   Washington, D.C. 20234

b. 8:30 A.M.–5:00 P.M., Monday–Friday

c. Open to the public for on-site use only. Interlibrary loan service is available.

d. Patricia W. Berger, Chief Librarian

2. Overall, the library holds some 150,000 volumes and subscribes to more than 2,500 journals. No accurate count of materials relating to the USSR was possible.

3. Chemistry, mathematics, physics, and statistics are the subjects of strength.

4. The library receives approximately ninety Soviet scientific and technical journals. Runs for many begin in the 1930s; at least a dozen begin in the 1920s; and a few start at the turn of this century.

A45 National Gallery of Art Library

1 a. *Fourth Street and Constitution Avenue, NW*
Washington, D.C. 20565
(202) 842-6517

   b. Noon-5:00 P.M., Monday
   10:00 A.M.–4:00 P.M., Tuesday–Friday (subject to change)

   c. Researchers may request permission for on-site use of materials not readily available elsewhere in the area. Interlibrary loan service and photocopying facilities are available.

   d. J. M. Edelstein, Librarian

2. Holdings total approximately 118,000 volumes. In addition, the library receives all major art periodicals. This fine-arts collection is strongest in the fields of European and American painting, sculpture, decorative arts, and other objects in the gallery's holdings. There are valuable items here for Russian/Soviet-area specialists as well and in substantial enough number to make the library a very useful resource.

3 a. An estimate of total pertinent holdings and their content cannot be provided; some material is presently uncataloged. The more important items, however, can be described. Through informal exchange agreements with Soviet museums and galleries—such as the Pushkin, Tretiakov, and particularly the Hermitage—the gallery library receives art publications, exhibition catalogs, guides to collections, and texts. Works cover both art and architecture; the collection is much better for recent times than for earlier periods. (The exchange agreements are of fairly recent origin but should become increasingly important in future years.) It is likely that Russian/Soviet-area materials will grow in number here.

In addition, it should be noted that the library receives all major Western art books—scholarly and popular. The Russianist can thus do research on Western art history as it relates to Russian-area art history and on many related subjects.

4. See the entry for the National Gallery of Art Photographic Archives (F9).

A46 National Geographic Society Library

1 a. *1146 Sixteenth Street, NW*
Washington, D.C. 20036
(202) 857-7783 (Reference)
(202) 857-7785 (Circulation)
(202) 857-7787 (Head Librarian)

   b. 8:30 A.M.–5:00 P.M., Monday–Friday

c. Open to the public for on-site use. Interlibrary loan service is available with other specialized libraries within the District of Columbia. Photocopying facilities are not available.

d. Virginia Carter Hills, Head Librarian
Susan Fifer, Head, Information Services
Patricia Smith, Head, Technical Services

2. The collection totals more than 70,000 volumes, primarily covering exploration, geography, and travel.

3 a. The shelflist, which is perhaps not the best indicator of holdings, shows some 550 volumes on Russia and about 100 on Siberia. These totals are for a number of subject categories combined, although most items would relate to ethnography, and geography. Most are in English; some are translations. Significant portions of the holdings, particularly for Siberia, are from the eighteenth and nineteenth centuries. For the category of geography and ethnography the collection deserves a B/C rating, although it is weak in maps (see point 4).

4. The library has at least seventeen periodicals or serials from the USSR. More than half are in Russian, and most deal with geography or related sciences.
Virtually all maps of the society are sent to the map department (see entry E7).

5. The library contains extensive vertical-file material, including more than two drawers on Russia per se and many other folders on specific aspects of the country. The arrangement is by geographic area and by subject, the latter also having a geographic breakdown.
It should be noted that the library has the only complete set of Hakluyt Society publications in the area.
The bibliography department of the library holds copies of the bibliographies prepared for stories published in the *National Geographic* magazine.

6. For the *National Geographic* the library has a unique and fascinating reference tool: a card index lists virtually all mentions of any geographic area, country, city, or body of water that have ever appeared in the magazine. Not just titles of pieces but even one-line references in the body of a story can be easily located through this index. The Public Reference Service (202/857-7059) promptly answers questions based on this index. Every six months the society publishes *National Geographic Index*; under the same title, three cumulations have appeared, for 1888–1946, 1947–76, and 1977–81.

A47 National Institute of Education (Education Department)—Educational Research Library

1 a. *1832 M Street, NW, Sixth floor*
Washington, D.C. 20208
(202) 254-5060

Branch Library:
400 Maryland Avenue, SW
Washington, D.C. 20202
(202) 245-8853

b. 10:00 A.M.–4:00 P.M., Monday–Friday

c. Open to the public. Interlibrary loan service and photocopying services are available.

d. Charles Missar, Supervisory Librarian

2. The library holds approximately 150,000 items, an extensive reference document and microform collection, and receives some 800 current periodicals and newspapers. Holdings pertain to almost all aspects and levels of education.

3 a. Nearly 200 titles dealing with Russian/Soviet education were measured in the shelflist. All other subject categories fell below the D level. The education category rates a B.

4. The library now receives a handful of English-language periodicals covering Russia/USSR, but none in Russian. Some titles received are not retained, however, and others have incomplete runs.

5. The library has about 500 Soviet textbooks, uncataloged and in random order. Most titles are on science and technology, although many are in the social sciences. These books might be a fine resource for the student of Soviet education.

Virtually all Educational Resources Information Center (ERIC) publications and materials are available at the library. (ERIC is a part of the work of the Educational Reference Center, located one floor above the library [see entry G5].) Together, the library and the center form the heart of the Educational Resource Division of the National Institute of Education.

6. *The Periodical Holdings List: Educational Research Library* (1978) is available.

A48 National Library of Medicine (NLM)

1 a. *8600 Rockville Pike*
Bethesda, Maryland 20209
(301) 496-6095 (Reference)
(301) 496-5405 (History of Medicine Division)
(301) 496-5511 (Interlibrary Loan Service)

b. Regular hours (Labor Day to Memorial Day):
8:30 A.M.–9:00 P.M., Monday–Thursday
8:30 A.M.–6:00 P.M., Friday
8:30 A.M.–5:00 P.M., Saturday

Summer hours (Memorial Day to Labor Day):
8:30 A.M.–5:00 P.M., Monday–Saturday
Stack service ends thirty minutes before closing time.

History of Medicine Collection:
8:30 A.M.–4:45 P.M., Monday–Friday

c. Open to the public. Interlibrary loan service and photocopying facilities are available.

d. Martin M. Cummings, M.D., Director

2. NLM, the largest collection of its kind in the world, consists of about 2.5 million items; more than half the material is bound volumes, the remainder comprises audiovisual items, manuscripts, medical theses, microforms, and prints and photographs.

Library holdings cover some forty medical subjects and related fields of science and technology. Currently the library receives more than 20,000 serial titles.

3. The library's materials are divided largely between the General Collection—monographs and serials published after 1870—and the History of Medicine Collection (pre-1871 publications mostly but later works also). Taken altogether, Russian medical literature here is the greatest collection, in quantity and quality, outside the Soviet Union.

For a number of reasons, it is very difficult to judge the size and value of NLM's Russian/Soviet holdings. Like the fields of science and technology, clinical and technical medical literature—the core of the library's holdings—is not broken down by geographic areas primarily. The material is usually arranged by subject and then by geographic area within that subject. Moreover, the division of holdings according to date of publication almost precludes a total count from one consolidated shelflist. By mid-1983, however, virtually all records for cataloged printed works will be in computerized form. Finally, data for some nineteenth-century materials have not been integrated with the main catalog.

Shelflist measurements can at least indicate the relative strengths of the NLM collection. They show that the library has by far the most titles in the field of Russian public health (several hundred volumes). For the history of Russian medicine, NLM also has a large number of books. Another strength is the subject of the medical profession and a related topic, the practice of medicine. For a wide variety of specific, clinical, or technical aspects of medicine, the library also has volumes relating to Russia/USSR. The most interesting of these subjects might be that of psychiatry. In a number of these fields, the collection has materials relating not only to Russia but also to the Baltic area.

For the category of sociology (particularly health and medicine) the NLM collection rates an evaluation of A. Holdings also are on a high level for aspects of history (of science, primarily).

But what should be stressed is the many thousand volumes at NLM that relate to many different sides of Russian/Soviet society. A tremendous wealth of information for social scientists is here, much of it virtually untapped. Examples of what can be found include psychiatric studies of Russian writers, radicals, and rulers; details on Russian/Soviet hospitals, officials, and populace caught in the grip of war and plague; ethnographic and anthropological data; investigations of social customs, manners, the standard of living, and the way of life of people in the Russian Empire and the USSR; and much, much more.

There is no way scholars of Russia/Soviet Union can do serious research by mail, at a distance from NLM. Long searches and some hard digging, plus the generous help of the staff, will be necessary before Russianists can hope that the library will yield its vast treasures to them. Their efforts, however, will be more than worthwhile.

4. Another way to attempt to gauge NLM's Russian holdings is to look at certain special collections, which are more easily measured than the total collection.

In the 1880s the library's catalog showed that some thirty Russian serial titles were received. By 1907 more than 200 periodicals from the Russian Empire appeared in the listings. In 1958 NLM staff estimated that the library received and cataloged roughly seventy-five to eighty percent of all substantive medical publications of the USSR; the figure would be at least as high today. As of August 1982, of approximately 24,000 serial titles received at NLM, 5 percent or about 1,212 titles were of USSR origin and 5.2 percent or 1,262 titles were in Russian or contained some Russian articles.

The Documents Collection of the library includes more than 100,000 items from U.S., foreign, and international agencies. Soviet publications are well represented.

A CATLINE search (see point 6) conducted in 1982 showed 26,698 monograph or periodical titles either entirely or partially in Russian. Of these, 16,891 titles have been cataloged since 1965. The remaining were cataloged earlier and the records have only recently been computerized. By mid-1983, records for all cataloged printed works in Russian will be available in CATLINE.

5.   The History of Medicine Division has three collections of pertinent materials shelved not by subject but by geographic area. Twenty-five boxes of medical theses are from Tartu (Dorpat, Yurev) University, mostly from the nineteenth century. At an average sixty-five theses per box, there would be about 1,600 theses here. Theses from all other Russian medical schools are cased in another sixty boxes; these appear to total about 3,100 items and they date from the nineteenth and twentieth centuries. Finally, there are forty-three boxes of Russian material on miscellaneous medical topics. These roughly 850 items are from the nineteenth and (mostly) twentieth centuries. Some, if not all, of these holdings will be found in the library's *Index-Catalogue* (see point 6).

The division also has in its rare book room some eighteen Russian medical works from the eighteenth century.

This library has some papers of interest to the Russianist. The papers of Albert Baird Hastings, 1915–76, fifty-four boxes and several volumes, include correspondence, a diary, and permits from 1943–44 when he was a biochemist and a physician in the Soviet Union. Approximately fifty-five items in six folders relate to his experiences in the USSR. James Sprigg Wilson was chief surgeon of the medical corps with the American Expeditionary Forces (A.E.F.) at Vladivostok in Siberia. His papers, 1918–30, thirty items, include letters, photos, and other items that pertain to the A.E.F.

6.   Important nonpublished aides are NLM's several computerized search services. In the mid-1960s the library developed its computerized Medical Literature Analysis and Retrieval System (MEDLARS) to produce the huge bibliography known as the *Index Medicus* (see following). By 1971 an online retrieval system had come into being: MEDLINE (MEDLARS Online). MEDLINE currently is a data base containing citations to approximately 500,000 items from 3,000 biomedical journals. References are from the current year and the two preceding years; other back files cover the biomedical literature from 1966 to 1979. SDILINE (Selective Dissemination of Information) is a part of MEDLINE and contains only the current month's citations. Every month the library updates MEDLINE and replaces SDILINE. One can search MEDLINE by words appearing in article titles and/or abstracts or by some 14,000 medical subject headings (MeSH), singly or in combination. Searchers have a variety of approaches available (e.g., language, date of publication, names, and titles) and may have references come online at computer terminals or printed offline for mailing. Citations may be brief or complete, as the user desires. CATLINE (Catalog Online) is NLM's data base containing more than 450,000 references to monographs and serials in the NLM collection. Searchers may use this computerized catalog in much the same way as MEDLINE.

SERLINE (Serials Online) is a data base with bibliographic and other information for approximately 38,000 biomedical serial titles, current and ceased (including 1,262 Russian-language serials).

Other computerized data bases of some interest: TOXLINE (Toxicology Information Online, with more than 600,000 bibliographic references); CANCERLIT/ Literature (Cancer Online, the National Cancer Institute's data base of more than 270,000 bibliographic citations); CANCERPROJ (National Cancer Institute's online data base with summaries of ongoing cancer research projects in many countries); and

AVLINE (AudioVisuals Online), currently experimental. Still more data bases exist, but they seem to involve purely technical or library matters.

More than 1,600 medical schools and other facilities throughout the country have access to the above data bases, including MEDLINE and CATLINE.

Of the many published bibliographic tools available to researchers, the most important for materials in the History of Medicine Division is undoubtedly the *Index-Catalogue of the Library of the Surgeon General's Office.* Five multivolume series of this catalog appeared between 1880 and 1961, covering books printed through 1950. The catalog is arranged by author and subject, and contains citations to not only books but also periodical articles, making it of enormous value to scholars. A rather rapid survey of the first series of the *Index-Catalogue* (16 vols., 1880–95) revealed approximately 500–600 citations of articles and perhaps 200 of books on Russian subjects. Fairly extensive cross-references aid any search, but these figures are perhaps only a small part of the wealth of Russian references in just the first series alone.

The annual *Army Medical Library Author Catalog* began publication in 1950 and, after many name changes, ceased publication in 1965 under the title *National Library of Medicine Catalog.* Quinquennial cumulations of this catalog appeared in 1955 and thereafter. Unlike the *Index-Catalogue,* this catalog contains only monograph citations as does the publication that followed it: *National Library of Medicine Current Catalog.* This fully computerized book catalog is published quarterly.

For periodical literature the researcher should consult the *Index Medicus,* a monthly listing of current medical writing that has appeared intermittently, under a variety of titles, since 1879, and regularly since the late 1930s. Scholars should consult NLM staff members for details on this index and other publications that supplement it for certain years or, in some cases, merged with it (for example, the American Medical Association's *Quarterly Cumulative Index to Current Medical Literature,* 1916–26). Currently the library produces the *Index Medicus* and its other catalogs and recurring bibliographies through the MEDLARS system.

Other publications of NLM and/or the Health and Human Services Department of value to users of this library: *Index of NLM Serial Titles* (1981); *International Bibliography of Medicolegal Serials, 1736–1967,* by Jaroslav Nemec (1969), which has a geographic index—by city within each country—for the place of origin of serials. All titles listed are in the NLM collection, but the bibliography does not indicate which other libraries hold each title; Directory of Biomedical Institutions in the USSR, by Mordecai Hoseh (1965); *Guide, to Russian Medical Literature,* ed. Scott Adams and Frank B. Rogers, M.D. (1958), which is still very useful.

In addition, all publications in the series *Soviet Health Studies* (fifteen to date) produced by the John E. Fogarty International Center for Advanced Study in the Health Sciences, at the National Institutes of Health, are of interest. A longer list of these publications will be found in the entry for this center within the description of the Health and Human Services Department in the U.S. Government agencies section of this guide (entry K19). Three of these studies of primary importance for NLM users are: *A Bibliography of Soviet Sources on Medicine and Public Health in the U.S.S.R.,* comp. Lee Perkins (1975); *Soviet Biomedical Institutions: A Directory* (1974); *Soviet Medicine: A Bibliography of Bibliographies* (1973).

Finally, some Soviet publications are tools to note; NLM would have the majority of titles listed in these bibliographies and catalogs: *Meditsinskaia periodicheskaia pechat' Rossii i SSSR (1792–1962),* by M. M. Levit (Moscow, 1963); *Sistematicheskii katalog otechestvennykh periodicheskikh i prodolzhaiushchikhsia izdanii po meditsine 1792–1960,* comp. E. N. Chernova et al. (Leningrad, 1965).

NLM has published a lengthy description of itself: *Communication in the Service of American Health . . . A Bicentennial Report from the National Library of Medicine*

(1976). The library also has available without charge a handy guide to its facilities and services.

National Museum of American Art and National Portrait Gallery Library (Smithsonian Institution)   See entry B2

A49   National Museum of American History (formerly National Museum of History and Technology) Library (Smithsonian Institution)

1 a.   *Twelfth Street and Constitution Avenue, NW*
Washington, D.C. 20560
(202) 357-2414

b.   8:45 A.M.–5:15 P.M.,   Monday–Friday

c.   Open to the public for on-site use. Interlibrary loan service and photocopying facilities are available.

d.   Rhoda Ratner, Branch Librarian

2.   The library has scattered holdings relating to Russia/USSR throughout its collection of more than 150,000 volumes. Some ten to fifteen Soviet periodicals, largely on military and museum matters, are received.

3 a.   Pertinent materials here are on such subjects as the applied arts and sciences, history of science, military and naval affairs, numismatics, and philately. Russian-area holdings are not substantial but may be of value on specific topics. Researchers should check the library's catalogs for their own particular interests.

6.   *Guide to Manuscript Collections in the Museum of History and Technology* (1979) is available for consultation. For a description of Russian-related manuscripts maintained by various divisions of the museum, see entry C10.

A50   National Museum of Natural History (Smithsonian Institution)— Anthropology Branch Library

1 a.   *Tenth Street and Constitution Avenue, NW*
Washington, D.C. 20560
(202) 357-1819

b.   1:00–5:00 P.M.,   Monday–Friday

c.   Open to serious researchers, by appointment only. Interlibrary loan service and photocopying facilities are available through the central library in the Natural History Building.

d.   Janette Saquet, Anthropology Librarian

2.   The library holds more than 50,000 books and currently receives approximately 3,000 periodicals. Russian holdings amount to about seventy-five linear feet; dispersed throughout the library, the materials deal mostly with ethnology and archaeology. Some periodicals are from the USSR.

6. There is no published catalog or description of the library holdings. Researchers are advised to consult the staff for further information on Russian/Soviet-related materials.

A51 National Oceanic and Atmospheric Administration (Commerce Department)—Library Information Services Division, Silver Spring Center

1 a. *8060 Thirteenth Street, Room 816*
Silver Spring, Maryland 20910
(301) 427-7800

b. 8:00 A.M.–4:30 P.M., Monday–Friday

c. Open to the public for on-site use. Interlibrary loan service and photocopying facilities are available.

d. Ann Juneau, Librarian

2. The library contains about 150,000 volumes, plus weather maps and other meteorological data. It is one of the most comprehensive collections on climatology, hydrology, and meteorology in the world. Between 500 and 1,000 volumes pertain to the USSR. (A more precise count of Soviet-area materials was impossible due to the lack of an adequate method of measurement for these subjects in the library's two different shelflists.)

3. Virtually all holdings are in the fields of hydrology and meteorology. For these subjects the collection rates an A.

4. Researchers should inquire of reference staffers concerning scattered special materials dealing with the USSR.

5. The most noteworthy holding relating to Russia is a series of weather observations and reports dating from the last quarter of the nineteenth century.

A52 Naval Observatory Library (Navy Department)

1 a. *Thirty-fourth Street and Massachusetts Avenue, NW*
Washington, D.C. 20390
(202) 254-4525

b. 8:00 A.M.–4:30 P.M., Monday–Friday

c. Open to researchers, by appointment. Limited interlibrary loan service and photocopying facilities are available.

d. Brenda Corbin, Librarian

2. The total collection of the library numbers approximately 75,000 volumes, including bound periodicals. Russian holdings are sizable: exceeding 5,000 volumes.

3. Soviet-area specialists will be most interested in the library's almost complete runs of publications from all Russian/Soviet observatories. For example, the run from the famous Pulkovo Observatory starts fairly early in the nineteenth century. The library

currently has exchange agreements with Soviet observatories and the USSR Academy of Sciences to ensure that it continues to receive these publications. In general, the collections are very strong in astronomy and the space sciences.

4.   At present the library receives about twenty periodicals from the USSR, excluding serials such as the observatory publications noted above.

6.   *Catalog of the Naval Observatory Library,* 6 vols., was published in 1976 by G.K. Hall.

A53   Navy Department Library

1 a.   *Washington Navy Yard, Building 220*
M and Eighth streets, SE
Washington, D.C. 20374
(202) 433-4131

b.   10:00 A.M.–4:30 P.M.,   Monday–Friday

c.   Open to the public for on-site use. Interlibrary loan service and photocopying facilities are available.

d.   Stanley Kalkus, Director

2.   The library holds more than 150,000 volumes, some 10,000 microfilm rolls, and several hundred current periodicals.

3.   The strength of this library for Russianists lies in its holdings on history and military affairs. Approximately 1,000 titles relate to Russia/USSR. For specific topics, the library is a fairly good resource. For example, on the Russo-Japanese War there are roughly eighty titles. Not much of the material is in Russian. For the two categories just noted, the library seems to be at the rank of D. Other subjects fairly well represented here, in general terms at least, are geography, government, international law and diplomacy, politics, and nearly all naval topics.

5.   The library has an incomplete but extensive run of the important serial *Morskoi sbornik.* There are at least 100 volumes from the years 1853–1911. Although not unique, this title would almost certainly be more conveniently and efficiently used in the Navy Department Library's open stacks than at, say, the Library of Congress. Since 1970 the library has also been receiving translations from the *Soviet Digest* under the title *Morskoi sbornik.*

6.   The *Navy Department Library: A Brief Description* is a small but informative brochure published by the Naval History Division. It is available without charge.

NOTE: There are more than twenty other Navy Department libraries in the Washington area. Because almost all are restricted and/or narrowly technical, entries for most do not appear in this guide. Researchers can obtain more information about them from the Navy Department Library or from the publication of the American Society for Information Science entitled *Library and Reference Facilities in the Area of the District of Columbia* in the selective bibliography at the end of this volume.

A54 Patent Office Scientific Library (Commerce Department)

1 a. *Location:*
2021 Jefferson Davis Highway
Arlington, Virginia

Mail:
Washington, D.C. 20231
(703) 557-2955
(703) 557-2957 (Reference)
(703) 557-3545 (Foreign Patent Services)

b. 8:30 A.M.–5:00 P.M., Monday–Friday

c. Open to the public. Interlibrary loan service and photocopying facilities are available.

d. Dora Weinstein, Head, Users' Services
Barrington Balthrop, Chief, Foreign Patent Services and Record Section

2. This repository holds approximately 200,000 books, thousands of bound periodicals, and millions of foreign patents, bound or on microfilm. Currently 1,700 periodicals are received.

3. The library represents a major resource, particularly for the student of the history of Russian science and technology. Holdings include more than fifty monographs on patents and inventions (in Russian and English), plus up to 100 dictionaries and reference works. Sample items: *Register of Inventions Published in the USSR 1896-June 1963* (one vol. only); statistical tables from 1858; and a work on state paper manufacturing (1893). Seventeen periodicals are of interest: most are no longer active, roughly half are on patents and the rest on more general topics, and about half are in English.

4 5. The heart of the collection consists of the patents themselves. The library has received patents from the Soviet Union from November 1925 to April 1928 and then from March 1959 to the present. In the more recent period, patent runs are fairly complete. Those from 1959 through 1970 appear most in bound volumes on the shelves. From circa 1970 the Russian patents are on microfilm and total some 394 cartridges in 1982.

6. The library has three card catalogs: the main catalog is arranged by author, title, and subject, but entries are often not found under each heading ("Russia" and "USSR" may both be used as headings); the patent periodicals catalog is arranged geographically, with Russian titles filed under "USSR"; and the general periodicals catalog lists its titles under "Russia," not "USSR."
 The library has three valuable publications: *World Patents Indexes* (July 1974–) and *Central Patents Index* (since February 1970), both published by Derwent, with indexes by country and by type of patent, and *Soviet Inventions Illustrated* (since 1962). (Access to the Derwent publications is restricted.) Some of the earlier periodicals noted in point 3 would also be of great help. Finally, Russianists might want to consult Dora Weinstein, who is a staff translator as well as head of Users' Services, concerning the library's Russian/Soviet holdings.

Population Reference Bureau Library   See entry H25

Rand Corporation Library   See entry H26

**Russian Orthodox Church of Saint John the Baptist—Library
See entry P6**

**Saint Sophia Religious Association of Ukrainian Catholics, Inc.,
Library   See entry P9**

**A55   School of Advanced International Studies (SAIS) (Johns Hopkins
University)—Mason Library**

1 a.   *1740 Massachusetts Avenue, NW*
Washington, D.C. 20036
(202) 785-6296

  b.   Academic year:
8:30 A.M.–10:00 P.M.,   Monday–Thursday
8:30 A.M.–6:00 P.M.,   Friday
10:00 A.M.–5:00 P.M.,   Saturday
Noon–9:00 P.M.,   Sunday
When classes are not in session:
8:30 A.M.–5:00 P.M.,   Monday–Friday

  c.   Open to researchers for on-site use, for limited periods of up to one month. A
fee is charged for borrowing privileges and for extensions of research visits beyond
one month. Interlibrary loan service and photocopying facilities are available.

  d.   Peter J. Promen, Director

2.   The total collection numbers some 90,000 volumes, with Russian/Soviet holdings
of more than 1,800 titles.

3.   The vast majority of books in the total collection are English-language secondary
literature published since 1950 with subject strengths primarily in economics and
international relations.

4.   The periodical collection totals 800 titles of which twenty pertain to the USSR.
Of the library's fifty newspaper subscriptions, only one, *Pravda,* is of interest to
Russianists.

**School of Ukrainian Studies of Greater Washington Library
See entry M60**

Scottish Rite Supreme Council Library   See entry B8

A56 Senate Library

1 a. *Capitol Building, S-332*
Washington, D.C. 20510
(202) 224-7106

b. 9:00 A.M.–5:00 P.M., Monday–Friday

c. Access requires a letter from one's senator. Interlibrary loan service is not available; photocopying facilities are available.

d. Roger K. Haley, Head Librarian

3. The library holds all Senate and House documents: bills, hearings publications, legislation, reports, and so on. It is thus an invaluable research facility for scholars interested in U.S.-Soviet relations, American domestic policies and politics related to the USSR, congressional action and attitudes with respect to the Soviet Union, and many more topics.

6. *General Information and Services of the Senate Library* (1971) is a useful guide to the facilities.

SRI International—Strategic Studies Center—Library   See Entry H28

A57 State Department Library

1 a. *State Department Building, Room 3239*
2201 C Street, NW
Washington, D.C. 20520
(202) 632-0535/1099

b. 8:15 A.M.–5:00 P.M., Monday–Friday

c. The library is closed to other than State Department, Agency for International Development, and Arms Control and Disarmament Agency employees. Unique materials (not available elsewhere in the area) can, however, be made available to outsiders. (Nonemployees cannot do in-depth research here.) Call ahead for clearance.

d. Conrad Eaton, Librarian

2. In 1982 the library contained some 700,000 volumes. Annual accessions come to about 16,000 volumes, thirty to forty percent of which are from foreign countries. Current issues of 125 periodicals are available in the Reading Room, as are several foreign telephone directories; total periodical titles are about 1,000.

3 a. In 1976 the staff made all the measurements below; evaluations are thus based entirely on quantity. As a general Russian collection, the State Department Library surpasses the U.S. Information Agency Library but falls below the University of Maryland libraries and, of course, LC.

b. The subject categories and evaluations are as follows:

Subject	Number of Titles	Rating
Philosophy and Religion	155	D
History	5,290	B/A
Geography and Ethnography	200	B
Economics	3,410	B/A
Sociology	345	C
Politics and Government	1,620	B/A
Foreign Relations	125	C/B
Law	Unmeasured	
Education	165	B
Fine Arts	60	Below D
Language	265	C
Literature	300	D
Military Affairs	240	B
Bibliography and Reference	285	C
Ukrainians	70	D
Byelorussians	25	D/C
Baltic Nationalities	350	C
Caucasian Nationalities	255	C/B
Central Asian Nationalities	305	C/B
Siberian Nationalities	240	B

4.   The library currently receives about thirty-five periodicals from the Soviet Union in Russian and English and about twelve periodicals on the USSR published in the West. Many runs go back to at least the 1930s or 1940s, although they may be incomplete. *Izvestiia* and *Pravda* are here on microfilm.

This is a deposit library for U.S. Government documents, thus a major resource for research on them. The library per se has no map collection of note. The Maps Library at the State Department and the Naval Yard Map Library are closed to outsiders; they fall under the Maps and Publications Office of the department (202/632-9674).

6.   There are two card catalogs. The first is a regular dictionary catalog, arranged alphabetically by author, title, and subject. The second is a geographic catalog and of greatest interest to area specialists.

The library publishes a monthly acquisitions list and also irregular selective bibliographies, such as "Periodicals on the Soviet Union" (April 15, 1976). The Bureau of Intelligence and Research publishes a bimonthly *Russian Book List* for Russian-language materials it receives. Much of this collection would eventually come to the library.

A library handbook entitled *Department of State Library,* available without charge, is particularly valuable for including a list of other reference collections in the department.

A58   Textile Museum Library

1 a.   *2320 S Street, NW*
Washington, D.C. 20008
(202) 667-0441

b.   10:00 A.M.–5:00 P.M.,   Wednesday–Friday
10:00 A.M.–1:00 P.M.,   Saturday

c. Open to the public for on-site use. Interlibrary loan service is not available. Limited photocopying facilities are available.

d. Katherine Freshley, Librarian

2. There are about 10,000 titles in the library. Some 300 of these will be of particular interest to the Russian/Soviet specialist.

3 a. For this specialized collection only the fine arts category applies. The holdings rate about a C in one or two aspects of this category. Most titles are on the subjects of costume, embroidery, rugs, tapestry, and textiles. The areas covered include Russia, the Caucasus, Central Asia, Moldavia/Bessarabia, and Scythia. There are also some books on art in general, Russian culture, archaeology, and travel.

4. The library conducts a regular exchange of materials (articles, catalogs, and some periodicals) with the Hermitage Museum in Leningrad.

6. There are no published materials on the library's holdings, but see point 4 in the description of the Textile Museum (entry C16).

A59 Transportation Department Library

1 a. *Main Library:*
400 Seventh Street, SW, Room 2200
Washington, D.C. 20590
(202) 426-2565 (Director)
(202) 426-1792 (Reference)
(202) 426-2563 (Law)

Branch (Air Transportation and Aeronautics):
800 Independence Avenue, SW, Room 930
Washington, D.C. 20590
(202) 426-3611 (Reference)
(202) 426-3604 (Law)

b. Full service hours, both libraries:
8:30 A.M.–5:00 P.M., Monday–Friday

c. Open to the public for on-site use. Interlibrary loan service and photocopying facilities are available.

d. Lucile E. Beaver, Library Director

2. Combined holdings of the libraries total more than 300,000 hard-copy documents, 125,000 microform documents, and 2,170 current journal titles. The libraries also have more than 100 subscriptions to abstracting services.

3 a. Russian holdings of the libraries nearly all fall into the economics subject category. Among the materials here are some on Russian highways, maritime affairs, and railroads. Another 280 items are uncataloged books and pamphlets, many published prior to 1960, dealing largely with Russian roads. In addition, the branch library appears to have some reports and other material, in small amounts, relating to Soviet air transport.
    The collections rank at the B level for the field of transportation (but not economics as a whole).

6. The library has an index file for periodical literature on many aspects of transportation. There are approximately 800,000 four-by-six-inch cards in this special file, which date from about 1930. Materials on Russia/USSR, in English mostly, are noted here, although not in great numbers at present.

This reference index file has been microfilmed as *Transportation Masterfile, 1921–1971* in 140 reels, with a supplement covering 1971–74 in 7 reels.

The library publishes *Transportation: Current Literature,* weekly; and other special bibliographies, irregularly.

Treasury Department Library   See entry K34

Ukrainian Catholic Seminary Library   See entry P12

A60   United Nations Information Centre

1 a. *2101 L Street, NW, Suite 209*
Washington, D.C. 20037
(202) 296-5370

   b. 9:00 A.M.–5:00 P.M., Monday-Friday
Library:
9:00 A.M.–1:00 P.M., Monday-Friday

   c. Open to the public. Interlibrary loan service and photocopying facilities are available.

   d. Helen Macsherry, Reference Assistant/Librarian

2-5. The collection includes all official UN records and documents since 1969. A large amount of UN sales publications (nonofficial) are also here. The library's extensive reference section deserves mention as well.

It would be difficult to assess the extent and significance of this facility's holdings that relate to the USSR.

A61   U.S. Information Agency (USIA) Library

1 a. *Main Library:*
1750 Pennsylvania Avenue, NW, Room 1011
Washington, D.C. 20547
(202) 724-9214 (Librarian)
(The Voice of America Branch of this library is quite small and of negligible importance.)

   b. 8:45 A.M.–5:30 P.M., Monday-Friday

   c. Closed to the public; researchers, however, may receive permission from the Office of Public Liaison (202/724-9606) to use unique materials. Interlibrary loan service and photocopying facilities are available.

   d. Jeanne Zeydel, Librarian

2-3.   There are several different collections to note at the main library. Of principal interest to Russian/Soviet-area scholars is the Russian Language Collection, in Room 904, which contains approximately 12,000 books, 6,000 periodical volumes, and 1,000 reels of microfilm (newspapers and serials). Not all holdings are cataloged. The title of the collection is slightly misleading: it holds all materials in Cyrillic. The figures immediately following, taken from the collection's separate shelflist, show that it is strongest in economics, history, and Soviet foreign policy and international relations

Subject	Number of Titles	Rating
Philosophy and Religion	505	B
History	2,830 total (850 Russia/USSR only)	B
Geography and Ethnography	120	C
Economics	2,200	B
Sociology	375	B/C
Politics and Government	905	B
Foreign Relations	620	B/A
Law	310	C
Education	150	B/C
Fine Arts	180	D/C
Language	135	D/C
Literature	605	D/C
Military Affairs	215	B
Bibliography and Reference	260	C
Ukrainians	75	D
Byelorussians	14	D
Baltic Nationalities	150	C/D
Caucasian Nationalities	40	D
Central Asian Nationalities	125	D/C
Siberian Nationalities	50	C
Science	150	not rated
Technology	230	not rated

Because all holdings are in Cyrillic, every call number was measured in its entirety. Geographic areas other than Russia/USSR are thus reflected in the above counts. Pamphlets, arranged by subject (LC call number), are in forty boxes throughout the collection. They are not a part of the title measurements just given.

A part-time librarian is on duty Monday through Thursday, 9:00 A.M. to 5:00 P.M. (202/724-9263). Access would be easiest at these times.

Evaluation of subject categories are based on the library's total holdings.

4.   The USIA Archives (Katherine T. Shimabukuro, branch chief, 202/523-4362), a special collection of the library, holds an extensive collection of books and historical records (such as annual reports, congressional documents, directories) related to the USIA, U.S. International Communication Agency, and their predecessor agencies, dating from 1933 to the present. At this point, miscellaneous agency records and other documents may also be found here. In addition, the archive contains a comprehensive collection of USIA (and its predecessor agencies) publications, including *America*

Illustrated. This collection is unique in that USIA is forbidden to distribute these materials in the U.S.

6.   The library publishes the monthly *Selected List of Russian Language Acquisitions*, arranged by author.

Washington Post Library   See entry Q24

B Archives and Manuscript Depositories

Introductory Note

Among the billions of records stored in the National Archives and Records Service (NARS) (entry B6) the Russianist will find considerable primary research material in almost every topic area; documents on Russian-American relations are a particular strength at NARS. The Manuscript Division of the Library of Congress (entry B4) offers less volume—a "mere" 10,000 items—but comparable diversity; the papers of American ambassadors to Russia, those of explorer-author-journalist George Kennan, and the (as yet restricted) Vladimir Nabokov Collection are among the riches there. Beyond these two superb facilities the Soviet area scholar will find the archive/manuscript collections within the Smithsonian system very valuable for specialized holdings: the Smithsonian Institution Archives (entry B11) include interesting items on Russian Alaska; the collections in the Archives of Amercan Art and National Museum of American Art/National Portrait Gallery Library (entry B2) have an abundance of fascinating material on Russian/Soviet émigré artists; and the library of the Freer Gallery of Art (entry B3) holds a major collection of Armenian manuscripts.

NOTE: Many other libraries hold archival or manuscript materials, generally of individuals; these items are described in the Library section (A) under point

5. Furthermore, many vertical-file collections consisting primarily of printed matter are described in entries for associations, government agencies, libraries, etc.

Air Force Department—Office of Air Force History   See entry K2

American Federation of Labor and Congress of Industrial Organizations Library   See entry A3

American Latvian Association in the United States   See entry M11

B1   American Red Cross Archives

1 a. *Main Building:*
   430 Seventeenth Street, NW
   Washington, D.C. 20006
   (202) 737-8300
   Archives:
   431 Eighteenth Street, NW
   Washington, D.C. 20006
   (202) 857-3712

   b. Archives: 8:30 A.M.–4:45 P.M., Monday-Friday

   c. Open to researchers, by appointment.

   d. Photocopying facilities are available.

   e. Odette Binns, Archivist
      Elizabeth Hooks, Photo Librarian
      Rudy Clemen, Information Research Specialist

2.   The American Red Cross is a largely voluntary organization dedicated to preventing or alleviating human suffering caused by natural calamities or manmade disasters at home and abroad. It interacts with other Red Cross Organizations (including the Russian Red Cross) through its participation in the International Committee of the Red Cross and League of Red Cross Societies.

Red Cross archival material is arranged chronologically in five record groups. There are Russian-area holdings in each of these five groups. The first three groups, covering the years 1881 to 1946, however, have been transferred to the National Archives and Records Service (NARS) where they are filed in Record Group 200 (National Archives Gift Collection). Included in this material (some 33.31 cubic meters) are correspondence, memoranda, publications, and reports relating to Red Cross relief operations undertaken in Russia, Siberia, Armenia, Estonia, Finland, Latvia, and Lithuania as a result of droughts, epidemics, famines, floods, and wars. A list of all Russian/Soviet items in the three groups is available at the Red Cross Archives (but not at NARS).

3.   The two record groups kept at the Red Cross Archives have an undetermined but significant amount of Soviet-related material. Record Group 4 (1947-64; 152 drawers) contains correspondence with the Alliance of Red Cross and Red Crescent Societies of the USSR (Russian Red Cross) and materials on prisoners in the Soviet Union. Record Group 5 (since 1965) has later correspondence of the same kind.

Materials from the current files—which are restricted—are transferred to this record group after three years.

4. There are no published research tools, but the list noted in point 2 is very valuable. There is also a country-coded record book covering correspondence in each record group.

NOTE: The Red Cross Library, located on the third floor of the Eighteenth Street building, maintains a photograph collection that includes seven albums covering activities of the Siberian Commission, 1918–20.

B2 Archives of American Art *and* Library of the National Museum of American Art and National Portrait Gallery (NMAA/NPG) (Smithsonian Institution)

1 a. *American Art and Portrait Gallery Building*
Eighth and F streets, NW
Washington, D.C. 20560
(202) 357-2781 (Archives)
(202) 357-1886 (Library)

b. 10:00 A.M.–5:00 P.M., Monday-Friday

c. Open to researchers, who should secure a pass from the entrance guards. Some archival materials are restricted.

d. Limited photocopying facilities are available.

e. Archives:
William Woolfenden, Director (in New York)
Garnett McCoy, Senior Curator
Arthur Breton, Curator of Manuscripts
Library:
Cecilia Chin, Director

2. The library contains at least 40,000 volumes covering the fine arts, particularly in America. Art historians, especially those studying émigrés from the Russian Empire or USSR who came to this country, should find good material here.

3. The holdings of greatest interest in both the Archives of American Art and the NMAA/NPG Library—which are separate and distinct, although housed in the same building—will probably be the archival and vertical-file material. For artists who left Russia/USSR to come to America, the collections hold, in many cases, large amounts of valuable, fascinating information. A comprehensive list of items cannot be attempted here, but the following descriptive list should indicate the treasures in store for researchers. The list is arranged by artist, homeland, and type of material available.
Alexander Archipenko. Kiev, Ukraine. Two tape recordings (1962 and n.d.); letters, photos, slides, writings, notes, business records, and other printed matter (17,000 items, dated 1912–66), available on microfilm (archives). The library has other vertical-file material.
David Burliuk. Russia. One hundred and eighty-five items, dated 1925–67, including letters, photos, slides, and other pieces, most on microfilm. The library also has materials for Burliuk.

Marc Chagall—Vitebsk, Byelorussia—an undated interview (archives). The library has a number of envelopes with secondary-source material.

Naum Gabo. Russia. Envelope with clippings and/or catalogs.

Jacques Lipchitz. Lithuania. Four interviews, most from the 1960s (archives). The library has several envelopes with clippings and other material.

Adja Yunkers. Riga, Latvia. More than 300 items in the archives, including printed matter (1946–65) and two interviews from 1968–69; textual material on microfilm. The library holds some envelopes with more information.

The archives also has holdings on many artists born in various parts of the Russian Empire, who left the country while still fairly young. Among them are Boris Anisfeld, Saul Baizerman, Ilya Bolotowsky, Serge Chermayeff, Nicolai Cikovsky, Gleb N. Derujinsky, John D. Graham (Debrovski), Morris Kantor, Louis Lozowick, Louis Ribak, Joseph Schillinger, Ben Shahn, Moses and Raphael Soyer, Nahum Tschacbasov, Abraham Walkowitz, Max Weber, and Feodor Zakharov. The library also has vertical-file material on some of these individuals.

In addition, other collections of Americans or Russians in the U.S. sometimes have items of interest. Researchers will find small amounts of material in the papers of Senator William Benton, an art collector who traveled to the USSR in the 1950s and 1960s; William Merritt Berger, who sketched Russian literary figures in the late nineteenth century; Maxim Karolik, whose family letters are in Russian; and William Reinhold Valentiner, whose diary discusses Russian-German relations after World War I. The papers of Rockwell Kent, Hilla Rebay, and Theodore Roszak are also in this collection. Of some slight interest might also be the papers of Alfred Hamilton Barr, who wrote on Russian music, and of Thomas Eakins, who discussed the 1867 attempt on Alexander II's life in letters to family and friends. All of the above are in the Archives of American Art.

4. In 1972 Garnett McCoy published *Archives of American Art: A Directory of Resources* (New York: R. R. Bowker), which itemizes many of the holdings. The ten-volume *The Card Catalog of the Manuscript Collections of the Archives of American Art* (Scholarly Resources, Inc., 1981) is available in many university and major art libraries. This is a reproduction of the card catalog of the Manuscript Collections of the Archives of American Art exactly as arranged at the time of publication.

For those researchers who can go to any of the five offices of the archives (the others are in Boston, Detroit, New York, and San Francisco), the card catalog will be of great value. Office records are more up-to-date for new or changed collections.

NOTE: The archives has five offices coast-to-coast (see immediately preceding) where researchers can find most of the materials they need because nearly three-quarters of the holdings have been microfilmed. Interlibrary loan service for microfilm is available. Unfilmed collections are available for use in the Washington office only, by appointment.

Army Center of Military History (Army Department)   See entry K4

Catholic University of America—Mullen Library   See entry A10

B3   Freer Gallery of Art Library (Smithsonian Institution)

1 a. *Jefferson Drive at Twelfth Street, SW*
Washington, D.C. 20560
(202) 357-2091

b. 10:00 A.M.–5:00 P.M., Monday-Friday

c. Open to the public. Interlibrary loan service, except for the slide collection (oriental art), is not available.

d. Photocopying and microfilming facilities are available.

e. Ellen A. Nollman, Librarian

2-3. The library holds a major collection of Armenian manuscripts. There are 119 folios of the four gospels of the New Testament. The manuscripts, on vellum, date from the eleventh century.

The library also has one Mongolian xylograph (wood engraving), apparently once part of a larger collection now housed at the Library of Congress (Asian Division). (The staff does not consider it strictly Mongolian, so it would be difficult to locate by that description alone.) The subject of the xylograph is undetermined, but it probably concerns religious or cultural matters.

4. The Armenian holdings are the subject of No. 6 in the series of Freer Gallery of Art Oriental Studies: *Armenian Manuscripts in the Freer Gallery of Art,* by Sirarpie Der Nersessian (1963).

Georgetown University—Lauinger Library   See entry A23

Hillwood Museum Archives   See entry A27

Library of Congress—Asian, Law, and Music Divisions Manuscripts   See entry A37

B4   Library of Congress—Manuscript Division

1 a. *James Madison Memorial Building, First Floor, Room LM-102*
    Washington, D.C. 20540
    (202) 287-5383

b. 8:30 A.M.–5:00 P.M., Monday-Saturday

c. Open to researchers; proper identification and registration are required. Restrictions on the use of certain materials are for reasons of national security or have been imposed by donors.

d. Subject to preservation and copyright restraints, most manuscripts may be photocopied for research use. There are coin-operated photocopying machines and a microreader-printer in the spacious Manuscript Reading Room. The Library's Photoduplication Service (202/287-5654) also provides a full range of copying facilities. Special permission is required for use of cameras in the reading room. With few exceptions, microfilm reproductions of manuscripts are available for consultation through interlibrary loan service. Publication of manuscripts requires prior clearance. A leaflet concerning photocopying and publication of manuscripts is available.

e. James H. Hutson, Chief
    David Wigdor, Specialist, Twentieth Century Political History

2. The division houses approximately 10,000 separate collections. No accurate estimate of Russian/Soviet material is possible, but holdings are extensive.

3. There is no method of locating Russian/Soviet-area items by subject or geographic location. Considerable work has been done, however, in identifying and describing materials of primary interest to Russianists in many of the division's collections: the archive/manuscript survey *The Russian Empire and the Soviet Union: A Guide to Manuscripts and Archival Materials in the United States* (Boston: G. K. Hall, 1981), by Steven A. Grant and John H. Brown, gives summary descriptions of the Russian/Soviet items in 194 groups among the holdings (see pp. 124–37).

It would obviously be bootless to attempt to reproduce all the information contained in this larger study in the pages of the present guide (the more so as a copy of the Grant-Brown volume is available for reference in the division reading room). It will suffice here to offer an abridged version of the earlier work supplemented by some additional material provided by the division staff on recent accessions. The researcher stands reminded, in any event, that no guide can substitute for on-site inspection of a resource as large and diffuse as this one.

Cleveland Abbe Papers, 1850–1916. Astronomer and meteorologist. Included is correspondence with Otto Struve, director of the Pulkovo Observatory, and Abbe's letters to his family when he was guest astronomer at the Pulkovo Observatory, 1865–66. The letters deal not only with scientific matters but also with Russian social and cultural life and include descriptions of Saint Petersburg and its outskirts.

Academy of Natural Sciences of Philadelphia Records, 1812–1925. Included are thirty-eight reels of microfilm containing references to several Russian organizations, including the Academy of Sciences (Leningrad) and Legation imperiale de Russie aux Etats-Unis.

Carl William Ackerman Papers, 1933–70. Journalist, educator, public-relations consultant. Included are two boxes of notes, memoranda, and telegrams on Ackerman's journey to Russia in 1918–19, when he traveled to Ekaterinburg and interviewed alleged eyewitnesses to the execution of Nicholas II. There is also material on Ackerman's visit to Baku, Moscow, and Stalingrad in 1945.

Adams Family Collection, 1776–1914. Included are copies of letters of John Quincy Adams to A. H. Everett that touch on Adams's activities in Russia, where he was U.S. minister from 1809 to 1814.

Henry Tureman Allen Papers, 1806–1933. U.S. military attaché in Saint Petersburg, 1890–95, and commander of the American forces of occupation on the Rhine until 1923. Included are correspondence, journals, military reports, Russian government decrees, and photographs that deal with U.S.-Russian relations, the Russo-Japanese War, and Soviet policy toward Rumania and Poland after World War I.

American Council of Learned Societies Records, 1919–46. Included are fifteen boxes of correspondence, financial reports, literary manuscripts, and office files pertaining to Russian studies in secondary schools; Slavic grants; U.S.-USSR exchanges of scholars in the humanities and social sciences; the Russian national character; Russian art, music, and painting; and Soviet patriotism.

American Institute of Aeronautics and Astronautics Papers. Two boxes of reports and (especially) printed materials and newspaper clippings pertain to Russian engineers and aviators.

American Peace Commission to Versailles Papers, 1917–19. Included are ten reports on conditions in Russia in the 1910s.

American Psychological Association Records, 1912–72. Three boxes of material reflect the association's contacts with Russia and interest in Russian scientific developments. Included are reports by a group of U.S. psychologists who visited the Soviet Union in 1960.

Hannah Arendt Papers, 1935–75. Included is correspondence pertaining to the Academic Committee on Soviet Jewry and to the conference on the Status of Soviet Jews, 1967–70.

Henry Harley Arnold Papers, 1907–50. U.S. general. Included is a considerable amount of material pertaining to Russian-American relations during World War II.

L. K. Artamonov Papers, 1897–1929. Russian army officer. Memoirs, photographs, reports, and other materials pertain to the Special Russian Mission to Abyssinia, 1897–99, in which Colonel Artamonov took part.

Alexis Vasilevich Babine Papers, 1901–30. Born in Russia and educated in the U.S., Babine was—after the revolution—superintendent of schools in the Vologda area, instructor at the University of Saratov, and assistant to the American embassy in Moscow. He eventually emigrated to the U.S. Five boxes and one large folder of materials pertain to Babine's life in postrevolutionary Russia, to the Bolsheviks, and to Russian universities.

Newton Diehl Baker Papers, 1898–1962. Secretary of war during the Wilson administration, 1916–21, and author of *Bolshevism, Fascism, and Capitalism* (1932). Among the Russian-related materials here are memoranda on John Cadahy's book *Archangel: The American War with Russia* and on the North Russian and Siberian expeditions. Both memoranda are dated 1924.

Wharton Barker Papers, 1870–1920. Philadelphia financier and publicist, Barker participated in various business ventures in Russia during the late nineteenth century. Materials reflect Barker's interest in Russian railway concessions and trade, the Russian navy, Russian-American relations, and Ukrainian coal fields. Among his principal correspondents was Konstantin Petrovich Pobedonostsev.

Clara Harlowe Barton Papers, 1834–1918. Philanthropist and founder of the American Red Cross, Barton was concerned with the Russian famine of 1894 and participated in a Red Cross conference held in Saint Petersburg in 1902. Several folders of materials pertain to these contacts with Russia.

Bayard Family Papers, 1797–1885. Included are correspondence, diplomatic documents, and a diary of James A. Bayard (1767–1815) documenting his mission to Saint Petersburg as a member of a U.S. delegation to end the War of 1812 under Russian mediation.

Edward L. Bernays Papers, 1897–1965. Public-relations counsel. Included are materials dealing with Diaghilev's Ballet Russe and with the Russian exposition of 1929 in the U.S.

Blackwell Family Papers, 1830–1959. Three boxes of materials reflect the interest of Alice Stone Blackwell (1857–1950), a reformer, author, and editor, in Russia and Russian poetry, which she translated. Included is Blackwell's correspondence (1904–38) with the "grandmother of the revolution," Catherine Breshkovskaia.

Tasker Howard Bliss Papers, 1870–1930. Army officer, scholar, diplomat, Bliss was active in World War I. Several boxes of material, business correspondence, intelligence reports from the U.S. military attaché in Petrograd, maps, memoranda, pertain to Russia, especially in the years 1918–19. Subjects include the Allied intervention, anti-Bolshevik forces, the murder of Nicholas II and his family, political conditions in Russia, Russian POWs in Germany, and the situation in Estonia, Latvia, Lithuania, and the Ukraine around the time of the revolution.

Charles Eustis Bohlen Papers, 1940–70. U.S. ambassador to the USSR, 1953–57. Among Bohlen's papers are research notes, drafts of *Witness to History,* and correspondence pertaining to the Soviet Union and to Bohlen's views on Soviet aims and intentions in the post–World War II era.

Bollingen Foundation Records, 1939–73. Two folders of correspondence relate to Vladimir Nabokov's translation of *Eugene Onegin.* Also included are letters on the publication of scholarly monographs in Slavic studies between 1957 and 1962.

Boris Leo Brasol Papers, 1919–52. Prosecuting attorney under the Imperial Russian government, 1910–16, Brasol was second lieutenant in the Imperial Russian guard, 1914–16, and lawyer in New York specializing in Russian law, 1918–53. Included are six boxes of "political correspondence," 1922–46; four boxes of "anti-Soviet correspondence," 1919–48; six boxes on the "Russian situation"; three boxes of correspondence on other matters; and ten boxes of Brasol's works on Russian literature and drama.

Mark Lambert Bristol Papers, 1887–1939. Naval officer. Six folders of materials pertain to Russia, including dispatches sent by Newton Alexander McCully regarding the Denikin campaign, January–April 1920, and the Wrangel campaign, April–October 1920. Other subjects include Russian relief work, 1922–23, and Russian refugees, 1934–35.

Simon Cameron Papers, 1824–92. U.S. minister to Russia, January-November 1862. The general correspondence covers the months Cameron was in Russia.

George Washington Campbell Papers, 1793–1886. U.S. minister to Russia, 1819–20. A few items pertain to Campbell's diplomatic service in Saint Petersburg.

John Randolph Clay Papers. Contains the photostat negative of a draft of a report, 1824, by Clay, then secretary of the U.S. Legation, Russia, to William Wilkins, U.S. minister at Saint Petersburg.

Confederate States of America Records, 1861–65. Included are materials (microfilm) on Lucius Q. C. Lamar's mission to Russia.

Josephus Daniels Papers, 1806–1948. Secretary of the navy, 1912–21. One folder of materials pertains to conditions in Russia, 1917–21, as seen by Americans both inside and outside the country.

Joseph Edward Davies Papers, 1860–1957. U.S. ambassador to the Soviet Union, 1936–38, Davies was special envoy to confer with Stalin in May-June 1943, and special adviser to President Harry S. Truman and Secretary of State James F. Byrnes at the Potsdam conference, July–August 1945. More than ten boxes of material (including correspondence, diaries, and memoranda) contain references to Soviet personalities in the 1930s, lend-lease to Russia, and international conferences in the World War II era. Also included are materials used by Davies for his book *Mission to Moscow* and its sequel.

Peter A. Demens (P. A. Tverskoi) Papers, 1893–1911. Russian-born writer and entrepreneur; wrote about the U.S. for Russian publications. Included are drafts of articles and letters, newspaper clippings, and other materials (mostly in Russian) illustrating Demens's interests and career.

Ira Clarence Eaker Papers, 1918–60. U.S. general. Included is material on a U.S. military mission to Moscow on May 5, 1944 and on March 20, 1945.

Herbert Feis Papers. Economist and historian. Included are five boxes of materials used by Feis for his books on Russia.

John Watson Foster Papers, 1872–1917. Two instructions from the U.S. Secretary of State William M. Evarts pertain to Foster's service as U.S. minister to Russia, 1880–82.

George Gamow Papers, 1915–75. Born in Odessa, Gamow was professor at the University of Leningrad, 1931–33, and, after his emigration to the U.S., professor at George Washington University. Included is an annotated typescript, "Getaway from Russia," and various correspondence.

Edmond Charles Genet Papers, 1756–1795. Included are materials pertaining to Genet's diplomatic service in Russia (1787–89) as secretary to Comte de Ségur, French minister at the court of Catherine II.

German Captured Materials. Some twenty boxes of materials pertain to Russia, 1938–44. Subjects covered include Germans in Russia; Russian literature in the libraries of Russian towns occupied by Germans, 1942; Soviet agriculture; religion in Russia and other matters.

Albert Gleaves Papers, 1803–1946. Commander of the U.S. Asiatic fleet, 1919–21. Included are references to the Japanese army in Russia after World War I, evacuation of Czechoslovak troops from Russia, and conditions in Russia after the revolution.

Maksim Gorki Papers, 1922–38. Contains correspondence (original and copies) between Gorki and Khodasevich (1923–25); and a lecture (in Russian) by Khodasevich.

Adam Hrabia Gurowski Papers, 1848–98. Author, panslavist, scholar, Gurowski emigrated to U.S., where he wrote *Russia as It Is* (1854). Contains a biography of Gurowski by Julius Bing; notes taken by Gurowski, evidently for his book on Russia; and letters from American readers to Gurowski regarding his *Russia as It Is*.

Green Haywood Hackworth Papers, 1919–73. Hackworth accompanied Secretary of State Cordell Hull to the Moscow Conference, 1943. Included are materials on Soviet interests, 1944–45, UN Conference delegates in San Francisco from the USSR, April–May 1945; the Yalta Voting Formula; and the Tehran Conference.

Leland Harrison Papers, 1915–47. Diplomatic secretary, American Commission to Negotiate Peace. Included are six folders with correspondence and reports pertaining to Bolshevik Russia, to the activities of the Japanese and Germans in postrevolutionary Russia, and to a tentative plan for a Russian relief mission for the American Commission to Negotiate the Peace.

Philip Caryl Jessup Papers, 1902–55. Jurist, biographer, educator. Contains documentation on the Russian Institute, Columbia University, 1946–47, and Russian studies, 1943.

John Paul Jones (part of the Peter Force Collection). U.S. naval officer. Materials pertain to Jones's service in Russia in the 1780s.

George Kennan Papers, 1840–1937. Siberian explorer, author, and journalist; cousin of diplomat George F. Kennan's grandfather. These papers can be divided into three parts: (1) 110 boxes of autobiographical materials, lecture materials, newspaper clippings, notes, and published articles, much of which pertains to Russia. Among the subjects dealt with are the Black Sea, bureaucracy, the Caucasus, Central Asia, civil service, Constitutional Democrats, courts, the Crimea, Czargrad, Dukhobors, education, Finland, Friends of Russian Freedom, Georgia, Irkutsk, Jews, Kalmucks, Kazan', labor unions, the Lena river strike, liberals, Moscow, nationalism, nihilism, the nobility, Novgorod, the Octobrists, Odessa, Petropavlosk fortress, prisons, religion, revolution, Saint Petersburg, Siberia, the Social Democrats, socialism, terrorism, Tomsk, the Union of the Russian People, and the Y.M.C.A. (2) seven boxes of diaries, journals, and notebooks, 1865–1924. (3) eighteen boxes of correspondence, 1895–1937. Correspondents include numerous government, cultural, and business figures from both Russia and the United States.

John Adams Kingsbury Papers, 1940–60. Medical doctor and social worker, Kingsbury visited Russia, took part in Russian-related organizations in the U.S., appeared before the Subversive Activities Control Board to explain the activities of the National Council of Soviet-American Friendship, and wrote about Soviet medicine. Four boxes of materials reflect Kingsbury's interest in the Soviet Union and Soviet medicine.

Alan Goodrich Kirk Papers, 1919–61. U.S. ambassador to the USSR, 1949–52. A few items pertain to Kirk's service in Moscow.

Ivan Alekseevich Korzukhin Papers, 1900–1931. A manuscript book, "Materialy po istorii Chukhotskogo predpriiatiia," which deals with the several unsuccessful efforts made by Korzukhin, a geologist, and others to exploit mineral resources, particularly gold, in the Chukhotsk peninsula and surrounding area. The volume is illustrated with photos and a map.

Breckinridge Long Papers, 1840–1948. Third assistant secretary of state under

Woodrow Wilson, 1917–20. Included are materials pertaining to the Allied intervention in Siberia, the American Red Cross in Russia, and the Russian railway system. There is also a mimeographed account of a conference of the members of the Russian Constituent Assembly, January 8–12, 1921.

McCook Family Papers, 1827–1963. Included is one folder of materials (mostly correspondence) on Alexander McCook's visit to Russia in 1896 as a U.S. representative to the coronation of the tsar.

Newton Alexander McCully Papers, 1917–27. U.S. naval officer. Included are McCully's diaries in 1918, when he commanded U.S. naval forces in north Russia, and in 1920, when he was special agent of the State Department in south Russia.

George von Lengerke Meyer Papers, 1901–17. U.S. ambassador to Russia, 1905–7. Included are correspondence and a diary documenting Meyer's diplomatic service in Russia, Nicholas II, the Duma, social life in Saint Petersburg, and the negotiations leading to the termination of the Russo-Japanese War.

Montgomery Family Papers, 1771–1974. Boxes 21, 22, and 23 contain materials (primarily correspondence) pertaining to the activities of the Armenia–America Society, 1919-23, of which George Redington Montgomery (1870–1945) was director, 1920–23. The society aimed to bring peace in both Turkish and Russian Armenia and assist Armenians in establishing a self-supporting nation.

Roland Slettor Morris Papers, 1910–43. U.S. ambassador to Japan, 1917–20; Morris went on a special mission to Siberia, 1918. Three boxes of correspondence, maps, memoranda, and reports pertain to Russia and the Far East, conditions in Siberia during the Russian Civil War, the Japanese intervention in Siberia, and the Third Communist International.

Vladimir Vladimirovich Nabokov Collection, 1923–58. Contains manuscripts, typescripts, galley proofs, and corrected copies of Nabokov's novels, poems, articles, translations, book reviews, and other writings. Works in English include *Conclusive Evidence, Invitation to a Beheading, Pale Fire* (on index cards), *The Real Life of Sebastian Knight,* and other works. Works in Russian include *Drugie berega, Dar', Izobrazhenie Val'sa,* and *Tragediia Gospodina Morna.* There is also a translation of *Eugene Onegin* and notes in regard to *The Song of Igor's Campaign.* Finally, there are several folders of general and special correspondence with Nabokov's agent, with Aldanov, Khodasevich, and Lukash, and with other writers and poets. The collection is restricted.

George William Norris Papers, 1864–1944. U.S. senator from Nebraska; Norris visited Russia in 1923, favored U.S. recognition of the Soviet Union. Included are several folders of documents on American prisoners in Russia, 1920; the Anna Lerner case, 1924; the Captain Paxton Hibben case; and American recognition of the Soviet regime.

J. Robert Oppenheimer Papers, 1927–67. Physicist. Three folders of materials (including letters from George F. Kennan) pertain to Russia.

Francis le Jau Parker Papers, 1916–34. U.S. army officer, Parker was an attaché in Petrograd, 1917, and observer with the Russian army. Five folders of correspondence, reports, telegrams, newspaper clippings, and maps pertain to the Russian army in the 1910s, Parker's view on Russia's political future, and to other Russian-related subjects.

Leo Pasvolsky Papers, 1937–53. Born in Pavlograd, Pasvolsky was the editor of the *Russkoe slovo,* 1917–20, and *Amerikanskii ezhegodnik,* 1917–18, and later a State Department official and economist. Included is some material pertaining to foreign policy and to conferences after and during World War II, including the Crimea Conference, 1945.

Robert Porter Patterson Papers, 1940–51. Under secretary of war and secretary of war, 1940–47. Included is a report by Averell Harriman on developments in the Soviet Union as reflected in the Soviet press.

Gifford Pinchot Papers, 1830–47. Agriculturalist, governor, and conservationist. Included are notes on a trip to Russia in 1902 and materials on Bolshevism, communism, foreign forests, and Russia.

Konstantin Petrovich Pobedonostsev Papers. Correspondence of Pobedonostsev. The original material is located in the Lenin Library, Moscow.

Poushkin Society of America Minutes, 1934–55. Included are minutes, programs, correspondence, literary contest essays, postcards, newspaper clippings, and a card index to the words of Boris Godunov. Much of the material documents the activities of the society and Russian émigré life and literature.

John Randolph of Roanoke Papers, 1806–32. U.S. minister to Russia, 1830–31. Included are a diary and letterbook by John Randolph Clay, nephew of Henry Clay who held diplomatic posts in Russia in the 1830s.

Elihu Root Papers, 1863–1937. U.S. secretary of state, 1905–09; ambassador extraordinary at the head of the Special U.S. Diplomatic Mission to Russia, 1917. Several folders of materials pertain to Root's mission to Russia, including correspondence, maps, invitations, telegrams, calendars, and appointment books. There are also reports on Rear Admiral Glennon's movements in Russia, on the activities of John R. Mott with the mission, and on the requirements, in dollars, of the Russian government according to the Russian minister of finance.

Edward L. Rowny Papers, 1973–79. U.S. General, representative of Joint Chiefs of Staff to U.S.-Soviet Strategic Arms Limitation Talks. Included are originals and photocopies of documents, back channel messages, memoranda, and papers pertaining to Rowny's role in the SALT negotiations. The collection is restricted.

Charles Edward Russell Papers, 1914–18. Russell served on the Special Diplomatic Mission to Russia, 1917, and wrote *Unchained Russia* (1918). Included are Russell's "Diaries of an Amateur Diplomat," which cover his Russian journey in 1917. Ten folders of materials (including correspondence, reports, drafts of articles, notes, and postcards) deal with Russia in the late 1910s.

Russia Miscellany. Circa 1759–1917. Included in four containers are the following items: "Zapiska ob ustanovke flinbers-bara u kompasov"; letters patent conferring the order of Saint Alexander Nevsky on George Thomas Marye, U.S. ambassador to Russia, February 24, 1916, signed by Nicholas II; incomplete monthly lists of officers attending lectures at the Nicolaevsky Academy of the General Staff, Saint Petersburg, 1881; a thanksgiving manuscript book for the victory of Russian troops over the king of Prussia at Frankfurt, August 1, 1759; a printed copy of the land decree of October 26, 1917; and other materials.

Russia—Moscow. Included in three containers are copies of the following materials: Instructions to Count Pahlen from Alexander I, 1809; "Projet de dépêche à M. de Stoeckl" (1854); Instructions to Baron Tuyll from Alexander I, 1817; papers of the Ruling Senate—Instructions to scientists of the Bering Expedition, 1732–33, fifty-four pages; materials, 1868, from the archives of the Russian legation in Washington with translations by Hunter Miller; photostat negatives of signed autograph documents, sixty-two sheets, various sizes, pertaining to treaty negotiations leading up to the treaty of 1832 between the U.S. and Russia, in French.

Russian Orthodox Church in Alaska. Typescript, fifteen volumes. "Documents Relative to the History of Alaska," made by the staff of the Alaska History Research Project at the University of Alaska, 1936–38. Included are calendars, indexes, transcripts of documents, and excerpts and translations of some of the records of the Russian-American Company (at the National Archives in Washington, D.C.) and of the following documents at the Manuscript Division: Russian Orthodox Greek Catholic Church records, Yudin Collection, Russia-Petrograd, Russia-Moscow, Russia-Miscellany, and Russia-Valaam.

Russian Orthodox Greek Catholic Church in Alaska Records, 1772–1936. Donated to the Library of Congress by Russian Church officials in 1928 and 1964, these voluminous records (some 1,015 containers) consist primarily of ecclesiastical documents dealing with the administration of Alaskan parishes. Documents include registers of births, marriages, and deaths; records of confession and communion; reports about churches and lists of clergy; records of divine services; records of income and expenditures of church funds; registers of converts to orthodoxy. There are also twenty-three diaries and travel journals spanning the years 1828–97; Imperial decrees beginning with Catherine the Great; letters, 1870, on the proposed union of the Russian Orthodox Church with the American Episcopal Church; private correspondence to clerics in Alaska from V. K. Sabler, Professor I. Glubokovskii (Saint Petersburg Ecclesiastical Seminary), Professor N. Dobrov (Moscow Theological Seminary), and many others. Finally, there are documents pertaining to the church and the Russian-American Company before the purchase of Alaska.

Russia—Petrograd. Twelve containers include copies of materials made by Frank A. Golder in the Petrograd archives in 1914. Most of the material deals with Bering's expeditions, activities of the Russian-American Company and of Russians in Alaska, and sale of Alaska to the United States.

Russia—Philanthropic Societies Papers, 1865–76. Reports, account books, and photographs relating to charitable and philanthropic organizations in Russia, including the Bratoliubovnoe obshchestvo, Benevolent Society for Governesses and French Teachers in Russia, and Community for the Sisters of Charity at Pskov.

Russia—Valaam. Consists of four photographs of original drawings from Valaam monastery of the Elevoi, Kodiak, and Lisnoi Islands during 1819 made by the monk Kanowsky from memory in 1866. The materials were collected by Frank A. Golder.

Eugene Schuyler. Diplomat, author, and scholar. Included are materials pertaining to Schuyler's service as secretary of the American legation in Saint Petersburg, 1873–76, and to his book *Turkistan: Notes of a Journey in Russian Turkistan, Khokand, Bukhara, and Kuldja* (1876). There is also material relating to the advance of Russians into Central Asia, the Balkan question, and the Treaty of Berlin, 1878.

Hugh Lenox Scott Papers, 1845–1934. Army officer and public official. Included is correspondence and reports by Scott during his membership, 1917–19, on the Root mission to Russia.

William Sowden Sims Papers, 1856–1951. Some family letters pertain to Sims's service in Russia, where he was U.S. naval attaché in the late 1890s.

Joseph Stalin Papers. A photograph of a published handwritten note praising Lenin, 1925, with a typewritten English translation. The note appeared in *Rabochaia gazeta*, 17 (January 1925).

William Harrison Standley Papers, 1895–1963. U.S. ambassador to the Soviet Union, 1942–43. Included are drafts of Standley's book *Admiral Ambassador to Russia*. There is also correspondence pertaining to the anticommunist causes with which Standley was associated in the 1950s.

Laurence Adolph Steinhardt Papers, 1929–50. U.S. ambassador to Russia, 1939–41, Steinhardt handled the arrangements of the first lend-lease shipments to the Soviet Union. Included are some materials on Russia and Russian-Turkish relations.

Georgii Gustavovich Telberg Papers, 1915–40. Russian-born author, lecturer, and government official, Telberg participated in the Kerensky government. Various materials (primarily Telberg's autobiography, and also newspaper clippings and lecture notes) relate to life in Russia, the Russian revolution, and emigration.

Dimitry Tuneeff Papers. Included are Tuneeff's master's thesis, "Russian Libraries," (1932) and a biographical sketch, 1931, of G. V. Yudin.

Volga Province-Russia Records. Spanning the late eighteenth and early nineteenth centuries, these fifty-four items, which include official documents and service records, pertain to the service and family history of the Ivanovs, a noble Russian family that lived in the Volga region.

Vozdushnye puti Records, 1902–67. Contains three boxes of correspondence (1941–67) to R. N. Grynberg, the editor and publisher of *Vozdushnye puti*. Correspondents include Natalie Baranoff, Joseph Brodsky, Max Hayward, Roman Jakobson, Vladimir Nabokov, Aleksei Mikhailovich Remizov, Gleb Petrovich Struve, and others. In addition, there are three boxes of literary manuscripts, newspaper clippings, and photos (of Khodasevich, Mayakovskii, Nabokov, and others).

Gennadii Vasil'ievitch Yudin—Russian-American Company Records, 1876–1930. Correspondence, reports, tariffs, cargo registers, ships' logs, and other materials dealing with the exploration and colonization of Alaska by the Russian-American Company. Available on microfilm.

The following collections also contain Russian/Soviet material: Edward Goodrich Acheson; Henry Justin Allen; Joseph Wright Alsop; Chandler Parsons Anderson; Austria-Staatskanzlei; Turpin C. Bannister; John Davis Batchelder; Becker Family; William Edgar Borah; Breckinridge Family; Browning Family; James Bryce; Anson and Edward L. Burlingame; S. E. Burrows; Harold Hitz Burton; Thomas Capek; Truman Capote; James McKeen Cattell; Philander Chase; Raymond Clapper; Columbia University Oral History Collection; George Albert Converse; Clarence Seward Darrow; Elmer Holmes Davis; Norman H. Davis; Denmark (Danske Kaniellis Udenrigske Afdeling); George Vernon Denny; Lavinia L. Dock; George Fielding Eliot; Janet Flanner and Solita Solano (Flanner-Solano); Ford Peace Plan; France—Ministère des affaires étrangères; Frederick II of Prussia; John Philip Frey; Harry Augustus Garfield; Arthur Huntington Gleason; William Crawford Gorgas; Great Britain—Foreign Office; Frank Lester Greene; Hale Family; Elija Walker Halford; Hamilton (ship); John Marshall Harlan; Florence Jaffray Harriman; Burton Harrison Family; John Haynes Holmes; Harold L. Ickes; George Frederick Kunz; Gisella Rabinerson Lachman; William Daniel Leahy; Irvine Luther Lenroot; Nicholas Low; William Gibbs McAdoo; James Patrick McGranery; Alfred Thayer Mahan; William Alexander Marshall; James Murray Mason; William F. Megee and Samuel Nightingale; Ogden Livingston Mills; William Mitchell; John Bassett Moore; Maria Moransky; Alfred Mordecai; National American Woman Suffrage Association; Vladimir Ivanovich Nemirovich-Danchenko; Simon Newcomb; Reinhold Niebuhr; John Callan O'Laughlin; William Orr; Garfield Bromley Oxnam; Palmer-Loper Families; Charles Ross Parke; Joseph and Elizabeth Pennell; John Joseph Pershing; Amos Richard Eno Pinchot; Gregory Goodwin Pincus; Viacheslav Konstantinovich Pleve; Louis Freeland Post; Mary Edith Powel; Joseph Pulitzer; Grigorii Efimovich Rasputin; Jesse Robinson; Kermit Roosevelt; Igor Ivanovich Sikorsky; Smirnov Archive; Carl Andrew Spaatz; Lawrence Edmund Spivak; John Frank Stevens; Stevenson Family; Michael Wolf Strauss; Oscar Solomon Strauss; Arthur Sweetser; Raymond Swing; Thomas de Witt Talmage; Stephen Timoshenko; John Willard Toland; Ukrainian Congress Committee of America; Hoyt Sanford Vandenberg; Thomas James Walsh; Stanley Washburn; Boris Weinberg; William Allen White; Bertram David Wolfe; Levi and Charles Levi Woodbury; Wilbur and Orville Wright; and Gregory Ignatius Zatkovitch.

Among other division collections worthy of examination by the Russianist, two groups in particular stand out: the papers of U.S. presidents and secretaries of state. The former encompasses twenty-three series (from Washington to Coolidge); all are on microfilm and have name indexes. Of the latter—which include the papers of roughly half the men who served in the post—particularly fruitful collections for the Russianist may prove those of Henry Clay, Bainbridge Colby, Charles Evans Hughes, Cordell Hull, Robert Lansing, and Henry Kissinger (restricted). The recently acquired microfilmed editions of the papers and diaries of Henry L. Stimson and the papers of Frank B. Kellogg may also contain noteworthy material.

4. Of most importance is probably the ongoing publication of *The National Union Catalog of Manuscript Collections (NUCMC)* (since 1959). By 1982, nineteen volumes (including indexes) had appeared. *NUCMC* describes many LC holdings. Earlier inventories include *Handbook of Manuscripts in the Library of Congress* (1918); *List of Manuscript Collections in the Library Of Congress to July 1931,* by Curtis W. Garrison (1932); and *List of Manuscript Collections Received in the Library of Congress, July 1931 to July 1938,* by C. Percy Powell (1939). Manuscript accessions are described in *Annual Report of the Librarian of Congress* (1897–) and, since 1943, in *Quarterly Journal of the Library of Congress* (formerly, the *Library of Congress Quarterly Journal of Acquisitions*). In the Manuscript Reading Room is a dictionary catalog listing all catalog collections by "title"—i.e., by personal or place name in general. At present the catalog is in two parts and both must be consulted.

The most complete list of holdings is unpublished; it is the computerized descriptive listing kept at the Reading Room desk. A printout is made every six months, showing the size of most collections and indicating if finding aids exist for them. This tool should be the most useful for scholars who come to work in the division. Since 1958 the division has been publishing "registers" for some of its holdings. The majority of collections that have guides for use, however, have unpublished registers or finding aids. A card file in the Reading Room shows for which collections these guides exist. All Presidential Paper collections and more than 150 other personal paper collections have card indexes for them.

The division makes available without charge two brief guides: "Manuscript Division: Library of Congress" and "Catalogs, Indexes, Finding Aids."

Maryland University Libraries   See entry A39

B5   Marine Corps (Navy Department)—History and Museums Division

1 a. *Washington Navy Yard*
M at Eighth streets, Building 58
Washington, D.C. 20374
(202) 433-3840 (Administration)

b. 8:00 A.M.–4:30 P.M., Monday–Friday

c. Open to researchers, by appointment.

d. Photocopying facilities are not available.

e. Brigadier General E. H. Simmons, Director
Colonel O. M. Whipple, Jr., Deputy Director for History
H. I. Shaw, Chief Historian
Benis M. Frank, Director, Oral History Program
Colonel F. B. Nihart, Deputy Director for Museums
Charles Anthony Wood, Head, Collections Sections
Ken Smith-Christmas, Registrar

2. At present an estimate of total holdings pertaining to Russia/USSR cannot be made. There are some items of interest in each of the two branches of this division.

It should be noted that the Washington museum has a sister branch at the Quantico Marine Base in northern Virginia, which holds weapons and physical objects, some relating to the USSR. The Quantico museum, however, is not within the bounds covered by this guide.

3.   The museum branch collection of personal papers has the diary, stereopticon slides, and other materials of Henry Clay Cochrane relating to the coronation of Tsar Alexander III. Cochrane, a marine officer, was in attendance at the ceremonies.

The same branch should, in the near future, have the papers of Major General David Rowan Nimmer and of his wife. Nimmer was a naval attaché in Moscow, 1934–35. When these papers become available, which may not be for some time, they should be of considerable value for Soviet-area specialists. Russianists should check with the staff (Charles Wood) concerning these two sets of papers and others relating to their field of interest.

The Oral History Collection contains a taped interview with General Nimmer conducted by Major Thomas E. Donnelly. The transcription runs to 117 pages. A restriction on use of the material is pending. In the interview Nimmer discusses his service as assistant naval attaché in Moscow, 1934–35, the question of recognition of the Soviet government, and the opening of the U.S. embassy. Researchers should consult Benis Frank for other interviews of potential significance for Soviet-area specialists.

4.   In 1975 the History and Museums Division published *Marine Corps Oral History Collection Catalog* as a historical reference pamphlet. In the same series of pamphlets, *Marine Corps Personal Papers Collection Catalog* appeared in 1980 (3d rev. ed.).

A list of all artifacts has been computerized; an inventory of manuscripts and personal papers has not yet been computerized.

National Aeronautics and Space Administration—Headquarters History Office   See entry K25

B6   National Archives and Records Service (NARS) (General Services Administration)

1 a.   *Eighth Street and Pennsylvania Avenue, NW*
Washington, D.C. 20408
(entrance from Pennsylvania Avenue only)
(202) 523-3232 (Central Research Room)
(202)523-3218 (General Information)

b.   Central Research Room (and Microfilm Research Room):
8:45 A.M.–10:00 P.M., Monday.–Friday
9:00 A.M.–5:00 P.M., Saturday
Branch Research Rooms:
9:00 A.M.–5:00 P.M., Monday–Friday

c.   Open to researchers over the age of sixteen. Users must obtain a National Archives research pass (available in room 200B), for which appropriate identification is required. Some material may be restricted.

d.   Extensive photocopying facilities are available. Some Russian/Soviet material is available on microfilm; researchers should check *Catalog of National Archives Mi-*

crofilm Publications (1974; suppl. 1979) to see if the particular record groups they want are listed.

    e. Robert Warner, Archivist of the United States

2-3. One hardly knows where to begin with a resource as large and important, but relatively "unorganized," as NARS. In Washington it must share equal billing with LC as a scholarly research facility in almost every field. Recent estimates of its size are that it contains more than one million cubic feet of material, equaling some three billion records. Among these holdings are six million photographs, five million maps and charts, 100,000 films, and 80,000 sound recordings. Deposited here are the past records (from 1774) of all branches of the federal government and materials collected by them as well. NARS has been accurately described as "the nation's memory."

    All materials at NARS are organized into record groups, one for every agency as a whole, or subdivision of it, and for other governmental bodies or organizations. What makes holdings difficult to use is that there is thus no subject arrangement; any government agency or body may produce or acquire information about any and all subjects.

    In approaching this massive collection of data, therefore, the Russianist would be well advised to consult two specialized guides that cover Russian/Soviet material at NARS. The first is an inhouse study compiled by Elizabeth Buck and published by NARS in 1952: *Records in the National Archives Relating to the Russian Empire and the Soviet Union*, Reference Information Paper No. 41 (hereafter, *Records*). In 1952 *Records* found relevant (Russian/Soviet) material in at least 92 record groups of the nearly 400 maintained at that time. *Records* performs the great service of arranging its citations under broad subject categories. Although this organizational scheme necessitates the repetition many times of references to several of the largest and most significant record groups, its advantages far outweigh its drawbacks. The eight subject categories used in the guide are: government and politics; diplomatic relations; military affairs; geography; economic affairs; social conditions; science, medicine, and public health; and emigration and Russian nationals in the U.S. Most categories are further broken down by specific topics and/or dates.

    In each case where individual holdings are noted or described, *Records* gives the Record Group (RG) number wherein the material can be found. An appendix supplies the names of the agencies that correspond to these numbers. For example, RG 59 is readily identified in the appendix as the General Records of the State Department. A second major reference tool in the 1952 guide is a subject, geographic, and personal name index, with almost 400 entries.

    Records is currently out of print. Copies of it are available for consultation, however, at NARS; moreover, a photocopy of the paper will be mailed without charge to researchers who address specific requests for it to the Civil Archives Division.

    The second specialized guide that the scholar will find of great value in preparing to use the Russian/Soviet holdings at NARS is the survey compiled by Steven A. Grant and John H. Brown: *The Russian Empire and Soviet Union: A Guide to Manuscripts and Archival Materials in the United States* (Boston: G. K. Hall, 1981). The entry covering NARS in this volume (pp. 149–67) goes some way toward updating *Records,* particularly in postwar accessions, and provides summary descriptions (some in considerable detail) of the Russian-related materials in 137 separate record groups.

    While there is no substitute for direct, on-site searches of the archives, a familiarity with the two guides described above (and with the more general NARS finding aids cited in point 4) can save the scholar considerable time and effort in focusing his or her research. One further note: it is always advisable to write or call ahead before a research trip to NARS; an archivist at the relevant branch can often provide invaluable information as to the availability, accessibility, condition, and location of material within a given record group.

In general, the greatest concentrations of Russian/Soviet holdings occur in the Records of the State Department (RG 59), Records of the Foreign Service Posts of the Department of State (RG 84), Records of Former Russian Agencies (RG 261), and in those groups directly related to wars, the military, defense, and intelligence (e.g., RGs 38, 45, 80, 98, 111, 120, 127, 165, 179, 182, 208, 211, 218, 226, 242, 256, 262, 263, 306, 330, and 342). Other rich groups include the General Records of the United States Government (RG 11), Records of the United States Bureau of Customs Service (RG 36), Records of United States Participation in International Conferences, Commissions, and Expositions (RG 43), Records of the Committee on Public Information (RG 63), Records of the Bureau of Foreign and Domestic Commerce (RG 151), National Archives Gift Collection (RG 200), Records of Presidential Committees, Commissions, and Boards (RG 220), and Records of the U.S. Senate and House of Representatives (RG 46 and 233 respectively). The following brief account of some of the significant holdings within these and other record groups (listed under the operating division or branch having primary archival control) is based largely on material in *Records* and the Grant-Brown volume. It should be noted, finally, that this description covers textual materials only; nontextual items in these record groups (i.e., films, photos, machine-readable materials, maps, and sound recordings) are treated in separate entries (F7, G7, E6, D7) in this volume.

CIVIL ARCHIVES DIVISION
(202) 523-3108
Daniel Goggin, Director

Diplomatic Branch
(202) 523-3174
Milton Gustafson, Chief

RG 11: General Records of the United States Government. Contains international treaties and agreements signed by the U.S. since 1778, including such Russian-related documents as the Convention Ceding Alaska, 1867; North Pacific Sealing Convention of 1911; and SALT I Treaty. See Preliminary Inventory (PI) 159.

RG 43: Records of the United States Participation in International Conferences, Commissions, and Expositions. Included are materials on several conferences with references to the USSR, e.g., the Third World Power Conference, 1936; Moscow Conference of Foreign Ministers, October 19–30, 1943; and Tehran Conference, 1943. There are also Russian-related materials in records pertaining to bodies such as the European Advisory Commission, 1943–46; Council of Foreign Ministers, 1945–50; Far Eastern Commission, 1945–51; Allied Council for Japan, 1946–52; U.S.-USSR Joint Commission on Korea, 1946–48; and others. See PI 76 and supplement.

RG 59: General Records of the Department of State. This extremely rich record group is a principal archival source for documentation on Russian-American diplomatic relations and an important source of political, economic, and social information on Russia/USSR. Indeed, RG 59 contains extensive data on almost every subject of interest to the researcher, as U.S. embassies, legations, and consulates collect information ranging far afield from strictly diplomatic concerns. The holdings date from as early as the 1760s and run through the latest year for which State Department documents are released to the public (approximately twenty-five years after the date of issue). The Communications series within the record group, each of which contains Russian-related materials, are dispatches from consular offices, 1789–1906; instructions to consular officers, 1800–1906; notes to foreign missions in the United States, 1806–1906; diplomatic dispatches, 1808–1906; instructions to diplomatic representatives, 1829–1906; numerical file, 1906–10; decimal file, 1910–latest year of release. In addition to the wealth of information in these central series, the Russianist will find material of unique value in various special "lot files" (office files and working papers not integrated into the central files). Among these are collections pertaining to specific events and people, including Records of the Kosloff Affair, 1815–16; Records of the International Commission on the North Sea Incident, 12–25 November, 1905; "Sisson Documents," 1917–21; Records of the State Department Mission to South Russia, 1920; Records of (State Department official) Harley A. Notter, 1939–50; and (Dean) Acheson Files, 1941–47. Also pertinent to Russian/Soviet-area research are a number of more "general" lot files, e.g., Records of the Foreign Service Buildings Office, 1911–48; Records of the Office of the Counselor—general records, 1916–28; Records of the Division of Eastern European Affairs, 1917–41; Records of the War History Branch, 1938–50; Records of the Bureau of Intelligence and Research, 1941–61. Finally, scattered Russian/Soviet material can be found in various miscellaneous files (e.g., miscellaneous manuscripts; miscellaneous petitions and memorials; miscellaneous memoranda of conversations of the secretary of state, 1893–98).

The researcher is referred to both *Records* and *Grant-Brown* (see above) for descriptions of these materials. In addition, the State Department's annual *Foreign Relations of the United States* series serves as a valuable finding aid to the record group (along with NARS PI 157 and Special Lists [SL] 7 and 37). Also useful is "State Department Records in the National Archives: A Profile," by Milton O. Gustafson in *Prologue: the Journal of the National Archives* (Winter 1970). The complete State Department central files through 1910—as well as much later material—are available on microfilm.

RG 76: Records of Boundary and Claims Commissions and Arbitrations. Included are documents relating to miscellaneous claims of U.S. citizens against Russia for the loss of vessels or cargoes seized, 1807–81, and other Russian-related materials. See PIs 170 and 177.

RG 84: Records of the Foreign Service Posts of the Department of State. Many records in this group are duplicated by documents in RG 59, but there are also original materials, a large number of which pertain to trade and consular activities. The personal correspondence, 1916–18, of Ambassador David R. Francis is also here. See PI 60 and SL 9.

RG 256: Records of the American Commission to Negotiate Peace. Included are studies and other materials pertaining to Russian nationalities and the condition of the army in Russia at the time of the revolution. See Inventory 9 and PI 89.

RG 353: Records of Interdepartmental and Intradepartmental Committees (State Department). Included are materials pertaining to U.S.-Soviet relations, in particular among the series Records of Interdepartmental and Intradepartmental Committees Maintained by the Executive Secretariat (U.S. Lend-Lease and Surplus Settlement Committee, 1945–46), USSR Country Committee, 1946–48, and Records of the Joint U.S.A.-USSR Documentary Publication Project on Russian–American Relations, 1765–1815.

RG 360: Records of the Continental and Confederation Congresses and the Constitutional Convention. Included are materials pertaining to Francis Dana's mission as U.S. envoy to Saint Petersburg in the 1780s; to John Paul Jones's service in Russia; and to other topics of early Russian-American relations.

Judicial and Fiscal Branch
(202) 523-3059
Clarence Lyons, Chief

RG 26: Records of the United States Coast Guard. Included is an Alaska File with correspondence from the secretary of state regarding U.S. nationals seized by Russian authorities for illegal fur-sealing activities. Correspondence and communications of the Bering Sea Patrol, 1926–40, are also here.

RG 36: Records of the United States Customs Service. The Customs Service records also contain an Alaska File (cf. RG 26) that includes documents on how the treaty of 1867 influenced the Russian church in Alaska and on other Russian Alaska matters.

RG 39: Records of the Bureau of Accounts (Treasury). Included are twenty-six boxes of materials pertaining to U.S.-USSR fiscal relations, 1917–41. Among the documents are letters, memoranda, reports, claim files, newspaper clippings and publications that shed light on a wealth of topics: loans to Imperial Russia in World War I; economic, financial, and political conditions in Russia, 1917–20; Soviet representatives in the U.S., 1918–40; recognition of the USSR 1921–33; and much more. (Note: records relating to the Baltic States are filed separately from those of the USSR.)

RG 51: Records of the Office of Management and Budget. Files on specific legislation relating to Russia/USSR are interspersed in the general legislation files, 1921–38; general subject files, 1921–38; general legislative history files, 1939–68; and subject files of the director, 1939–68.

RG 56: General Records of the Department of the Treasury. Included is a folder of correspondence—from the office of the secretary of the Treasury, 1917–33 and 1933–56—pertaining to assistance to Russia during World War I, the purchase of Russian gold, and the deterioration of U.S.-Soviet relations after 1946. The group also contains material on Russian participation at the Chicago World's Columbian Exposition of 1893 and other matters. See PI 187.

RG 60: General Records of the Department of Justice. Included are documents from 1916 pertaining to claims that Russian nationals were using the Russian consulate in Chicago as a savings depository. There are also files on the Justice Department's handling of communist activities in the U.S., 1919–39, and documents pertaining to the enactment of the North Pacific Sealing Convention.

RG 63: Records of the Committee on Public Information. The Russian Division of the foreign section of this committee (Creel Committee) has records on American propaganda campaigns in the Soviet Union, 1918–19. Among these are leaflets, bulletins, and news clippings from the Russian and Siberian press and photostats on the "German-Bolshevik conspiracy" (see also RG 130).

RG 65: Records of the Federal Bureau of Investigation. The main series of records here are microfilmed FBI investigative case files, 1907–23, 956 rolls of microfilm, titled Miscellaneous, Mexican, and Old German Files. Investigation case files contain information on persons and organizations associated with socialist, communist, anarchist, and Russian activities in the U.S.

RG 82: Records of the Federal Reserve System. Included are materials pertaining to the Russian Embargo, 1918–43; Amtorg Trading Corp., 1924–30; Eesti Bank (Estonia), 1924–54; Latvijas Banka (Latvia), 1926–54; Lietuvos Bankas (Lithuania), 1931–54; and State Bank of the USSR, 1948.

RG 85: Records of the Immigration and Naturalization Service. The passenger arrival records, 1883–1954 (11,476 rolls of microfilm), contain the names of Russian immigrants to the U.S. Also included here are ship and airplane passenger and crew lists and other materials.

RG 104: Records of the Bureau of the Mint. Included are a number of reports by U.S. diplomats on Russian currency and Russia's acquisition of gold and silver coins, circa 1870–1915.

RG 113: Records of the Allied Purchasing Division. Contains material pertaining to Russian contracts and to the political situation in Russia, 1917–18.

RG 130: Records of the White House Office. Included are documents on the "German-Bolshevik conspiracy," 1918, obtained in Russia by Edgar Sisson at the request of President Wilson.

RG 220: Records of Temporary Committees, Commissions, and Boards. Included are the records of the Subversive Activities Control Board, 1951–73, which contain materials on communist organizations, and records of the National Aeronautics and Space Council, 1958–73. See PIs 43 and 190.

RG 272: Records of the President's Commission on the Assassination of President Kennedy. Included are name files for Lee Harvey Oswald, the accused assassin; his Russian-born wife, Marina; and persons with knowledge of Oswald's life in the Soviet Union (including defector Iurii Nosenko). Other material concerning Oswald's residence in the USSR, much of it published, is also here. See Inventory 5.

Legislative and Natural Resources Branch
(202) 523-3238
Trudy Peterson, Chief

RG 22: Records of the Fish and Wildlife Service. Included are materials pertaining to the North Pacific Sealing Convention, the Russian fur-seal industry in the Pribilov Islands (early nineteenth century) and salmon fishing/canning operations in Siberia.

RG 46: Records of the United States Senate. Included are the files of the Senate Committee on Foreign Relations, which contain hearings, committee papers, and petitions relating to such topics as U.S. concern for conditions in Russia during the revolution; American attitudes toward recognition of the Soviet Union; the U-2 incident; and the summit conference of 1960. Considerable material on the situation of Jews in the Soviet Union is also here. See PIs 23, 48 and 62, and SL 32.

RG 54: Records of the Bureau of Plant Industry, Soils, and Agricultural Engineering. Included are materials on the exchange of agricultural data with the USSR, 1922–36. See PI 66.

RG 57: Records of the Geological Survey. Included are materials on coal production in Russia, 1913–20, and Russian hydrological classification and terminology.

RG 69: Records of the Works Projects Administration. Contains a bibliography of research on civilian defense and protection against air raids in the Soviet Union.

RG 83: Records of the Bureau of Agricultural Economics. Included are materials on Russian crop area and production, 1864–1916; economic conditions, 1930–31; agricultural insurance; and rural credit. There are also materials on lend-lease to Russia and various studies pertaining to Russian agriculture.

RG 95: Records of the Forest Service. Included are various materials on forestry in Russia, 1915–20. See PI 18.

RG 115: Records of the Bureau of Reclamation. Included is material on irrigation in Turkestan, Siberia, and Russia, 1899–1903 and 1922–29. See PI 109.

RG 126: Records of the Office of Territories. Included are letters on Siberian mail delivery and materials on Soviet warships in the Philippines during World War II and communist activities in the islands, 1917–36 (filed under "Bolsheviki"). See PIs 151 and 154.

RG 166: Records of the Foreign Agricultural Service. Included are reports on various aspects of Russian agriculture by U.S. diplomats, agricultural attachés, and special agents in Russia, 1903–45. RG 166 also has material on wood resources in the USSR, 1920–39; economic conditions in Russia, 1942–45; and Soviet foreign trade.

RG 180: Records of the Commodity Exchange Authority. Contains a Soviet government study of future markets, 1927–38. See PI 112.

RG 233: Records of the United States House of Representatives. Contains the records of the House Committee on Foreign Affairs and House Committee on Un-American Activities. Included are materials on American attitudes toward Russia, the Bolshevik revolution, and the independence of Eastern European areas, including the Ukraine. There are also numerous bills, petitions, and resolutions pertaining to the abrogation of the U.S.-Russian commercial treaty of 1832, interest payments on

Russian Imperial government bonds, and many other Russian-related subjects. See PIs 11, 70, and 113.

RG 350: Records of the Bureau of Insular Affairs. Included are materials on Russian refugees in the Philippines, Russian consuls to and from Cuba, and Russian vessels served by the U.S. See Inventory 3 and SLs 2–5.

Industrial and Social Branch
(202) 523-3119
Franklin Burch, Chief

RG 14: Records of the U.S. Railroad Administration. Included are materials on the construction of 200 American locomotives for the Russian government and Soviet attempts to get this equipment; on seniority rights of former Russian Railway Service Corps employees who went back to work in the U.S. 1919–22; and on the unwillingness of Seattle longshoremen to ship arms and munitions to Siberia.

RG 20: Records of the Office of the Special Adviser to the President on Foreign Trade. Data on exports and imports between the U.S. and USSR, 1922–34, are here, as well as copies of commercial agreements, 1934–35, between the Soviet government and England, France, and Latvia.

RG 32: Records of the United States Shipping Board. Contains memoranda and correspondence pertaining to coal, fuel, and other supplies for Russian relief, 1919–21, and to the regulation of passenger travel between the USSR and the U.S. by a commercial treaty, 1933–34. See PI 97.

RG 40: General Records of the Department of Commerce. Included are correspondence, reports, and memoranda regarding commercial opportunities for American business in Russia, the purchase of Russian products, and statistics of Russian trade with the U.S. and other countries.

RG 41: Records of the Bureau of Marine Inspection and Navigation. Data on Russian merchant and war ships in the early 1900s are here, along with U.S. diplomatic documents from Riga on Soviet regulation of travel abroad by Soviet nationals and considerable material on U.S.-Latvian maritime relations.

RG 90: Records of the Public Health Service. Included are the records of a U.S. Public Health Marine Hospital in Western Latvia, 1909–13, which document emigration, epidemics, and health conditions in the Baltic area. Also here are a (translated) report of the Imperial Plague Commission, 1912, concerning measures against cholera on the railways; copies of U.S. consular reports on epidemics and other health matters in the Soviet Union, 1924–38; a copy of a report by Joseph E. Davies on Sochi, 1938; an account by Dr. O. H. Cox on Moscow hospitals and other medical establishments; and reports and correspondence on the Soviet Institute of Hematology and Blood Transfusion, 1940. See PI 141.

RG 102: Records of the Children's Bureau. Included are a League of Nations account of medical support for the USSR, 1921–22, and the names of people in the USSR involved in child care, July 1933. See PI 184.

RG 151: Records of the Bureau of Foreign and Domestic Commerce. Contains an extensive collection of correspondence and reports on the economy and foreign trade of Russia in the first half of the twentieth century. Included in the central file are materials on business conditions, credit, currency, development of natural resources, exchange rates, foreign loans, Imperial and Soviet bonds, labor conditions, trade regulations, and other topics for specific periods. RG 151 also contains correspondence pertaining to Japanese commerce in Siberia, car production in the USSR, U.S. famine relief in Russia and documents on the Soviet oil industry, 1920–30, in Baku and elsewhere.

RG 174: General Records of the Department of Labor. Included are materials on the selection of labor representatives to the Root Mission to Russia; deportation of C. A. K. Martens, chosen in 1919 to establish trade relations with the U.S.; Soviet labor pamphlets on the Russian army in World War I; and anti-Bolshevik activities.

RG 178: Records of the United States Maritime Commission. The series Cargo, Mail, and Passenger Reports, 1918–46, contains information on sailings of the U.S. merchant marine fleet from Soviet ports by year and name of ship.

RG 211: Records of the War Manpower Commission. Contains considerable documentation on Soviet labor from 1921 on, including data on absenteeism, migration of agricultural workers, social insurance, and trade unions. Also here are materials on Soviet industry, vocational training, welfare programs, veterans' pensions, and economic destruction during World War II. There is an index to publications pertaining to the USSR. See Inventory 6.

RG 219: Records of the Office of Defense Transportation. Included are a report by a U.S. organization on how to improve Soviet railroads, 1930; reports on the mail and communications system in the USSR, 1941–45; and information on freight to be shipped from the U.S. to the Soviet Union, 1942–45.

RG 248: Records of the War Shipping Administration. Included are the Records of the Office for the Russian Shipping Area, which pertain to the development of Soviet and East European shipping programs, 1941–46. Also here are documents on U.S. lend-lease to the USSR; reports by the OSS on Russian nationalities and political organization in northeastern Siberia; data on Soviet mineral and other exports to the U.S.; and reports on Soviet economic conditions and potential. See PI 30.

RG 250: Records of the Office of War Mobilization and Reconversion. Included are materials on war relief in the USSR and on U.S. agricultural goods sent to the Soviet Union, 1941–45. See PI 25.

RG 262: Records of the Foreign Broadcast Intelligence Service. Included are transcripts of broadcasts from the USSR related to economic, military, and other matters. See PI 115.

GENERAL ARCHIVES DIVISION
Washington National Records Center
4205 Suitland Road
Suitland, Maryland

Mail:
Washington, D.C. 20409
(301) 763-7410
Daniel Goggin, Director
(Daily shuttle service is available from main Archives building.)

RG 5: Records of the United States Grain Corporation. Included are materials relating to the Baltic and Polish missions of the American Relief Administration and economic conditions of southern Russia after World War I.

RG 19: Records of the Bureau of Ships. Included are materials on tools and equipment bought by the Amtorg Corp., 1937–39, and correspondence on lend-lease naval equipment to the Soviet Union, 1941–45. See PI 133.

RG 61: Records of the War Industries Board. Included are various materials pertaining to U.S. contracts with Russia, 1917–18. See PI 1.

RG 70: Records of the Bureau of Mines. Contains materials on various aspects of Russian mine and oil production, including U.S. use of Russian oil resources, 1917–21; influence of the world oil situation on Russia and Sakhalin Island, 1917–22; and petroleum resources of Baku and Azerbaizhan, 1919–21.

RG 77: Records of the Office of the Chief of Engineers. Included is a report on

Russian iron production, 1870; drawings/plans on civil projects in Vladivostok and elsewhere; and materials on U.S. support of the Russian Railway Service Corps.

RG 112: Records of the Office of the Surgeon General. Included are documents relating to lend-lease and reciprocal aid programs to Russia during World War II.

RG 153: Records of the Office of the Judge Advocate General (Army). Contains reports of investigations of criminal acts by Nazis (German and non-German) in the USSR and Soviet citizens against other Soviet citizens and persons of other nationalities. Also included are trial records of Nazis that shed light on the Katyn Forest massacre, extermination of Soviet Jews, and participation of Soviet judges in the International Military Tribunal, Far East.

RG 169: Records of the Foreign Economic Administration. Included is considerable material on the Harriman mission to Moscow, 1941–42, to negotiate lend-lease to the Soviet Union. Also included are a "History of Lend-Lease" completed by the State Department and materials on exports to the USSR during World War II. See PI 29.

RG 182: Records of the War Trade Board. Included are documents on contacts of Russian companies with Germany in the 1910s; the Russian budget during World War I; trade between Russia and the U.S.; and Russian exports and imports, 1917–19. See PI 100.

RG 208: Records of the Office of War Information. Included are reports (as well as photos, speech recordings, and films) on the Soviet military, 1942–45; USSR air command in Alaska during World War II; Yalta Conference; Soviet delegates to the signing of the UN Charter, 1945; lend-lease to the USSR; and economy of the Ukraine, 1942–45. See PI 56.

RG 232: Records of the Petroleum Administrative Board. Included are materials on the oil resources of Asiatic Russia, Estonia, Latvia, Lithuania, and Sakhalin Island, 1925–29.

RG 253: Records of the Petroleum Administration for War. Included is much material on the lend-lease of oil goods to the USSR and on Soviet petroleum resources, needs, and production. See PI 31.

RG 255: Records of the National Aeronautics and Space Administration. Contains materials on Soviet aviation, 1915–63, including photographs, reports, and translated documents.

RG 260: Records of the United Stated Occupation Headquarters, World War II. Included are materials on the administration of Germany and Austria by the Allies and the USSR; Berlin Airlift; industrial dismemberment of Germany; and German war reparations.

RG 261: Records of Former Russian Agencies. Consists of records of Imperial Russian Agencies obtained by the Department of State. Among them are the records of the Russian-American Company, 1802 and 1817–67; records of Russian consulates in the U.S. and Canada, 1862–1922; and records of the Russian Supply Committee, 1914–22.

RG 331: Records of Allied Operational and Occupation Headquarters, World War II. Contains materials on Russian-Allied military activities; missions of the Supreme Headquarters, Allied Expeditionary Force (SHAEF) to Russia; handling of censorship by Soviet and American authorities; and procurement of supplies for the USSR.

RG 338: Records of the United States Army Commands. Among the holdings are documentation on Soviet troop movements and U.S.-Soviet troop contacts in Central Europe; Intelligence Division interrogation reports on persons in the USSR or in Soviet-controlled nations, 1943–49; materials on Nazi criminal acts in the USSR and against Soviet citizens abroad.

RG 341: Records of Headquarters United States Air Force. Included are correspondence, intelligence reports, aerial photos, radar reports, charts, and air attaché reports pertaining to the USSR.

RG 407: Records of the Adjutant General's Office. Includes correspondence, reports, etc., on lend-lease to the USSR; the Berlin blockade, 1948; Russian atomic bomb developments, 1949–54; and U.S.-USSR joint occupation policies after World War II.

MILITARY ARCHIVES DIVISION
(202) 523-3089
Dr. Gary Ryan, Acting director

Navy and Old Army Branch
(202) 523-3229
Dr. Gary Ryan, Chief

Modern Military Branch
(202) 523-3340
Robert Wolfe, Chief

NOTE: In general, pre-1940 records are the domain of the Navy and Old Army Branch, while the Modern Military Branch oversees post-1940 materials. Certain record groups are maintained jointly by both branches.

RG 18: Records of the Army Air Forces. Included are materials on various aspects of Soviet aviation in the 1930s.

RG 24: Records of the Bureau of Naval Personnel. Included are logs of vessels in Russian waters, circa 1880–1945, and logs of ships assisting the Allied intervention in Russia; also considerable materials on Soviet aviation, artillery, and navy personnel in World War II. See PI 123.

RG 38: Records of the Office of the Chief of Naval Intelligence. A very rich group, RG 38 includes naval attaché reports, 1892–1946, dealing with Russian military affairs and with political, economic, social, and diplomatic matters. Among the topics covered in detail are the Russo-Japanese War, the Russian Civil War, the Five-Year Plans, the Russo-Finnish War of 1939–40, World War II, communism, and ethnic and political minorities in the USSR.

RG 45: Naval Records Collection of the Office of Naval Records and Library. Voluminous material on various naval matters is here, from the activities of John Paul Jones, 1778–91, to the activities of U.S. submarines off the Russian Pacific coast. Included are the Asiatic Squadron letters (21 vols.), 1865–85; data on Russian economic and diplomatic affairs, 1890–1916; and much more.

RG 52: Records of the Bureau of Medicine and Surgery. Bureau correspondence, 1941–46, includes studies of casualties in Russia, bulletins on sanitary and health conditions, Soviet medical handbooks, course lists of the Russian Medical Academy, and intelligence reports from 1922 on relief work in Russia and health conditions in the Ukraine. See PI 6.

RG 72: Records of the Bureau of Aeronautics. Numerous information bulletins from World War II deal with the allocation of raw/finished materials in the USSR, the Soviet Meteorology Mission of 1943, U.S.-USSR photographic exchange, translation of Soviet technical data, and war relief efforts by Soviet civilians. See PI 26.

RG 80: General Records of the Department of the Navy. Included are the James Forrestal papers, 1940–47, with speeches, letters, memos, and articles on lend-lease supplies and the Russian political situation; comments on communist theory and practice, the Five-Year Plans, and Soviet personalities; and minutes of the American Top Policy Group, 1944–47. Also here are naval records on Bolshevik activities in the Soviet Union, 1919–26; and correspondence on the Amtorg Trading Corporation's activities in the U.S., 1939–42.

RG 92: Records of the Office of the Quartermaster General. Included are various materials on the equipment, supply, transportation, and organization of the Russian army, 1890–1914.

RG 94: Records of the Adjutant General's Office. Contains reports and other materials by U.S. military observers during the Crimean and Russo-Japanese wars. See PI 17.

RG 107: Records of the Office of the Secretary of War. Included is documentation concerning lend-lease, U.S.-Soviet relations, and Soviet internal affairs, 1940–47. Considerable material—correspondence, directives, and reports—on Soviet domestic and foreign affairs from assistant secretaries of war and air in the 1940s is also here.

RG 120: Records of the American Expeditionary Forces (World War I). The records of the American Expeditionary Forces, North Russia, 1917–19, include materials of the chief of the American military mission, the inspector general, judge advocate, and chief surgeon. AEF GHQ (Intelligence) has information on the military, political, and social conditions in Russia, both before and after the intervention. GHQ—Office of the Commander in Chief, 1917–20, contains materials on the repatriation of Russian POWs in Germany after 1918, U.S. relief supplies for Russia, and conditions in Russia. GHQ—General Staff has material on the Kerensky government; the movement of Russian revolutionaries between Switzerland and Germany, March–April 1917; Finnish anti-Bolshevik forces and intentions; and other matters pertaining to Russia circa 1917.

RG 160: Records of Headquarters Army Service Forces. There is extensive Russian-related material (largely for the period 1940–46) in the records of the following divisions and branches: International Division, 1940–47; Mission Branch; Civilian Supply Branch; Control Division; and Strategic Logistics Branch.

RG 165: Records of the War Department General and Special Staffs. Extensive Russian-related material may be found in the following series: Military Intelligence Division Correspondence, 1917–41; English Translations of Foreign Intelligence Documents, 1919–47; War Plans Division Correspondence, 1920–42; German Military Records Relating to World War I; Office of the Chief of Staff, 1942–47; Director of Intelligence; Operations Division, 1942–49.

RG 179: Records of the War Production Board. Included are extensive materials documenting U.S. lend-lease to the Soviet Union. See PI 15.

RG 218: Records of the United States Joint Chiefs of Staff. Included are the records of the United Joint Chiefs of Staff (JCS) and the Combined Chiefs of Staff (CCS) in the central decimal and geographic decimal files, 1942–56, with information on Soviet armed forces during and after World War II, post-war occupation of Austria and Germany, Soviet domination of Eastern Europe, Soviet influence worldwide, conditions in the USSR, Soviet weapons, and U.S. plans for war in case of Soviet attack. The records of the Munitions Assignment Board are also here.

RG 226: Records of the Office of Strategic Services. Contains intelligence, naval, and military reports on Soviet natural resources, nationality problems, and other social, political, military, and economic matters.

RG 242: National Archives Collection of Foreign Records Seized, 1941–. Extensive series of microfilms of captured Nazi documents and other World War II materials pertaining to Russia are in this group. Pertinent series include: Records from the Heere-archiv, 1679–1947; Miscellaneous Records, 1815–1945; Library of German microfilms, 1870–1945; Miscellaneous Russian Records, 1870–1947; Records of the All-Union Communist Party, Smolensk District, 1917–41; Records of the National Socialist German Workers' Party, 1915–42; Records of Other Reich Ministries and Offices, 1919–45; Italian Records, 1922–43; Japanese Records, 1928–47; Records of German Air Force Commands, 1932–45; Records of the Soviet Purchasing Commission at Prague, 1936–41; Records of the Reich Commissioner for the Strengthening of Germandom, 1939–45; Records of the Reich Ministry for the Occupied Eastern Territories, 1942–45; and Records Seized by U.S. Military Forces in Korea. RG 242 has a published index and supplement.

RG 319: Records of the Army Staff. Included are materials on U.S.-USSR policies in occupied countries after World War II (Austria, Germany, Japan); military contingency planning toward the USSR; and Soviet military potential and activities.

RG 330: Records of the Office of the Secretary of Defense. Included are vast (but scattered) materials dealing with war planning directed toward the USSR. Subjects discussed include strategic and tactical nuclear weapons; European Defense Community agreements; the Mutual Defense Assistance Program, 1950–52; the Mutual Security Act, 1953; the Soviet wartime and post-war roles; and Soviet-Iranian relations.

RG 333: Records of International Military Agencies. Records of the Tripartite Naval Commission, 1941–47, contain correspondence, memoranda, and messages among commission members representing the U.S., Great Britain, and the USSR. Other references to the USSR can be found in the Records of the United Nations Command, 1950–57. See PI 127.

RG 334: Records of Interservice Agencies. Records of the United States Military Mission to Moscow, 1943–45, contain documents on the shuttle-bombing of Axis-occupied Europe (Operation Frantic). Also in this group are the Records of the National War College, 1943–54, with library files on Soviet domestic affairs, military capability, and foreign relations.

RG 335: Records of the Office of the Secretary of the Army. Contains documentation on the Berlin airlift, the Soviet explosion of the atomic bomb, Soviet military strength, and Soviet natural resources.

RG 340: Records of the Office of the Secretary of the Air Force. Included are documents on preparing for war against the USSR, 1948–50.

RG 395: Records of the U.S. Army Overseas Operations and Commands. Included are the records of the American Expeditionary Forces in Siberia, 1918–20, consisting mostly of war diaries from Vladivostok.

RG 457: Records of the National Security Agency/Central Security Office. Included are comprehensive reports of economic, military, political, psychological, subversive, and other conditions in the USSR.

SCIENCE AND TECHNOLOGY ARCHIVES DIVISION
(202) 523-1408
Albert Leisinger, Director

Center for Polar and Scientific Archives
(202) 523-3223
Franklin Burch, Acting Director

RG 227: Records of the Office of Scientific Research and Development. Included are materials on Soviet achievements in various fields of medicine; a report describing Soviet bauxite resources, 1928–44; and material on rodent control in Soviet agriculture.

RG 307: Records of the National Science Foundation (NSF). Included are English translations of Russian studies on the Antarctic and records relating to the Joint U.S.-USSR Commission on Scientific and Technical Cooperation. See also NSF Director's Files.

PRINTED DOCUMENTS DIVISION
(202) 523-3049
Pat Andrews, Director

Printed Archives Branch
(202) 763-3920
Nancy Menan, Chief

RG 287: Publications of the United States Government. This is a complete collection of all government documents printed by the Government Printing Office (GPO), including various reports and documents pertaining to Russia/USSR. Documents are available through the Archives Library (202/523-3286).

4. In addition to the guides and finding aids already noted—Reference Information Paper No. 41 *(Records)*, the *Grant-Brown* volume, and the *Catalog of National Archives Microfilm Publications*—various other publications will prove valuable to the researcher. These include:

Guide to the National Archives of the United States (1974). The most important general catalog of NARS holdings is updated regularly and maintained in looseleaf form in division offices for consultation.

Select List of Publications of the National Archives and Records Service, rev. (1977). This useful guide lists the inventories, preliminary inventories, and special lists that accompany many record groups (some of which have been cited in the text above) as well as NARS reference information papers and conference papers. At least three conference papers—*Captured German and Related Records,* ed. Robert Wolfe; *The National Archives and Foreign Relations Research,* ed. Milton O. Gustafson; and *World War II: An Account of Its Documents,* eds. James E. O'Neill and Robert W. Krauskopf—are of interest to the Russianist.

List of Record Groups of the National Archives and Records Service (January 1981). A compilation of statistical information, this booklet provides physical measurements of the material in each RG and breaks down the material by type and by archival unit of control (division/branch).

A Researcher's Guide to the National Archives, rev. (1977). An introductory leaflet.
Regulations for the Public Use of Records in the National Archives, rev. (1976).
Location of Records and Fees for Reproduction Services in the National Archives and Records Service, rev. (1979).
General Restrictions on Access to Records in the United States (1976).

Other information sheets are available from the Central Research staff. The most important finding aids for Russianists will probably be the elaborate name index cards for different departments. These indexes are kept in Room 5W and staff members there can be of assistance in using them. The most complete indexes are those for the State, Commerce, and Justice departments. Researchers will usually find it best to start their searches with these name index cards and to use them as they go through the actual materials.

For recent information on acquisitions by the National Archives see: *Prologue: The Journal of the National Archives* (quarterly); the American Historical Association's *AHA Newsletter* (nine issues per year); Phi Alpha Theta's *The Historian* (quarterly); and the *Newsletter* (quarterly) of the Society for Historians of American Foreign Relations.

NOTE: See also entries D7, E6, F7, G7, and Q12.

National Library of Medicine   See entry A48

B7   Naval Historical Center (Navy Department)—Operational Archives Branch

1 a. *Washington Navy Yard*
M at Eighth streets, SE, Building 210
Washington, D.C. 20374
(202) 433-3171

b. 7:30 A.M.–4:30 P.M.,   Monday–Friday

c. Most of the collection is open to the public for on-site use.

d. Limited photocopying facilities are available.

e. Dean C. Allard, Director

2–3.   The Operational Archives has a number of items of interest for Russian-area scholars. In the Early Records Collection is the two-volume diary of Vice Admiral Newton A. McCully and a few associated papers. McCully was a naval attaché in Saint Petersburg in 1904–5. More important, he was an observer with the Russian forces in the Russo-Japanese War, saw the siege and fall of Port Arthur, and also was on hand at the Battle of Mukden. He traveled through Mongolia and northern China on his return to the U.S. In 1914 he returned to Saint Petersburg, again as naval attaché, but in the fall of 1917 he was sent to France. He became commander of U.S. naval forces in northern Russia in September 1918, a post he left in June 1919. The Operational Archives holds the original of the diary, though a copy is available at the National Archives. The diary has also appeared in published form—replete with sketches, maps, and other valuable information—as *The McCully Report: The Russo-Japanese War, 1904–1905*, ed. Richard A. von Doenhoff (Annapolis: U.S. Naval Institute Press, 1977).

Among the Records from Foreign Sources are German officers' reports, essays, and analyses of the military situation vis-à-vis the Soviet Union. Most are from the 1930s and 1940s, some in German and others in English. The basic collection of German naval records for that period is held on microfilm at NARS. Some duplicate materials from the collection are in the Operational Archives.

In the various groups among the Records Organized by the Operational Archives is extensive material on convoys to Russia in World War II; some reports and other materials from U.S. naval attachés in Moscow in the 1940s; and limited material on lend-lease and international conferences involving the Soviet Union.

4.   The useful guide *Information for Visitors to the Operational Archives* (1978) and a current list of the office's open collections are available without charge.

Office of Air Force History (Air Force Department)—Library
    See entry A1

B8   Scottish Rite Supreme Council Archives and Library

1 a. *1733 Sixteenth Street, NW*
       Washington, D.C. 20009
       (202) 232-3579, ext. 39 (Library), ext. 32 (Archives)

   b. 8:00 A.M. 4:00 P.M.,   Monday–Friday (Library)
       8:00 A.M.–3:30 P.M.,   Monday–Friday (Archives)

   c. Open to the public but, especially for the archives, by appointment.

   d. Interlibrary loan service and photocopying facilities are available.

   e. Inge Baum, Librarian
       Aemile Pouler, Keeper, Archives

2–3.   The archives contain an unusual item: a letter from an organization of Russian Masons, dated 1817, asking for recognition from the supreme council. Archivist Aemile Pouler has published the letter with commentary in the council's monthly *The New Age* (October 1973).

The library proper contains approximately 200,000 books and pamphlets, about a third of which are on the Freemason movement worldwide. Some articles or chapters in books concern the Masonic movement in Russia in the eighteenth and nineteenth centuries. An even more important resource for Russianists, however, would be the library's contacts with most other Masonic libraries and repositories. Researchers can obtain invaluable help in locating useful materials for studying the movement in Russia and its contacts with international Freemasonry.

Senate Historical Office   See entry K30

B9   Seventh-Day Adventists—General Conference—Archives

1 a. *6840 Eastern Avenue, NW*
       Takoma Park
       Washington, D.C. 20212
       (202) 722-6373

   b. 8:30 A.M.–5:30 P.M.,   Monday–Thursday
       8:30 A.M.–Noon,   Friday

   c. Open to the public.

   d. Interlibrary loan service is not available, but photocopying facilities are available.

   e. Neal C. Wilson, President
       Alf Lohne, Vice President in Charge of USSR Region
       F. Donald Yost, Archivist

2–3.   The General Conference of Seventh-Day Adventists has been active in teaching, mission work, and—under the auspices of the Seventh-Day Adventist World Service—relief work in many parts of the world. The Takoma Park office is the headquarters of the General Conference. It serves as the administrative center and liaison between the U.S. and foreign operations.

This organization includes more than 400 Adventist churches in the Soviet Union with a membership in excess of 30,000. Regular exchanges of representatives between the U.S. and Soviet branches take place: in June 1981, Mssrs. Wilson and Lohne visited the Soviet Union; in October 1981, two Soviet Adventist pastors attended an annual council in Washington.

The Conference's Department of Archives and Statistics maintains files dating from 1896 with information concerning Adventism in Russia/USSR. The material includes correspondence between Russian/Soviet church pastors and the headquarters here, as well as magazine articles on the Conference's activities in the USSR and minutes of the General Conference's committee meetings. The most interesting documents in the collection may be those concerning the 1924 Adventist schism in the USSR; the Takoma Park archives are a unique source of information on this event.

4.   The General Conference publishes *Yearbook,* which includes missionary statistics for Adventist worldwide activities; the weekly *Adventist Review*; and the quarterly *World Missions Report.* Each is published by the Review and Herald Publishing Association under the general editorship of Howard Rampton. The 1982 edition of the *Yearbook* contains names and addresses of local Seventh-day Adventist church leaders in the USSR.

B10   Sisters of Mercy of the Union—Office of Archives

1 a.   *1320 Fenwick Lane, Suite 500*
Silver Spring, Maryland 20910
(301) 587-6310

b.   9:00 A.M.–5:00 P.M.,   Monday–Wednesday

c.   Open to researchers, by appointment.

d.   Photocopying facilities are available.

e.   Molly McMahon, Archival Technician

2–3.   Crimean materials in this collection include photocopies of "Mission of the Sisters of Mercy in the Military Hospitals of the East 1854–1856," two volumes, by Sr. Francis Bridgeman, and diaries of Sr. M. Joseph Croke and Mother M. Clare Moore who served in the Crimea. The originals of these materials are preserved in Kinsale, Ireland. Also included is the original copy of "Remembrances of Crimea," by M. Joseph Lynch.

B11   Smithsonian Institution Archives

1 a.   *Arts and Industries Building, Room 2135*
900 Jefferson Drive, SW
Washington, D.C. 20560
(202) 357-1420

b.   9:00 A.M.–5:00 P.M.,   Monday–Friday

c. Open to the public.

d. Photocopying facilities are available.

e. William A. Deiss, Acting Archivist

2. The archives contain some 7,300 cubic feet of materials, most concerning American science and the broad range of activities of the Smithsonian (entry K31) with its various branches. A thoroughgoing search for Russian/Soviet materials could not be undertaken. Enough was found, however, to indicate that researchers in the Soviet field can find much of value in the archives.

3. Some examples of items located in the collections:

Gustav Wilhelm Belfrage Papers, 1866–82. Contains a small amount of material, in the form of letters, on entomology in Russia and the exchange of specimens.

Joseph A. and John Randolph Clay Papers, 1841–66. Another fairly small collection as pertains to Russia includes accounts, correspondence, and lists covering the mineralogical specimens received by the Clays from Russia. An unpublished finding aid can be consulted.

William H. Dall Papers, circa 1839–58 (Record Unit 7073). Contains letters, diaries, and notebooks on Russian America (Alaska) during the nineteenth century and up to the 1920s. The political and commercial situations in Alaska, Sitka society, and other matters related to Russia are reflected in the holdings. An unpublished finding aid can be consulted.

Robert Kennicott Papers, 1863–65 (Record Unit 7072). Three letters, two to Roderick MacFarlane of Winnipeg, Canada, bear on Kennicott's experiences exploring Russian Alaska.

National Institute, Records, 1839–63 (Record Unit 7058). Some references to Russia occur here. An unpublished finding aid can be consulted.

National Zoological Park Records, 1887–1965 (Record Unit 74). In Series 14, Box 163, Folder 2, is correspondence concerning exchanges of animals with the Soviet Union in 1938–39. An unpublished finding aid can be consulted.

Registrar, 1834–1958 accretions to 1976 (Record Unit 6999T). These records (circa 405 cubic feet) include some correspondence with Russian/Soviet scientists and are partially microfilmed. A card index can be consulted.

U.S. National Museum, Permanent Administrative Files, 1877–1975 (Record Unit 192). These files include the correspondence of Russian/Soviet scientists and records concerning the Smithsonian-Harvard 1912 expedition to the Altai Mountains in Siberia. Inquire concerning special conditions of access. An unpublished finding aid can be consulted.

Special Order, Drawer 1. Correspondence on microfilm of the Smithsonian Institution with Russians in the nineteenth century. An unpublished index can be consulted.

Leonhard Stejneger Papers, 1867–1943 (Record Unit 7074). Included are correspondence, notes, photos, and writings on fur seals and the hunting of them in the North Pacific and Bering Sea, plus meteorological and ethnographical information relating to the Russian Empire (late nineteenth century to 1920s). An unpublished finding aid can be consulted.

Western Union Telegraph Expedition Collection, 1864–67 (Record Unit 7213). Also known as the Russian-American Telegraph Expedition, this ambitious project studied the feasibility of establishing communications with Europe via Alaska, the Bering Straits, and Siberia. Three divisions worked in Canada, Russian-America (Alaska), and Asia. Robert Kennicott headed the Russian-American division, which also made natural history collections. Members of the Scientific Corps that went to Alaska included Henry M. Bannister, William H. Dall, and Henry W. Elliott. This collection contains correspondence (mostly to Spencer F. Baird), copies of reports, copies of Kennicott's notes on natural history, and clippings.

Again it should be stressed that on-site inspection might uncover much more pertinent material in the archives.

4. *Finding Aid: Guide to the Smithsonian Archives* (1978) is useful to researchers.

U.S. Information Agency—Library   See entry A61

C Museums, Galleries, and Art Collections

Museum, Gallery, and Art Collection Entry Format (C)

1. General Information
   a. *address; telephone number(s)*
   b. hours of service
   c. conditions of access
   d. photocopying facilities
   e. name/title of director and heads of relevant divisions
2. Size and Holdings Pertaining to Russia/USSR
3. Description of Holdings Pertaining to Russia/USSR
4. Bibliographic Aids Facilitating Use of Collection

Introductory Note

The Washington area features a number of museum and gallery collections of great interest for Russianists. The collection of Russian decorative art at the Hillwood Museum (entry C3) and that of Russian coins and medals in the National Museum of American History (entry C10) are the best in their respective fields outside the Soviet Union. Russian/Soviet émigré art is well represented in small but impressive collections at the Hirshhorn Museum (entry C4), National Museum of American Art (entry C9), and Phillips Collection (entry C14). The Textile Museum (entry C16) should not be overlooked by those interested in Central Asian rugs and furnishings. Philatelists will find the National Philatelic Collections of the National Museum of American History (entry C10) an outstanding resource.

C1 Anderson House (The Society of Cincinnati)

1 a. *2118 Massachusetts Avenue, NW*
   Washington, D.C. 20008
   (202) 785-2040

b. 1:00–4:00 P.M.,   Tuesday–Saturday (Museum Collection)
July and August: closed Saturday
10:00 A.M.–4:00 P.M.,   Monday–Friday (Library)

c. Open to the public; library facilities available by appointment.

e. John D. Kilbourne, Director, Anderson House Museum

2–3.   The museum collection contains many Oriental art objects but also includes about a half-dozen Russian icons from the seventeenth and eighteenth centuries and a malachite cup on a pedestal (about three feet tall). The icons include: *Image of the Sleepless Eye* (eighteenth century), *Lady of Vladimirskaia* (seventeenth century), *Saturday of All Saints* (eighteenth century), and *Madonna and Child* (seventeenth century).

B'nai B'rith Klutznick Museum   See entry M27

C2   Corcoran Gallery of Art

1 a. *Seventeenth Street and New York Avenue, NW*
Washington, D.C. 20006
(202) 638-3211

b. 10:00 A.M.–4:30 P.M.,   Tuesday–Wednesday and Friday–Sunday
10:00 A.M.–9:00 P.M.,   Thursday
Closed Mondays and major holidays.

c. Open to the public.

e. Michael Botwinick, Director
Jane Livingston, Associate Director and Chief Curator
Edward Nygren, Curator of Collections
Linda Simmons, Associate Curator of Collections

2–3.   Though the gallery's collection consists largely of works by American artists, Russian/Soviet paintings have also been featured at the Corcoran. Two former gallery properties—Ivan Aivasonskii's late-nineteenth-century commemorative works *The Relief Ship* and *Distributing Supplies*—were sold at auction in 1978–79. In the fall of 1981, the gallery displayed thirty-eight portraits of prominent figures from Russian arts and letters painted by Soviet émigré artist Gabriel Glickman. The Glickman exhibition was opened with musical accompaniment for and commentary on the portraits by Mstislav Rostropovich, conductor of the National Symphony Orchestra.

C3   Hillwood Museum

1 a. *4155 Linnean Avenue, NW*
Washington, D.C. 20008
(202) 686-5807

b–c.   The museum is open to the public, by appointment. A guide leads small groups on a tour of the house.

e. Roy D. R. Betteley, Director
   Katrina V. H. Taylor, Curator
   Hillwood is operated by the Marjorie Merriweather Post Foundation of the District of Columbia.

2.　The museum holds an extensive collection (at least 2,000 items) of the works of Russian gold- and silversmiths, porcelain, glassware, textiles, furniture, and other decorative-art objects. Some fifty paintings and seventy icons are also here. This is perhaps the largest collection of Russian decorative art outside the Soviet Union.

3.　The following descriptive list can only highlight some of the extraordinary treasures of this magnificent museum. The holdings include:
   A watch of Peter the Great, more than two inches in diameter, of gold set with a miniature of his wife, Catherine I, and with diamonds.
   The only imperial Russian crown outside the USSR—the nuptial crown of Marie Alexandrovna, bride of (later) Tsar Alexander II, and then worn by successive tsarinas-to-be at their weddings.
   Two imperial Easter eggs by Fabergé, including the famous "Pink Egg"—a present from Nicholas II to his mother in 1914.
   Outstanding examples of Russian porcelain, such as four services from the Frances Gardner Factory commissioned by Catherine the Great for use at the state dinners given annually for the knights of the four imperial orders (Saint Andrew, Saint George, Saint Alexander Nevsky, and Saint Vladimir), painted with the ribbons and badges of each order.
   A notebook of Elizabeth I, framed in silver cloth and gold, and a solid platinum box, covered with worked gold, commemorating the coronation of Nicholas I.
   Approximately thirty portraits of members of the imperial family and other Russian nobility, including several of Catherine the Great, and one of Princess Dashkova by the finest Russian portrait painter of the eighteenth century, Dmitry Levitsky.
   Karl Briullov's portrait, *Countess Samoilova and Her Foster Daughter* (1832–34), 106 by 79 inches, an oil on canvas and very important in the history of Russian painting.
   Konstantin Makovskii's imposing oil painting, *The Boyar Wedding* (1883), approximately 96 by 180 inches.
   Some twenty landscapes and scenes, most from the early twentieth century.
   Many chalices from the seventeenth to the nineteenth centuries, of silver and gold, including one in gold with diamonds by I. W. Buch commissioned in 1791 by Catherine the Great.
   Niello work on silver, mostly boxes of the eighteenth and nineteenth centuries.
   Tapestries, including one for an imperial palace, woven with wool and silver thread in the early part of the nineteenth century.
   Icons from the seventeenth and eighteenth centuries; a portable iconostasis; and a pair of Royal Doors from another, much larger iconostasis.
   But there is so much more than this that the collection must be seen in person to be appreciated.

4.　The collection has been cataloged and photographed. The former curator of the museum, Marvin C. Ross, prepared two catalogs of parts of the collection: *The Art of Karl Fabergé and His Contemporaries* (1965) and *Russian Porcelains* (1968), both published by the University of Oklahoma Press, Norman. Each is out of print.
   A booklet entitled *Notes on Hillwood* by Marjorie Merriweather Post is useful for acquainting oneself with the basic holdings and can be obtained at the museum.

C4   Hirshhorn Museum and Sculpture Garden (Smithsonian Institution)

1 a.   *Eighth Street and Independence Avenue, SW*
Washington, D.C. 20560
(202) 357-2700 (Smithsonian Information)
(202) 357-1618 (Public Affairs Office)
(202) 357-3222 (Library)
(202) 357-3281 (Registrar)
(202) 357-3235 (Education Department)
(202) 357-3230 (Department of Painting and Sculpture)

b.   Galleries:
10:00 A.M.–5:30 P.M. every day; closed Christmas Day
Departmental offices and research collections:
8:45 A.M.–5:15 P.M.,   Monday–Friday

c.   Open to the public. Many pertinent holdings are not on permanent display but in storage. To make arrangements to examine these items, write or call to the Department of Painting and Sculpture (202/357-3230), requesting an appointment with the staff.

d.   Many objects in the collection have been photographed; the museum sells black-and-white prints of these negatives (currently for $3.50 each). For a fee of fifty dollars the staff will take black-and-white photos of previously unphotographed works. Visitors may take nonflash, handheld photos of any work on permanent exhibit.

e.   Abram Lerner, Director
Stephen Weil, Deputy Director

2.   The museum holds some thirty to thirty-five works by émigré Russian (and other nationalities) artists.

3.   Among the émigré artists represented are Alexander Archipenko, Saul Baizerman, David Burliuk, Naum Gabo, Jacques Lipchitz, Louis Lozowick, Antoine Pevsner, Serge Poliakoff, Mark Rothko, Raphael Soyer, Pavel Tchelitchew, Vitaly Komar, and Alexander Melamid.
(Also of interest here is a thirty-five-foot-long mixed-media construction, *The History of the Russian Revolution from Marx to Mayakovsky,* created by American artist Larry Rivers in 1965; it is installed on the second floor of the museum.)

4.   No comprehensive guide to the holdings is available. The most complete listing of works in the collections is in the museum's inaugural catalog, *The Hirshhorn Museum and Sculpture Garden* (New York: Abrams, 1974).
In 1976 (May–October) the museum held a major exhibition entitled *The Golden Door: Artist-Immigrants of America, 1876–1976,* which featured works of several émigrés from the Russian Empire/Soviet Union. A catalog of the same title was published by the Smithsonian Institution Press. A fact sheet, photographs of the works, and documentary materials pertinent to the exhibition have been available.
From November 20, 1980, to February 16, 1981, the exhibition *Avant-Garde in Russia, 1920–1930: New Perspectives* was held in the museum. This exhibition included more than 450 objects illuminating Russian visual arts of the period. A catalog on the exhibition has been published by the Los Angeles County Museum of Art and is distributed by MIT press.
The museum's unpublished computer masterlist is a valuable guide to relevant holdings; it is arranged by artists' names and is available to researchers.

C5 Judaic Museum

1 a. *6125 Montrose Road*
   Rockville, Maryland 20852
   (301) 881-0100

 b. 9:00 A.M.–11:00 P.M., Monday–Thursday, Sunday
   9:00 A.M.–5:00 P.M., Friday
   Closed national and Jewish holidays.

 c. Open to the public.

 d. Photocopying services are not available; posters of some of the items in the museum may be purchased.

 e. Susan Morganstern, Director

2–3.   The Judaic Museum is affiliated with the Jewish Community Center of Greater Washington. Among the museum's permanent display holdings is a series of twenty-four original lithographs (circa 1920s) by Abel Pann collectively entitled "In the Name of the Czar." The series reflects the artist's memories of Russian pogroms during the 1880s. This collection is unique to the Washington area.
   The museum also displays the work of various Soviet émigré artists from time to time; many of these items are for sale.

4.   A catalog of the holdings, prepared in 1980, is available without charge.

C6 Liros Gallery

1 a. *626 North Washington Street*
   Alexandria, Virginia 22314
   (703) 549-7881

 b. 9:00 A.M.–5:30 P.M., Monday–Saturday

 c. Open to the public.

 e. Serge Liros, President

2.   This private art gallery offers Russian art work for sale. The number of items on hand and on display varies from time to time. Visitors can usually expect to find at least twenty to twenty-five different pieces displayed.

3.   The gallery carries mostly Russian icons, from the seventeenth to the nineteenth centuries in general, although occasionally items from earlier or later times are available. No works come directly (recently) from the Soviet Union; most are from the collections of emigrants. Liros also offers oil paintings, watercolors, and old prints from the eighteenth to the nineteenth centuries. Some prints, published in England, Germany, or elsewhere in the West, may have Russian subjects.

NOTE: The proprietor can appraise Russian icons and welcomes discussions about Russian art.

C7 National Air and Space Museum (Smithsonian Institution)

1 a. *Seventh Street and Independence Avenue, SW*
   Washington, D.C. 20560
   (202) 357-2700

   b. Galleries:
   April 1–Labor Day:
   10:00 A.M.–9:00 P.M. everyday
   Labor Day–April 1:
   10:00 A.M.–5:30 P.M. every day; closed Christmas Day
   Departmental offices and research collections:
   8:45 A.M.–5:15 P.M., Monday–Friday

   c. Open to the public (access to the library, however, is by appointment only; see entry A41).

   d. Photocopy services are available.

   e. Walter J. Boyne, Director
   Paul A. Hanle, Chairperson, Space Science and Exploration Department
   Donald S. Lopez, Chairperson, Aeronautics Department

2–3. Pertinent items are on display in at least three different sections of the museum. In the Rocketry and Space Flight Gallery is a model, about thirty-nine inches high, of a spaceship concept developed by Konstantin Tsiolkovskii circa 1903–15. The model itself was built circa 1971.

In the Milestones of Flight Gallery is displayed a full-size replica of the Sputnik I, the first manmade earth satellite. And in the Space Hall is another full-size replica of the Soiuz spaceship, linked to an Apollo craft, used in the joint U.S.-USSR Apollo-Soiuz mission.

Each of these objects is on long-term loan from the Soviet Union.

C8 National Gallery of Art

1 a. *Sixth Street and Constitution Avenue, NW*
   Washington, D.C. 20565
   (202) 737-4215

   b. Galleries:
   April 1–Labor Day:
   10:00 A.M.–9:00 P.M., Monday–Saturday
   Noon–9:00 P.M., Sundays
   Labor Day–April 1:
   10:00 A.M.–5:00 P.M., Monday–Saturday
   Noon–9:00 P.M., Sundays
   Closed Christmas Day.
   Departmental offices and research collections:
   8:45 A.M.–5:15 P.M., Monday–Friday

   d. Most of the works have been photographed (in black and white); copies may be purchased from the publications and sales staff (202/842-6466). Arrangements for special photography may be made through the Department of Photographic Services (202/842-6230).

Visitors may take nonflash, handheld photos of any work on permanent exhibit. To use a tripod, permission must be obtained from the Department of Photographic Services.

   e. J. Carter Brown, Director
      E. A. Carmean, Curator, Twentieth-Century Art Department
      Dr. Andrew Robison, Head, Prints Department

2. At present the gallery has a rather small number of holdings relating to Russia/USSR, including some 29 prints and a few other items.

3. Marc Chagall's *Houses at Vitebsk* (painting no. 2644), paper on canvas from 1917, is here. The painting measures 18⅝ by 24 inches. About sixteen of the prints come directly from Russia; the remainder were made by Russian/Soviet émigré artists of the twentieth century.

It should also be noted that the National Gallery of Art, begun with generous gifts from Andrew W. Mellon, holds Mr. Mellon's collection of paintings acquired from the Hermitage Gallery in Leningrad. These twenty-odd works include paintings only from Western artists, such as Botticelli, Chardin, Jan van Eyck, Frans Hals (two), Perugino, Raphael (two), Rembrandt (five), Rubens, Titian, van Dyck (four), Veronese, and Velázquez.

C9 National Museum of American Art (Smithsonian Institution) (*formerly* National Collection of Fine Arts)

1 a. *Ninth and G streets, NW*
     Washington, D.C. 20560
     (202) 357-2700 (Information)

   b. Galleries:
      10:00 A.M.–5:30 P.M. every day; closed Christmas Day
      Departmental offices and research collections:
      8:45 A.M.–5:15 P.M., Monday–Friday

   c. Open to the public. Most pertinent holdings are not on premanent display but are in storage. To make arangements to examine these items, write or call ahead to the Office of the Registrar (202/357-1381), requesting an appointment with the staff.

   d. Many objects in the collection have been photographed; the museum sells back-and-white prints of these negatives (currently for five dollars each). Visitors may take nonflash, handheld photos of any work on permanent display. To use a flash attachment or tripod, permission must be obtained from the Office of Visual Resources (202/357-1626).

   e. Charles Eldredge, Director

2. Approximately fifty works pertain to Russia/USSR.

3. Most pertinent works are paintings; some are sculptures and prints. The artists, born in the areas noted, became U.S. citizens after emigrating:
  Russia: Ilya Bolotowsky, David Burliuk, Moses Soyer, Raphael Soyer, Max Weber, and Feodor Zakharov.

Ukraine: Alexander Archipenko, Alexander Liberman, and Louis Lozowick.
Byelorussia: Saul Baizerman, Nicolai Cikovsky, and Morris Kantor.
Lithuania: Jacques Lipchitz, Paul Puzinas, and Ben Shahn.
Latvia: Adja Yunkers.
Armenia: Arshile Gorky (Vosdang Manooz Adoian).
Siberia: Abraham Walkowitz.

NOTE: Many of these artists left their homeland at a very early age and thus cannot be considered as having produced art wholly within the art traditions of their respective countries. Also, the list is not comprehensive; a complete search of the collection was impossible because of its great size.

C10 National Museum of American History (Smithsonian Institution) (*formerly* National Museum of History and Technology)

1 a. *Twelfth Street and Constitution Avenue, NW*
Washington, D.C. 20560
(202) 357-3129 (Information)

b. Galleries:
10:00 A.M.–5:30 P.M. everyday; closed Christmas Day
Departmental offices and research collections:
8:45 A.M.–5:15 P.M., Monday–Friday

c. Open to the public. Appointments are required for visiting research facilities and viewing items in storage.

d. Visitors may take photos of any work on permanent exhibit. Photos intended for publication must by cleared with the Office of Public Affairs. Color transparencies and black-and-white photos of many objects on exhibit are on sale in the museum gift shop. Photocopying facilities are available through the departmental offices.

e. Roger G. Kennedy, Director

2. The primary objective of the museum is to document through artifacts the cultural, scientific, and technological history of America. Materials from, or related to, foreign areas are generally collected for comparative purposes or to highlight the international influences on American development. The museum has a large number of unusual and fascinating items relating to Russia/USSR; as these are scattered among many different divisions, no complete count is possible. Researchers should not consider the following description as comprehensive.

NATIONAL PHILATELIC COLLECTIONS
(202) 357-1796

Herbert R. Collins, Executive Director
Reidar Norby, Curator

This department manages a collection of more than fifteen million items, including several thousand Russian and Soviet stamps dating from 1857 to the present. There is also a special collection of *zemstvo* postage stamps.
The unit's large library holds some Russian books and periodicals on philately not

readily available elsewhere in the area. There is no printed catalog or description of holdings.

The library is currently being reorganized and is open to researchers by appointment only.

NATIONAL NUMISMATIC COLLECTIONS
(202) 357-1798
Elvira Clain-Stefanelli, Historian

This unit maintains the most important collection of Russian coins in the West: the Willis H. du Pont Collection of Russian Coins and Medals (also known as the Prince Georgii Mikhailovich Collection). Included are more than 6,000 coins—dating largely from the period 1700–1915—and some 4,000 silver and bronze medals. Only Leningrad's Hermitage Museum has a broader selection. For bibliographies covering this collection (exclusive of its ancient coins), see point 4.

The National Numismatic Collections also has a collection of Russian paper currencies dating from about 1800; it is extremely strong for the years during World War I and immediately afterward.

DEPARTMENT OF SOCIAL AND CULTURAL HISTORY
(202) 357-2735
Ian Golovin and Elizabeth Harris, Cochairpersons

The Division of Ceramics and Glass (Susan Myers, curator, 202/357-1786) maintains a small collection of Russian porcelains, including five pieces from the eighteenth century, some thirty to forty from the nineteenth, and a smattering of twentieth-century pieces. In addition, the division has two eighteenth-century engraved glass goblets and a small selection of Russian enamelware and malachite vases.

The Division of Community Life (Richard Ahlborn, curator, 202/357-2385) features some Russian decorative metal castings, samovars, kettles, metal crosses, and some 200–250 icons from the turn of the century (made by Russian Old Believers who emigrated to America). Also here are scattered Slavic objets d'art—a few silver cigarette cases, pairs of metal candlesticks, and decorated Ukrainian Easter eggs *(pysanky)*—and a collection of artifacts from Russian Alaska. Researchers seeking further information on the division's Russian holdings should consult Mrs. Vera Espinola, the staff specialist in the field.

The Division of Political History (Herbert Collins, Margaret Klapthor, and Edith Mayo, curators, 202/357-2008) has custody of the Gustavus Vasa Fox Collection containing documents and sixty-eight articles relating to Fox's 1866 mission to Tsar Alexander II and to visits of Russian dignitaries to the U.S. in the 1870s. The objects include a snuff box presented to Fox by the tsar; a handful of medals; a malachite box from the City of Saint Petersburg; a silver salver presented by a Russian nobleman; and some five presentation scrolls given Fox by various Russian cities. (See bibliography under point 4.)

The Russian-related holdings of other divisions within the department appear to be of purely incidental note. The Division of Costume (202/357-3185) has a brooch and three seals from a Russian noble family. The Division of Graphic Arts (202/357-2877) includes a few etchings by Nikolai Massaloff among its small Russian selection. The Division of Textiles (202/357-1889) has samples of needlework by Russian immigrants to America. Finally, the Division of Musical Instruments (202/357-1707) includes several brass trombones with decorative bells of Russian origin.

DEPARTMENT OF THE HISTORY OF SCIENCE AND TECHNOLOGY
(202) 357-1963
Bernard Finn, Chairman

The Division of Medical Sciences (Audrey Davis and Ramunas Kondratas, curators, 202/357-2274) features a nineteenth-century silver hearing aid, twelve surgical staplers, various prophylactics and contraceptive devices of Russian origin, and some medicinal plants grown in Siberia.

Among the Russian artifacts in the Division of Electricity and Modern Physics (John Schlebecker, and George Sharrer, curators, 202/357-1840) are a seventeenth-century lodestone in period casing; a pre-World War I Russian army field telephone and wireless; a Soviet short wave receiver from the 1920s (made for distribution in England); a receiver of Soviet origin powered by a thermoelectric generator (designed for use in rural areas); several experimental television tubes made by the Russian-born pioneer in the field, Vladimir Zvorykin; and a specimen of the U.S.-Soviet hotline telephone system dating from 1963.

The Division of Mathematics (Uta Merzbach, curator, 202/357-2392) features an abacus from Moscow (eighteenth century), an early-twentieth-century calculator from Saint Petersburg, and descriptive material on the history of computing in Russia.

The Division of Mechanical and Civil Engineering (Robert Vogel, curator, 202/357-2058) has custody of the papers of John A. Beemer containing various materials (correspondence, reports, maps, plans, drawings) pertaining to Beemer's work as a consulting engineer for the Soviet government on the Samgory irrigation project in Georgia, 1929–31.

The Division of Military History (Donald Kloster, curator, 202/357-1883) features some twenty-five Russian weapons. Included are swords, rifles, and other pieces dating from the eighteenth to the twentieth centuries. Also included is a collection of military propaganda posters from World War I Russia and World War II USSR. The division maintains a small reference library.

The Division of Transportation (Robert Post and John White, curators, 202/357-1438) has custody of the papers of Joseph Francis, a nineteenth-century inventor and manufacturer who pioneered many developments in boat design and construction. Francis worked in Russia from 1858 to 1862; his papers include documents and letters concerning shipbuilding and testing in Russia (in Russian and English), Russian patents, and the emancipation of the serfs.

Incidental Russian/Soviet items among the collections of other divisions in the department include an album with numerous photographs of Armenians in Turkey, circa World War I, in the Division of Naval History (202/357-2249); a threshing stone brought from Russia to America by German Mennonites in 1870 in the collection of the Division of Extractive Industries (202/357-2095); and Soviet watches of recent make kept by the Division of Mechanisms (202/357-2371).

4.   There is no comprehensive guide to the museum as a whole. Perhaps the most complete listing of holdings is the bicentennial exhibition catalog *A Nation of Nations,* ed. Peter Marzio (1976).

For individual holdings, the following titles will be of value:

Georgii Mikhailovich, grand duke of Russia. *Monety tsarstvovanii Imperatritsy Anny Ioannovny i Imperatora Ioanna III.* Saint Petersburg, 1901.

———. *Monety tsarstvovanii Imperatritsy Elisavety I i Imperatora Petra III.* 2 vols. Saint Petersburg, 1896.

———. *Monety tsarstvovaniia Ekateriny II.* 2 vols. Saint Petersburg, 1894.

———. *Monety tsarstvovanii Imperatora Pavla I i Imperatora Aleksandra I.* Saint Petersburg, 1891.

———. *Monety tsarstvovaniia Nikolaia I.* Saint Petersburg, 1890.

————. *Monety tsarstvovaniia Aleksandra II.* Saint Petersburg, 1888.
Immanuel M. Casanowicz. *The Gustavus Vasa Fox Collection of Russian Souvenirs in the United States National Museum.* Proceedings of the U.S. National Museum 38, No. 1725. Washington, D.C., 1910.
Dr. Vladimir Clain-Stefanelli, former historian, published a *History of the National Numismatic Collection* in Contributions from the Museum of History and Technology Paper 31 (Washington, D.C.: Smithsonian Institution Press, 1968). Other useful publications based on the museum's numismatic collections include *The Beauty and Lore of Coins, Currency and Metals,* by Elvira and Vladimir Clain-Stefanelli (Melbourne: Lansdowne, 1975) and *Das grosse Buch der Munzen und Medaillen mit Munzkatalog Europa von 1900 bis heute,* by the same authors and Gunter Schon (Munich: Battenberg, 1976).
Finally, the paper-bound *Guide to Manuscript Collections in the Museum of History and Technology* (1978) is available for consultation in the museum library.

C11 National Museum of Natural History (Smithsonian Institution)

1 a. *Tenth Street and Constitution Avenue, NW*
Washington, D.C. 20560
(202) 357-2700

 b. Galleries:
10:00 A.M.–5:30 P.M. every day; closed Christmas Day
Departmental offices and research collections:
9:00 A.M.–4:00 P.M., Monday–Friday.

 c. Open to the public. Appointments are required for visiting research facilities and viewing items in storage.

 d. Visitors may take photos of any work on permanent exhibit. The museum also has available photographic services.

 e. Dr. Richard S. Fiske, Director

2. Not many divisions of the museum arrange their holdings geographically, therefore, no count of Russian-related material is very significant. Suffice it to say that substantial resources are here for Russianists among the approximately sixty-five to seventy million individual items in the collections.

3. Much of what serious researchers might want to examine is in the research collections, not on display. In addition to the specimens themselves, the expertise of many staff members will be of importance for scholars in the Soviet field.
The Department of Anthropology has approximately 200 archaeological specimens (a relatively small number) from "Russia" and a small amount of pottery from Armenia. It also has a significant collection of materials that deal with Arctic Siberia in general and with the Chukchi people in particular.
The gems section of the Department of Minerals Sciences holds a magnificent statue of Saint George; a dragon in gold and platinum (with diamonds, rubies, and malachite) created in 1882 for Tsar Alexander III; and approximately a dozen Russian carvings on different materials from the late eighteenth century.
In addition, the museum collects flora and fauna specimens from around the world, including the Soviet Union. The Departments of Botany, Vertebrate Zoology, and others have many fascinating examples of plants and animals from the USSR: a

Siberian tiger, a now-extinct species of sea cow, Kamchatka and Altai regions mammals, and various flowers. Among those who take some interest in the Soviet area are Stanwyn G. Shetler in the Department of Botany and George Watson, curator of the Department of Vertebrate Zoology.

4. No published catalogs or inventories exist at present. There are, however, many different card catalogs to aid researchers and, for the staff, a computerized inventory.

C12 National Portrait Gallery (Smithsonian Institution)

1 a. *Eighth and F streets, NW*
Washington, D.C. 20560
(202) 357-2866 (Office of Public Affairs)

b. Galleries:
10:00 A.M.–5:30 P.M. every day; closed Christmas Day
Departmental offices and research collections:
8:45 A.M.–5:15 P.M., Monday–Friday

c. Open to the public.

d. Visitors may take photos with a handheld camera or purchase photos of any work in the permanent collection.

e. Alan M. Fern, Director

2–3. Among the few items for Russianists here is a portrait of violinist Fritz Kreisler by Boris Chaliapin dated 1943. The work is gouache and colored pencil on artist board.

In 1978 the National Portrait Gallery acquired the rights to past and future *Time* magazine covers (which include portraits of various Soviet and Russian personalities). About 1,000 covers were done by Boris Chaliapin.

4. A useful research aid, *National Portrait Gallery, Smithsonian Institution: Permanent Collection Illustrated Checklist* (Washington, D.C.: Smithsonian Institution Press, 1982), is compiled every two years; each edition is cumulative.

C13 National Rifle Association Firearms Museum

1 a. *1600 Rhode Island Avenue, NW*
Washington, D.C. 20036
(202) 828-6194

b. 10:00 A.M.–4:00 P.M. every day; closed major holidays

c. Open to the public.

d. Visitors must purchase photos of items in the collection.

e. Dan R. Abbey, Jr., Curator

2–3. The museum contains some one to two dozen examples of Russian/Soviet firearms, dating from the nineteenth century to World War II; sabres are also displayed periodically. A small amount of reading material might also prove to be of interest.

4.   The published guide to the museum would be too general to help anyone interested primarily in the Russian-area holdings.

C14 Phillips Collection

1 a.   *1600 Twenty First Street, NW*
Washington, D.C. 20009
(202) 387-2151

b.   10:00 A.M.–5:00 P.M.,   Tuesday–Saturday
2:00-7:00 P.M.,   Sundays
Closed Mondays and holidays.

c.   Open to the public.

d.   Black-and-white and color photos and 35-mm slides of most paintings in the collection are available.

e.   Laughlin Phillips, Director
Willem de Looper, Curator

2.   The collection contains thirty to forty paintings pertaining to Russia/USSR.

3.   The pertinent works are all by persons who have emigrated from Russia or the Soviet Union. Artists represented include Kandinsky, Rothko, Shahn, Walkowitz, and Weber.

4.   In 1952 the museum published an illustrated inventory of its holdings; it is still available. A new catalog, however, is currently in the planning stages, with 1983 as the tentative publication date. Scholars may also wish to consult *Museums Discovered: The Phillips Collection,* by Eleanor Green (New York: Shorewood Fine Arts Books, 1981), available at the museum shop. The book contains some 200 color reproductions of paintings and a number of descriptive essays on the artists represented.

C15 Rowe House Gallery

1 a.   *1834 Wisconsin Avenue, NW*
Washington, D.C. 20007
(202) 965-2688

b.   10:00 A.M.–6:00 P.M.,   Monday–Saturday

c.   Open to the public.

d.   In the past the management has allowed visitors to photograph items on display.

e.   Carl Rowe, Manager
Betsy Rowe, Secretary

2–4.   In the spring of 1976 the Rowe House gallery held a major exhibit of art by recent émigrés from the USSR. A brochure on the exhibit, giving details about the artists and their work, was published and plans were made to expand the gallery's activities in Soviet émigré art (a vertical-file collection of materials relating to émigré artists displayed in the gallery was begun). Since that time, however, the gallery's interest in this area has declined considerably; at present Rowe House is a minor resource for Russianists.

Saint Sophia Religious Association of Ukrainian Catholics, Inc.—Washington Branch   See entry P9

C16   Textile Museum

1 a. *2320 S Street, NW*
      Washington, D.C. 20008
      (202) 667-0441

   b. 10:00 A.M.–5:00 P.M.,   Tuesday–Saturday
       1:00 P.M.–5:00 P.M.,   Sunday (curators are available Monday–Friday)

   c. Open to the public. (A two-dollar donation is appreciated.)

   d. Limited photocopying facilities are available. Black-and-white photos of some of the museum's pieces are for sale.

   e. Patricia Fiske, Director

2. About 325 items pertain to Russia/USSR.

3. The museum has approximately 150 rugs and furnishings from Central Asia. It has twenty to twenty-five Turkmen embroidered covers and woven silks. Most of these holdings date from the late nineteenth and early twentieth centuries. From the eastern and southern Caucasus the museum has about 120 seventeenth-to-nineteenth century rugs and another twenty to twenty-five embroidered covers. The museum features rotating exhibits that might occasionally display a few items from the above; exhibits limited to a geographic area of interest to the Russian/Soviet scholar are also mounted regularly (see point 4). But nearly all these items are kept in storage as a rule and can be seen only by appointment with a member of the museum staff.

4. The museum has published two catalogs for exhibits of interest to the Russian/Soviet-area specialist: *Early Caucasian Rugs,* by Charles Grant Ellis (1975); and *Turkmen Tribal Carpets and Traditions,* eds. Louise Mackie and Jon Thompson (1980). The exhibit on which the second volume was based, staged by the museum in the fall of 1980, was the most extensive of its kind ever organized in the West.

NOTE: Every Saturday, year-round, at 10:30 A.M., the museum has "rug mornings": an expert gives an informal talk about the rugs of a particular geographic area. Turkmen or Caucasian rugs, for example, are the subject of a talk once a month or so. The public may attend, without charge; moreover, people may bring their own rugs to discuss with the expert after the talk.

   The museum also holds occasional lecture series, the topics of which may be of interest to the Soviet-area scholar. An annual convention held at the museum focuses on a specific topic (which may also be the topic of a current exhibition). Caucasian and Turkmen rugs were recently featured.

NOTE: Although an adequate listing of the private art collections in the Washington area is not feasible here, the reader should be aware of such collections as potential resources for research. The types of art work to be found run the gamut of fine and applied/decorative art. There are excellent examples of modern painting, icons, ceramics, glassware, jewelry, tapestry, and carpetry. In the last category, for example, are some magnificent collections of oriental rugs. Although the majority of holdings are probably from the nineteenth and twentieth centuries, some earlier items are here as well. Collectors include people from the academic world; the government—particularly present and past members of the State Department, who have traveled often or stayed long in the USSR; and the émigré community. Some collections, because of the mobility of their owners, are not permanently located in this area.

There are a few people in the area whom interested scholars might contact to find out about some collections. Professor Norton Dodge, Saint Mary's College of Maryland Economics Department (Saint Mary's City, Maryland 20686), has much knowledge of post-Stalin, unofficial Soviet art holdings. Most art work of this type consists of paintings and graphics. Professor Dodge can be contacted at the college at telephone number (301) 863-7100.

Norton Dodge is also the director of the Modern Soviet Art Collection and Archive, which, located in Mechanicsville, Maryland, is some forty miles from Washington and thus outside the bounds taken as the limits for this guide. Researchers might note this resource, however; it contains at least 1,000 paintings, prints, and drawings—samples of post-Stalin unofficial art. In addition, the archive holds several thousand photos and slides, plus other reference material, on the subject. The holdings are not fully cataloged. The Modern Soviet Art Collection and Archive is administered by the Cremona Foundation in Mechanicsville, Maryland 20659, of which Professor Dodge is president (301/884-3140). A noteworthy adjunct activity of this foundation—although again well beyond the geographical range of this volume—is the Contemporary Russian Art Center of America, located at 599 Broadway, eleventh floor, New York, New York 10012 (telephone number: 212/431-9148).

Professor Helen Yakobson, of the George Washington University Department of Slavic Languages and Literatures, is another source of information on private art collections in the Washington area. Her telephone number is (202) 676-6336.

Both references given above are knowledgeable primarily about the art of the Russian people. For more information about nationalities and minorities in the Soviet Union (with respect to their art), scholars should probably contact some of the various cultural organizations listed in the Associations section (M).

D Collections of Music and Other Sound Recordings

Music and Other Sound Recordings Collection Entry Format (D)

1. General Information
   a. *address; telephone number(s)*
   b. hours of service
   c. conditions of access
   d. name/title of director and key staff members

2. Size of Holdings Pertaining to Russia/USSR

3. Description of Holdings Pertaining to Russia/USSR

4. Facilities for Study and Use
   a. availability of audiovisual equipment
   b. reservation requirements
   c. fees charged
   d. photocopying facilities

5. Bibliographic Aids Facilitating Use of Collection

Introductory Note

For Russianists, the principal collections of music and other sound recordings are found at the Library of Congress (entries D3–D4), the University of Maryland (entries D5–D6), and the National Archives and Records Service (entry D7). LC's Motion Picture, Broadcasting, and Recorded Sound Division features, among other things, some 15,000 Soviet and pre-Soviet 78-rpm recordings; the library's Archive of Folk Culture is also a potentially rich vein. At Maryland, the university's Language Media Center offers a modest but diverse collection of tapes. More important, however, are the International Piano Archives at Maryland, which should soon achieve considerable reknown for their extensive and unique recital recordings by Russian-born virtuosi. The holdings of the National Archives—Soviet political speeches, trial testimony, wartime radio broadcasts, and much more—constitute a fascinating collection for students of Soviet history.

For more detail on collections of musical and other sound recordings, the reader will find useful the forthcoming *Scholars' Guide to Washington, D.C., for Audio Resources,* by James R. Heintze, scheduled for publication by the Smithsonian Institution Press in 1984.

American Latvian Theatre   See entry M12

D1   The American University Library—Record-Score Collection

1 a. *Kreeger Building, Room 218*
Massachusetts and Nebraska avenues, NW
Washington, D.C. 20016
(202) 686-2165

   b. 9:00 A.M.–7:30 P.M.,   Monday–Friday
9:00 A.M.–1:00 P.M.,   Saturday
Closed Sunday.

   c. Open to the public for on-site use. Sound recordings do not circulate.

   d. James R. Heintze, Librarian

2–3.   The library has a small collection of disc recordings of Russian folk music, eighteenth-century choral music, and folk songs in the International Series of Nonesuch Records and the Ethnic Folkways Library. Representative titles include, for example, *A Heritage of Folk Song from Old Russia,* Nonesuch 72010, and *Folk Music of the U.S.S.R.,* Folkways FE 4535.

   The library also has more than 100 disc recordings of classical Russian music representing major composers and works. Russian-born contemporary composers and performers are well represented, including Alexander Dudyukhin, Grigory Feigin, Valentin Feigin, Vladimir Ivanovsky, Kiril Kondrashin, Yevgeny Mravinsky, Ivan Petrov, Sviatoslav Richter, Gennady Rozhdestvensky, Mstislav Rostropovich, Maksim Shostakovich, Igor Shukov, Yevgeny Svetlanov, and Galina Vishnevskaya. Russian orchestras represented in the collection include the Bolshoi Theater Orchestra, Moscow Radio Symphony Orchestra, and Philharmonic Symphony Orchestras of Leningrad and Moscow. One particularly noteworthy series in the collection is the Melodiya recordings (thirty-five discs) produced in the USSR.

4a–d.   Listening equipment is available on-site, on a first-come, first-served basis. Recordings may be copied on-site, with special permission only.

5.   In addition to author-title and subject catalogs, the library has a number of reference aids for discographies of Russian music (e.g., the *International Bibliography of Discographies* (1975). Reference service for the collection is also provided by staff specialists.

D2   Folklife Program (Smithsonian Institution)—Music and Recorded Sound Collection

1 a. *2600 L'Enfant Plaza*
Washington, D.C. 20560
(202) 287-3424

b. 9:00 A.M.–5:00 P.M., Monday–Friday

c. Open to the public, by appointment.

d. Ralph Rinzler, Director
Richard Derbyshire, Archivist

2–3. The ongoing program of folkloric exhibitions and special activities presented by the Smithsonian's Office of Folklife Programs has included both American and international participants. Many of these activities have been preserved on tape. The total collection of recorded performances (on audiotape, videotape, and photographic film) amounts to more than 10,000 recorded hours. Certain recordings may be of interest to the Russianist, including tapes of performances by two groups of Russian Old Believers from California and two groups of Ukrainian émigrés. These performances include songs and folkloric stories recorded in 1975–76 at the annual Folklife Festival. They are partly in English and partly in the original languages.

In addition, there is a collection of family histories (recorded in English, 1974–77, 1981) gathered among Russian and Ukrainian émigrés; these emphasize the regional traditions of the areas from which the families emigrated. Another collection of audiotapes includes the emigration stories of a number of Russian and Ukrainian families (recorded in English, 1976-78). Some recordings have been transcribed and are available in print.

4. Listening equipment is available on-site; reservations are required.

D3 Library of Congress—American Folklife Center—Archive of Folk Culture

1 a. *Thomas Jefferson Building, Room G-152*
10 First Street, SE
Washington, D.C. 20540
(202) 287-5510

b. 8:30 A.M.–5:00 P.M., Monday–Friday

c. Open to the public.

d. Joseph C. Hickerson, Head

2–3. The Archive of Folk Culture (originally called the Archive of Folk Song) was established within LC's Music Division in 1928 as a national repository for documentary manuscripts and sound recordings of American folk music. In 1978 it merged with the American Folklife Center to form a new administrative body within LC.

The archive presently controls more than 35,000 field recordings—cylinders, discs, tapes, and wires, containing more than 300,000 items of folklore—and more than 100,000 sheets of manuscript material. The staff maintains a vertical file for written materials bearing on the collection. Under "Russia" is one small folder containing pamphlets, book reviews, correspondence, and a descriptive list of one set of recordings (Molokane sect items). Noncommercial recordings and tapes are listed in an accessions card catalog. A search under a wide variety of subject and geographic headings turned up nine cards under "Russia," "Russian-American," or similar designations; three under "Finland"; four under "Lithuanian"; one under "Mongolian Folk Music"; two under "Ukrainian"; two under "Estonia"; and three under "Lapland" and "Lappish." Finally, in the manuscripts and microfilm card catalog, one item appears under "Russia"—a piano, vocal score—and one under "Ukraine."

It will be readily apparent that these descriptions cannot do justice to the riches that lie here for Russianists. The Soviet-area specialist will simply have to come in person and dig in the different catalogs—as well as request the continual help of staff members—to locate desired materials.

4 a.   A reading room and listening equipment are available.

   b.   Reservations to use listening equipment should be made at least a day in advance.

   c.   No fee is charged for using listening equipment.

   d.   Recording laboratory facilities in which all forms of recorded sound can be reproduced are available. A fee is charged for this service. More than eighty-five phonodiscs have been produced and are for sale. A catalog is available without charge from the archive. Russianists should also note that several LPs in the Folk Music in America series include performances by Russian immigrants to America.

5.   To facilitate use of the collection, the archive has published *An Inventory of the Bibliographies and Other Reference and Finding Aids Prepared by the Archive of Folk Culture, Library of Congress* (1982). The reading room's reference collection of more than 3,500 books and periodicals includes *Ethnomusicology: A Study of Its Nature, Its Problems, Methods and Representative Personalities to Which Is Added a Bibliography*, by Jaap Junst (The Hague, 1974) and the American journal *Ethnomusicology*; both are indispensable for folk music research. The archive also prepares the serialized "Current Bibliography" for the journal *Ethnomusicology*. For general information and a brief history of the archive, a four-page descriptive brochure is available.

D4   Library of Congress—Motion Picture, Broadcasting, and Recorded Sound Division

1 a.   *James Madison Memorial Building, Room 113*
   101 Independence Avenue, SE
   Washington, D.C. 20540
   (202) 287-5509 (Sound Recordings)

   b.   8:30 A.M.–5:00 P.M.,   Monday–Friday

   c.   Open to the public.

   d.   Paul Spehr, Acting Chief
   James Smart, Reference Librarian (sound recordings)

2.   No complete measurement of Russian/Soviet-related materials among the massive holdings—more than one million items—of the division's recorded sound collection could be undertaken. It is certain in any case, that the collection is an extremely valuable resource for Russianists.

3.   The collection may be divided into three components. The largest portion of the holdings comprises noncommercial recordings—approximately 700,000 items. Remaining materials are divided between pre-LP commercial recordings (200,000 items) and commercial LP recordings, domestic and foreign (250,000 items). No shelflist or geographic index exists for these materials; more important—and more unfortunate—most of it is uncataloged (although there is a catalog of about 175,000 NBC Radio Archive recordings, 1927–70). Sample measurements taken by the division staff in 1982 yielded the following results. In the catalog of commercial LPs, for Tchaikovskii:

1,100 titles; Prokof'ev: 600 titles; Glinka: 90 titles; Glazunov: 70 titles; Dargomyzhskii: 15 titles; and under Russia/Russian (various languages), title and subject: 250 titles These figures are even more misleading in that only longer works—generally one-half an LP or longer—appear in the catalog.

Presently scheduled to be completed by May 1983 is a composer/author, title, performer catalog of the circa 200,000 pre-LP commercial disc recordings in the collection. This collection includes the LC's fairly extensive Soviet and pre-Soviet 78-rpm recordings totaling at least 15,000 items. Also in progress is a project to acquire basic composer/author, title, and performer location information for the 200,000 Armed Forces Radio and Television Service (AFRTS) disc collection.

Measurements made in the separate index of noncommercial recordings showed for Tchaikovskii: 105 cards, some with multiple titles (as with many entries below); Prokof'ev: 61 cards; Shostakovich: 18 cards; Glazunov: 13 cards; Glinka: 7 cards; and under Russia/Russian: 42 cards. (Note: names are not standardized in this index.)

The inadequacy of the method used to measure this section's holdings means that one must rely more than usually on the knowledge of the staff. Discussions with them revealed some most interesting materials. In the partially cataloged pre-LP commercial recording collection there are many Rachmaninoff items, including some unpublished test pressings; a large number of Shaliapin recordings, some again unpublished; very rare recordings of other Russian singers of imperial times, recorded about the turn of this century; and Stravinskii performing on a player-piano roll. One special item in the noncommercial recordings is an unpublished tape of the playing of Alexander Siloti. In the commercial LP and noncommercial recordings collections the researcher will find many items by political and literary figures such as Lenin, Khrushchev, Molotov, Solzhenitsyn, Stalin, Tolstoi, and the poets Evtushenko and Voznesenskii. The section also maintains a collection of Voice of America transcriptions, an Office of War Information collection, and a National Press Club collection. Finally, it has obtained and continues to acquire a huge number of UN recordings—of committee meetings and General Assembly sessions mostly—from 1945 to the 1960s. These recordings are in the original languages. Plans exist to acquire Security Council recordings as well.

4 b. Materials may be listened to only between the hours of 9–12 A.M. each weekday. Reservations to use listening equipment should be made about a week in advance.

c–d. LC has its own recording laboratory that can reproduce all forms of recorded sound. A fee is charged for this service. The laboratory also produces and sells phonodiscs.

5. The cataloged audio holdings appear in the comprehensive catalog *Music, Books on Music, and Sound Recordings,* which is a part of the *National Union Catalog* (NUC). This catalog, issued semiannually with annual and quinquennial cumulations, replaced the earlier *Library of Congress Catalog: Music and Phonorecords,* a quinquennial cumulation also published as part of the NUC. Another semiannual catalog, *Catalog of Copyright Entries: Sound Recordings,* lists sound recordings registered for copyright since the 1972 copyright legislation (not all of which are in the division's collections). Finally, there is a pamphlet on audio collections, *Sound Recordings* (1979), available without charge from the division.

D5 Maryland University Language Media Center

1 a. *Foreign Language Building, Room 1202*
College Park, Maryland 20742
(301) 454-5728

b. 8:00 A.M.–10:00 P.M., Monday–Thursday
8:00 A.M.–4:00 P.M., Friday
10:00 A.M.–3:00 P.M., Saturday
Closed Sundays, holidays, and the week of final exams

c. Open to researchers with the permission of a faculty member.

d. Recordings may be copied on-site, with the permission of the center's director.

e. James E. Royalty, Director

2–3. The Language Media Center has tapes for three different Russian-language textbooks; about forty tapes of Russian music (e.g., "Balalaika Favorites," "Songs and Dances of Old Russia," Soviet jazz and rock and roll); forty tapes of plays (by Chekhov, Gogol, Gor'kii, and others); twenty tapes of poetry readings (poems by Akhmatova, Nekrasov, Pasternak, Evtushenko, and others); twenty excerpts from novels and short stories (by authors such as Dostoevskii, Lermontov, Pushkin, and Tolstoi); tapes of interviews (with Medvedev and Rostropovich among others); various speeches by Lenin; and a series of tapes made from early recordings entitled Writers Speak (with the actual voices of Gor'kii, Tolstoi and others).

4 a. Tape recorders are available for listening to the tapes.

b. Reservations to use listening equipment should be made in advance.

c–d. No fee is charged for using listening equipment.

D6 Maryland University—Music Library and Music Room

1 a. *Hornbake Library, Room 3210*
College Park, Maryland 20742
(301) 454-3036

b. 8:00 A.M.–11:00 P.M., Monday–Thursday
8:00 A.M.–6:00 P.M., Friday
10:00 A.M.–6:00 P.M., Saturday
Noon–11:00 P.M., Sunday
For information on summer hours, call (301) 454-2853.

c. Open to the public for on-site use. Materials in the general collection are unrestricted (but see point 4).

d. Neil Ratliff, Fine Arts Librarian and Head, Music Library

2–3. In addition to the standard resources on Russian music common to most major university music libraries (e.g., multivolume sets of the complete works of Tchaikovskii, Musorgskii, and others), the Music Library features a unique collection with considerable material of interest to the Russianist: the International Piano Archives at Maryland. Within the archives are some twenty-five 78-rpm shellac records of Soviet manufacture featuring such performers as Emil Gilels and Shostakovich; an open-reel tape collection of some 1,100 recital recordings (many unique) featuring performances by such masters as Vladimir Ashkenazy, Aleksandr Brailowsky, Shura Cherkassky, Aleksandr Cherepnin, Nikolai Medtner, Svyatoslav Richter, and Vladimir Horowitz; a large collection of early-twentieth-century reproducing piano rolls, a spot check of which revealed performances by Aleksandr Borovsky, Ossip Gabrilowitsch, Leopold

Godowsky, Joseph Lhévinne, Sergei Prokofieff, Sergei Rachmaninoff, and Igor Stravinsky; a collection of nineteenth-century piano scores, with works by (again from a spot check) Anton Arensky, Tchaikovskii, Aleksandr Glazunov, Glinka, Dmitrii Kabalevskii, Anatolii Liadov, Medtner, Prokofieff, Rachmaninoff, Anton Rubinstein, and Aleksandr Scriabin (including a copy of his two-piano version of the Third Piano Concerto, unique outside the Soviet Union); and a collection of manuscripts of piano music, including an autograph manuscript of a piano trio by Anton Rubinstein.

4 a–d. Access to the archives is by appointment only. Researchers are allowed to play the open-reel tapes themselves (earphones provided), and the staff will play the 78-rpm records by request. The piano rolls—despite the lack of a player piano—are accessible for study and reproduction; a substantial fee is charged to commercially reproduce the rolls. The archives has also published a catalog of the reproducing piano rolls. Photocopying of public-domain printed music scores is also allowed; reproduction of other materials in the archives is possible only if cleared through university legal counsel.

5. A card catalog provides access to the general collection. The entire Piano Archives collection has been put on a computer-output microfilm catalog—the only such project of its kind in the U.S.

Namysto Singing Ensemble See entry M46

D7 National Archives and Records Service (NARS) (General Services Administration)—Special Archives Division—Motion Picture, Sound, and Video Branch

1 a. *Pennsylvania Avenue at Eighth Street, NW*
Washington, D.C. 20408
(entrance from Pennsylvania Avenue only)
(202) 523-3267

b. 8:45 A.M.–5:00 P.M., Monday–Friday

c. Open to researchers over the age of sixteen by appointment. Users must obtain a National Archives research pass (available in room 200B), for which appropriate identification is required. Some materials may be restricted.

d. Les Waffen, Reference Supervisor

2. Various record groups contain many fascinating items.

3. Some pertinent items are recordings of speeches by Soviet personalities made in the USSR or abroad. Other materials include speeches by numerous West European and U.S. figures about the Soviet Union. Major foreign policy speeches of U.S. presidents and other world leaders will be found in recorded form here. Radio broadcast recordings—covering news stories, commentaries, discussions, interviews, reports, and much more—can all contain material of value to the Russianist. For the majority of relevant materials in this branch, however, there is no way to measure and detail the holdings. The researcher must look for specific materials, with the help of the staff, in a variety of different record groups. (Note: Transcripts for Soviet-related materials can be found in the appropriate record groups in the other divisions

and branches of the archives, with other textual holdings.) Partial card catalogs (arranged by subject, name, and title) exist for much of the collection; a card file of titles for record groups is arranged in numerical order. Some of the finding aids noted below in point 5 will also provide some assistance. A brief survey of some of the record groups containing Russian-related material is offered below.

RG 59: General Records of the Department of State. Includes recordings of addresses by Secretaries of State John Foster Dulles, Cordell Hall, and Christian Herter.

RG 160: Records of Headquarters Army Service Forces. Contains thirty-three phonograph records (LP) used in Russian-language training.

RG 200: National Archives Gift Collection. Contains the following speeches: five by J. Stalin, from 1936–45, five to forty-two minutes long; two by L. Trotskii (in English), three and eleven minutes long; a 1938 League of Nations address by Maksim Litvinov, seventy minutes long; a 1953 talk by V. Molotov, fifteen minutes long; a 1959 speech to the National Press Club by Khrushchev (with an English summary) ninety minutes long; and a recording of a meeting of early Soviet government officials entitled "Lenin and the Peoples' Commissars," sixty minutes long.

RG 208: Records of the Office of War Information. Includes speeches by delegates of the USSR, Byelorussia, and the Ukraine at the ceremony marking the signing of the UN Charter in 1945; also recordings from the 1945 Yalta Conference and other major international conferences (e.g., Casablanca, 1942; and Dumbarton Oaks, 1944).

RG 238: National Archives Collection of World War II Crimes Records. Contains some 300 sound recordings from the International Military Tribunal at Nuremburg, 1945–46, with the voices and testimony of Russian witnesses and prosecutors.

RG 262: Records of the Foreign Broadcast Intelligence Service. Contains a speech by Stalin recorded in November 1942 by the BBC and a wealth of other material from the Foreign Broadcast Intelligence Service, including recordings of monitored shortwave broadcasts from Radio Moscow during World War II.

RG 263: Records of the Central Intelligence Agency. Contains a speech by Khrushchev delivered at Kiev in October 1949, when he was first secretary of the Central Committee of the Ukrainian Communist Party.

4 a. Tape recorders are available for listening to the material on tape recordings; and phonographs, for disc recordings.

b. Reservations to use listening equipment should be made in advance.

c–d. No fee is charged for listening or for duplicating materials, if the researcher brings his own tape and does the recording himself. A fee is charged for having the staff duplicate items.

5. The following inventories for division holdings are available without charge in the division office, room 18E: *Audiovisual Records in the National Archives Relating to World War II*, by Mayfield S. Bray and William T. Murphy (1980); *The Crucial Decade: Voices of the Postwar Era, 1945–1954* (1977); *Sound Recordings in the Audiovisual Archives Division of the National Archives*, by Mayfield S. Bray and Leslie C. Waffen (1972); *Sound Recordings: Voices of World War II, 1937–1945* (1971).

D8   National Public Radio—Audio Library

1 a. *2025 M Street, NW*
Washington, D.C. 20036
(202) 822-2061 (Reference)

b. 9:00 A.M.–5:00 P.M., Monday–Friday

c. Open to the public on a restricted basis.

d. Susan Bau, Librarian

2–3. Regular newscasts and special programs are tape-recorded and stored in the library. A substantial number of items on a variety of newsworthy subjects relate to the USSR.

4 a. Tapes may be listened to on equipment at the library.

d. Copies of tapes may be purchased for noncommercial use.

5. All programs since 1971 are cataloged. The catalog has a geographic breakdown, so that USSR-related items should be easy to locate.

Radio Liberty and Radio Free Europe Recordings   See entries Q16–Q17

Senate Historical Office—Oral History Project   See entry K30

Voice of America   See entry Q22

E Map Collections

Map Collection Entry Format (E)

1. General Information
    a. *address; telephone number(s)*
    b. hours of service
    c. conditions of access
    d. photocopying facilities
    e. name/title of director

2. Size of Holdings Pertaining to Russia/USSR

3. Description of Holdings Pertaining to Russia/USSR

4. Bibliographic Aids Facilitating Use of Collection

Introductory Note

Russian-related map collections in the Washington area are few but incomparable. The Library of Congress Geography and Map Division (entry E4) has a considerable amount of Russian/Soviet material (at least 13,000 items) among its massive holdings. This is by far the best general collection in the nation. The Cartographic and Architectural Branch at the National Archives and Records Service (entry E6) offers extensive resources for the Russianist; scattered among the record groups are such treasures as original charts from the North Pacific Surveying Expedition of 1854–55 (in RG 37); maps of the American Expeditionary Forces during World War I (RG 120); and German air reconnaissance and maps of the eastern front during World War II (RG 242). The third noteworthy collection is that of the Interior Department's Geological Survey Library (entry E2), which includes some 2,000 maps covering Soviet water resources, wildlife, vegetation, etc.

Central Intelligence Agency Map Collection   See entry K6

E1 Defense Mapping Agency (DMA) Hydrographic/Topographic Center (Defense Department)

1 a. *6500 Brookes Lane, NW*
Washington, D.C. 20315
(202) 227-2080 (Support Division)

b. 8:30 A.M.–3:00 P.M., Monday–Friday

c. The DMA map collections are not open to the public. Access is restricted to researchers affiliated with the Defense Department's Mapping, Charting, and Geodetic Community.

d. Photocopying facilities are available only for Defense Department and other U.S. Government organizations. Copies of a few unclassified maps are available through public sale (see point 4).

e. Captain W. C. Palmer, USN, Director
Elmer T. Childress, Chief, Support Division, Scientific Data Department

2–3. The center's library collection contains approximately one million maps; 190,000 charts; 65,000 books, periodicals, and documents; and 4,500,000 place names. The number of USSR-related maps and charts is difficult to estimate.

Holdings include topographic maps (depicting special features such as vegetation, roads, railroads, land and ocean areas, cities, towns, and airfields), aeronautical charts (depicting essential topography, obstructions, aids to navigation, and other pertinent information for air use), and nautical charts (showing navigable waters and adjacent land areas, marine obstructions, aids to navigation, and other information for mariners). Maps range in scale from city plans at 1:15,000 or larger to maps covering large areas at 1:1,000,000 scale or smaller. Many maps are classified. The classification is usually related to source, scale, and date or to restrictions imposed by international agreements.

A substantial number of maps produced by DMA, however, are not available to the public. As a service to libraries throughout the country, the agency has provided hundreds of unclassified maps to so-called DMA repositories; among these are the libraries of George Washington University and the University of Maryland.

4. There is no published inventory of the complete collection. A catalog of unclassified maps, which must be continually updated as new maps are released, is available at DMA repositories. This catalog will show researchers which maps the repository holds.

Selected topographic maps, aeronautical, and nautical charts are available for purchase. For further information and a copy of the *DMA Price List of Maps and Charts for Public Sale,* contact the Customer Services and Sales Management Division (202/227-2816).

E2 Geological Survey Library (Interior Department)

1 a. *12201 Sunrise Valley Drive*
Reston, Virginia 22092
(703) 860-6671/6672 (Reference)
(703) 860-6679 (Catalogers)

b. 7:15 A.M.–4:15 P.M., Monday–Friday

c. Maps are available to the public, but researchers should call the library two or three days in advance to arrange a visit to the warehouse in which all foreign maps are now stored (in Herndon, Virginia, some three miles from the library). Maps circulate to employees of the Geological Survey and the Interior Department. For others there is interlibrary loan service.

d. The library has a very limited capacity to copy maps. It directs those who want maps copied to local photocopying firms, which provide this service for a fee. In addition, researchers may purchase some maps from the Survey's Public Inquiries Office (703/860-7184) and National Cartographic Information Center (formerly the Map Information Office; 703/860-6045).

e. Barbara Chappell, Chief, Reference and Circulation Section

2. In the collection of roughly 225,000 maps, approximately 2,000 pertain to the Soviet Union.

3. Maps are labeled and arranged by geographic area, subject, scale, and date. The major part of Russia/USSR holdings are for the country as a whole, divided into more than thirty subject categories: coal, ground water, paleogeology, permafrost, vegetation, volcanoes, water, etc. Among maps covering just part of the country, most are on Siberia and European Russia, with others on Arctic, Armenia, the Baltic, Caucasus, Central Asia, the Ukraine, and White Russia (Byelorussia).

4. In 1978 the library put the map holdings onto a computerized system—OCLC (Online Computer Library Center). For maps published by the Geological Survey itself, a large part of the collection, the following catalogs provide bibliographic aid: *Publications of the Geological Survey, 1879–1961* and *Publications of the Geological Survey, 1962–1970,* both available without charge from the Geological Survey Distribution Center (1200 South Eads Street, Arlington, Va. 22202); and for current maps—*New Publications of the Geological Survey,* issued monthly with annual cumulations, available without charge from the Survey, above address, mail stop 39.

In addition, a bibliography by Mark Pangborn for major geologic maps in the library appears in *Geologic Reference Sources,* by Dederick C. Ward and Marjorie W. Wheeler (Metuchen, N.J.: Scarecrow Press, 1972). A second edition, published in 1981, updates this information. Finally, as an ongoing, informal project, some staff members prepare a selective monthly list of map accessions, which the American Geological Institute (5205 Leesburg Pike, Falls Church, Va. 22041) publishes in its journal *Geotimes.*

E3 George Washington University—Gelman Library Map Collection

1 a. *2130 H Street, NW*
Washington, D.C. 20052
(202) 676-6047

b. 8:30 A.M.–10:00 P.M., Monday–Friday
10:00 A.M.–6:00 P.M., Saturday
Noon–10:00 P.M., Sunday
These hours are for access to the map collection. For general library hours, call 202/676-6845.

c. Open to the public for on-site use.

  d. Photocopying facilities are available for letter-sized reproductions.

  e. Joan K. Lippincott, Head, Reference Department

2–3. Gelman Library is a repository for both the Defense Mapping Agency (DMA) Hydrographic/Topographic Center and U.S. Geological Survey. The library's map collection, located in the Reference Room, is substantial but contains only a modest selection of maps of particular interest to the Russianist: some 450 maps from the DMA series of Eastern Europe (including the USSR) and Western, Central, and Eastern Siberia are here.

4. There are no inventories of or guides to the general collection. An index for each DMA series, however, is available.

E4 Library of Congress—Geography and Map Division

1 a. *James Madison Memorial Building, Room B01*
      101 Independence Avenue, SE
      Washington, D.C. 20540
      (202) 287-6277 (Maps)

  b. Reading Room:
      8:30 A.M.–5:00 P.M., Monday–Friday
      8:30 A.M.–12:30 P.M., Saturday
      Closed Sundays and holidays.

  c. Open to the public; visitors must register. Limited interlibrary loan service is available.

  d. Limited photocopying facilities are available.

  e. John A. Wolter, Chief

2. The collections total several million items (atlases, globes, maps, etc.). Russian/ Soviet materials amount to at least 13,000 items.

3. The division's resources may best be described under four separate rubrics: maps, atlases, reference materials, and the vault collection.

MAPS. These holdings are most extensive: more than 3.5 million. The collection is composed of three parts. First, there is the MARC file, consisting of single-sheet maps cataloged by the LC computer system (MARC). Subject access for MARC maps is available through a card catalog, while subject, author, and title access is available through computer terminals located in the reading room. Almost all cataloged single maps have been acquired since 1968. Second is the title collection (also single-sheet maps) accessioned before 1968. Only a few of these maps appear in the shelflist; the rest are unclassified and uncataloged. These map files, however, are arranged in geographical order by continent and/or country, then in chronological order or by subject, and finally by geographic subdivision of the country (e.g., region, administrative division, city). Within the subdivisions, chronological and subject orders are again maintained. The third part of the map collection is the series file of multiple-sheet maps. These maps are cataloged and appear in the map shelflist (some in MARC cataloging). They are arranged geographically by continent and country, then by scale. A separate shelflist for just these series maps exists, but it is duplicated in the overall map shelflist entries. There is also a graphic index map for each series, which shows by shading the division's holdings of individual sheets.

It is easy to ascertain the division's holdings of MARC and series maps. Being entirely controlled, they form the largest part of the shelflist of maps. Although the major portion of the title collection (pre-MARC single maps) is unclassified and uncataloged, some USSR maps have been cataloged because of the greater interest in this area in the 1950s. Therefore, the following shelflist measurements may be understood to include all MARC and series files and an unknown but relatively small percentage of the titled maps.

Call numbers	Area	Number of titles
G 7000–7012, 7060–7063	USSR, Russia	1,480
7020–7054	Baltic	95
7090–7093	Byelorussia	35
7100–7103	Ukraine	135
7110–7113	Moldavia	10
7120–7153	Caucasus	135
7200–7202	Russia in Asia	10
7210–7263, 7405–7407	Central Asia	160
7270–7340	Siberia, Far East	240

Total: 2,300 maps (roughly twenty-seven inches at eighty-five maps per inch)

As a supplement to these measurements, a simple drawer count of the title collection yields the following figures: USSR—by date: eleven drawers; by subject: fifty-four drawers; by region and natural feature: sixty-nine drawers; by republic: fifty-three drawers; by cities: thirty-eight drawers. Estonia, Latvia, Lithuania—by date: four drawers; by subject: two drawers; by region, province, and city: five drawers. Total number of drawers counted in the title collection: 248. A very rough estimate of maps per drawer is forty. Thus, the title map file would hold approximately 9,920 maps, according to this calculation.

If one adds together these two totals for maps, the division's holdings come to a minimum of 12,000 single-sheet maps and multiple-sheet series. This figure, moreover, is almost undoubtedly low.

Maps of Poland measure 10.1 inches in the shelflist and amount to fifty-two drawers in the title collection, for a total of more than 3,000 items. For Finland, the figures are 2.1 inches and twenty-four drawers, or about 1,100 maps. (The call numbers are G 6520–6524 and G 6960–6964, 7080–7083, respectively.)

ATLASES. Atlases represent a much smaller proportion of the division's materials than do maps (perhaps thirty-eight to thirty-nine thousand items total). The following shelflist measurements reveal the disparity clearly:

Call number	Area	Number of items
G 2110–2118, 2140-2143	Russia/RSFSR	365
2120–2139	Baltic	20
2145–2148	Byelorussia	10
2150–2153	Ukraine	20
2155–2158	Caucasus	20
2160–2162	Russia in Asia	10
2165–2168, 2202.C4,. A	Central Asia	15
2170–2193	Siberia, Far East	20

Total: 480 atlases (roughly 5.7 inches at eighty-five titles per inch)

There were 1.9 inches measured for Poland (G 1950–1954) or roughly 162 atlases and 7 inches for Finland (G 2075–2079) or roughly sixty atlases.

One author/title/subject card catalog for atlases is located in the reading room.

REFERENCE MATERIALS. The division maintains a card catalog for articles and books on mapmaking and cartography—*Bibliography of Cartography,* arranged by author and subject/geographic heading. Most entries are available in the division's own holdings or those of LC as a whole. Uses of this index extend beyond locating literature on the two subjects mentioned above. A wide variety of topics (which are objects of mapmaking) are found as subject headings under country entries: e.g., agriculture, climate, population, and many more. Some measurements: Russia—170 titles; USSR—155 titles; Baltic area, Estonia, Latvia, Lithuania—22 titles; Siberia—15 titles; Armenia—11 titles; Central Asia—2 titles.

Cards in this catalog are often thinner than standard-weight index cards and titles do not often exceed one card. Hence, a calculation of ninety-five titles per inch seems warranted here. The results: about 415 entries for just the headings listed.

THE VAULT COLLECTION. Some materials of the division are deemed rare (including atlases, globes, maps) or are termed manuscripts and stored in a vault. Two sets of cards catalog this collection, one labeled "Locked Cases," the other "MSS and Rare." About twenty items—mostly nineteenth-century maps—appear in the first set under "Russia"; eleven items—again maps, one from the eighteenth century, most from the nineteenth—are in the second.

The public reading room is well equipped for map study, with good lighting and large tables on which to spread out materials. The staff of specialists is most helpful for both locating and using maps. In addition, a large collection of reference materials is at hand for the researcher, and the division receives a substantial number of periodicals.

4. The following publications are of interest in facilitating access to the collections: *A List of Geographical Atlases in the Library of Congress, with Bibliographical Notes,* vols. 1–4, comp. P. L. Phillips, issued 1909–20; vols. 5–6 issued 1958–63; vols. 7–8, comp. Clara E. LeGear, issued 1973–74; *Bibliography of Cartography,* 5 vols. (Boston: G. K. Hall, 1973), and a two-volume supplement (1980); *Geography and Map Division* (1977); *Guide to Geographical Bibliographies and Reference Works in Russian or on the Soviet Union,* by Chauncy D. Harris (Chicago: University of Chicago Press, 1975).

E5   Maryland University—McKeldin Library—Government Documents/ Maps Room

1 a. *Third Floor, Room 3110*
College Park, Maryland 20742
(301) 454-3034

   b. 8:00 A.M.–11:00 P.M.,   Monday–Friday
8:00 A.M.–6:00 P.M.,   Friday
10:00 A.M.–6:00 P.M.,   Saturday
Noon–11:00 P.M.,   Sunday

   c. Open to the public for on-site use.

   d. Photocopying facilities are available for letter-sized reproductions.

   e. LeRoy Schwarzkopf, Map Librarian

2–3.   The university library serves as a repository for both the Defense Mapping Agency Hydrographic/Topographic Center (since 1950) and U.S. Geological Survey (since 1977). For the Russianist, however, the collection is not a major resource. Mr. Schwarzkopf, the map librarian, indicates that among the collection's 70,000 sheets, only a few Defense Mapping Agency maps (produced when that agency was known as the U.S. Army Map Service) cover the USSR, and that other holdings pertaining to the Soviet Union are very limited.

4.   There is no general guide to the collection. Index sheets for each map series, however, are available.

E6   National Archives and Records Service (NARS) (General Services Administration)—Cartographic and Architectural Branch (NNSC)

1 a.   *Location:*
841 South Pickett Street
Alexandria, Virginia
(703) 756-6700

Mail:
Eighth Street and Pennsylvania Avenue, NW
Washington, D.C. 20408

b.   8:45 A.M.–5:00 P.M.,   Monday–Friday

c.   Open to all researchers over the age of sixteen with a National Archives research pass (obtainable at the South Pickett Street facility).

d.   A variety of photocopying facilities are available.

e.   William Cunliffe, Chief

2.   Among the records in the center are more than 2 million maps and 7.5 million aerial photographs, comprising one of the world's largest accumulations of cartographic materials. Russian/Soviet maps and charts, either produced or collected by different U.S. agencies, are scattered in many record groups and, therefore, render a numerical estimate impossible. Some significant holdings pertaining to Russia are described below under the Record Group (RG) numbers into which the holdings are organized.

3.   RG 11: General Records of the United States Government. Contains small-scale maps of the Russian Empire in the eighteenth and nineteenth centuries, showing political and administrative divisions, place names, physical features, water drainage, and transportation systems.
   RG 22: Records of the Fish and Wildlife Service. Contains manuscript and annotated maps plus field notebooks showing Bering Sea islands with fur seals, 1872–1918.
   RG 37: Records of the Hydrographic Office. Includes original charts from the North Pacific Surveying Expedition, 1854–55, relating to Bering Strait, Saint Lawrence Bay, Seniavine Straits, Providence Bay, Nikolski Anchorage on Komandorski Island, eastern shore of Sea of Okhotsk, harbor of Ayan, Sakhalin Island, de Kastri Bay, northern Kurile Islands, Vladivostok harbor, and Wrangel Island. There are also annotated manuscripts and printed charts relating to routes of explorers in northern Siberia, Professor Adolf Erik Nordenskiold's voyage along the north coast of Siberia, 1878, the loss of the U.S.S. *Jeanette* and landings at the mouth of the Lena River, 1881–

82, and the location of Russian settlements in Alaska, circa 1867. For the years 1939–45 there are hydrographic charts and topographic maps of coastal waters and some harbors of the USSR, plus naval aviation charts and other maps or charts.

RG 38: Records of the Office of the Chief of Naval Intelligence. Includes general maps of Russia and contiguous areas, plus an incomplete set of large-scale topographic maps of Poland and western Russia, circa 1900–1916; terrain maps of the Russo-Japanese War; and large-scale maps of the Dardanelles Campaign, 1915–16.

RG 45: Naval Records Collection of the Office of Naval Records and Library. Contains hydrographic charts and maps of the Vladivostok region and other maps showing the Allied intervention in the civil war, including British maps and charts of the Baltic and Arctic regions.

RG 46: Records of the United States Senate. Contains maps of the Crimean War.

RG 76: Records of Boundary and Claims Commissions and Arbitrations. Contains maps of Russian origin used by the U.S. in the 1903 Convention regarding the U.S. Alaskan Boundary.

RG 77: Records of the Office of the Chief of Engineers. This is one of the largest and most diverse groups, containing small-scale maps of Napoleon's 1812 invasion of the Russian Empire; maps showing early World War I events and military situations; manuscript maps relating to the American Expeditionary Forces in Siberia, 1918; and small-scale maps of the U.S. Engineer Corps showing transportation facilities in the nineteenth and twentieth centuries. Here also are small-scale maps from Soviet sources of Russia's natural resources; large-scale topographic maps of parts of twentieth-century Russia; and many more small-scale maps of the USSR (1921–45) showing terrain, place names, vegetation, and political-administrative divisions.

RG 83: Records of the Bureau of Agricultural Economics. Contains maps indicating crop and livestock distribution in Russia, 1916–21.

RG 120: Records of the American Expeditionary Forces (World War I). This group includes maps relating to operations in northern Russia (n.d., fourteen items); maps accompanying reports from military missions (1918–19, twenty-nine items); enemy forces maps, eastern front (1917–19, twenty-six items); maps of areas not on the western front (1918–19, eighty-six items), showing fronts, situations, and orders of battle in Italy, the Balkans, Eastern Europe, the Near East, Rumania, Russia, and Portugal; a 1:500,000 topographic map of the Vladivostok area (1909); 1:420,000 planimetric maps of Russia (1918–19, ten items); situation maps—Russia and Siberia (1918–19, thirty-five items); and enemy order of battle maps—eastern front (1917–19, twenty-six items.

RG 165: Records of the War Department General and Special Staffs. Contains maps of the Russo-Japanese War, including ones of the Battle of the Yalu River and some large-scale topographic maps.

RG 226: Records of the Office of Strategic Services. Another large and valuable group, RG 226 has small-scale maps dating from World War II, showing population, terrain, economic—particularly mineral—resources, Soviet fisheries, transportation, plus maps of the political and administrative divisions of the USSR.

RG 242: National Archives Collection of Foreign Records Seized 1941–. The Cartographic Records in this group, covering 1934–45, include more than 30,000 items, among which are air reconnaissance maps of the eastern front, maps of the disposition of Red Army units, situation maps prepared by the Soviets and Russian maps from captured World War II records.

RG 253: Records of the Petroleum Administration for War. Includes maps of Soviet oil resources, petroleum refineries, and other geological information.

RG 256: Records of the American Mission to Negotiate Peace. Cartographic records here include a "Russia and Poland Division," which contains 152 items illustrating the problems of establishing an independent Poland. There are also maps showing

Eastern Europe, Armenia, and Russian settlements in Central Asia as well as maps with agricultural data from 1916–21.

RG 324: Records of the Board on Geographic Names. Includes fifteen volumes of gazetteers of the Soviet Union in 1953 and 1959 that give the correct spelling of many geographic names, longitude and latitude figures, etc.

4. The basic inventory for all Russian holdings at NARS—*Records in the National Archives Relating to the Russian Empire and the Soviet Union,* Reference Information Paper No. 41 (August 1952)—is of value for cartographic materials. Most information given above in the descriptive list came from this publication, a photocopy of which may be obtained without charge by forwarding a written request to the Civil Archives Division.

Of some use also will be *Preliminary Inventory of the Cartographic Records of the American Expeditionary Forces, 1917–21,* comp. Franklin W. Burch (1966), Preliminary Inventory No. 165; the *Guide to Cartographic Records in the National Archives,* by Charlotte M. Ashby et al. (1971); and U.S. Hydrographic Office, *Manuscripts Charts in the National Archives, 1838–1908,* by William J. Heynen (1978). A list of available guides, inventories, and unpublished finding aids, along with other useful information on the center, is provided in the pamphlet *Cartographic Archives Division,* General Information Leaflet No. 26 (reprinted 1976).

E7 National Geographic Society—Cartographic Division Map Library

1 a. *Membership Center Building*
11555 Darnestown Road (Maryland Route 28)
Gaithersburg, Maryland 20760

Mail:
1146 Sixteenth Street, NW
Washington, D.C. 20036
(202) 857-7000 Ext. 1401

b. 7:30 A.M.–5:00 P.M., Monday–Friday

c. Open to the public by appointment. Maps from this collection may also be made available to scholars through the National Geographic Society Library (entry A46); maps requested early in the morning should be ready at the library the same afternoon.

d. Photocopying facilities are available through the Gaithersburg facility.

e. Margery Barkdull, Map Librarian

2–3. The collection is estimated to contain more than 85,000 maps. The cartographic material ranges from topographic, administrative, subject, and highway maps of the U.S. and foreign areas to lunar maps, nautical and aeronautical charts, and city plans. Holdings include almost every map produced by the National Geographic Society. (Maps of the Soviet Union, other than those produced by the society, are generally obtained by the division through the Kamkin bookstore, see Appendix IV.) At present, the collection contains approximately twenty-five maps of the Soviet Union. A good selection of atlases, gazetteers and reference books is also available. Although the geographic scope is global, coverage of the U.S. and Europe predominates, followed by Asia, Africa, and Central and South America.

4. The collection is arranged geographically. The card catalog is also organized geographically with a further breakdown by region and country and division within countries.

Maps published by the society are available at the Explorers Hall sales desk (202/ 857-7589), located at Seventeenth and M streets, NW, Washington, D.C.

F Film Collections (Still Photographs and Motion Pictures)

Film Collection Entry Format (F)

1. General Information
   a. *address; telephone number(s)*
   b. hours of service
   c. conditions of access
   d. name/title of director and key staff members

2. Size of Holdings Pertaining to Russia/USSR

3. Description of Holdings Pertaining to Russia/USSR

4. Facilities for Study and Use
   a. availability of audiovisual equipment
   b. reservation requirements
   c. fees charged
   d. photocopying facilities

5. Bibliographic Aids Facilitating Use of Collection

Introductory Note

Various depositories in the Washington area hold fine collections of Russian-related still photographs and motion pictures. For photographs, the Prints and Photographs Division of the Library of Congress (entry F6) is the best single source. The holdings of the Still Picture Branch of the National Archives and Records Service (entry F7) include many thousands of photographs of interest to the Russianist as well. Art scholars will find the photographic archives at the National Gallery of Art (entry F9) an excellent resource for the study of Russian painting.

Students of Russian/Soviet cinema may arrange to see a number of excellent feature films without charge through (or at) the Soviet embassy (entry F3), Prince George's County Public Libraries (entry F13), Northern Virginia Community College (entry F12), Folger Shakespeare Library (entry F4), and Library of Congress (Motion Picture, Broadcasting, and Recorded Sound Division, entry F5). The latter also contains a good collection of documentary newsreel and television films about Russia/USSR; a more extensive (and eclectic) group of noncommercial productions is maintained by the National Archives and Records Service in its Motion Picture, Sound, and Video Branch (entry F7).

For more detail on cinematography, consult the volume in this series entitled *Scholars' Guide to Washington, D.C., Film and Video Collections,* by Bonnie G. Rowan (Washington, D.C.: Smithsonian Institution Press, 1980).

American Red Cross Archives   See entry B1

Army Library (Army Department)   See entry A8

Central Intelligence Agency—Film Collection   See entry K6

F1   Defense Audiovisual Agency

1 a.   *Anacostia Naval Station, Building 168*
  Washington, D.C. 20374
  (202) 433-2166

  b.   9:00 A.M.–3:00 P.M., Monday–Friday
  closed 11:00 A.M.–noon

  c.   Open to the public, by appointment.

  d.   Jack Carter, Chief

2.   The agency's collection numbers approximately one million color and black-and-white photographs taken within the past twenty-five years, including 500–1,000 related directly to the USSR.

3.   Almost all items are unclassified, including the Soviet materials. In five notebooks (approximately forty to fifty photos in each) are photographs from World War II, either taken in the Soviet Union or related to the USSR (e.g., depicting lend-lease operations or supplies).

The agency has many photos of Soviet ships; among the subjects is the aircraft carrier *Kiev.* Some 150 pictures, mostly of poor quality, are of Russian aircraft from different times, showing at least twenty-five different types of planes. There are also some photos of Soviet missiles on parade at May Day celebrations in Red Square.

Several special collections here—on World War II and the Korean and Vietnam conflicts—may hold photographs of some value for the Soviet-area scholar.

The agency holds negatives for most of the still photos in the collection of the Naval Historical Center's photographic section. (The agency itself was created in 1981 through the merger of the Air Force Central Still Photographic Depository, Naval Photographic Center, and equivalent departments of the army and marines.)

4 c.   A fee is charged for any research or searching requested of them by visitors. No other fees are charged for work done by the outside researcher himself.

  d.   Copies of the holdings are available for a fee.

5.   The staff maintains a visual print file arranged by subject and geographic area; these file prints are kept in binders on open shelves for the use of researchers. A

naval card drawer file is arranged by subject, by class of ship, and by name. There is a cross-indexing system.

F2 Dumbarton Oaks—Center for Byzantine Studies (Harvard University) Photograph Collection

1 a. *1703 Thirty-second Street, NW*
Washington, D.C. 20007
(202) 342-3246

b. 9:00 A.M.–5:00 P.M., Monday–Friday

c. Researchers must supply a letter of recommendation and call for an appointment. No groups and no tours can be accommodated.

d. Charlotte Kroll Burk, Photoarchivist, Byzantine Photograph Collection

2-3. The Photograph Collection has more than 1,500 black-and-white prints pertaining to Byzantine/medieval Russia (USSR), including Armenia and Georgia. The collection is arranged geographically by medium. Prints pertaining to "Russian" interests are cataloged as follows: architecture (266), mosaic (82), sculpture (195), and wallpainting (671). One may note a microfiche publication on Armenian architecture, black-and-white prints of Byzantine manuscripts in Russian collections, and a limited number of 35-mm color slides of Byzantine Russian art.

4 b. Reservations are required; the staff requests at least a week's notice. See also point 1c.

c. No fees are charged for viewing photographs.

d. No copies are available or are permitted to be made. Photographs, however, are available from the negative collections. Full photograph source information is available to the researcher.

F3 Embassy of the USSR—Film Library

1 a. *1706 Eighteenth Street, NW*
Washington, D.C. 20009
(202) 347-1355

b. 9:00 A.M.–Noon, Monday–Friday

c. Open to the public.

d. Anatolii Diuzhev, Counselor (Cultural Affairs)

2-3. The Soviet embassy's film collection includes approximately 100 titles. Among these are short documentaries (most in English but some in Russian) exploring various aspects of Soviet life, geography, nature, republics of the USSR, industry, agriculture, culture, history, sports, and children; historical films covering such topics as World War II and the life of Lenin; contemporary Soviet feature films (e.g., *Oblomov, Moscow Does Not Believe in Tears*); and more.

4 a.   No viewing facilities are presently available at the embassy, although construction of a screening room is planned.

b.   Borrowing is handled by mail and in person. Reservations should be made in a letter containing information on the organization assuming responsibility for the film(s). Borrowers who can pick up films at the Film Library can usually get them on short notice.

c.   No fees are charged.

5.   A descriptive catalog is available.

F4   Folger Shakespeare Library

1 a.   *201 East Capitol Street, SE*
Washington, D.C. 20003
(202) 544-4600

b.   8:45 A.M.–4:45 P.M., Monday–Friday
8:45 A.M.–Noon, 1:00–4:30 P.M., Saturday (films cannot be viewed on Saturday)

c.   Open to researchers. Only one person at a time may view the films.

d.   O. B. Hardison, Jr., Director
Catherine Sentman, Film Archivist

2-3.   The Folger has several Soviet Shakespearean films, including *Gamlet* (1964) and *Korol' Lir* (1971), both directed by G. Kozintsev, and *Otello* (1955), directed by S. Youtkevich. The library also has a complete collection of Shakespeare's plays translated into Russian, Soviet scholarly works dealing with Shakespeare, and accounts of Russia by Western travelers in the early modern period.

4 a.   A console editor is available for viewing films.

b.   Reservations are required for either a morning or afternoon viewing session.

c.   No fees are charged.

d.   Copies for purchase or rental are not available.

5.   *A Shakespeare Filmography* (Washington, D.C.: Folger Shakespeare Library, 1979) describes feature films based on the works of Shakespeare.

Hillwood Museum Library and Archives   See entry A27

Howard University Audiovisual Center   See entry J9

International Labour Office   See entry A32

F5 Library of Congress—Motion Picture, Broadcasting, and Recorded Sound Division

1 a. *James Madison Memorial Building, Room 338*
101 Independence Avenue, SE
Washington, D.C. 20540
(202) 287-5840 (motion pictures)

b. 8:30 A.M.–4:30 P.M., Monday–Friday

c. Open to researchers past the high-school level; undergraduate college students must provide a letter of recommendation from a supervising professor to use the facilities.

d. Paul Spehr, Acting Chief
Emily Sieger, Reference Librarian (film/TV)

2. There are approximately 100 documentary, newsreel, or television films and an undetermined number of feature films, most made in the U.S., which are about Russia/ USSR.

3. The films in this collection, listed in a subject-entry card catalog under "Russia," are primarily documentaries that treat the history, culture, and people of the Soviet Union. There are newsreels, parts of television series, dramatizations and informational movies made in the U.S., Western Europe, and the USSR. The films cover a broad range of subjects, including the Soviet economy, industry, travel in the USSR, major historical events, and literary figures. None appear to be of outstanding quality or interest. Researchers might find here, among captured German films from the Russian campaign of World War II, some notable items; the division staff also indicates that the Julian Bryan collection (with scenes of Moscow, Leningrad, and Soviet agriculture in the 1930s) and an American Friends Service Committee film from the early 1920s *(America's Gift to Famine Stricken Russia)* may provide some useful material for the Russianist.

Feature films in the collection (some ten to fifteen in all) also represent a minor resource. There are virtually no early Russian/Soviet classics—no Eisenstein, no Dovzhenko, only one Pudovkin *(The End of Saint Petersburg,* 1927). More recent Soviet cinema is likewise scarcely represented (although Grigorii Chukrai's *Ballad of a Soldier,* 1960, is here). Western films on Russian themes which may be of interest include Warner Brothers' *Mission to Moscow* (1943); *Bolshevism on Trial* (1919, silent); Josef von Sternberg's *The Scarlet Empress* (1934); *The First Circle* (1972), a Danish adaption of the Solzhenitsyn novel, dubbed in English; and a handful of other cinematic versions of literary works.

A recent acquisition of interest is the twenty-hour television documentary series *The Unknown War* that covers the conflict on the eastern front, 1941–45. The controversial series, first telecast in 1978, is a U.S.-Soviet coproduction; most archival footage is from Russian sources and unfamiliar to Western audiences.

4 a-c. The division provides individual screening devices with earphones for viewing (about the size of a large television set screen). No fees are charged, but reservations should be made well in advance. The collection is not available for public projection, rental, or loan.

5.   There is no comprehensive published catalog or inventory of motion pictures. The division does, however, have custody of descriptive materials (continuities, plot synopses, pressbooks) for films in its possession registered for copyright after 1912.

A brochure prepared by the division, *Film and Television* (1979), is available without charge.

F6   Library of Congress—Prints and Photographs Division

1 a.   *James Madison Memorial Building, Room 337*
First Street and Independence Avenue, SE
Washington, D.C. 20540
(202) 287-6394

b.   8:30 A.M.–5:00 P.M., Monday–Friday

c.   Open to the public. Researchers should make arrangements in advance if they wish to use unprocessed collections.

d.   Oliver Jensen, Chief

2.   This is perhaps the largest still-picture collection in the area for Russianists and for scholars in general. Although there is no way to measure accurately the total amount of Soviet-area material, an approximation would be that there are more than 12,000 individual photographs and negatives, prints, posters, woodcuts, and slides by count, plus an additional twelve linear feet of photos in file drawers, plus thirty-eight drawers of posters.

3.   At the present time it is very difficult to locate all the still picture items that relate to any particular country or geographic area. The division's catalogs are of some help but many photographs are uncataloged, dispersed among different collections, or listed in ways not obvious to the Russianist trying to use the resources here. Staff help is thus indispensable for finding desired materials.

The subjects about which researchers will find the most still pictures here are: the USSR in World War II; Russians and Russia in the period of World War I, the revolutions, and the civil war; architecture in the Soviet Union/Russia; émigrés after 1917; Siberia; the Russo-Japanese War; the Russian imperial family; and places of historical or other particular interest. Most collections, especially the larger ones, can best be described simply by lot numbers and the name of the collecting person or agency. No names are assigned to smaller groups as a rule, and lot numbers alone must suffice to identify them. The Vanderbilt catalog noted in point 5 will prove frustrating (though valuable) to use for a guide to holdings, because the names it assigns to collections are frequently no longer used for the pictures described. The five largest groups of pictures appear to be the following:

Office of War Information Collection. These 625 photographs occupy some four feet of space in two file drawers (lots 11595–11605; 11640); they concern military and civilian aspects of World War II, including agriculture, combat, families, medicine, POWs, and transportation in the USSR.

American Red Cross Collection. Another four feet (two drawers) of photos are here, these dealing with Russia at the end of World War I and after, showing the care of the ill, the injured, and the young; religious subjects; and the new regime.

Collection under "Russia" in the geographic file. Some two feet of photographs depict mostly buildings and other architectural structures.

Carpenter Collection (lots 11469 and 11470). This group includes ninety photographs of post-1917 émigrés plus 349 photographs of scenes and people in the USSR circa 1930. Many are from the book *The Homesick Million.*

Prokudin-Gorskii Collection (lots 10332–10343). The approximately 2,700 photo-prints (and the plates from which they were taken) comprise a unique record of the Russian Empire in the years 1905–15: many subjects photographed have either disappeared since or not been reproduced satisfactorily by other photographers. The areas shown include much of the Volga River basin, the Marinsky Canal region, parts of western Russia/Byelorussia/Poland where Napoleon invaded and important rail lines lie, the Ural Mountains and their industries, Central Asia, western Siberia, and the Caucasus. Few people are in the photos (though Tolstoi at Yasnaya Polyana is here), but they include churches, public buildings, street views, landscapes, railroads, farming and industrial scenes, and much art work. Many of the best photos in this collection are reproduced in color in the book *Photographs for the Tsar* (New York: Dial Press, 1980).

An important stereograph collection from the late nineteenth and early twentieth centuries includes scenes of the Russo-Japanese War (lot 11691); the two capitals and their churches, palaces, kremlins; Kiev and other towns; Cossacks; the imperial family; foreign visitors to Russia; landscapes; economic activities; and a variety of ceremonial affairs.

On specific subjects there are the following lots of photographs and photo prints, plus prints, lithographs, and other items.

The Crimean War—photocopies (uncounted) of contemporary prints and drawings showing battle scenes (Balaklava and Sevastopol), fortifications, ports, hospitals, etc. (lot 4708).

Russo-Turkish War of 1877–78—some fifty-seven wood engravings and seventeen lithographs of Rumania, Bulgaria, military operations, Russian troops, war atrocities, and combat (lots 8240 and 8488).

Russo-Japanese War—more than seventy-five individual photos, four albums of photographs, more than eighty stereo views, twenty-nine postcards, and several lithographs show almost every aspect of the war and the peace conference afterward at Portsmouth, New Hampshire (lots 2559 ["Noble Collection"], 2624 ["Noble Collection"], 3372, 7702, 7729 ["Pershing Collection"], 7776, 8223, and 8631).

World War I—more than 200 photos detail Red Cross relief work, Russian and Allied troops in Russia and France, Russian POWs in Germany and the Eastern Front (lots 3635, 5712 ["Van Norman Collection"], 11166–63, 11170, and 11457). (See also under "Siberia," following, and the "Red Cross Collection," preceding.) World War II—there are perhaps two to three thousand photos, almost all on U.S. Army efforts to supply the USSR through Iran but also on Soviet troops in China and of a June 1942 concert in Washington, D.C., for the anniversary of Germany's invasion of the Soviet Union (with Paul Robeson, a balalaika orchestra, and Madame Litvinov) (lots 159 [on microfilm], 3098 ["Pauley Mission Collection"], and 5178 ["Persian Gulf Command Collection"]). Note: The most important holding on this subject is noted under "Office of War Information Collection."

Russian Imperial Family—a large number of prints, photos, and glass negatives picturing the tsar and his family made after 1900, some taken during their internment at Tsarskoe Selo in 1917 (lots 11119 and 11148).

Bolshevik (and Menshevik) Party History—about 480 glass lantern slides showing aspects of the social-democratic movement in Russia, historical development of both party factions, and significant events up to the revolution (lots 5827–5838 ["Diafato Collection"—from Glavuchtekhprom narkomprosa RSFSR]).

Siberia—more than 875 photos, 400 drawings, and twenty postcards depict nearly every side of Siberian (and Mongolian) life, people, flora, fauna, buildings, etc. Some material from World War I is of Red Cross and troop activity. More than 100 fascinating photos date from 1885 to 1910, and all the drawings from 1860 to 1910, some showing exiled prisoners. The color lithograph postcards are dated 1899. More recent photos are of a collective farm, Irkutsk, Lake Baikal and Ulan Ude in the 1950s (lots 2444, 2691, 3327 ["Fugiwara Collection"], 4487 ["Bayard Taylor Collection"], 7043 ["Kuznetsov Collection"], 7198, 7213, 8700–8701, 8715, 9760 ["Jackson Collection"], and 9917, plus lots 2916–2919, 3027, 3029–3030, 3052–3053, all "Red Cross Collection").

On a large variety of other topics there are the following general or small collections:

A large poster collection (thirty-eight drawers) from the revolution and civil war years, World War II, and the present; twenty-five drawers are filled with original stencil designs issued during World War II by the TASS news agency, and much of the remainder of the collection is on domestic economic (agriculture, industry) and social (education, health, and welfare) matters. Except for one drawer, these holdings are uncataloged. A smaller number of TASS posters (lot 2692) were part of the Soviet war effort in the 1940s. Boxes and boxes of TASS postcards are also here.

Twelve photo prints from about 1900 are on the diverting subject of toys and learning aids; the objects are on display at a museum or show of some kind (lot 7017).

Twelfth-century Byzantine frescoes on the walls of the Church of the Savior at Nereditsa are the theme of about 164 mounted photo prints in lot 4027 ("Russian Imperial Collection").

Georgia and the Caucasus are pictured in some 740 photo prints (in ten portfolios) dating from about the turn of the century (lot 7576 "Harbord Collection").

Lot 2746 contains lithographs depicting the history of Nizhni Novgorod (now Gorki) from 1171 to the eighteenth century; these thirteen small pictures are undated.

Eighty-three glass lantern slides from the "Diafoto Collection" are of various aspects of life in the USSR circa 1939 (lots 5839, 5842, and 5849).

More than 400 photos picture Soviet life and culture in the late 1940s (lots 5258–5270).

Russian personalities appear in numerous photos from diverse groups: artists, intellectuals, and scientists of the turn of the century are the subjects of clippings in an album in lot 7048; Khrushchev is with John F. Kennedy in a few photos from June 1961 in Vienna (lot 10499); and Russian-Americans or Russians in America in the years 1938–43 are in photos in lots 37, 1335, and 1811.

There are sixty-six photographs in a portfolio in lot 7354 that show the celebration of the three-hundredth anniversary of the annexation of the Ukraine to Muscovy.

Eighteen ninety-two is the date of fifteen photo prints, mounted in a portfolio, of churches and monasteries at Uglich, on the Volga north of Moscow (lot 7042).

A railroad line along the Dniester River and through the Ukraine and gold mining are featured in photos of lots 7044 and 6999 respectively (thirty prints of the first, nine of the second), called the "Russian Southwest Railway Collection" and the "Russian Gold Mining Collection."

A number of photographs transferred from the George Kennan Papers (in the Manuscript Division) are here.

Five prints of A. M. Rodchenko—examples of modern art—are cataloged in the Master Photographs Collection.

What other still picture treasures on Russia/USSR lie here undiscovered is uncertain. At least five collections described in a 1955 catalog are either lost or scattered; a search more thorough than was possible for this guide might turn up the following: "Kun Collection"—750 photos of Turkestan in 1871–72; "William Eleroy Curtis Collection"—a part of nearly 2,000 photographs are from nineteenth-century Russia; "Alexander II Collection"—twenty-five mounted photos of designs (models) for a mausoleum for Tsar Alexander II; "Kalugin Collection"—twenty-five prints of late nineteenth-century Russian scenes; and the "Bristol Collection"—an album of photos of refugees from the civil war years in Constantinople.

In any event, there are several other collections of interest here: two of Japanese woodcuts and another of postcards and miscellanea stand out. The woodcuts, in color, are prints of a Russian naval visit to the islands in 1804–5 336 ("Chadbourne Collection") and of the Russo-Japanese War ("Noyes Collection"). The "Babine Collection" lot 7047 contains about 100 postcards of people, places, and events of the Russian Revolution of 1905 and of World War I; two lengthy scrolls showing nineteenth-century parade arrangements; an 1883 parade schema; a children's card game; and other items. The staff also indicates that among the division's graphic art holdings—including the Master Drawings collection; the Popular and Applied Graphic Art Collection, lot 9887; and a collection of original prints by contemporary Soviet artists—the Russianist will find considerable noteworthy material.

4. For still pictures, 1 a–c do not apply. Materials not copyrighted or restricted can be copied by the LC Photoduplication Service according to a schedule of fees. Photographic copies, photostats, microfilm, slides, and blue line prints are the available forms of copying.

5. There are no published catalogs or inventories of still pictures. The best reference tool available for collections of prints, photos, and posters is the badly outdated and confusing *Guide to the Special Collections of Prints and Photographs in the Library of Congress,* by Paul Vanderbilt (1955). The best part of this publication may be the detailed descriptions it provides of the history and contents of the hundreds of collections listed; these descriptions may permit researchers to find materials otherwise not (or inadequately) cataloged.

There are several catalogs for still picture items; these are usually arranged by subject, geographic area or country, or the name of the collection. But the catalogs must be used with care and the help of the staff to yield satisfactory results.

For prints, a subject file exists; folder 7004 lists Russian-area material, but the listing is far from complete.

Many of the collections have been described in articles in the *Quarterly Journal of Current Acquisitions* (now the *Quarterly Journal of the Library of Congress*); two examples are the Red Cross Collection (February 1945) and some of the TASS poster collection (October–December 1944). Again, the Vanderbilt guide noted earlier describes most of the more important holdings.

Martin Luther King, Jr., Memorial Library   See entry A38

Maryland University Library   See entry A39

National Aeronautics and Space Administration—Audiovisual Section See entry K25

National Air and Space Museum Library   See entry A41

National Arboretum Library   See entry A42

F7   National Archives and Records Service (NARS) (General Services Administration)—Special Archives Division—Motion Picture, Sound, and Video Branch; Still Picture Branch

1 a. *Eighth Street and Pennsylvania Avenue, NW*
Washington, D.C. 20408
(entrance from Pennsylvania Avenue only)
(202) 786-0041 (Video, Audio)
(202) 523-3054 (Still)

b. 8:45 A.M.–5:00 P.M., Monday–Friday

c. Open to researchers over the age of sixteen. Users must obtain a National Archives research pass (obtainable in room 200B), for which appropriate identification is required. Some materials may be restricted.

d. William Murphy, Chief, Motion Picture and Sound Recording Branch
Joe Thomas, Chief, Still Picture Branch

2. The division (internally designated NNV) holds hundreds of films relating to Russia/USSR in the Motion Picture and Sound Recording Branch (NNVM). Many thousands of photographs of interest to the Russianist are stored by the Still Picture Branch (NNVP). This is clearly a major resource in both categories.

3. This description will discuss motion and still picture holdings separately, arranged by record group number. No thorough search of all record groups was undertaken; the data given here rely upon past and present NARS staff findings and are not complete.

Motion pictures (in the form of edited and unedited outtakes, newsreels, information and training films, documentaries, and a few feature films):
RG 64: Records of the National Archives and Records Service. All items here are from World War II. Included are Soviet newsreels, training films, and the film *June 13, 1942* on military activities in the USSR during the Nazi invasion.
RG 75: Records of the Bureau of Indian Affairs. Contains a one-reel film, from 1921, *A Trip to the Arctic with Uncle Sam,* which documents a trip of the vessel *Bear* from the Aleutian Islands to Siberia.
RG 96: Records of the Farmers Home Administration. Contains a 1936 silent film (16-mm, eighteen minutes long), *Agricultural and Industrial Cooperatives in Russia and England.*
RG 107: Records of the Office of the Secretary of War. Included are films on Soviet troops in Thuringia, Allied Council in Berlin, and Russian Commission in Korea.
RG 111: Records of the Office of the Chief Signal Officer. This is one of the most important collections. It contains about thirty Russian newsreels (about twelve minutes long), most on World War II but others on agriculture, factories, industry, mining, and plants; and a number of Signal Corps films. Among the latter are two on the Russo-Japanese War; three on American intervention in Siberia and Archangel *(339th Infantry in Northern Russia, American Expeditionary Forces in Siberia,* and *Siberian War Reviews);* and some from World War II, including the nearly two-hour *Battle of Russia* showing action at Stalingrad and elsewhere.
RG 131: Records of the Office of Alien Property. Contains a film from the 1920s produced by the Hamburg-American Line, *The Soviet Union.*
RG 200: National Archives Gift Collection. The second of the four most significant

groups, RG 200 has a 1905 Paramount newsreel on the Russo-Japanese War and a second showing the breakdown of the tsarist army in World War I, with Russian soldiers surrendering to the Germans. Another film depicts Russian transportation and the Trans-Siberian Railroad, 1917–18. From the time of World War II there are Movietone and Paramount newsreels on the fighting in the East of Europe; the features *Finland Fights* and *Mission to Moscow*; and March of Time films, *Russians Nobody Knows*, *Answer to Stalin*, and *As Russia Sees It*. From these and later years come newsreels and features on Soviet culture, military equipment, diplomats abroad, and foreigners in the USSR; the Universal Newsreel Library collection—containing hundreds of films on Russian topics made over a thirty-year span—is a particularly rich lode for the Russianist. The CBS series Eyewitness to History shows Khrushchev's 1959 visit to the U.S. and 1960 trip to France. Still other holdings are about communism in Russia, Richard Nixon's trip to the USSR and the American Trade Fair in 1959, the 1960 Paris Summit Meeting, the Kennedy-Khrushchev meeting in Vienna (1961), and the Nuclear Test Ban Treaty signing of 1963. There are more than 500 pertinent items in this RG.

RG 207: General Records of the Department of Housing and Urban Development. The one germane item in this collection concerns housing and planning in the Soviet Union.

RG 208: Records of the Office of War Information. This is the third of the most important holdings. Here are some eighty-six Russian newsreels of the same kind as in RG 111; they are short and depict such aspects of the war as the the Eastern Front, the home front and civilian life, prisoners of war, generals and political leaders, and the war's destruction. In either this collection or in RG 111 there are Russian-made films like *Moscow Strikes Back,* with English narration, and many Russian-language pictures; instructional and training films; short subjects on May Day festivals; and longer documentaries entitled *The Red Army* and *Russian Tanks.* Finally, RG 208 contains a series of newsreels sponsored by the Office of War Information, made in Russia, called Russian News (1942–45).

RG 233: Records of the United States House of Representatives. Contains a four-reel film of the hearings of the Kersten Committee (Select Committee to investigate the incorporation of the Baltic States into the USSR).

RG 242: National Archives Collection of Foreign Records Seized, 1941–. This is the fourth and last of the noteworthy collections. It contains a large number of pre– and post-war Russian newsreels, educational films, documentaries, and feature films (see the Naval Photographic Center [NPC] series and elsewhere) on social conditions, science, technology, agriculture, industry, mining, transportation, fishing, lumbering, medicine, housing, travel, schools and religion in the Soviet Union. Other pictures show Russian culture, history, and the Kremlin. *The Death of Lenin* has segments on Lenin in 1918–24 and on Stalin. Other subjects of films here are Soviet political meetings (the Presidium, joint sessions of soviets), the fall of Berlin in 1945, the meeting of Soviet troops with the Western allies on the Elbe, and the socialization process in various Soviet republics. Some anti-American works are also present. Moreover, there are seized Italian, Japanese, and German newsreels, the latter showing German-Soviet battles and also the signing of the Nazi-Soviet Pact of 1939.

RG 306: Records of the United States Information Agency. Recent accessions of large numbers of edited and unedited films, 1937–77, produced or acquired by this agency include such titles as *The Mission of Apollo-Soyuz, The Missiles of October,* and *Conversation with Svetlana Alliluyeva.*

RG 326: Records of the Atomic Energy Commission. Includes Russian educational documentary films, circa 1964, on the peaceful uses of atomic energy.

RG 342: Records of the United States Air Force Commands, Activities, and Organizations. Contains motion pictures with documentation on the 1949 May Day celebration, the defense of Moscow, Igor Sikorsky, Stalin, and Molotov.

Still Pictures (including photographs, negatives, and a few posters):
RG 18: Records of the Army Air Forces. Contains fifteen photos from 1924 of the Kamchatka Peninsula.
RG 19: Records of the Bureau of Ships. Contains some thirty photos of Russian naval vessels in 1900 and 1915.
RG 26: Records of the United States Coast Guard. The Alaska file in this group contains eight photos from 1891 of Siberian natives loading reindeer aboard the vessel *Bear* (see RG 75 above); natives in Holy Cross Bay, Saint Lawrence Bay, and East Cape are also shown. Photos of approximately fifty Soviet merchant ships in San Francisco harbor, 1941–43, may also be found here.
RG 30: Records of the Bureau of Public Roads. Contains six photos showing Russian road machinery and a crowned dirt road, 1914 (filed under "Foreign").
RG 38: Records of the Office of the Chief of Naval Intelligence. Contains some twenty photographs of Soviet leaders who took part in the San Francisco United Nations conference in 1945; also a number of undated pictures of maps.
RG 44: Records of the Office of Government Reports. Contains twelve examples of Soviet War posters and propaganda from 1942–45.
RG 59: General Records of the Department of State. Contains photos of the 1903 International Court of Justice at The Hague, the signing of the Russian-Japanese peace treaty in 1905, and the floor plans and assembly room of the Hall of Nobility in Petrograd (1915).
RG 77: Records of the Office of the Chief of Engineers. This is one of the five to six largest holdings: 500 photographs are of the 1918–19 American intervention in Siberia; they are in an album and captioned. Some photos also show the forces in North Russia. Other pictures are of military operations and peace demonstrations in the Russian army (1917).
RG 80: General Records of the Department of the Navy. Contains more than one hundred photos of Russian ships, planes, places and officers, and enlisted personnel filed under geographic names and headings (e.g., Airplanes—Foreign—Russia, Merchant Ships).
RG 111: Records of the Office of the Chief Signal Officer. The largest collection, RG 111 has some 600 photos of the Expeditionary Forces in Siberia (early 1920s) and about 300 of those at Archangel (1918–19), for which there are caption lists, plus about 3,000 photos of the Russo-Japanese War. These magnificent photo collections show details of nearly every aspect of military operations, personnel, and local scenes and sites. There are pictures of Kolchak and the White forces and of Bolshevik prisoners, in the American Expeditionary Force (AEF) group.
RG 121: Records of the Public Buildings Services. From 1939 there are seven negatives of posters rendered by American artists showing Russian/Soviet life. A small number of photos here are of paintings of the fur-seal industry in the Pribilov Islands, 1872–90.
RG 131: Records of the Office of Alien Property. Some twenty photographs picture Soviet tourist resorts on the Hamburg-American Line, 1926, and another eight are of Soviet diplomats, 1940–41. There is also a cartoon of Stalin.
RG 151: Records of the Bureau of Foreign and Domestic Commerce and Successor Agencies. The thirty photos here illustrate magazine articles of about 1930—on agriculture, public buildings, shipping and the "new cities" of Soviet Russia.
RG 165: Records of the War Department General and Special Staffs. This is another of the large and varied groups. From 1864 there is one photo of the Russian imperial family, from 1870 a negative of a big map of Russian America. About ten 1900 photos

of the China Relief Mission show Russian military personnel and equipment and 125 prints from 1905 depict battles and personalities of the Russo-Japanese War. A large number of pictures are from World War I, including eight of Russian troops and equipment in France; 100 of Lithuania, Rostov, Sevastopol, and Brest-Litovsk at the time of the peace negotiations (Trotskii appears in some); twenty-five of military and diplomatic personalities, including Kerenskii; and some 200 of U.S. commissions to Russia, Russian commissions to the U.S., the Bolsheviks, Lenin, Kolchak, Ekaterina Breshkovskaia, peace conference delegates, and prisoners of war in Russia. A final batch of 250 photos from 1941–45 are of Soviet armaments (mostly of Soviet origin). An inventory card is available for this last group of pictures.

RG 200: National Archives Gift Collection. Contains about 200 photographs of the German Forty-seventh Army Corps invasion of the USSR, 1941; an inventory card is available. Here also are another twenty-seven prints showing the Soviet occupation of Vienna, 1945; there is a list of captions for these photographs.

RG 208: Records of the Office of War Information. This very large group of photos has items from World War II: 1,500 photos of the Russian air command in Alaska, the Soviet Navy in Finland, ground troops in the Baltic and Eastern Europe, prisoners of war, the lend-lease operation; and 190 of diplomatic and military personalities such as Gromyko, Litvinov, and Stalin.

RG 238: National Archives Collection of World War II Crimes Records. Contains some twenty-five to thirty photos of the Soviet legal and military personnel who collaborated with the U.S. counsel in the prosecution of Axis war criminals.

RG 242: National Archives Collection of Foreign Records Seized, 1941–. Includes some 250 photos from Joachim von Ribbentrop's album showing the signing of the 1939 Nazi-Soviet Pact, Molotov's 1940 visit to Berlin, and other views of Molotov and Stalin. An inventory card exists for these items. There are also an undetermined number of photographs of German Waffen SS units' operations in the USSR, 1943–44.

RG 255: Records of the National Aeronautics and Space Administration. Includes some photos of different types of Soviet aircraft.

RG 306: Records of the United States Information Agency. Contains the second-largest recorded amount of Russian/Soviet material. Covering the years 1917–50 are some 2,000 photos and negatives of important personalities (e.g., Chicherin, Dzerzhinskii, Ehrenburg, Kerenskii, Lenin, Maiskii, Stalin, Tomskii, Trotskii and Zinov'ev); of the 1921 Volga region famine; on agriculture, civil war orphans, industry, and labor; and on various conferences of World War II. The holdings were part of the *New York Times* Paris office file taken over by the USIA. Access is unrestricted, and an index to the items exists. In RG 306 also are photos of Soviet political meetings, schools, prominent personalities, and many other subjects. These prints have restricted access a name/subject index is available for them. There are also Russian-related materials in the records of the International Press Service of the State Department, 1948–53, and Photographic Library of the USIA, 1953–65.

RG 342: Records of the United States Air Force Commands, Activities, and Organization. Contains some ninety photographs of the Soviet Berlin zone, in 1945.

RG 395: Records of United States Army Overseas Operations and Commands. Contains duplicates of the 600 photos on the Siberian intervention in RG 111. They are on a caption list available at the archives.

4 a.   Individual screening devices are available for both 16- and 35-mm film; basic instruction will be provided, but researchers must operate the equipment themselves.

b.   Researchers must reserve the viewers in advance. Depending upon how busy the branch is, there may be virtually no wait or one of a few days.

c. All services are provided without charge except those described in 4d.

d. Subject to copyright laws and other restrictions, researchers may make video or audio copies using their own equipment; the staff will duplicate items for a fee (a price list and order forms are available). Certain government-produced or distributed films can also be purchased or rented from the NARS Stock Film Library in Arlington, Virginia (703/557-1114) and from the National Audiovisual Center (General Services Administration) in Capitol Heights, Maryland (301/763-1896).

5.   At present there are no published finding aids; a number of card catalogs (generally arranged by subject, name, and title) are the principal research tools. There are also several mimeographed caption lists and preliminary inventories that, while sometimes very incomplete and partly outdated, will provide much useful information to researchers. The record groups for which pertinent caption lists exist have been noted above in the listings themselves. The other aids include: *Still Pictures in the Audiovisual Archives Division of the National Archives,* by Mayfield S. Bray (1972); *Motion Pictures in the Audiovisual Archives Division of the National Archives,* by Mayfield S. Bray and William T. Murphy (1972); *Audiovisual Records in the National Archives Relating to World War II,* by Mayfield S. Bray and William T. Murphy (circa 1970).

Copies of these titles are available for consultation at the branches and, while the supply lasts, free to those who request a copy.

Currently the staff is also working on a list of motion picture film titles for publication.

F8   National Audiovisual Center (General Services Administration)

1 a.   *Location:*
Capitol Heights, Maryland
(301) 763-1896

Mail:
Washington, D.C. 20409

b.   8:00 A.M.–4:30 P.M., Monday–Friday

c.   Open to the public by appointment only.

d.   John H. McLean, Director

2-3.   The National Audiovisual Center was established in 1969: to serve as the central clearinghouse for all U.S. Government-produced audiovisual materials and to make federally produced audiovisual materials available to the public through distribution services (i.e., loan referrals, rentals, and sales).

In 1982 the center maintained more than 12,000 titles of audiovisual materials (mostly 16-mm motion pictures) for sale and/or rental. At least three films pertain to the USSR: *The Rise of the Soviet Navy* (1969); *The Road to the Wall* (1962), concerning the Berlin wall; and *The Battle of Russia* (1945).

4 a.   Screening facilities are available on-site.

b.   Screenings are conducted free of charge for purchasers; appointments are required.

c-d.   The center maintains a list of prices for all items for sale and rental.

5. The center maintains a master data file on more than 20,000 audiovisual materials produced by the U.S. Government; the file is constantly updated. At the same time, the center has published a catalog entitled *Reference List of U.S. Government Produced Audiovisual Materials* (1978), with a 1980 supplement both of which are available without charge from this office. The brochure *National Audiovisual Center, Services to the Public* is also available without charge.

F9   National Gallery of Art—Photographic Archives

1 a.   *Fourth Street and Constitution Avenue, NW*
Washington, D.C. 20565
(202) 842-6026

b-c.   Closed to the public. Open to researchers by appointment only.

d.   Ruth Philbrick, Curator

2-3.   There are some 1,200 photographs here of Russian paintings. The photos, all taken in this century, show various schools of painting of the fifteenth to the eighteenth centuries and also works of the nineteenth and twentieth centuries. The photos are arranged in roughly chronological order, according to the period of the work shown, and then by geographic area.

Russianists should note that the archives staff is attempting to set up an exchange of materials with the Hermitage Museum in Leningrad. Thus the future potential of the archives for research in the Soviet field is substantial.

National Geographic Society Film Collection   See entry M51

National Library of Medicine   See entry A48

F10   National Museum of Natural History (Smithsonian Institution)— National Anthropological Archives Photograph Collection

1 a.   *Natural History Building, Room 60-A*
Tenth Street and Constitution Avenue, NW
Washington, D.C. 20560
(202) 357-1986

b.   9:00 A.M.–5:00 P.M., Monday–Friday

c.   Open to the public by appointment.

d.   Herman Viola, Director
Paula R. Fleming, Assistant Director
James R. Glenn, Archivist

2-3.   The Photograph Collection consists of an estimated 150,000 items (mainly black-and-white photographs), the majority of which date from the 1860s to 1930s. Since the primary focus of the collection is Native American peoples, coverage on Russia/ USSR is relatively limited. There are approximately 200–300 photographs of various

European Russians as well as some Siberian Eskimo material. These holdings remain uncataloged and dispersed throughout the collection.

4 c-d. Photocopying facilities are available.

5. A card index is maintained.

National Space Science Data Center   See entry G8

F11   Naval Historical Center (Navy Department)—Curator Branch—Photographic Section

1 a. *Washington Navy Yard*
M at Eighth streets, SE
Washington, D.C. 20374
(202) 433-2765

  b. 9:00 A.M.–4:00 P.M., Monday–Friday

  c. Open to researchers by appointments. (Mail inquiries should be addressed to the center *without* specifying the branch or section.)

2. The archives have at least 500 photos relating to the Soviet Union and prerevolutionary Russia.

3. These unclassified photographs are overwhelmingly of ships. The greatest concentration of items dates from the 1950s. Photos of the pre-Soviet era are in less abundance, and for the 1930s–40s the holdings are not very good. More recent photos may also be found in the collections of the Defense Audiovisual Agency (entry F1).

4 c-d. Prints of some holdings should be available from the Defense Audiovisual Agency. Orders for reproduction can be directed there.

5. An index arranged by name, class of ship or aircraft, and place where the photo was taken is maintained.

F12   Northern Virginia Community College (Loudoun Campus)—Film Collection

NOTE: The Northern Virginia Community College (NOVA) film collection is shared by the five campuses of the college—Alexandria (703/845-6226), Annandale (703/323-3127), Manassas (703/368-0184), Woodbridge (703/670-2191), and Loudoun (703/323-4566). The Russian/Soviet films are located at the Loudoun campus, but they may be requested and sent to any campus. There is a single catalog.

1 a. *Loudoun Campus Learning Resource Center*
1000 Harry Flood Byrd Highway, Room 217B
Sterling, Virginia 22170
(703) 323-4566
(703) 323-4507 (after hours and Saturdays)

b. During the school year: 8:00 A.M.–10:00 P.M., Monday–Thursday
8:00 A.M.–5:00 P.M., Friday

c. Open to the public on-site use.

d. Bernadine C. Thomas, Director

2-3. This collection of approximately 1,000 films, all purchased since 1970, serves the academic programs at the college. Six of the thirteen feature films in the collection are Russian; included are three by Eisenstein *(Alexander Nevsky, Ivan the Terrible,* and *Ten Days that Shook the World*) and Pudovkin's *Mother.*

4 a. Projectors and video analysis equipment are available.

b. Reservations are not required, but researchers should call ahead to check on the availability of a specific title.

5. A descriptive film catalog with elaborate indexing is maintained at each learning resource center and at other locations on each campus. A card file for videotapes is also maintained.

F13 Prince George's County Public Libraries

1 a. *Administrative Offices:*
6532 Adelphi Road
Hyattsville, Maryland 20782
(301) 699-3500 (Films Service)

b. 9:00 a.m–5:00 P.M., Monday–Friday
Hours vary slightly for branches and between winter and summer.

c. Any adult eighteen years of age or older with a Prince George's County Memorial Library borrower's card or a borrower's card from a library participating in the Maryland Public Library Service Agreement may borrow films. Nonresidents who do not otherwise qualify to borrow films may pay an annual nonresident fee and obtain full borrowing privileges (including films) for the year.
Films cannot be used for commercial or fundraising activities. They cannot be televised or duplicated in any way.
Borrowers may pick up and return films to any one of twenty different branches of the library or the offices above, but reservations must be made at the administrative offices. The number of films borrowed at one time is not limited.
The loan period is overnight on weekdays (i.e., pick up one morning, afternoon, or evening requires return by closing time the following day). Films picked up on Friday or Saturday, however, may be returned on Monday.

d. Kent Moore, Head, Films Division

2. This collection of 16-mm films has an extraordinary number of excellent domestic and foreign feature films, silent and sound. It may be the largest holding of Soviet feature motion pictures in the area, containing at present more than ten of the most significant classics of Soviet cinema. It also has a number of Western-made films based on Russian/Soviet literary works or otherwise relating to the USSR.

3. Among the pictures available to borrowers are:
By Sergei Eisentein—*Strike* (1924), his first film; *Battleship Potemkin* (1925)—the

most famous film by this or any other Soviet director; *Ten Days that Shook the World* (or *October*; 1927), a tribute to the 1917 revolution on its tenth anniversary; *The General Line* (or *Old and New*; 1929), on the Soviet peasant just before collectivization; *Alexander Nevsky* (1937), the medieval epic of Slavs versus Teutons, and anti-Nazi propaganda of great fascination; *Ivan the Terrible,* parts 1 and 2 (1945–46), his final, unfinished masterwork.

By V. I. Pudovkin—*Mother* (1926), a fine adaptation of the Gor'kii novel; *Storm over Asia* (1927), Mongols against British Expeditionary Forces in Siberia; *End of Saint Petersburg* (1927), commissioned to celebrate the October Revolution and interesting to compare with Eisenstein's *Ten Days.*

By Alexander Dovzhenko—*Arsenal* (1929), about World War I and the revolt in Kiev.

By Dziga Vertov—*Man with a Movie Camera* (1928), a highly experimental, engrossing "documentary." *The Colt*, a 1960 adaptation of a Sholokhov short story (about forty minutes long).

The Birth of Soviet Cinema (1972), a documentary on Soviet cinema in the 1920s, including clips from many of the films listed above (about fifty minutes long).

Shorter documentaries are available on Soviet ballet, folk dancing, and the Stalin-Trotskii struggle of the 1920s. All Russian-language films have English subtitles. Their physical quality ranges from fair to good.

4 a.   Borrowers must furnish their own 16-mm sound projector.

b.   Reservations for films are not required, but more popular films usually need to be reserved a month or two ahead. Reservations can be made up to two years in advance in person, by mail, or by phone and only at the administrative offices.

c.   The rental fee ranges from one to four dollars depending on the film's length.

5.   The library publishes an annual *Film Catalog* plus periodic supplementary listings, which is for sale at all branches (current price is three dollars).

Senate Historical Office   See entry K30

F14   Suburban Washington Library Film Service

1 a.   *Alexandria Library Film Service*
5651 Rayburn Avenue
Alexandria, Virginia 22311
(703) 998-0650

Arlington County Department of Libraries Film Service
1015 North Quincy Street
Arlington, Virginia 22201
(703) 527-4777

Fairfax County Public Library Film Service
5502 Port Royal Road
Springfield, Virginia 22151
(703) 321-9166

Montgomery County Department of Public Libraries Film Service
99 Maryland Avenue
Rockville, Maryland 20850
(301) 279-1944

Loudoun County Public Library Film Service
52 West Market Street
Leesburg, Virginia 22075
(703) 777-0369

b. Hours vary among the participating libraries. Borrowers should call in advance.

c. Films are loaned to adults for a twenty-four-hour period according to the regulations of the member library system. Borrowers usually must have a borrower's card from the participating library system. Films may not be loaned to public schools for curricular purposes nor may they be used for commercial or fundraising activities.

2-3. Out of a total collection of some 4,000 16-mm films, fourteen pertain to Russia/USSR. Six are documentaries that portray various regions of the country (e.g., Siberia, Leningrad) or give overviews of the USSR in general. The other eight are film versions of literature classics (e.g., Gogol's *The Overcoat*).

4 a. Viewing facilities are not available. Borrowers must furnish their own 16-mm projector.

b. Reservations for films should be made three weeks in advance.

c. No fees are charged.

d. Films cannot be shown on television or duplicated in any manner.

5. The *Suburban Washington Library Film Service Catalog* (1981), plus supplements, may be purchased for $3.50 at any of the participating library film service offices or branches.

Washington Post **Library   See entry Q24**

G Data Banks

Data Bank Entry Format (G)

1. General Information
    a. *address; telephone number(s)*
    b. hours of service
    c. conditions of access (including fees charged for information retrieval)
    d. name/title of director and key staff members

2. Description of Data Files (hard-data and bibliographic-reference)

3. Bibliographic Aids Facilitating Use of Storage Media

Introductory Note

Many Washington-area government agencies, libraries, and research organizations maintain their own series of subscriptions to a wide variety of data banks that can be drawn upon throughout the U.S. and, in many cases, throughout the world. The listing included here is primarily of those data-base systems developed or prepared in Washington containing significant resource material of potential interest to Soviet-area specialists. Because of the nature of the medium, the majority of the collections listed below are of scientific or economic data.

G1   Agency for International Development (AID)—Economic and Social Data Bank

1 a. *Economic and Social Data Services Division*
      Office of Development Information and Utilization
      Scientific and Technical Bureau
      Pomponio Plaza, Room 509
      1735 North Lynn Street
      Arlington, Virginia 22209
      (703) 235-9170

   b. 8:45 A.M.–5:30 P.M., Monday–Friday

c. The data bank is primarily for the use of AID personnel. At present individual researchers cannot use the Economic and Social Division's terminals; the staff, however, will conduct data searches on specific topics for researchers as time permits.

d. Anette Binnendijk, Division Chief

2. AID's Economic and Social Data Bank contains some 450 worldwide (macro) country-level data elements (variables) obtained from the World Bank/IMF, UN, Agriculture Department, AID, Census Bureau, and other U.S. Government agencies. These variables include such major social and economic indicators as population, birth/death rates, life expectancy, literacy, national accounts, central government expenditures, international trade (by commodity and trading partner), agricultural and food production, and military expenditures. The data spans a thirty-year period for many categories. While the majority of the material collected pertains to developing nations, scattered data on the Soviet Union and other socialist countries also figure in; of these, the demographic and trade data are the most complete. Researchers should note that the data are received and included without being edited (with the exception of the AID official file); thus their reliability is directly related to the accuracy of the source material.

3. Many of the data bank's statistics are available in hard-copy form.

G2 Agriculture Department (USDA)—International Economics Division

1 a. *500 Twelfth Street, SW*
Washington, D.C. 20250
(202) 382-9831

b. 8:30 A.M.–5:00 P.M., Monday–Friday

c. The data base is maintained primarily for internal use; researchers should make special arrangements to visit the center.

d. Ed Overton, Data Coordinator, Economic Research Service

2. Data files of direct or indirect use to students of Soviet economics include indexes of world agricultural production from 1950 to the present compiled by the Agriculture Department; USDA-generated data on international grain-crop acreage and yields; international trade data compiled by the UN (1967–present); trade and production data (1966–present) compiled by the UN Food and Agriculture Organization (FAO); and population data by country (1950–present) compiled by AID.

In addition, the Data Systems Division (Eldon Hildebrandt, director, 202/447-5255), of the department's Foreign Agricultural Service, maintains USDA-generated machine-readable data on foreign agricultural production, supply and distribution (1960–present); and extensive U.S. Census Bureau data on U.S. trade with foreign countries.

Arms Control and Disarmament Agency—Documents Data Base
See entry K3

Brookings Institution—Social Science Computation Center   See entry H7

Census Bureau Data Bases   See entry G3

G3 Commerce Department Data Bases

1 a. *Fourteenth Street between Constitution Avenue and E Street, NW*
Washington, D.C. 20230
(202) 377-2000 (Information)

2. Data bases of interest to USSR-area specialists may be found in several bureaus, divisions, and subunits of the Commerce Department. The availability of tapes to researchers for use or purchase varies from office to office.

CENSUS BUREAU

The Foreign Trade Division (FTD) can make available magnetic tapes of foreign trade statistics of the U.S., including U.S. imports from and exports to the USSR. The FTD Trade Information Office (301/763-5140) can provide order forms and additional information. Ruth Mangarro of the FTD's Special Reports Branch (301/763-7700) can help researchers obtain tapes of import and export statistics designed to meet specific research needs.

INTERNATIONAL TRADE ADMINISTRATION

The Office of Trade Data and Analysis (202/377-2456) maintains a data base containing perhaps the most extensive computerized East-West trade information in the D.C. area. Online are data on U.S. trade with all other countries individually (1969–present). Offline are figures for the trade of the fourteen largest Western countries with each socialist country. Information desired may generally be obtained in one day (overnight). Researchers have free access to runs made by the office. Robert Teal (202/377-5994) is the staff specialist on East-West trade.

NATIONAL BUREAU OF STANDARDS

In the Reference Department (301/921-2228) is the highly technical National Standard Reference Data System (NSRDS) through which the accuracy of data reported in primary research literature (including literature from the Soviet Union) on the physical and chemical properties of well-characterized materials or systems is assessed, and compilations of critically evaluated data that serve as reliable standards for the scientific and technical community are prepared. Copies of the *National Standard Reference Data System Publications List, 1964–1980*—which includes a section on Russian translations—are available without charge.

G4 Defense Technical Information Center (DTIC) (Defense Department)

1 a. *Cameron Station, Building 5*
Alexandria, Virginia 22314
(703) 274-7633 (Documentation Information)

   b. 7:30 A.M.–4:00 P.M., Monday–Friday

   c. Open only to Defense Department (DOD) personnel and authorized staff members of research organizations under DOD contract.

   d. Hubert E. Sauter, Administrator

2. DTIC is a computerized repository of more than 1.4 million classified and unclassified research reports produced or funded by the DOD. Virtually all formal research results from projects funded by DOD are deposited here. The strength of the collection is in the physical sciences, technology, and engineering as they relate to national defense and military matters. Some social science research pertinent to the USSR may also be in the facility. The bibliographic data base is on computer tape; full reports are available on microfiche. Declassified materials in the data base may be purchased through the National Technical Information Service (entry Q13), which announces the DTIC reports released to it through the publication *Government Reports, Announcements, and Indexes.*

3. DTIC distributes a confidential biweekly *Technical Abstracts Bulletin* of recent acquistions to registered users of DOD contracts. No published bibliographies of DTIC holdings are available to the public.

G5   Educational Resources Information Center (ERIC)

1 a. *National Institute of Education (NIE)*
Education Department
1200 Nineteenth Street, NW
Washington, D.C. 20208
(202) 254-7934 (Information)
(202) 254-5500 (Central ERIC)

b. 8:00 A.M.–4:30 P.M., Monday–Friday

c. Open to the public; the data base may be accessed at several points nationwide. For the (biennial) *Directory of ERIC Search Services* which lists organizations providing computerized searches of the ERIC data base and the various fee schedules, write ERIC Processing and Reference Facility, 4833 Rugby Avenue, Suite 301, Bethesda, Maryland 20814, telephone number (301/656-9723).

d. Charles Hoover, Chief

2. ERIC is a national information system designed to provide ready access to descriptions of exemplary programs, research and development efforts, and related information that can be used in developing more effective educational programs. Central ERIC and its sixteen clearinghouses nationwide (each specializing in a different multi-discipline educational area) collect documents (current research findings, project and technical reports, speeches, and unpublished manuscripts, books, and professional journal articles) and screen them. Items selected are abstracted, indexed, cataloged, annotated, entered into the ERIC computer data base and announced in ERIC reference publications. The data base may be searched manually or by computer according to author, subject, or institution descriptors. The full text of the documents cited may be purchased in microfiche or hard copy form from: ERIC Document Reproduction Service, P.O. Box 190, Arlington, Virginia 22210.

The system presently contains more than 400,000 items, some 1,000 of which pertain to Soviet education.

3. Several handbooks, indexes, and pamphlets published by or for ERIC are available.

Resources in Education (RIE) is a monthly abstract journal announcing recently completed research reports, descriptions of outstanding programs, and other educational documents. Each issue contains subject, author, and institutional source indexes. Semiannual cumulative indexes are available.

Current Index to Journals in Education (CIJE) is a monthly guide to more than 750 education-related periodicals, indexed by subject, author, and journal title. Annual cumulative indexes are available.

Thesaurus of ERIC Descriptors contains the vocabulary used to index documents entered into ERIC.

The biennial *Directory of ERIC Microfiche Collections* lists collections in the U.S. and overseas.

The series *ERIC Information Analysis Products* provides bibliographies of substantive publications entered into the system and previously announced in RIE or CIJE.

Pocket Guide to ERIC is the most recent brochure introducing ERIC to potential users.

Institute for Defense Analyses—Computer Facility   See entry H20

G6   International Reporting Information Systems (IRIS)

1 a. *1725 Jefferson Davis Highway, Eighth Floor*
    Arlington, Virginia 22202
    (703) 892-1600

  b. 8:30 A.M.–5:30 P.M., Monday–Friday
    9:00 A.M.–12:00 P.M., Saturday

  c. Open to subscribers only.

  d. Gustaf Douglas, Chairperson
    Barry Kelly, Chief Executive Officer
    Paul H. Boeker, Senior Vice President, Information and Analysis
    Lee T. Feldman, Senior Vice President, Systems and Services

2. IRIS is an international information and analysis service designed to provide its clients—businesses, government agencies, and international organizations—with timely, comprehensive coverage of commercial, economic, and political developments throughout the world. At the heart of the IRIS system is its computer-sort capability, which continuously takes in a mass of data collected from international, national, and local wire services, newspapers, selected periodicals, broadcasts, and government releases. A large full-time staff of leading international analysts and a worldwide correspondent network of experienced journalists and other professionals support IRIS's advanced computer technology. Through a sophisticated software profile system that defines the individual information requirements of each IRIS client, the IRIS computer screens information in seven languages (including Russian) and delivers it to IRIS expert analysts who further distill the information into concise English-language reports. These reports are automatically sent to each client terminal. The subscriber to the IRIS system receives this customized monitoring and further in-depth evaluation to meet specific needs and interests. Consultations and management briefings with IRIS regional, country, and sectoral experts are also made available to the IRIS client.

3. Training on the IRIS system is provided to clients to facilitate search, processing, and storage of information.

NOTE: IRIS suspended operations in early 1983.

International Trade Commission—Data Bank   See entry K22

Justice Department—JURIS System   See entry K23

Library of Congress—LOCIS; National Referral Center   See entry A37

National Aeronautics and Space Administration—RECON System   See entry K25

National Agricultural Library—AGRICOLA   See entry A40

G7   National Archives and Records Service (NARS)—Machine-Readable Archives Branch (NNSR)

1 a.   *Eighth Street and Pennsylvania Avenue, NW*
Washington, D.C. 20408
(entrance from Pennsylvania Avenue only)
(202) 724-1080 (Reference)

b.   8:45 A.M.–5:15 P.M., Monday–Friday

c.   Open to the public; substantial fees are charged for documentation and computer processing. Reproduction services include copying card-to-card, tape-to-card, card-to-tape, tape-to-tape, tape-to-printout, extracts of specified information, electrostatic copying and microfiche. Tape-to-tape copying is $86 per reel. Computer time is calculated on the basis of $172 per hour, with a $57 minimum for tape-to-printout copying and a $287 minimum for tape-to-printout-extract copying. A complete fee schedule is available.

d.   Trudy H. Peterson, Chief

2.   The Machine-Readable Archives Branch, founded in 1969, locates current records on tape of government agencies, determines whether they should be made permanent and whether they should come to the National Archives and, if the agency agrees, accessions these machine-readable materials for NARS. The branch retains physical control (and legal custody) of the records. Thus this section of the archives has some nontextual holdings from different record groups. Researchers must check with staff members of various divisions and this branch, as well as in guides and inventories, to determine if the material they want is in machine-readable form. At present, the following record groups are known to include machine-readable data pertinent to Russian/Soviet studies:

RG 77: Records of the Office of the Chief of Engineers. This group contains one reel of machine-readable data from 1970 pertaining to Soviet trade with the United States.

RG 166: Records of the Foreign Agricultural Service. Data on the Soviet Union are included in statistics on U.S. agricultural imports and exports, which are contained in two files in this group. In *U.S. Agricultural Imports and Exports Trade History* data coverage is worldwide in scope, covering 1,700 agricultural or agriculture-related imports and approximately 800 agricultural or agriculture-related exports beginning in January 1967 and updated semiannually for the six-month period prior to the most current two years.

RG 197: Records of the Civil Aeronautics Board. Included here are machine-readable data from 1962 to the present pertaining to air traffic between the U.S. and the USSR by U.S. carriers.

RG 354: Records of the Economic Research Service. This group contains data (1961–71) on trade between the USSR and the member countries of the Organization for Economic Cooperation and Development.

3. The division's *Catalog of Machine-Readable Records in the National Archives of the United States* (1977) is currently out of print; a new edition is being prepared for publication in 1983.

National Bureau of Standards Data Bases   See entry G3

National Library of Medicine Data Bases   See entry A48

G8   National Space Science Data Center (National Aeronautics and Space Administration)

1 a.   *Goddard Space Flight Center, Building 26*
Greenbelt, Maryland 20771
(301) 344-7000

b.   8:00 A.M.–4:30 P.M., Monday–Friday

c.   Open to researchers, by appointment.

d.   James I. Vette, Director (301/344-7354)

2-3.   The Science Data Center maintains various data bases, computerized and otherwise. Bibliographic information, substantive data, reports and other "hard" materials on satellites and space programs of the U.S. and other countries can be found here. The Soviet Union is well represented, both in its own publications and in Western sources (most are translated). The great variety and quantity of materials available at the center make it impossible to catalog the pertinent holdings in any detail.

Staff members could indicate that among items that Russianists would find here would be photographs (e.g., up to forty on or since the Soviet Zond program), materials on the Apollo-Soiuz joint space effort, much information of Soviet satellite programs since Sputnik, and similar holdings.

Unlike the case at many computer facilities, there is normally no charge for outside researchers to use the data bases at the Goddard Center. Many brochures and informational publications are available without charge, including *Data and Distribution Services,* a basic guide to the center. Researchers may also ask to be placed on the center's distribution list for mailings. A catalog of the collection has also been issued.

G9   New York Times Information Service, Inc.—Washington Office

1 a.   *1111 Nineteenth Street, Suite 510*
Rosslyn, Virginia 22209
(703) 243-7220

b. 9:00 A.M.–5:00 P.M., Monday–Friday

c. A search costs fifty dollars for next-day or seventy-five for same-day service plus two dollars per abstract. Abstracts vary from 3 to 100 lines in length.

d. Sharon Taylor, Regional Manager

2. This computerized data base contains more than two million abstracts of news stories, editorials, and other significant items from the *New York Times* (since 1969) and more than sixty other national and international publications.

Researchers may make use of the Retail Service that can search the base for such subjects as U.S.-Soviet relations, international affairs, the foreign policies of the U.S. and the USSR, military and defense questions.

3. Researchers may write or call the Information Bank for more information about its services and a free brochure about the data base.

Senate Historical Office   See entry K30

SRI Institute Data Base   See entry H28

State Department—FAIM Data Base   See entry K32

Transportation Department—TRISNET   See entry K33

G10   United Nations Environment Program/International Referral System (UNEP/INFOTERRA)—U.S. International Environmental Referral Center (USIERC)

1 a. *U.S. Environmental Protection Agency*
401 M Street, SW (PM-213)
Washington, D.C. 20460
(202) 382-5917

b. 8:00 A.M.–4:30 P.M., Monday–Friday

c. Open to the public.

d. Carol Alexander, Director
Charlene S. Sayers, Source Coordinator

2. UNEP was created in 1972 as an independent UN agency with headquarters in Nairobi, Kenya. INFOTERRA, established within the UNEP structure, is a network of more than 100 national and sectoral Focal Points in participating countries (including the U.S. and USSR) that identify and register sources of environmental information and transmit these sources in a unified format to the system's central data bank in Geneva, Switzerland. The U.S. National Focal Point, named the U.S. International Environment Referral Center (USIERC), was established in 1975 within the U.S. Environmental Protection Agency. The Soviet Focal Point is the Department of International Economic, Scientific, and Technical Organizations of the State Committee for Science and Technology in Moscow.

The data consist of more than 7,000 sources of environmental information classified into approximately 1,000 computer-coded subject areas (from "air pollution" and "energy sources" to "land use" and "waste-water treatment") and fed into the continually updated *INFOTERRA International Directory* (ten volumes), which is accessed manually by the USIERC staff. The data can be searched geographically as well as topically. At present the *Directory* lists forty-eight separate Soviet sources. U.S. sources concerned with Soviet environmental questions appear in the U.S. national file. INFOTERRA neither stores information nor answers substantive questions; its task is to enable the potential user of environmental information to locate the most appropriate source of the information required.

3. Information services on INFOTERRA are available without charge. The *U.S. Directory of Environmental Sources,* 4th ed. (February 1981) is available for purchase (sixty-four dollars hard copy, four dollars microfiche) from National Technical Information Service (Q13).

ORGANIZATIONS

H Research Centers and Information Offices

Research Center and Information Office Entry Format (H)

1. *Address; Telephone Number(s)*

2. Founding Date

3. Chief Official and Title

4. Staff, Research, and/or Teaching Personnel

5. Parental Organizations

6. Principal Fields of Research and Other Activities

7. Library/Special Research Facilities (including specialized collections and unique equipment; availability to nonmenbers)

8. Recurring Meetings Sponsored by the Organization (open or closed)

9. Publications or Other Media

10. Affiliated Organizations

Introductory Note

Washington is the home of some of the nation's most prestigious research organizations, and many of these institutions are actively involved in research on Russia/USSR and its nationality components. Several of the institutions, such as the Kennan Institute for Advanced Studies (entry H23), National Council for Soviet and East European Research (entry H24), and George Washington University's Institute for Sino-Soviet Studies (entry H15), focus their work almost exclusively on Russian/Soviet-related issues and are therefore of great value to the Russianist. These, along with the many other organizations listed in this section of the *Guide,* vie for government contracts for economic, legal, military, political, and technical research. The Soviet Union—as the foremost adversary of the United States—is often the subject of these contracts.

When approaching the entries in this section, the scholar should bear in mind that many of these research organizations are advocates for a particular ideological stance, and this fact may be reflected in their work. Also, programs and personnel tend to change rapidly; a Soviet-related program may disappear from the activities of one organization only to reappear with another one at a later date.

For locating research centers not included in this section, scholars may contact the Commerce Department (entry K8), which monitors foreign contracts obtained by U.S. firms. It may also be fruitful to consult the lists prepared by various government agencies (particularly the State Department [entry K32], U.S. Information Agency [entry K35], and the Defense Department [entry K12]) for contracts awarded by U.S. Government agencies for work on or in foreign countries.

H1 Advanced International Studies Institute (AISI) (University of Miami)

1. *East-West Towers, Suite 1122*
   4330 East-West Highway
   Bethesda, Maryland 20814
   (301) 951-0818

2. 1978

3. Mose L. Harvey, Director
   Dodd L. Harvey, Director of Publications

6. AISI, associated with the University of Miami at Coral Gables, Florida, undertakes interdisciplinary research in international affairs and U.S. foreign policy; its primary focus is on Soviet studies.

7. The institute maintains a small reference library that contains one of the most complete Soviet-related collections of the Foreign Broadcast Information Service (entry Q7) and Joint Publications Research Service (entry Q10). Special arrangements can be made for visitors to use the library.

8. On occasion, AISI sponsors seminars on international affairs in which experts from the academic, business, and government communities participate.

9. AISI produces several series of publications including *Soviet World Outlook* (monthly), *AISI Special Reports* (occasional), *Occasional Papers in International Affairs,* and *Monographs in International Affairs.* A descriptive brochure on AISI containing a list of publications is available without charge. Titles of interest to the Russianist include: *Soviet Strategic Power and Doctrine: The Quest for Superiority,* by Mark E. Miller (1982); and *Crisis in Central America,* by Cleto DiGiovanni and Mose L. Harvey (1982).

H2 American Enterprise Institute for Public Policy Research (AEI)

1. *1150 Seventeenth Street, NW*
   Washington, D.C. 20036
   (202) 862-5800

2. 1943

3. William J. Baroody, Jr., President
   Richard B. Madden, Chairperson of the Board

4. AEI employs a full-time staff of 125, including directors of the various AEI divisions and resident scholars. Robert J. Pranger is the director of foreign and adjunct policy studies.

6. AEI is a nonprofit, nonpartisan research organization. The institute produces scholarly studies of public issues. In domestic affairs it works on questions of economics, energy, government and politics, health policy, law and regulation, and legislative analysis. AEI's foreign affairs and defense program brings together specialists from the academic, business, and government communities to study defense policy, diplomatic politics, ethical-philosophical questions of international relations, international cultural affairs, resources and technology, and other matters. Much of this work will interest Russianists.

An educational organization as well, AEI has a broad program of dissemination of information and research, as detailed in points 8 and 9.

7. The institute maintains a small library, but it does not represent a research resource for Russianists.

8. AEI occasionally permits graduate students to participate in its seminars. The Conversation with . . . series gives scholars and experts from business, government, labor, and the news media an opportunity to meet and discuss important public policy matters.

For further information about conferences and meetings sponsored by AEI, write to Marvin Esch, director, Seminars and Programs, or to Robert Pranger, director, International Programs. Researchers may be placed on the promotional mailing list to receive the quarterly *Memorandum* with news of AEI issuances and activities.

9. The institute has an extensive publication program. Of most interest to Soviet-area specialists will be the foreign affairs studies and special analyses, many of which directly or indirectly concern the USSR. Legislative analyses and the results of debates, meetings, and symposia on foreign affairs and defense questions have also appeared. Some studies of note are: *Soviet Advances in the Middle East,* by George Lenczowski (1972). *Soviet Trends: Implications for U.S. Security,* by William R. Kintner and Robert L. Pfaltzgraff, Jr. (1971), *U.S.-Soviet Detente: Past and Future,* by Vladimir Petrov (1975). The institute's annual report and annual list of AEI publications is available without charge.

To its own staff and to legislative and executive branches of the federal government AEI distributes the daily *News Digest* that summarizes major stories from some fifty daily American newspapers, news programs of the three main television networks, and the wire services.

AEI publishes five periodicals: *AEI Economist*; *Foreign Policy and Defense Review,* *Inflation Watch*; *Public Opinion*; and *Regulation.*

AEI also produces, and some 500 television and radio stations broadcast, an ongoing series of public affairs programs with distinguished guests participating in discussion and question-and-answer sessions. Referred to as Public Policy Forums, these programs have featured academicians, journalists, and politicians with a variety of views on important national and international issues. One-hour video and audio cassettes of these programs are available to schools and the public.

For college and university libraries worldwide, AEI has established Public Policy Research centers, which it supplies with all its research and reference materials, including publications and the audio cassettes of its telecasts.

H3   American University—Foreign Area Studies (FAS)

1.   *5010 Wisconsin Avenue, NW*
     Washington, D.C. 20016
     (202) 686-2769

2.   FAS, 1955.

3.   William Evans-Smith, Director

4.   FAS employs more than thirty persons, some eighteen of whom are professional researchers working in various multidisciplinary teams. Other staff members provide library, editorial, secretarial, and administrative services.

5.   FAS is an integral part of American University, though located off-campus, and is operated under a contract between the university and the Army Department.

6.   FAS publishes books in a series entitled Country Studies, which evaluate contemporary society in particular countries. Attention is given to the various elements of society—describing origins and traditions, dominant beliefs and values, the community of interests and forms of association, and the nature of access to economic and political power. Of paramount consideration are the expectations of the people; their affections and disaffections; and their attitudes toward each other, toward the social, political, economic, and national security systems under which they live, and toward the conditions of their daily life. Although focusing on the present, each study strives toward a dynamic rather than a static portrayal. Contemporary society is examined in the context of its historical antecedents, current development, and pressures for and against further change—all with a view to revealing past trends and future possibilities. The publications vary from 300 to 800 pages, with a 450-page average. Optimum use is made of figures and tables for presentation of maps and statistical material, and half-tone photography and country specific illustrations are featured. Country Studies are available on the Soviet Union and all East European countries.

7.   The FAS library is an unusual facility. Designed to meet the special research needs of FAS staff, the holdings reflect an emphasis on the most current and reliable (secondary) sources of information on more than 100 nations covered in the publications. Periodical subscriptions account for the major part of acquisitions. Some unusual scholarly materials, not readily available elsewhere in the area, may also be be found here. The library can provide bibliographic assistance for its own and other Washington collections, has photocopying facilities, and is open to researchers. Russianists interested in using the facility should call FAS for more information.

9.   Country Studies may be purchased from GPO bookstores throughout the United States.

H4   Analytic Services, Inc. (ANSER)

1.   *400 Army-Navy Drive*
     Arlington, Virginia 22202
     (703) 979-0700

2.   1958

3. John A. England, President
(General inquiries should be directed to Robin Taylor, personnel manager.)

4. The technical staff (researchers and analysts) numbers 120.

6. ANSER is an independent, nonprofit research corporation. It produces studies and analyses to assist government agencies, primarily the air force, in development planning, requirements assessment, program evaluation, and resource allocation. Most of the work is classified and concerns weapons systems, technical aircraft questions, and similar matters.

7. Use of the library is strictly limited to the staff.

9. ANSER's catalog of publications is not available to a general audience, but researchers may receive a descriptive brochure without charge.

H5 Atlantic Council of the United States

1. *1616 H Street, NW*
Washington, D.C. 20006
(202) 347-9353

2. 1962

3. Kenneth Rush, Chairperson
June Haley, Librarian

4. The council employs a full-time staff of about ten. The number of people associated with the council's Working Groups at any particular time ranges from 200 to 300 individuals drawn from the academic, business, and government communities.

5. The Atlantic Council of the United States is the American member of the North Atlantic Treaty Organization (there are similar organizations in each NATO country).

6. A nonprofit organization working to encourage and strengthen economic, military, political, and social ties and institutions between NATO and OECD nations, the council considers a wide range of issues and problems. Many research projects, which are carried on by Working Groups of fifty or so individuals, inevitably relate to the Soviet Union and Soviet-American relations.

7. The council's library of more than 1,500 books and 150 current periodicals is open to researchers for on-site use. Appointments are recommended.

9. The research and policy recommendations of the council's working groups often appear in published form as articles in *The Atlantic Community Quarterly* or in *Policy Papers* or as monographs. Recent *Policy Paper* titles include: *Toward a Consensus on Military Service* (1982), *The Credibility of the NATO Deterrent: Bringing the NATO Deterrent up to Date* (1981), and *The Soviet Merchant Marine: Economic and Strategic Challenge to the West* (1979).
    The council also publishes a monthly newsletter, *Atlantic Community News*. A brief descriptive brochure, *Issues and Options: The Work Program of the Atlantic Council of the United States,* and a publication list are available without charge.

10. The council is affiliated with the Paris-headquartered Atlantic Institute for International Affairs, American Council of Young Political Leaders (entry N2), and Committee on Atlantic Studies.

H6 Battelle Memorial Institute—Washington Operations

1. *2030 M Street, NW*
    Washington, D.C. 20036
    (202) 785-8400

2. 1925

3. George Johnson, Vice President and Director, Washington Operations

4. The Washington office employs approximately 100–110 people. One or two staff analysts here have had many years of work in the Soviet field.

5. The institute is headquartered in Columbus, Ohio.

6. Battelle produces research for both government and industry. Its work is not confined to Soviet or even international affairs. Among the subjects it does examine are East-West trade; economic, political, and social trends in the USSR; and Soviet industry and technology.

7. The main library and research facilities for the institute are located in Columbus. For example, all materials received from the Soviet Union are sent to Ohio.

9. The annual bibliography *Papers and Articles Published* may be obtained from Columbus. Recent lists have contained a number of titles in the Soviet field.

H7 Brookings Institution

1. *1775 Massachusetts Avenue, NW*
    Washington, D.C. 20036
    (202) 797-6000

2. 1927 (merging three earlier existing institutions)

3. Bruce MacLaury, President

4. The institution's Research Programs maintain a staff of about thirty-one senior fellows, eleven research associates, twenty-nine research assistants, and a number of consultants and other supportive staff. Each program also has a large associated staff. The Advanced Study Program, Social Science Computation Center, and Publications staff add another fifty-five personnel members.

6. Brookings is a private, non-profit organization producing research and disseminating information on economics, foreign policy, government, and the social sciences. There is a research program for each of the first three subjects; other divisions are noted under point 4.

  The Advanced Study Program conducts conferences, roundtable discussions, seminars, and other activities designed to bring together government officials (federal, state, and local) and people from academia, business, and other areas.

  In addition, the institution makes the following awards to researchers: appointments in the Guest Scholar, Visiting Professor, and Younger Scholar Programs; Economic Policy Fellowships; Federal Executive Fellowships; Research Fellowships; and Science Policy Fellowships.

7. The Brookings library is a minor resource for Russianists: it contains a total of approximately 500–600 books on economics, history, and political science in the Russian/Soviet area. It is also a depository for UN publications. (Telephone: 202/797-6240.)

The Social Science Computational Center (202/797-6180) has a computer data base of mostly numerical data and offers a number of related computer and computational services. The center is for staff members but also serves other nonprofit users, with a strong preference for organizations over individuals. A fee schedule for use is available, and researchers should telephone before visiting to check on the availability of staff assistance.

8. The institution sponsors a series of seminars and roundtable luncheons through the Research and the Advanced Study programs. They are usually attended by invitation only.

9. Brookings issues an annual list of its publications in print and in preparation. Recent titles of note: *Diplomacy of Power: Soviet Armed Forces as a Political Instrument*, by Stephen S. Kaplan(1981); *Soviet Leadership in Transition*, by Jerry F. Hough, (1980); *Soviet Air Power in Transition*, by Robert P. Berman (1978); and *The Soviet Military Buildup and U.S. Defense Spending*, by Barry M. Blechman et al. (1977).

Carnegie Endowment for International Peace—Washington Office
See entry M28

H8   Center for Defense Information (CDI)

1. *303 Capitol Gallery West*
   600 Maryland Avenue, SW
   Washington, D.C. 20024
   (202) 484-9490

2. 1972

3. Rear Admiral (ret.) Gene R. La Rocque, Director

4. The center has a staff of five analysts, up to five research interns, and five administrative workers. The Soviet-area specialist is David T. Johnson.

5. CDI is a project of the New York-based Fund for Peace.

6. U.S. military and foreign policy are the center's main fields of research. Of interest to Soviet-area researchers will be the work on Soviet military capability and economic or political questions related to the military in the USSR. In studying current defense issues, CDI seeks to present an alternate view to that of the Pentagon.

7. The library, with a collection of some 3,000 volumes, is strong in government documents, Defense Department publications, and (post-1960) congressional hearings that bear on military and foreign affairs matters. Its periodical holdings on the same subjects are extensive. Only thirty to forty books in the library deal specifically with the Soviet military. The vertical file collection—with newspaper clippings, magazine articles, and press releases—has twenty folders relating to the USSR and its foreign policy and military. The library also has data on Soviet weaponry and a collection of CIA documents on Soviet and East Bloc governments, leadership, and economies.

Additionally, CDI maintains an audiovisual collection of about 150 videotapes, many of which concern the Soviet military.

The library is open to the public, 9:00 A.M. to 5:00 P.M., Monday through Friday; materials are not circulated.

8. On occasion the center sponsors a series of seminars on defense issues. Scholars should call for information and an invitation to these sessions, which are open to the public without charge.

9. CDI publishes a short (eight-to-twelve-pages) monthly newsletter, *The Defense Monitor,* devoted to selected military-related problems. The center also produces articles, conference reports, and monographs—the latter in a series called Military Monographs, some of which concern the Soviet Union. A title of interest is *Current Issues in U.S. Defense Policy,* ed. David T. Johnson and Barry R. Schneider (New York: Praeger, 1976).

10. CDI, Center for International Policy (entry H9), and the Center for National Security Studies (entry H10) are affiliated as projects of the Fund for Peace.

H9 Center for International Policy (formerly Institute for International Policy)

1. *120 Maryland Avenue, NE*
Washington, D.C. 20002
(202) 544-4666

2. 1975

3. Donald L. Ranard, Director

4. The center has a staff of about six professional analysts and some ten outside consultants.

5. The center is an affiliate of the New York-based Fund for Peace.

6. Research focuses on human rights issues but also covers U.S. national foreign policies (especially with Third World countries) and international affairs. Economic and financial relations—including trade and investment matters, foreign aid, and loans—are of major concern.

The staff also considers Soviet involvement in the Third World, particularly Indochina.

8. On occasion the center sponsors seminars and conferences on a variety of topics. Scholars should call for more information.

9. The bimonthly *International Policy Report* contains special studies on topics researched by the staff. The *Report* is distributed to many public officials, international and U.S. Government agencies, the media, and various organizations. The subscription rate is nine dollars per year.

10. The center is affiliated with the Center for Defense Information (entry H8) and Center for National Security Studies (entry H10). All are projects of the Fund for Peace.

H10 Center for National Security Studies (CNSS)

1. *122 Maryland Avenue, NE*
   Washington, D.C. 20002
   (202) 544-5380

2. 1974

3. Morton Halperin, Director

6. CNSS promotes its stated objective—"to reduce government secrecy, to limit the surveillance or manipulation of lawful political activity, and to protect the rights of Americans to write and speak on issues affecting the national security"—through litigation on behalf of victims of abuses by intelligence agencies and for release of documents under the Freedom of Information Act. The center staff also monitors legislation affecting intelligence agencies and government secrecy, testifies before congressional committees, appears on radio and television, and speaks before groups around the country. CNSS staff also writes and publishes books, reports, articles, and pamphlets on national security and civil liberties questions.

7. The library is a small facility containing some 2,000 books and reports, plus journals, newsletters, congressional hearings, and CIA documents obtained under the Freedom of Information Act. The library is open to researchers by appointment. Photocopying facilities are available.

9. CNSS issues a number of publications including a monthly newsletter, *First Principles,* several books and reports on various aspects of the security establishment, and two items of particular value for researchers seeking classified government documents: *Using the Freedom of Information Act: A Step-by-Step Guide* and *The 1983 Edition of Litigation under the Federal Freedom of Information Act and Privacy Act,* 7th ed. Also useful is the report *From Official Files: Abstracts of Documents on National Security and Civil Liberties Available from the Center for National Security Studies Library,* CNSS Report No. 102 3.

10. CNSS is affiliated with the New York-based Fund for Peace and the American Civil Liberties Union.

H11 Center for Naval Analyses (CNA)

1. *2000 North Beauregard Street*
   Alexandria, Virginia 22311
   (703) 998-3500

2. 1962 (formed by combining the Operations Evaluation Group [OEG], managed by the Massachusetts Institute of Technology, with the Institute of Naval Studies, then sponsored by the Institute for Defense Analysis; the OEG was the continuation of the Navy's Antisubmarine Operations Research Group, established in 1942).

3. David B. Kassing, President

6. CNA works almost exclusively on contract for the Defense Department. The bulk of the research is classified and concerns a broad range of naval questions. Among

the activities examined are air warfare, antisubmarine warfare, fleet air defense, naval communications, submarine warfare, and tactical development and evaluation. Naval science, systems, technology, and weapons are other subjects of major interest. Some nondefense research is carried out as well, such as studies of regulation and productivity and unemployment insurance.

The research groups that perform this work are Marine Corps Operations Analysis Group; Naval Studies Group; Operations Evaluation Group; and Public Research Institute.

7. CNA has a library and computer center. The library contains both classified and unclassified material and is unavailable for measurement. To use the Technical Reference Room researchers must obtain a security clearance by making a written request to the Chief of Naval Operations, Navy Department, Washington, D.C. 20350. Similar restrictions apply to the computer center.

9. There are two indexes to CNA publications, one for classified material and the other for unclassified.

The unclassified list is available without charge; the most recent edition is *Index of Selected Publications* (through December 1981), issued in March 1982. This index, the seventh in the series, is updated periodically. Requests for copies should be directed to the Management Information Office.

All formal classified research from CNA goes to the Defense Technical Information Center (entry G4); all publications cleared for public release are available at CNA and at NTIS (entry Q13).

The annual report of CNA, available on request, should also prove valuable to researchers. These publications include information pertaining to CNA's history, organization, management, and research program.

H12 Committee on the Present Danger

1. *1800 Massachusetts Avenue, NW*
   Washington, D.C. 20036
   (202) 466-7444

2. 1976

3. Charls Walker, Chair of the Executive Committee

4. The Committee employs an administrative staff of six; 193 members are on the board of directors.

6. A private, nonprofit organization, the committee is a research and educational group that studies such issues as foreign and defense policy, the U.S.-USSR military balance, and other international security issues. Funding for the committee comes from private individuals or foundations; there is no government support. All research activities are conducted in-house.

9. The committee issues reports on foreign and defense policy issues. Recent titles include: *Has America Become Number Two? An Assessment of American Defenses and the U.S.-USSR Military Balance* (1982) and *Is the Reagan Defense Program Adequate?* (1982).

H13 Dumbarton Oaks—Center for Byzantine Studies (Harvard University)

1. *1703 Thirty-second Street, NW*
    Washington, D.C. 20007
    (202) 342-3200

2. In November 1940 Dumbarton Oaks was given to Harvard University.

3. Giles Constable, Director

4. The center has a small staff of research scholars, librarians, curators, and editorial and adminstrative personnel.

5. Dumbarton Oaks is owned by Harvard University.

6. The Center for Byzantine Studies exists to promote the study of Byzantine civilization in all its aspects, including relations with neighboring cultures. Fields of investigation include the late Roman and early Christian period and the Middle Ages generally. Comparative studies of Byzantine cultural exchanges with the Latin West, and with Slavic and Near Eastern countries, are encouraged. Kievan Rus is thus within the center's scope of interests, as are Armenia and Georgia.
    Each year a limited number of fellowships are offered to qualified postgraduate and postdoctoral students of archaeology, art history, history, philology, theology, and other disciplines to support research at Dumbarton Oaks. Fellowships are normally awarded for a full academic year (September to May). Applications and more information about these fellowships may be obtained by writing to the assistant director, Dumbarton Oaks.

7. See entries in the Libraries section (entry A17) and Film and Still Picture Collections section (entry F2).

9. The center carries on an extensive publication program. Among the series of Dumbarton Oaks titles are bibliographies, catalogs, papers, studies, and texts. They are concerned with Byzantine matters, and works on Kievan Rus and related topics have appeared (e.g., A. A. Vasiliev's study of Rus attacks on Constantinople).

10. Of the three programs of research and publication at Dumbarton Oaks, the most extensive by far is that for Byzantine studies. The other two programs are in the field of pre-Columbian art and archaeology and in the history of landscape architecture.

Dwight D. Eisenhower Institute for Historical Research (Smithsonian Institution)   See entry K31

H14 General Research Corporation

1. *7655 Old Springhouse Road*
    McLean, Virginia 22102
    (703) 893-5900

2. 1961

3. Robert E. Wengler, President

4.   About 300 professional analysts and another 200 support workers are associated with General Research Corporation.

6.   This organization studies public interest/policy questions, including those concerning defense and foreign policy. In particular, part of its work is on Soviet armed forces, strategy, tactics, and military power in broader terms. It is a private, profit-seeking corporation.

7.   The library, containing nearly 30,000 books and pamphlets and about 350 current periodicals, is closed to the public. All material of interest to Soviet area specialists held by the library, according to the librarians, is at the Defense Technical Information Center (entry G4) and should be used there. Librarian, Robert Greathouse, may be reached at extension 675 of the corporation's phone number.

8.   General Research Corporation sponsors a number of meetings and seminars of potential interest to Russianists. They occur irregularly, however, and may be either open or closed to the public and cannot be detailed here. Those interested in further information must contact the organization directly.

9.   All publications noteworthy for Soviet area specialists are at the Defense Technical Information Center (entry G4) or National Technical Information Service (entry Q13); no list of these works is generally available to the public. Researchers may write or telephone Mr. Greathouse to inquire about publications.

H15   George Washington University—Institute for Sino-Soviet Studies (ISSS)

1.   *Location:*
Gelman Library, Suite 601
2130 H Street, NW
Washington, D.C. 20052
(202) 676-6340

Mail:
Institute for Sino-Soviet Studies
George Washington University
Washington, D.C. 20052

2.   1962

3.   Dr. Gaston J. Sigur, Director

4.   Research and teaching personnel of the institute number more than twenty full- and part-time professors in such disciplines as art, economics, geography, history, language and literature, laws and political science. Most members hold joint appointments with departments of George Washington University.

5.   ISSS is an integral part of the School of Public and International Affairs of George Washington University.

6.   The institute is designed to develop and promote graduate teaching and research programs in Russian/Soviet, East European, and East Asian studies. Though ISSS is not a degree-granting division of the university, it offers students in advanced degree programs courses in their country or region of specialization. All these courses are

part of the university's regularly scheduled offerings. (See the Slavic Languages and Literatures Department, entry J4).

Among the subjects taught are Sino-Soviet relations; Russian/Soviet economics, geography, history, law and political science; and Eurocommunism and comparative communist and socialist movements. Of particular note are two interuniversity colloquia, offered weekly during the academic year, the Soviet and East European Colloquium and the East Asia Colloquium. Topics of talks given at the colloquia, generally by scholars from outside the university, cover political science and history relating to the USSR, as well as economic questions, foreign relations (U.S.-USSR, Sino-Soviet), and more.

The institute supports research by offering to scholars from around the world an opportunity to come and use its facilities (office space, library) as visiting scholars. More information about this program may be obtained from ISSS. In addition, graduate students may apply for fellowships, assistantships, and loans.

7.   ISSS library is physically separate from the main university library. In the entry for the university library in the Libraries section (A24), institute holdings are included in the total figures because the card catalog includes these titles. Details on the ISSS collection, however, are given here rather than in the library entry.

Of the more than 8,000 volumes currently in the ISSS library, perhaps 5,000 relate to Russian/Soviet affairs. These titles are in both Russian and Western languages. The largest concentrations of materials are in the fields of political science and history, but there is also much here on social questions, economics, military affairs, and other subjects.

The library receives many periodicals from and relating to the Soviet Union. Of particular interest are reports by the Foreign Broadcast Information Service and translations by the Joint Publications Research Service. Other noteworthy items are the seventy-three-volume Arno Press series Russia Observed and thirty reels of microfilm material.

In general, researchers may make on-site use of the holdings without special permission.

8.   The weekly colloquia meetings have been noted in point 6. These meetings are open by invitation. The institute also sponsors occasional lectures or other presentations by experts in the Soviet field.

9.   Members' individual monographs are published by academic and commercial presses. ISSS offers reprints of selected articles and other staff publications and publishes a major quarterly, *Journal of Northeast Asian Studies*, which includes material relevant to the Soviet Union.

H16   Georgetown University—Center for Strategic and International Studies (CSIS)

1.   *1800 K Street, NW, Suite 400*
     Washington, D.C. 20006
     (202) 887-0200

2.   1962

3.   Dr. David Abshire, President

4.   Senior research personnel number about seventy; administrative support staff total about eighty.

5.   CSIS is an off-campus branch of Georgetown University, its only affiliation.

6.   The center engages in a broad range of studies on international affairs. Research, not teaching, is the basic aim of the staff, which also seeks to inform and educate Congress, the executive branch, and the public on major current issues.

Geographic and topical divisions of research are maintained at CSIS to facilitate ongoing work. In addition to Soviet studies, for example, there are projects on African, American, European, Latin American, Middle Eastern, and Pacific·Basin studies; also economics, energy, maritime policy, and politico-military programs.

CSIS is conducting a major examination of the significant trends and developments within the Soviet Union that will shape Soviet foreign policy during the next decade. The Soviet Union is facing critical choices in the demographic, economic, military, political, social and technological spheres, all of which will affect its behavior in the international arena.

The International Research Council, a group of distinguished scholars from around the world, assists and advises the center in its programs. In general, CSIS benefits from many diverse contacts with foreign affairs specialists in the government and in the academic community worldwide.

8.   CSIS sponsors a number of important conferences of potential interest to Russianists. Some are annual and not open to the general public (e.g. a Williamsburg, Virginia, conference held for selected members of Congress). Topics for discussion vary, and participants from different countries often contribute. The International Seminar Series presents discussions of current foreign and domestic issues, led by specialists from both the public and private sectors. Interested scholars should inquire about upcoming events and about gaining access to these conferences.

9.   CSIS has an active publication program. Its monograph series, Washington Papers, contains contributions from scholars worldwide on a variety of topics. Recent topics of interest to Soviet area specialists include *Religion in the USSR*, No. 78, *East-West Technology Transfer*, No. 75, and *Soviet Energy and Western Europe*, No. 90. CSIS publishes a journal, *The Washington Quarterly*, under the editorial direction of Professor Allen Weinstein. It is a review of international and strategic issues.

Other monographs from staff members and outside scholars also appear regularly, as do occasional papers with limited distribution. Many deal with Soviet affairs.

An informational brochure and lists of publications are available without charge.

H17 Government Research Corporation (GRC)

1.   *1730 M Street, NW*
     Washington, D.C. 20036
     (202) 857-1400

2.   1969

3.   Charles Heeter, Director, Trade and International Affairs

4.   The research division of GRC employs about twenty professionals and ten support workers.

6.   GRC is an independent research organization that provides the senior manage-

ment of private and public institutions with analyses of U.S. Government domestic and international policy. GRC research in international affairs inevitably involves the USSR.

7. GRC maintains an extensive library on current public policy affairs as well as many files on East-West trade. Access to the library is permitted on an individual basis and by appointment only.

8. On occasion GRC sponsors conferences on topical international affairs issues. A rather substantial attendance fee is charged.

9. GRC publications include the weekly *National Journal* and a series of periodic reports prepared for its retainer clients. A bibliographic list of reports and descriptive brochure are available without charge.

H18 Heritage Foundation

1. *513 C Street, NE*
   Washington, D.C. 20002
   (202) 546-4400

2. 1974

3. Edwin J. Feulner, Jr., President

4. The staff, including support personnel, numbers approximately 110; about fifteen professional analysts are concerned with foreign policy issues.

6. The Heritage Foundation is a nonprofit research organization that analyzes and disseminates information on a variety of public policy issues, both domestic and foreign, from a conservative point of view. The foundation accepts no U.S. Government funds. The permanent staff of policy analysts is augmented by a number of resident and associate fellows and scholars, often on a short-term basis. The foundation sponsors a continuing series of congressional briefings, lectures, symposia, and conferences to facilitate the exchange of ideas on public policy issues. Contemporary affairs as they relate to the USSR are a part of the Heritage Foundation's research interest, particularly in the fields of national security and defense.

   A principal activity of the Heritage Foundation is its Resource Bank. This liaison service links more than 1,000 scholars participating in its Academic Bank and 300 organizations in its Resource Bank to provide public policy information to members of Congress, government officials, academicians, and journalists. Members of the Academic Bank lecture, write articles, or testify before Congress on areas of their expertise. The Witness Program solicits input from these academics and organizations to help arrange testimony for congressional committees. The Communications Network helps provide speakers for other organizations and associations. The International Visitors Center gives foreign dignitaries the opportunity to participate in the Washington policymaking process by facilitating meetings and briefings on Capitol Hill. Finally, the Resource Bank's Talent Bank helps match qualified applicants with jobs, particularly on Capitol Hill. The Resource Bank is also the distribution center for the many Heritage Foundation publications described below.

7. A small library, consisting primarily of reference works and periodicals, is maintained for staff use only.

9. The Heritage Foundation issues about 150 publications per year. Among these

are: *Policy Review,* a quarterly journal of public policy with frequent articles on the USSR; Issue Bulletins, concise analyses of specific legislation; Backgrounders, studies of longer-range policy questions (a recent issue includes "The Mirror-Image Fallacy: Understanding the Soviet Union" [1982]); International Briefing, papers on policy questions in foreign countries; Institution Analyses, papers on various political interest groups and lobbies; Critical Issues Series, longer studies of contemporary issues; plus books and several monthly newsletters, including the *National Security Record,* which has such titles as *Soviet Violations of Arms Agreements* (1982) and *Soviet Support for International Terrorism* (1981). A publication of note is *Policy Digest,* a monthly newsletter circulated without charge to business executives, which provides one-page reviews of public policy studies. A recent title is "How the Russians See Us (and Want Us to See Them)," by M. Lenczowski,

A complete list of current publications and the Heritage Foundation's annual report are available.

H19 Historical Evaluation and Research Organization (HERO)

1.   *Location:*
      2301 Gallows Road
      Dunn Loring, Virginia
      (703) 560-6427

      Mail:
      P.O. Box 157
      Dunn Loring, Virginia 22027

2.   1962

3.   Colonel (ret.) Trevor N. Dupuy, President and Executive Director

4.   The small staff numbers about fifteen to twenty persons, including an editor and a director of research.

6.   HERO is a private, nonprofit research organization that studies military history— of all times and all nations. The staff is employed by T. N. Dupuy Associates (TNDA), a private company (see entry H29). Most of its work is done for the Defense Department. In general, the staff attempts to use historical analysis as an aid to setting national security policy. The center has established an Office for the Study of Soviet Military Affairs with two staff members and two consultants. The office offers a three-day, ongoing course for a fee, entitled "Understanding the Soviet Armed Forces." The course covers the contemporary, not the historical, Soviet military.

9.   HERO has issued some of the results of its research independently, through commercial publishers, and in conjunction with TNDA. No in-house publishing is currently being done.

H20 Institute for Defense Analyses (IDA)

1.   *1801 North Beauregard Street*
      Alexandria, Virginia 22311
      (703) 845-2000

2.   1956

3.   Dr. Alexander H. Flax, President

4.   The permanent staff numbers approximately 450. One-half are trained specialists in the natural, life, and social sciences or engineering. Administrative and other support workers make up the rest of the staff. These professionals are at times joined by outside experts as consultants or short-term employees.

5.   Originally formed by the Massachusetts Institute of Technology and four other universities, IDA has evolved into an autonomous organization.

6.   The issues studied by the staff are overwhelmingly concerned with defense, military affairs, weapons, and related matters. Most of the center's work is done on contract for the Defense Department, but some is for the Central Intelligence Agency and State Department. In recent years IDA has broadened its study of domestic problems for other government agencies such as the Transportation Housing and Urban Development; Justice and Health and Human Services departments.
    In addition, IDA encourages its staff to engage in independent research not on contract and to participate in professional societies, publish independently, and teach or lecture at local universities.

7.   IDA has both a classified and unclassified library. Inquiries about the library should be addressed to Evelyn Fass, manager, Technical Information Service (703/845-2040). For information about IDA's computer and for permission to use the libraries, computer and other facilities, researchers should contact Frederick G. Latreille, vice president and deputy general manager (703/845-2400).

9.   IDA's publications list is circulated to the defense community only. Most of its classified work goes to the Defense Technical Information Center (entry G4), while its unclassified work is released to the public through the National Technical Information Service (entry Q13).

H21 Institute for Foreign Policy Analysis, Inc.—Washington Office

1.   *1612 K Street, NW*
    Washington, D.C. 20006
    (202) 463-7942

2.   1976

3.   Robert L. Pfaltzgraff, Jr., Director

4.   The Washington Office employs about ten professional analysts and twelve support personnel.

6.   The Institute for Foreign Policy Analysis, headquartered in Cambridge, Massachusetts, studies a wide range of U.S. national security and foreign policy problems, many of which inevitably pertain directly to the USSR.

8.   The institute sponsors a series of German-, Franco-, and English-American Roundtables (frequently held in Washington, D.C.), which discuss issues related to NATO and the Warsaw Pact. Conferences and seminars on topical subjects are regularly conducted; the meetings are open by invitation only. Researchers should contact the office for more information.

9.   A number of the institute's publications deal with issues pertinent to the USSR. Its brief Foreign Policy Reports include *Defense Technology and the Atlantic Alliance:*

Competition or Collaboration? (1977). Among its Special Reports are *Eurocommunism and the Atlantic Alliance* (1977) and *The Neutron Bomb: Political, Technological, and Military Issues* (1978). The institute's Conference Reports include *NATO and Its Future: A German-American Roundtable* (1978) and *NATO: The Theater Nuclear Balance* (1978). Books include *The Atlantic Community in Crisis: A Redefinition of the Atlantic Relationship* (1978), *Soviet Military Strategy in Europe* (1979), and *U.S. Strategy at the Crossroads: Two Views* (1982). Each monograph contains a list of publications. A report of operations and a descriptive brochure are available without charge.

10.   The institute is associated with the Fletcher School of Law and Diplomacy of Tufts University in Massachusetts.

H22   Institute for Policy Studies (IPS)

1.   *1901 Q Street, NW*
Washington, D.C. 20009
(202) 234-9382

2.   1963

3.   Robert Borosage, Director

4.   IPS staff consists primarily of resident fellows; project directors and research associates affiliate with the organization on a temporary contract basis. Positions as research assistants and volunteer interns are also available. The total number employed is about 100.

6.   IPS is an independent, nonprofit center for "research, education, and social invention." IPS sponsors critical examinations of the assumptions and policies that define the American posture on domestic and international issues and offers alternative strategies and visions. The institute focuses on domestic policy, human rights, international economics, and national security. The National Security Program includes two projects related to the USSR: the Arms Race and Nuclear Weapons Project (William M. Arkin, director) and the U.S.-USSR Exchange (Marcus Raskin, director), a bilateral agreement dealing with arms control.

7.   The National Security Program maintains a library which may be of interest to Russianists. A large collection of clippings and reports, dating from the early 1970s, on all aspects of national security is maintained.
The library is open to researchers; appointments are recommended.

8.   IPS sponsors meetings and seminars regularly, often dealing with U.S. national security and U.S.-Soviet relations. Researchers may wish to be put on a mailing list to receive notice of these events, which are open to the public.

9.   IPS has an extensive publication program. Recent titles of interest include: *Dubious Specter: A Skeptical Look at the Soviet Nuclear Threat*, by Fred M. Kaplan (1980); *Rise and Fall of the Soviet Threat: Domestic Sources of the Cold War Consensus*, by Alan Wolfe (1981); and *Soviet Policy in the Arc of Crisis*, by Fred Halliday (1981). A publications catalog, issued periodically, is available.

10.   The Transnational Institute, located in Amsterdam, is the European research center of IPS.

H23 Kennan Institute for Advanced Russian Studies of the Woodrow Wilson International Center for Scholars

1. *Smithsonian Institution Building*
   1000 Jefferson Drive, SW
   Washington, D.C. 20560
   (202) 357-2415

2. 1974

3. Herbert Ellison, Secretary
   Honorable George F. Kennan, Chairperson, Academic Council

4. To advise the Kennan Institute on its programs and fellowship selections, there exists an academic council consisting of ten distinguished Russian/Soviet area scholars from around the country who are chosen on a rotating basis.

5. The Kennan Institute is a component of the Woodrow Wilson International Center for Scholars (Kennan Institute fellows are simultaneously fellows of the Wilson Center; see entry H31).

6. The Kennan Institute exists to provide a center in the Washington area where advanced research on Russia/USSR can be conveniently pursued by scholars, where hospitality and various forms of assistance can be offered to foreign and out-of-town visitors who come to Washington in connection with work of this nature, where encouragement and support can be given to the cultivation of Russian/Soviet studies throughout the country, and where liaison can be maintained with similarly placed institutions abroad.

The Residential Fellowship Program plays a central role in furthering these purposes. The Kennan Institute offers fellowships of two types:

(1) Senior fellowships that enable researchers in any field of the social sciences or humanities to carry out major research projects on Russia/USSR for periods of up to a year. The deadline for receipt of applications for the following academic year is October 1, and applicants are notified of appointment decisions in late January or early February. Soviet scholars are encouraged to apply.

(2) Short-term grants to advanced scholars having particular need for the library, archival, and other specialized resources of the Washington area. This program is open to scholars at the postdoctoral level and to persons from other fields with an equivalent degree of maturity and professional achievement. Short-term grants provide a per diem stipend for up to one month. Applicants are requested to submit a concise description of their research project, a statement on their preferred and alternate dates of residence in Washington, and one supporting letter from a qualified individual. Persons with common interests who would like to pursue their projects in Washington during the same period should indicate this preference on their application. Anyone wishing to consult with specific fellows of the Kennan Institute should also make note of this interest. Applications are reviewed by members of the institute's academic council at regular intervals throughout the year; closing dates for competitions are December 1, March 1, June 1, and September 1.

For more information and application materials, scholars should contact the Secretary, Kennan Institute for Advanced Russian Studies, Woodrow Wilson International Center for Scholars, Smithsonian Institution Building, Washington, D.C. 20560.

In 1982–83 Kennan Institute fellows and their projects included: Vassily P. Aksyonov ("The Paperscape: A Novel"), Cyril E. Black ("Modern Russian and Soviet

History in Comparative Context"), Robert W. Campbell ("Soviet Economic Constraints, Strategic Doctrine, and the Military Balance with the United States"), Timothy J. Colton ("Governing Moscow, 1917–1980"), Michael Confino ("Russia, 1880–1917: Society and Politics"), Sheila Fitzpatrick ("The Politics of Soviet Industrialization, 1928–1932"), Franklyn D. Holzman ("A Comparison of U.S. and Soviet Defense Expenditures and Their Implication for Policy"), Gail Lapidus ("Ethnonationalism and Political Stability in the USSR"), Walter Reich ("The Case of Soviet Psychiatry: A Study in Moral Judgment"), Thomas H. R. Rigby ("Revolutionary Absolutism: The Mono-Organizational Society and the New Class"), James P. Scanlan ("Marxism in the USSR: A Critical Survey of Current Soviet Philosophy"), Robert C. Tucker ("Stalin: A Study in History and Personality"), Tomas A. Venclova ("Lithuanian Culture, 1945–1975: Standardization Versus Nonconformity"), and Allan Wildman ("The End of the Russian Imperial Army").

The Kennan Institute's aim of facilitating Soviet-area studies is addressed in several continuing projects. First, with the American Film Institute and the Smithsonian Institution, it has sponsored public showings of both historic and contemporary films from the USSR. Second, with the Academy of Sciences of the USSR and the International Research and Exchanges Board (IREX), has prepared a directory of the academy's research institutes in the social sciences. Third, in cooperation with IREX, the Kennan Institute seeks to promote contact among qualified Soviet and American scholars and access by American specialists to the major scholarly resources of the USSR.

7.   The Kennan Institute's library is described in the Libraries section (entry A35).

8.   Among the activities sponsored by the Kennan Institute are noon discussions (on Wednesdays except in the summer), colloquia, conferences, and evening dialogues, all on topics of interest to Russian/Soviet-area specialists. Recent conferences have dealt with "The Formative Years of Soviet Culture," "Perspectives on the Contemporary Russian Language," "R and D and the Soviet Economy," "Scientific and Technical Cooperation and Exchange between the United States and the Soviet Union," "The Soviet Challenge in Science and Engineering Training Programs," "Soviet Economic Policy Alternatives in the 1980s," "Soviet Labor Management and Industrial Productivity," and "The Soviet Rural Economy."

Activities of the institute are listed in the Wilson Center's monthly *Calendar of Events*, for which area scholars may ask to be put on the mailing list. In addition, the institute reports its activities in the *Newsletter* of the American Association for the Advancement of Slavic Studies (AAASS).

9.   The Kennan Institute has a wide-ranging program of publications: papers from conferences and other meetings are often published in the series Occasional Papers, available from the institute's office; several reference aids for scholars in the Russian/ Soviet field have been prepared, including *A Scholars' Guide to Sources of Support for Research in Russian and Soviet Studies,* by Marc D. Zlotnik, *Soviet Research Institutes Project,* by Blair Ruble with Mark H. Teeter and Eleanor Sutter (1980–81, 3 vols. and suppl.); and *The Russian Empire and the Soviet Union: A Guide to Manuscript and Archival Materials in the United States,* by Steven A. Grant and John H. Brown (Boston: G. K. Hall, 1981); the monographic series Special Studies, the first volume entitled *Industrial Labor in the USSR,* edited by Arcadius Kahan and Blair Ruble (New York: Pergamon Press, 1979); a documentary collection, cosponsored by the National Archives and Record Service, State Department, and USSR Main Archival Administration, *The United States and Russia: The Beginnings of Relations, 1765–1815* (Washington, D.C., 1980); quinquennial report of the institute's activities, 1975–79. While the fellows make independent arrangements for the publication of their research, they are encouraged to contribute to the *Wilson Quarterly.*

10. The Kennan Institute maintains close contact with academic institutions involved with Soviet studies and also with professional associations such as the AAASS and its Washington chapter and with other organizations interested in promoting international studies.

H24 National Council for Soviet and East European Research

1. *1755 Massachusetts Avenue, NW*
   Washington, D.C. 20036
   (202) 387-0168

2. 1978

3. Vladimir I. Toumanoff, Executive Director

4. The full council of fifteen members review proposals for research. The program is administered by a staff of four in Washington.

6. The National Council is a private, autonomous academic body that receives funding from government agencies to develop a substantial and high-quality program of fundamental research dealing with Soviet and East European social, political, historical and economic development. Qualified applicants may be awarded long- or short-term contracts to study these areas. Of interest to Russianists, the council is the contracting agent for the University of Illinois Soviet émigré interviewing project.

8. As they relate to ongoing projects, the council conducts seminars in cooperation with such organizations as the Kennan Institute (entry H23) and the State Department (entry K32).

National Strategy Information Center—Washington Office   See entry M53

H25 Population Reference Bureau

1. *1337 Connecticut Avenue, NW*
   Washington, D.C. 20036
   (202) 785-4664

2. 1929

3. Dr. Robert P. Worrall, President

4. The research staff, including administrative support personnel, numbers about twenty.

6. The Population Reference Bureau is a nonprofit educational organization that compiles and disseminates demographic information on national and international population issues. It relies primarily on UN publications for Soviet data. Public reference services are provided.

7. A 15,000-volume research library is open to researchers, 8:30 A.M. to 4:30 P.M., Monday through Friday. Researchers may contact Janice Beattie, a technical-information specialist, for information. Interlibrary loan service is available.

9. The bureau publishes the newsletter *Intercom* (International Newsletter on Population); *Interchange*, a quarterly newsletter with a teaching module for teachers and educators; *Population Bulletin*, with in-depth reports on population trends and policies; the annual *World Population Data Sheet* with data on population, birth rates, death rates, life expectancy, infant mortality, etc.; and such special publications as *Population Handbook: Source Book on Population, 1970–1976*, with information on more than 1,000 publications, periodicals, organizations, and other sources of information on population, and *World Population Growth and Response, 1965–1975: A Decade of Global Action* (1976). Of particular interest to Russianists is the recent article in *Population Bulletin* (1982) entitled "The Soviet Union: Population Trends and Dilemmas," by Murray Feshbach.

H26 Rand Corporation—Washington Office

1. *2100 M Street, NW*
   Washington, D.C. 20037
   (202) 296-5000

2. 1948

3. Dr. Paul Hill, Director, Washington Operations

4. The Rand Corporation office in Washington employs approximately forty researchers and another forty full- and part-time support staff (librarians, research assistants, secretaries). Dr. Paul Kozar is a Soviet specialist.

5. The Washington office is an affiliate of the Rand Corporation of Santa Monica, California, a private, nonprofit research corporation.

6. Rand describes its own purpose as "research, and only that, on matters affecting the public interest," listing the following as research areas: air force logistics and support; applied science and technology; climate dynamics; communications; criminal justice; defense strategy and forces; economics, politics, and technology; education; energy, environment, and natural resources; health; housing; human resources; information systems; international studies; regional and urban problems; and research, development, and acquisition of systems. Organizationally, the corporation's research programs are divided into four branches: Domestic Programs Division, Institute for Civil Justice, National Security/Office of the Secretary of Defense (OSD) Division, and National Security/Project Rand Division. The corporation runs a computation center and the Rand Graduate Institute in California.

7. The library of the Washington office is closed to non-Rand personnel, but an interlibrary loan service is available for all nonclassified material, except Rand publications, which are only available through sale. Unclassified holdings are small—only a few thousand volumes—and are mostly in the social sciences.

9. Rand has a most extensive publication program. Each year several hundred technical reports and professional papers are issued under its own imprint; another large number of papers appears in journals; and commercial or university presses publish an additional ten to twenty Rand books. These publications are available at Rand itself, government documentation centers, and more than 350 subscription libraries worldwide. Quarterly and annual indexes, with abstracts of all publications, are in most university and public libraries. A special, cumulative, twenty-five-year index appeared in 1973. These indexes are available without charge to institutions and

organizations. Subscription libraries in the D.C. area (with dates of initial order) are: Army Library, Army Department (1970); George Mason University (1979); George Washington University Library (1970); Library of Congress (1953); and University of Maryland, Engineering Library (1966).

Rand also produces a large number of classified reports and working papers, which are not encompassed in the preceding paragraph and not available to the public.

Finally, Rand maintains selective bibliographies of its publications on fifty different subjects and geographic areas. One of these bibliographies is on USSR/Eastern Europe; others are on East-West trade, arms control, foreign policy. Copies of the bibliographies may be obtained without charge.

H27 Russian Information Research Service

1. *P.O. Box 1872*
   Rockville, Maryland 20850

2. 1982

3. Boris Shekhtman, President

4. The Russian Information Research Service is comprised of more than 300 Soviet-area scholars, most of whom are native speakers.

6. The service contracts with individuals, private and public organizations, and government agencies to research topics relating to Russian/Soviet issues.

8. The organization plans to hold seminars on the Russian language and translation.

9. At present there are no publications, but a descriptive brochure should be available in the near future.

H28 SRI International—Strategic Studies Center (SSC)—Washington Office

1. *Rosslyn Plaza, 1611 North Kent Street*
   Arlington, Virginia 22209
   (703) 524-2053

2. 1956 SRI and 1967 SSC, locally; 1946 SRI, Menlo Park, and 1954 SSC.

3. William F. Miller, President, SRI
   R. B. Foster, Senior Director, SSC

4. The center's research staff of economists, foreign-area specialists, political and social scientists, research analysts, and assistants numbers about twenty-five persons in Washington; nearly one-third are Soviet-area specialists. (SRI total personnel in Washington totals approximately 120.)

In addition, a supplementary research staff of senior scholars in the social sciences is employed by SSC. Most hold joint appointments, being full-time professors at various institutions of higher learning. A few are in the Russian/Soviet field.

On occasion a research problem requires specialized expertise, for which the center has agreements with about 100 consultants; about fifty of whom are used on a regular basis.

5. The center is an affiliate of the main headquarters of SRI International located in Menlo Park, California (no longer associated with Stanford University).

6. SRI's Strategic Studies Center is engaged in a comprehensive research program on major national security problems, designed to provide government planners with a range of policy options for supporting U.S. security interests and commitments. The center aims to assist decision-makers through analysis and evaluation of economic, military, political, and technological aspects of selected issues. SSC also seeks to provide leadership in discussion of defense and strategic matters through briefings and a publication program. The center works to improve the quality of such discussion both among the public generally and in congressional committees.

Analysis of the interactions between the U.S. and the USSR and between the U.S. and its allies (particularly West European) is an important part of the center's operations. To this end it has established relationships with U.S. and foreign research institutes also concerned with problems of global defense. Two of these institutes are Soviet: Institute of World Economy and International Relations (IMEMO) and Institute for the Study of the United States of America and Canada (IUSAC), both located in Moscow. Other institutes include Foundation for Science and Politics (Munich), French Institute of Strategic Studies (Paris), International Institute & Strategic Studies (London), Norwegian Institute of International Affairs (Oslo), Research Institute on Swedish National Defense (Stockholm), Stockholm International Peace Research Institute, and others in India, Iran, Israel, Japan, Korea, and Rumania. In the U.S. relationships are maintained with Center for Strategic and International Studies (Georgetown University, Washington, D.C.) (entry H16), Foreign Policy Research Institute (Philadelphia), Hoover Institute for War, Revolution, and Peace (Stanford University, California), and Washington Center for Foreign Policy Research (Johns Hopkins University, SAIS, Washington, D.C.) (entry J12).

7. The center maintains a specialized library, organized to provide research personnel access to open source literature and, on a need-to-know basis, classified materials for strategic analysis. The collection has works on Soviet, U.S., and Western European economics, foreign policies, military doctrines, and research activities, as well as data on special strategic problems of the Middle East and Asia.

A separate Russian Collection of some five to six thousand books covers Soviet economic, military, and political (party) affairs. Much of this material is in the Russian language. The SSC library also receives many Soviet journals and newspapers. With State Department approval, U.S. embassy book buyers in Moscow distribute items directly to the center.

Outside researchers would require special permission to use the research facilities of the SSC; they should call the center (ext. 204) for information about gaining access.

In Menlo Park SRI maintains a large-scale classified data bank for comparison and evaluation of U.S. and Soviet weapon systems and force postures. It includes characteristics, cost data, descriptions, and programs on both systems. Access is restricted to SSC project personnel. Classified holdings of the center total more than 6,000 documents.

8. The center regularly holds symposia (sponsored by SRI or others) on a variety of topics, sometimes as joint projects with government agencies, research organizations, or universities.

9. SSC has an extensive publication program for the exchange of literature information with research institutes worldwide and with other appropriate organizations. In addition to this dissemination of published material to government agencies, congressional staffs, university personnel, the public, and other research groups, center members contribute ideas directly to government studies.

10. SSC is not formally affiliated with other organizations but maintains relationships with a number of other research institutes as detailed in point 6.

H29 T. N. Dupuy Associates (TNDA)

1. *Location:*
   2301 Gallows Road
   Dunn Loring, Virginia
   (703) 560-6427

   Mail:
   P.O. Box 157
   Dunn Loring, Virginia, 22027

2. 1967

3. Colonel (ret.) T. N. Dupuy, President and Executive Director

4. TNDA employs the staff of Historical Evaluation and Research Organization (HERO), housed in the same building, for its work. HERO has about fifteen to twenty staff members (see entry H19).

6. TNDA is a private, profit-seeking organization established to research and write books on all aspects of military history. It works by contract.

9. TNDA publishes the informative biennial *Almanac of World Military Power.* Among other books put out by the staff, *A Documentary History of Arms Control and Disarmament,* by T. N. Dupuy and Gay Hammerman (New York and Dunn Loring, Va: R. R. Bowker and TNDA, 1973), and *Great Battles on the Eastern Front,* by T. N. Dupuy and Paul Martell (New York: Bobbs Merrill, 1982), might be of interest to Soviet area scholars.

H30 United Nations Information Centre

1. *2101 L Street NW, Suite 209*
   Washington, D.C. 20037
   (202) 296-5370

2. 1946

3. Marcial Tamayo, Acting Director
   Willard Hass, Information Officer

4. The research staff consists of about seven people.

6. The center provides services reflective of the main functions of the UN Office of Public Information. These include the use of press, radio, television, films, and exhibition for the dissemination of information. The Information Centre's primary goal is to establish direct contacts with representatives of the local press and information media, educational institutions, and governmental and nongovernmental organizations and to cooperate with them in providing a greater understanding of the aims and functions of the UN.

The center plays an important role in the observance of special UN occasions, such as UN Day and Human Rights Day, as well as publicity for current UN programs.

7. The Information Centre's library, the focal point of all research activities, is described in entry A60.

H31 Woodrow Wilson International Center for Scholars (WWICS)

1. *Smithsonian Institution Building*
   1000 Jefferson Drive, SW
   Washington, D.C. 20560
   (202) 357-2429

2. 1968

3. James H. Billington, Director

4. The center is governed by sixteen trustees appointed by the U.S. president, eight chosen from private life and eight from the public sector.

6. The WWICS was created by the U.S. Congress in 1968 as the nation's official living memorial to its twenty-eighth president. As a national institution with international interests, the center seeks to encourage the creative use of the unique human, archival, and institutional resources in the nation's capital for studies illuminating our understanding of the past and present.

Through its Residential Fellowship Program of advanced research the center seeks to commemorate both the scholarly depth and the public concerns of Woodrow Wilson. The center welcomes outstanding project proposals representing a wide diversity of scholarly interests and approaches from individuals throughout the world. It has no permanent or tenured fellows. Its fellowships are awarded, for periods ranging from four months to one year or more, in one broadly defined program and five more focused programs of research. The broadly defined program—focusing on history, culture, and society—enables the center to attract superior projects from the entire range of scholarship in the humanities and social sciences that promise to make major contributions to the understanding of the human condition or that attempt broad synthesis involving different fields or different cultures. The five designated programs are the Kennan Institute for Advanced Russian Studies (described in detail in entry H23), the Latin American Program, the International Security Studies Program, the East Asia Program, and the Program in American Society and Politics. The center also operates a Guest Scholar Program for the short-term use of the center's facilities by a small number of visiting scholars and specialists. Details and application procedure information are available on request.

7. The center has a working library containing 16,000 volumes of basic reference works, bibliographies, and essential monographs in the social sciences and humanities with an emphasis on the areas covered by the center's programs. The library subscribes to and maintains the back files of about 300 scholarly journals and periodicals. The librarian is Zdeněk V. David (202/357-2567).

8. The center's activities include frequent colloquia, evening seminars, and other discussions designed to foster intellectual community among the participants. These meetings are announced in the center's monthly *Calendar of Events,* for which area scholars may ask to be placed on the mailing list.

9. The *Wilson Quarterly* (circulation 100,000), begun in 1976, has carried occasional articles on Soviet culture, society, and foreign policy. Most notably, the journal published clusters of three articles and bibliographies on the mutual perceptions of the

U.S. and USSR (winter 1977 issue) and on the Soviet future (winter 1981). The center also sponsors the preparation and publication of *Scholars' Guides to Washington, D.C.,* available from the Smithsonian Institution Press (P.O. Box 1579, Washington, D.C. 20013). The guides survey the collections, institutions, and organizations pertinent to the study of particular geographic areas, such as Africa, Central and Eastern Europe, East Asia, Latin America and the Caribbean, the Middle East, Russia/Soviet Union, South Asia, Southeast Asia, and other world regions. A separate guide covers film and video collections in the Washington, D.C., area. The center's programs (Kennan Institute, Latin America, International Security Studies, and East Asia) publish *Occasional/Working Papers,* which are available upon request. Lists may be obtained from the Publications Office or individual program offices. The *Annual Report* and an occasional bulletin, the *Newsletter,* are sent to former fellows and other friends of the Wilson Center.

10. The Kennan Institute for Advanced Russian Studies, noted in point 6, is an integral part of the center; an entry for it appears in this section (H23).

J Academic Programs

Academic Program Entry Format (J)

1. *Address; Telephone Number(s)*

2. Chief Official and Title

3. Degrees and Subjects Offered; Programs/Activities

4. Library/Research Facilities

5. Publications

Introductory Note

The Washington metropolitan area offers a wide range of scholastic opportunities for both undergraduate and graduate studies. Students may either specialize in Russian literature and language or participate in an area-studies program. Through a special reciprocity system it is possible for students to enroll in courses at several institutions and receive credit from their home university. For further information on these programs and to learn more about the interests and academic activities of both faculties and students, researchers should contact the appropriate department heads. Department calendars of upcoming events are often available without charge.

Several Washington universities have established research centers that complement their academic programs. Such centers are described in the Research Centers and Information Offices section (H) of this *Guide*.

J1 American University—Russian Studies Program

1. *Asbury Building, Room 340*
   Washington, D.C. 20016
   (202) 686-2280

2. Dr. Vadim Medish, Professor and Coordinator, Russian Studies Program

3. Established in 1977 as an interdisciplinary program, this teaching program offers a wide variety of courses dealing with the Russian language, history, politics, economics, literature, culture, and civilization. The program offers an undergraduate

minor. B.A. and M.A. degrees in Russian studies are offered in conjunction with the Department of Language and Foreign Studies and School of International Service. On occasion lectures by distinguished speakers in Russia-related fields, symposia, and cultural events are presented. They are open to the public; for more information, contact the coordinator.

4. The university library contains numerous volumes pertaining to various aspects of Russia's past and present. Access is limited to students and faculty (see entry A6).

J2   American University—School of International Service (SIS)

1.   *Washington, D.C. 20016*
     (202) 686-2470

2.   Dr. William C. Olson, Dean
     Dr. F. Jackson Piotrow, Russian and Soviet Studies
     Dr. Linda L. Lubrano, Soviet Studies

3.   Established in 1958, the school offers such courses as modern Russian history, Soviet foreign policy and the domestic political system, comparative politics, and Soviet science policy. The program leads to a B.A., M.A., or Ph.D. degree in international studies. Courses in the program, now part of the College of Public and International Affairs, are designed to complement subjects taught under the Department of Language and Foreign Studies and elsewhere at the university.
     The Russian Studies Group draws interested faculty from all departments at the unversity for occasional discussions and other meetings.
     A Pan Ethnon society, comprised of students of international affairs, sponsors a series of talks on weekday afternoons, plus other (infrequent) events.

4.   The university library is described in entry A6.

J3   George Mason University—Department of Foreign Languages and Literature (Russian Section)

1.   *Fairfax, Virginia 22030*
     (703) 323-2231
     (703) 323-2241

2.   Dr. Leo Hecht, Chairperson, Russian Studies

3.   Begun in 1972, the B.A. degree program in the Russian Studies Department incorporates the study of the language, history, geography, literature, and culture of the USSR. The department often sponsors Russian-language symposiums, and individual faculty members are affiliated with such organizations as the American Association of Teachers of Slavic and East European Languages (AATSEEL) and American Association for the Advancement of Slavic Studies (AAASS).

4.   The university library (703/323-2616) has holdings relating to Russian and Soviet studies.

George Washington University—Institute for Sino-Soviet Studies (ISSS)   See entry H15

J4   George Washington University—Russian and East European Studies Program

1. *School of Public and International Affairs (SPIA)*
    Washington, D.C. 20052
    (202) 676-6240

2.   Dr. Charles Elliott, Director

3.   Established in 1970, the program for an M.A. degree in Russian studies is inter-disciplinary and is administered by the interdepartmental Russian and East European Studies Committee of the SPIA and Institute for Sino-Soviet Studies (ISSS) of George Washington University. Students may complete either a thirty-semester-hour program, including the writing of a master's thesis or a thirty-six-semester-hour program without a thesis requirement.

The student gains a broad knowledge of Russian affairs, with emphasis on the Soviet period, including the following subjects: economics and geography, foreign relations, internal and external affairs, literature and culture, military policy and strategy, and political thought and history.

The Cooperative Program in Russian and East European studies, a joint effort of George Washington University ISSS and Georgetown University Russian-area Studies Program, allows students at either of these institutions to take relevant courses at the other in fulfillment of course requirements. For further information, see the entry on the Institute for Sino-Soviet Studies (entry H15).

4.   Research facilities include the university's Gelman Library (entry A24), Slavic Department's holdings (entry J5), and ISSS library (entry H15).

5.   Program publications are issued by the ISSS.

J5   George Washington University—Slavic Languages and Literatures Department

1. *Gelman Library, Room 627*
    Washington, D.C. 20052
    (202) 676-6335

2.   Charles A. Moser, Chairperson

3.   The department offers a broad range of courses in Russian and some other Slavic languages, linguistics, literature, Russian culture and civilization, and other subjects. There are also "practical" courses such as that on business Russian.

The academic program leads to a B.A. degree in Russian literature and culture—in translation—and M.A. degree in Russian language or Russian literature. Students taking the education curriculum at the university may also earn a B.A. degree in education with a teaching field in Russian.

Staff members are also quite active in Washington-area Russian organizations, such as the Fund for the Relief of Russian Writers and Scientists in Exile (Litfund) (entry M36) and the International Dostoevsky Society (entry M37). Moreover, the department often sponsors films and lectures on topics of significance to Russianists. Its National Slavic Honor Society (Dobro Slovo) chapter plays a leading role in most of these events.

The department has about six full-time professors on the staff who engage in teaching and research.

Lectures, films, and other events sponsored by the department and Dobro Slovo are open to the public and announced ahead of time. Information about upcoming activities may be obtained from the department office.

4. The department maintains two collections separate from other university holdings (see entry A24). At present these collections are housed in the department offices. In the office proper is an English-language collection of Russian literature totaling a few hundred volumes. Next door are mainly Russian-language materials on history, language, linguistics, literature, and some basic reference works; these holdings amount to about another 850 titles, many of which are multivolume. Of special interest is the Belinkov Memorial Collection of nearly 150 titles on Soviet émigré and dissent movements. The department secretary doubles as librarian (preceding phone number); library hours are 9:00 A.M. to 5:00 P.M., Monday through Friday. A modern language laboratory facilitates study of Russian at the university.

J6   Georgetown University—Department of Russian

1. *Intercultural Center, Room 434*
   School of Languages and Linguistics
   Washington, D.C. 20057
   (202) 625-4811

2. Dr. Dmitry Grigorieff, Chairperson

3. Established in 1946, the department offers a wide selection of courses leading to B.A. and M.A. degrees in language and literature—given mostly in Russian. Courses taught include those on Russian culture and civilization, linguistics, medieval to modern literature, translation, and business Russian. Both undergraduate and graduate students may take a semester of study in the USSR.

The department has an active Russian Club that sponsors occasional films and lectures on topics of interest. Scholars should contact the department for further information.

4. Georgetown's library is described in entry A23. For Russian-language students a language laboratory with excellent audio and video equipment is available.

5. The School of Languages and Linguistics publishes occasional Working Papers in Linguistics, to which members of the Russian department contribute.

J7   Georgetown University—Foreign Service School

1. *Intercultural Center, Room 301*
   Washington, D.C. 20057
   (202) 625-4218

2. Peter F. Krogh, Dean

3.   Founded in 1919, the school's program of courses covers most aspects of Russian/ Soviet affairs, economics, foreign policy, history, and politics. In most respects the offerings are designed to give students not only broad general knowledge of the subjects but also practical learning for the chosen profession of government service. Students receive B.S. or M.S. degrees in Foreign Service.

In addition to the regular schedule of classes, the Foreign Service School also offers a host of so-called cocurricular activities: conferences, seminars, and talks, most open to the public and all accessible to researchers, in some cases by invitation. Many of these events concern Russian/Soviet affairs. For more information about these activities, contact the school and/or consult the publication noted in point 5.

The teaching faculty of the school is primarily drawn from professors in the departments of economics, government, and history of the College of Arts and Sciences; some are in the field of international relations as well.

4.   Georgetown's Lauinger Library is described in entry A23.

5.   The School of Foreign Service *Communique,* published quarterly, carries news of the school and upcoming events; copies are available without charge. Every two years the school sponsors the Conference on the Atlantic Community, the proceedings of which are published under the title *CONTACT.* The conferences deal with such topics as disarmament, NATO, and related matters of interest to the Soviet-area specialist. In addition, occasional papers of the faculty, published by the school, may be pertinent to the Russianist.

J8   Georgetown University—Russian Area Studies Program (RASP)

1.   *Intercultural Center*
Washington, D.C. 20057
(202) 625-4676

2.   Dr. William L. Stearman, Director

3.   RASP (established 1959) is a graduate program of Georgetown University. About twenty professors, nearly all members of different university departments, take part in the program. It is essentially a teaching program for graduate students only, leading to advanced degrees (M.A. and Ph.D.) in area studies. It also provides some course work for Ph.D. candidates in specific academic disciplines with a Russian/Soviet concentration. Disciplines in which courses are offered include economics, history, literature, political science, and philosophy. Much of the work is geared toward practical training for government or business careers that require expertise in the Soviet field. Eastern European studies are also included in the program.

Georgetown University's RASP program has close ties with the Sino-Soviet Institute (entry H15) at George Washington University. Both schools are members of the Consortium of Universities; students from either school may take courses at the other. For this reason, an attempt is made to have some course offerings complement each other at the two universities and to have students avail themselves of expertise at one school, which may not be available at the other. RASP encourages the enrollment of part-time students.

It is worth noting that Georgetown coordinates and administers the language study program of the New York-based Council of International Education Exchange in the D.C. area.

On occasion the program sponsors lectures and symposia on Russian/Soviet subjects, which are open to the public. Scholars should inquire for more information about scheduled events. Currently, and in conjunction with the National Strategy Information Center (entry M53), RASP is cosponsoring (with George Washington's Sino-Soviet Institute) a Defense Strategy Program for advanced graduate students, alumni, and others in defense-related work. The monthly meetings are open by invitation only.

4. Georgetown's library is described in entry A23.

J9   Howard University—German and Russian Studies

1. *Locke Hall, Room 368*
   Washington, D.C. 20059
   (202) 636-6755

2. Dr. Paul E. Logan, Chairperson

3. This academic department is primarily a teaching body, offering a full slate of courses in Russian civilization, language (including Old Church Slavonic), and literature. Staff members participate also in Howard's informal, interdisciplinary Russian area studies program with members of other departments such as history and political science. Students in the department may earn either B.A. or M.A. degrees in Russian language and literature. There are four full-time faculty members who are Russianists.

4. For its own students primarily, the department has a collection of some 500 books in Russian and English for the subjects taught by the faculty. The school also has a very modern, well-equipped language laboratory for Russian-language students (and other language students).

   The Audiovisual Center of the College of Liberal Arts, located on the second floor of Locke Hall, has several films, newsreels, and documentaries on Russia/USSR.

   Howard University's libraries are described in entry A30.

J10   Maryland University—Department of Germanic and Slavic Languages—Russian Section

1. *Foreign Languages Building (LL)*
   College Park, Maryland 20742
   (301) 454-4301/4302

2. Dr. Richard Brecht, Chairperson, German-Slavic Department

3. With a Slavic teaching staff comprising six full-time and additional part-time members, the department offers a full range of courses in the Russian language, linguistics, and literature—at present for undergraduates only. Among the offerings are courses on the structure and history of the Russian language within contemporary linguistic theory. Literature courses cover medieval to twentieth-century writings.

   A Russian Club and a chapter of the National Slavic Honor Society (Dobro Slovo) are active. On occasion the department sponsors lectures by outside speakers and films relating to Russia/USSR. Contact the department office for further information. Dr. Brecht, along with Dr. Dan Davidson of Bryn Mawr, is co-organizer of the periodic Soviet-American Conference on the Russian Language.

4. A small working library is maintained for students and includes works of literature, handbooks, and other basic reference tools. A modern-language laboratory aids students of Russian as well.

The Slavic collection at the university's McKeldin Library is, after the Library of Congress, the strongest in the area (see entry A39).

5. *Forum International,* ed. Dr. John Glad, is a scholarly journal devoted to Russian literature.

J11 Maryland University—Russian Area Studies Program

1. *History Department*
   College Park, Maryland 20742
   (301) 454-2843

2. John Lampe, Chairperson

3. The Russian Area Studies Program is designed at present for undergraduates and leads to a B.A. degree. Currently about eighteen faculty members, from five different disciplines (economics, history, political science, Slavic languages, and sociology) offer Russian-related courses for students in the program.

The activities involved in the program are intimately connected with those of the individual departments. Thus, lectures, films, concerts, and other events sponsored by departments are necessarily considered a part of the Russian Area Studies Program. In this respect, one should consult the preceding entry for the Maryland University Department of Germanic and Slavic Languages, Russian Section, for more information about the program.

Plans are proceeding for the establishment of a graduate program in Russian studies; the degree awarded will be a certificate.

4. The university library is described in entry A39.

J12 School of Advanced International Studies (SAIS) (Johns Hopkins University)

1. *1740 Massachusetts Avenue, NW*
   Washington, D.C. 20036
   (202) 785-6200

2. George R. Packard, Dean, SAIS

3. Established in 1943 as a graduate school, SAIS offers an interdisciplinary program leading to an M.A. degree or, for a smaller number of students, a Ph.D. degree. A one-year program leading to a Master of International Public Policy is available to midcareer business executives and government officials (U.S. and foreign).

Approximately thirty full-time and sixty-five part-time members make up the faculty. Part-time members are drawn from the large Washington community of academic, government, and international organizations. Practical and professional experience is matched with scholarly achievement in the faculty. Most of the language teachers are native speakers.

Students usually specialize in one geographic area while taking courses in international economics and general international affairs. An integral part of the program is language study: eight foreign languages are offered. A small number of full- and part-time faculty, including Professor Herbert S. Dinerstein, Bruce Parrott, and Dmitri Simes, offer courses in Soviet foreign policy, the dynamics of development in Russia and the USSR, comparative revolutionary systems, the Soviet economy, Marxist theory, Soviet economic history and policy, and other subjects.

SAIS draws heavily on the international affairs demands and expertise in the Washington area for placing students in a work-study program and for obtaining well-known guest lecturers and speakers. Other activities of SAIS include organizing and conducting conferences for corporation executives, diplomats, government officials, journalists, and scholars.

The Foreign Policy Institute is the publishing and research arm of SAIS. The institute attempts to integrate international policymaking with academia by sponsoring numerous projects, seminars, and weekly discussions and conferences. Contact the school for information about current schedules and to request access.

4. The SAIS library has some basic materials for Soviet-area research. See entry A55 in the Libraries section for more information.

5. Until recently SAIS had no publication program of its own. Currently the school issues *SAIS Review,* a journal devoted to international studies, and a monograph series featuring faculty members' reasearch. Descriptive brochures, including course listings and information about degree programs, are available without charge.

J13 Trinity College—Russian Department

1. *Main Building*
   Washington, D.C. 20017
   (202) 269-2286

2. Natalie Kalikin, Chairperson

3. The only member of the department, Natalie Kalikin teaches courses in Russian language and literature (the latter from medieval times to the Soviet period), history, drama, and art. Among other specialized offerings is a course in scientific Russian. Students may earn an undergraduate minor in Russian.

The school has a Russian Club, which is sometimes active in sponsoring films, guest lectures, and drama productions.

K U.S. Government Agencies

U.S. Government Agency Entry Format (K)

1. General Information
   a. *address; telephone number(s)*
   b. conditions of access
   c. name/title of director and heads of relevant divisions

2. Agency Functions, Programs, and Research Activities (in-house research, contract research, research grants, employment of outside consultants, and international exchange programs)

3. Agency Libraries and Reference Facilities

4. Internal Agency Records (unpublished materials and aids, indexes, vertical files, etc.)

5. Publications
   a. Published research products
   b. Research bibliographies

In the case of large, structurally complex agencies, a detailed description of relevant divisions follows the description of the organization as a whole; included is information on the above-numbered points.

Introductory Note

U.S. Government agencies and departments are among the most valuable resources in Washington for information on the Soviet Union. A vast number of government personnel are either directly or indirectly involved in projects related to the USSR, and most are very willing to discuss their work with visiting scholars. In addition, many government agencies allow private researchers to examine their libraries, reference collections, data banks, and other facilities, which contain records and documents not generally available elsewhere.

In obtaining access to those internal records and documents not publicly available, either from the agencies or departments generating the material or from the National Archives and Records Service (entry B6), researchers should be familiar with Freedom of Information Act procedures. The Freedom of Information Act (Public Law 89–487 of 1966, as amended by Public Laws 93–502 of 1974 and 94–409 of 1976) provides that any citizen has the right of access to, and can obtain copies of, any document, file, or other record in the possession of any federal agency or department, with specified exceptions (including certain personnel records and classified documents, the classification of which can be justified as essential to national security). Most government agencies have a Freedom of Information office or officer available to process requests for internal agency documents. When contacting these offices (in writing or by telephone), researchers should cite the Freedom of Information Act and make their requests as detailed and specific as possible. Researchers are not required to explain or justify their requests. Denials of requests may be appealed to the director of the agency. Such appeals are often successful, and rejected appeals may be challenged through court litigation. By law, agencies have ten working days in which to respond to an initial Freedom of Information Act request and twenty days in which to respond to an appeal. Researchers should note that agencies are permitted to charge rather substantial fees for document searches and the photocopying of released documents. Information on such fees should be requested when filing the initial request. In most cases, researchers are permitted to examine released records in person at the agency.

Several organizations in Washington can assist researchers in using (and litigating) Freedom of Information Act procedures. They include the Freedom of Information Clearinghouse. P.O. Box 19367 (2000 P Street, NW, Suite 700), Washington, D.C. 20036 (202/785-3704), which is a project of Ralph Nader's Center for the Study of Responsive Law; Campaign for Political Rights, 201 Massachusetts Avenue, NE, Washington, D.C. 20002 (202/547-4705); and Project on National Security and Civil Liberties, 122 Maryland Avenue, NE, Washington, D.C. 20002 (202/544-5380), an organization sponsored by the American Civil Liberties Union and Center for National Security Studies (entry H10). These organizations distribute without charge guides to Freedom of Information Act procedures. Another useful source of information is *Access Reports/Freedom of Information,* a biweekly newsletter published by the Washington Monitor, Inc., which reports on the latest developments in the Freedom of Information field (see entry Q23).

Researchers should be aware that bureaucratically inspired reorganizations of government offices are frequent; indeed, various agencies within the national intelligence community regularly reorganize their internal structures to disguise their function and confuse foreign observers. Elections also often lead to major administrative disruptions within the federal bureaucracy. As a result, many of the names and telephone numbers listed in the following entries are subject to change and must be considered as somewhat temporary. Researchers would be well advised to obtain the latest telephone numbers for various offices by consulting the most current edition of each government department's telephone directory. Some are updated on a quarterly basis. Most are available for purchase from the Government Printing Office (entry Q9). If all else fails, contact the Federal Information Center (202/755-8660) for assistance.

K1 Agriculture Department (USDA)

1 a. *Fourteenth Street and Independence Avenue, SW*
Washington, D.C. 20250
(202) 447-2791 (Information)

b. Department buildings are open to the public, but access is controlled; appointments are recommended.

2. Divisions of this department carry on substantive research concerning agriculture and related matters in the Soviet Union. Virtually all work is done in-house, with no research contracts or grants going to outside scholars for study of Soviet affairs. See the individual entries below.

3. See the National Agriculture Library (entry A40) and Data Services Center (entry G2).

4. Most important research records of the Foreign Agricultural Service and Economic Research Service—branches that study the USSR—are accessible to researchers. These are often working files, however, with natural limitations on their availability. In general, the department makes no effort to obtain or maintain records of private research on Soviet agriculture. Appropriate bibliographies and other publications are noted under each division.

5. Publications are described below with their respective entries.

INTERNATIONAL AFFAIRS AND COMMODITY PROGRAMS

FOREIGN AGRICULTURAL SERVICE (FAS)

USDA, South Building
Fourteenth Street and Independence Avenue, SW
(202) 447-3448 (Information)

Richard A. Smith, Administrator (202/447-3935)

International Trade Policy (ITP)
Asia, Africa, and Eastern Europe Division
(202) 382-1289

David Schoonover, Director

>   Eastern Europe and USSR Group
>   (202) 382-9061
>   Robert Harper, Leader

This unit works with other departments and USDA agencies on the agricultural aspects of general questions involving East-West trade legislation and policy.

International Agricultural Statistics (IAS)
Commodity Division
(202) 447-7233

Richard Cannon, Assistant Administrator

Units within IAS compile, analyze, and report near-term production data for crops and livestock in the USSR. IAS is also responsible for maintaining the agency's automated data system.

Many individual commodity divisions within this agency look at commodities of the USSR. Along with IAS, these divisions provide USDA with foreign market intelligence, including information on trade, supply, and utilization. Perhaps the most important of them is the Grain and Feed Division (202/447-6885). A current Soviet specialist in this division is Frank Gomme (202/447-7700).

Another section of FAS of potential value to researchers is the Office of the Assistant Administrator for Foreign Agricultural Affairs. The area officer for Europe (non-European Community) is currently Robert McConnell. This office can facilitate researchers' work in the USSR through the agricultural attaches there.

FAS publishes a number of works of great interest to Russianists:

Foreign Agriculture, a monthly subscription magazine (available without charge to certain individuals, institutions, and libraries). Likely to have about ten articles per year on the USSR; with annual index.

Foreign Agriculture Circulars, issued regularly on various commodities and export services. Each of twenty-four different commodity circulars, plus the *Weekly Roundup of World Production and Trade,* has its own mailing list.

Miscellaneous reports occasionally deal with the Soviet Union, e.g., no. 284: *USSR Sugar: Today and Tomorrow* (1978) and no. 289: *USSR Agricultural Trends 1955–77: A Historical Perspective* (1979). These publications are available without charge.

OFFICE OF INTERNATIONAL COOPERATION AND DEVELOPMENT (OICD)

USDA, Auditors Building
Fourteenth Street and Independence Avenue, SW
(202) 447-3157

Scientific and Technical Exchange Division
(202) 447-4445

Roger Neetz, Deputy Administrator

Douglas R. Freeman, Program Leader for Europe and Executive Secretary for U.S.-USSR Agricultural Agreement (202/382-8006)

This division in OICD administers all bilateral agreements on scientific and technical cooperation between USDA and foreign countries, including the U.S.-USSR Agreement on Agriculture signed in June 1973.

The Executive Secretariat executes decisions made by the Joint Committee established by the agreement. The U.S. chair of the Joint Committee is the under secretary for International Affairs and Commodity Programs in USDA. On the U.S. delegation to the Joint Committee are personnel from other USDA agencies in addition to OICD, including the Foreign Agricultural Service, Economic Research Service, Agricultural Research Service, and Cooperative State Research Service.

There are two working groups under the Joint Committee: one on agricultural research and technological development, and one on agricultural economic research and information. The Joint Committee and working groups usually meet once a year. There is a continuous exchange of agricultural specialists, planners and administrators, and materials and information under the agreement.

The executive secretary provides information about this work to scholars, businessmen, and scientists and confers with them on matters of programming. The secretariat staff is also in touch with agency personnel working on other U.S.-USSR bilateral agreements.

ECONOMIC RESEARCH SERVICE

500 Twelfth Street, SW

International Economics Division
Eastern Europe and USSR Branch
(202) 447-8380

Anton Malish, Chief

This branch is the Agriculture Department's primary source of agricultural intelligence and economic analysis on the USSR and Eastern Europe. The office maintains an extensive file of statistical data and research papers on major developments in Soviet agriculture. There are also complete data sets, in English, compiled from official Soviet and Eastern European sources. Memoranda on current work of the staff, known as Highlights, are kept on file and may be available to researchers. The office welcomes all inquiries on the current agricultural situation in the USSR and Eastern Europe.

Publications of interest to Russianists include: *The Agricultural Situation in the Soviet Union*, issued annually; *Outlook for U.S. Agriculture Exports*, issued quarterly; *Foreign Agricultural Trade of the United States*, issued monthly; and *World Agriculture Outlook and Situation*, issued quarterly.

National Economic Division
Agricultural History Branch
(202) 447-8183

Wayne Rasmussen, Supervisory Historian

Documentation Center
(202) 447-8684

Gerald Ogden, Director

The Documentation Center is a cooperative effort of USDA, National Agricultural Library, and American Agricultural Economic Association. Its function is to maintain a computerized bibliographic data base containing primarily American agricultural economists' articles, books, and papers. Researchers can find relevant references to English-language works here. For more information about the center, contact the director. A fee is charged for use of the computer.

NOTE: Wayne Rasmussen is the executive secretary of the Agricultural History Society.

AGRICULTURAL RESEARCH SERVICE
Beltsville, Maryland 20705
Overseas Labs and International Programs
(301) 344-2605

B. M. Kopacz, Director

Staff members generally actively participate in bilateral agreements on agriculture. Contact the office directly for information about personnel who play a role in this work.

A number of other USDA divisions participate to some degree in the projects of the agricultural (and other) bilateral agreements. Among these are:

FOREST SERVICE

International Forestry Staff
(202) 447-5748

Robert W. Brandt, Director

The staff works on the agricultural agreement (integrated pest control) and environmental and housing (building construction) agreements, with, respectively, the Environmental Protection Agency and Department of Housing and Urban Development.

SOIL CONSERVATION SERVICE (202/447-4531)

COOPERATIVE STATE RESEARCH SERVICE (202/447-4423)

Both services have contributed to the agricultural agreement, the Soil Conservation Service contributed to the now-expired science and technology agreement.

K2   Air Force Department

1 a. *The Pentagon*
Washington, D.C. 20330
(202) 545-6700 (Information)

  b. Access to the Pentagon is limited to persons with a security clearance, or by invitation.

2. Most research on the USSR is conducted in-house.

3. See entry A1 for the Office of Air Force History Library.

4. Internal records procedures are described in the Defense Department entry (entry K12).

5. Publications are discussed under relevant divisions.

NOTE: Readers are referred to the statements made at the start of the Defense Department entry (K12); they pertain to this agency also and should assist scholars who wish to know what resources exist for them in the Air Force Department.

OFFICE OF PUBLIC AFFAIRS (OFFICE OF THE SECRETARY)

Community Relations Division
(202) 697-1128

Staff members of this division answer inquiries from the general public and should be a researcher's initial contact point with the Air Force Department.

ADMINISTRATIVE ASSISTANT TO THE SECRETARY

News Clipping and Analysis Services Division
(202) 695-2884

Harry Zubkoff, Chief

The division maintains fairly extensive vertical-file collections (on shelves rather than in cabinets) on Air Force related subjects. The materials, newspaper clippings mostly, are chronologically arranged by subject. Russianists should thus be able to locate pertinent items rather easily. The division should be a major research resource for Soviet area specialists, although the office is not particularly designed to accommodate outside researchers. Therefore, researchers who wish to use the materials must call ahead to make arrangements.

DIRECTORATE OF ADMINISTRATION (OFFICE OF THE CHIEF OF STAFF)

Documentation Management
(202) 697-3491

James E. Dagwell

Two components of this office—the Air Force Freedom of Information Act Office (Kip Ward, 202/694-3488) and the Air Force Privacy Act Office (Mark Coon, 202/694-3431)—formulate Freedom of Information policy. The staff is helpful in locating desired materials and in directing Russianists to other sources of information. The actual performance of Freedom of Information requests is done by individual air force commands. Researchers who encounter problems in gaining access to or using documents might also want to contact the Office for Security Review (202/697-3222), for division reviews of research involving classified materials.

OFFICE OF AIR FORCE HISTORY (OFFICE OF THE CHIEF OF STAFF)
Bolling Air Force Base, Building 5681
Washington, D.C. 20332
(202) 767-5764

Richard H. Kohn, Chief

This office is an important resource for Russianists. The valuable archival resources of its library are described in entry A1. The staff can be most helpful in locating relevant research materials and in helping scholars gain access to them.

INTERNATIONAL AFFAIRS DIVISION (OFFICE OF THE CHIEF OF STAFF)
(202) 695-2251

Colonel Howard E. Lynch, Chief

Activities of this division include protocol affairs, disclosure policy, and matters related to munitions and exports.

AIR FORCE INTELLIGENCE SERVICE

Directorate of Soviet Affairs
Bolling Air Force Base, Building 520
Washington, D.C. 20332
(202) 767-4205

Colonel George Wish, Director

Staff members of the directorate perform most of the Soviet-area research, which is concentrated on military affairs. A limited amount of work is done by contract. Instead of employing scholars as consultants, the office usually hires qualified researchers as regular, full-time employees.

The directorate has its own research facility. It contains perhaps 10,000 Soviet books on military subjects. Currently the office also receives about fifty Soviet journals and newspapers relating to military questions; none of these titles, however, begins before the early 1970s. Access to the library is limited by security requirements and is further dependent upon permission of the director.

Since 1973 this office has been publishing a series of translations of Soviet military works under the general title Soviet Military Thought. Nineteen volumes have appeared thus far, and the project is slated to continue indefinitely. Another important publication series is the monthly *Soviet Press: Selected Translations,* which includes English texts of primarily military materials (sometimes the Russian text is also provided). An additional series, Studies in Communist Affairs, contains original analytical work. Finally, for in-house distribution, the directorate occasionally produces titles such as *The Education and Training of Soviet Air Force Officers* (1976).

K3 Arms Control and Disarmament Agency (ACDA)

1 a. *State Department*
320 Twenty-first Street, NW
Washington, D.C. 20451
(202) 632-8715

b. Access to the State Department building is limited to persons with an appointment.

2. ACDA sponsors both in-house and contract research. Subjects covered include the Soviet economy and levels of military spending; Soviet decision-making processes in the nuclear arms reduction talks; UN disarmament initiatives of the USSR; Soviet conventional forces and military posture in Europe; and Soviet nuclear proliferation policy and arms transfers.

The Office of Public Affairs (202/632-0392) offers consultative services and arranges briefings and other information/publication activities.

Among the more important divisions at ACDA that a researcher might want to contact for more specific information would be the following: Bureau of Strategic Programs (202/632-7017); Bureau of Multilateral Affairs (202/632-3635); Bureau of Verification and Intelligence (202/632-8090); Bureau of Nuclear and Weapons Control (202/632-3466).

3. The ACDA library is described in entry A7.

4. *ACDA External Research Reports,* which appears approximately semiannually, lists all unclassified reports prepared by contract for the agency.

The agency also maintains a computerized documents data base. Most of the materials are classified; a large proportion relate to the USSR. For most researchers, the only access to this computer system would be through Freedom of Information Officer Raymond O. Waters (202/632-0760). Requests for information should be in writing and should cite the act. A fee is charged for searches.

A huge vertical-file collection, dating to 1967, covering all aspects of arms control and disarmament, is in the Public Affairs Office. Researchers may have access to this tremendous resource, by appointment.

5 a. The following are only a few of the agency's publications of interest to Russianists: *Arms Control and Disarmament Agreements: Text and History of Negotiations* (1980); *Documents on Disarmament,* a two-volume set covers the period 1945–59, annual volumes, the years from 1960 through 1978; *World Military Expenditures and Arms Transfers, 1970–1979.*

K4 Army Department

1 a. *The Pentagon*
Washington, D.C. 20330
(202) 545-6700 (Information)

b. Access to the Pentagon is limited to persons with a security clearance, or by invitation.

2. Most research on the USSR is done in-house.

3. The army library is described in entry A8.

4. Internal records procedures are described in the Defense Department entry (K12).

5. Publications are described under relevant divisions.

NOTE: Readers are referred to the statements made at the start of the Defense Department entry (K12); they pertain to this agency also and should assist researchers who wish to know what resources exist for them in the Army Department.

CHIEF OF PUBLIC AFFAIRS (OFFICE OF THE SECRETARY)
Office of the Executive (202/697-4200)
Media Relations Division (202/697-7589)

These offices should be the researcher's first point of contact with the Army Department. The executive and the staff of the Media Relations Division provide general information about the U.S. Army and can put researchers in contact with the appropriate officers in specific divisions who can answer more detailed questions.

ASSISTANT CHIEF OF STAFF FOR INTELLIGENCE (OFFICE OF THE CHIEF OF STAFF)
(202) 695-3033

The office conducts in-house research relating to the USSR. The focus is on international military relations and potential Soviet military threats. Other concerns are biographic research, energy, and civil-military relations in the Soviet Union. The work is geared toward operational and policy questions. The office also contracts for research from outside organizations such as SRI International (entry H28).

This division sponsors translation projects of Soviet military journals, covering such topics as antiaircraft defense, military medicine, arms technology, and logistics. These publications are often available from NTIS. Another title from the office, *Handbook on the Soviet Ground Forces* (1975), is a GPO publication.

Within this office, Russianists should probably be aware of other pertinent sections: the Directorate of Foreign Intelligence under Colonel William P. Grace (202/697-3398) and the Intelligence Division under Colonel Donald G. Stephens (202/697-7533).

DEPUTY CHIEF OF STAFF FOR RESEARCH, DEVELOPMENT, AND AC-
QUISITION (OFFICE OF THE CHIEF OF STAFF)
(202) 697-8186

This office receives information, mostly of a technical nature, on armaments, munitions, and related matters. Although it is not geared especially toward specific (regional) threats, its work could be of some interest to Soviet-area specialists.

DEPUTY CHIEF OF STAFF FOR OPERATIONS AND PLANS (OFFICE OF
THE CHIEF OF STAFF)
(202) 695-2904

There are several directorates in this division that study questions of strategy, political-
military affairs, and war plans. The USSR figures in a large part of the work. Although
security and classification obstacles exist, staff members may be able to discuss some
aspects of their work with serious researchers.

THE ADJUTANT GENERAL (OFFICE OF THE CHIEF OF STAFF)
(202) 695-0163

Records Management Division
Hoffman 1
Alexandria, Virginia 22331
(703) 325-6183

Guy B. Oldaker, Chief

      Access and Release Branch (Freedom of Information)
      W. Anderson, Chief (703/325-6163)

      Programs Branch Policy
      John Henry Hatcher, Chief (703/325-6044)

      Declassification Operations Branch
      John Henry Hatcher, Chief (301/763-2442)

      Privacy and Rule Making Branch
      Richard Christian, Chief (703/325-6227)

The Records Management Division and its branches will be of great value to Russianists and other scholars. The Unofficial Historical Access Program and the Freedom
of Information Act bring much work their way: granting clearance and access to
classified materials, determining what has been or is being declassified, and helping
the National Archives and Records Service, particularly its regional centers. Researchers trying to locate specific army historical records and documents should contact
this division.

U.S. ARMY CENTER OF MILITARY HISTORY
Casimir Pulaski Building
20 Massachusetts Avenue, NW
Washington, D.C. 20314
(202) 272-0291

Brigadier General James L. Collins, Jr., Chief of Military History
David F. Trask, Chief Historian (202/272-0293)

Most of the center's research is done by staff specialists, but a small percentage of work is on a contract basis, usually with former center personnel. All aspects of military history, foreign and domestic, come under the scrutiny of this unit. A substantial amount of the unpublished material remains classified.

The center does not maintain any archival collection of official military records; these are kept at the National Archives and Records Service (entry B6). It is, however, the repository of U.S. Army unit histories, including a collection of 6,000 published and 5,000 to 6,000 unpublished historical studies prepared by U.S. Army unit historians. Some material used to prepare these studies is housed in the center's set of 100 files arranged geographically under the heading "Historians' Background Material Files." These files contain copies of war diaries, dispatches, telegrams, radio news broadcasts, press releases, operations reports, and statistics dealing with U.S. Army operations. The facility also maintains a 25,000-volume reference collection with a large number of army directories, publications, and regulations.

There is no published guide to the holdings, and the collection's card catalog is in the process of being revised and updated. For assistance in locating materials researchers should contact Chief of the Historical Records Branch Hannah M. Zeidlik (202/272-0317). Staff historians can also help scholars verify historical information, compile bibliographies, and locate military source materials in the National Archives and Records Service and other depositories, including the extensive Army Military History Research Collection at Carlisle Barracks, Pennsylvania 17013. An important resource for scholars, the facility is directed by Colonel Donald P. Shaw and houses some 300,000 bound volumes and 30,000 periodicals. Russianists will probably want to contact Colonel Shaw if their field is military history.

The center also coordinates a network of more than sixty army museums scattered around the country. The museums contain artifacts representing all facets of U.S. military history.

A center publication of interest is a projected three-volume study of the German struggle with the Soviet Union in World War II. The first part of the study is *Stalingrad to Berlin: The German Defeat in the East,* by Earl F. Ziemke (1968). Researchers may also want to obtain from GPO a copy of the catalog *Publications of the United States Center of Military History* (1979).

K5 Board for International Broadcasting (BIB)

1 a. *1201 Connecticut Avenue, NW*
Washington, D.C. 20036
(202) 254-8040

b. Open to the public.

c. Walter R. Roberts, Executive Director

2. The board offers some possibilities for contract research and occasionally uses scholars as consultants. This agency oversees Radio Free Europe (RFE) and Radio Liberty (RL) (entries Q16 and Q17).

4. Most bibliographic and research resources concerning RFE and RL are to be found within the offices of these organizations. Some program scripts and translations are at the board's offices, but more of this material and many tape recordings of broadcasts are at RFE and RL. After six months or so, these items are placed in warehouse storage.

5a.   The board publishes annual reports for the president and congress, to whom it is responsible.

K6   Central Intelligence Agency (CIA)

1 a.   *Location:*
Langley, Virginia
(202) 351-1100 (Information)
(202) 351-7676 (Public Affairs)

Mail:
Washington, D.C. 20505

b.   Closed to the public. Security clearance required for entry. Tours for large groups from academic, business, or other private organizations can be arranged through the Public Affairs Office.

2.   Soviet specialists are employed in the Directorate of Foreign Intelligence and other CIA units. Public access to these people is limited and researchers should direct inquiries concerning CIA analysts covering the Soviet Union to the Office of Public Affairs. Naturally, the CIA staff that Russianists would most like to contact is that for Soviet operations. The expertise and knowledge of these workers with respect to the USSR would be difficult to overestimate. They possess, in most cases, analytic, linguistic, and practical skills, plus, often, formal academic training and/or advanced degrees, all of which make the CIA Soviet specialists—desk officers, researchers, and especially field agents—an extraordinary resource for any researcher who can gain access to them.

Methodological research, model building, and technical studies are occasionally contracted out to academic or other private-sector specialists. Soviet-area specialists are also sometimes employed as consultants for regional studies. The coordinator for Academic Relations and External Analytical Support (202/351 5075) administers the CIA's research and consultancy program.

3.   The library (202/351-7701) is generally inaccessible to outside researchers. The unclassified monograph collection is indexed in the computerized Online Computer Library Center (OCLC) (see entries A22, E2).

Although no detailed descriptions of the library resources are possible here, some general remarks about them are appropriate. First, they are substantial and contain major holdings in the Russian/Soviet areas. Second, the library contains unclassified as well as classified material; items that are not readily available in the area may be borrowed from the CIA library on interlibrary loan by a number of libraries.

The map collection is large and also contains both classified and unclassified items. In virtually all cases, the latter holdings are duplicated by the map collections of the Library of Congress (entry E4) and Interior Department's Geological Survey (entry E2). Topological maps, aerial photography maps, and other such items with important strategic military and defense implications would also be an obvious part of this collection. Films here include documentaries, newsreels, and feature films, particularly from the World War II years and after.

4.   The internal records of the CIA are classified and unavailable to outside researchers except through Freedom of Information procedures, which are handled by the Information and Privacy Coordinator (202/351-7486). Research Publications, Inc. (entry Q18), publishes *Declassified Documents Quarterly Catalog,* which lists many

CIA documents, but there is no centralized collection of CIA documents released through Freedom of Information requests. Some staff members of congressional committees may be able to provide useful information in this regard.

5. The CIA produces a number of unclassified documents and maps that are available from different sources in the Washington area. Individual publications and full or tailored subscriptions of documents published after February 1, 1979, are available from the National Technical Information Service (NTIS) (entry Q13). Earlier publications available in hard copy or microfilm may be purchased from the Library of Congress Photoduplication Service, Washington, D.C. 20540 (202/287-5650). Maps and atlases and the *World Factbook* are available from GPO (entry Q9). To subscribe to all available CIA publications, for an annual fee of $225, write to the Document Expediting Project, Exchange and Gifts Division, Library of Congress, Washington, D.C. (202/287-9527). Some CIA publications of interest include *Economic Indicators Weekly Review, International Energy Statistical Review* (monthly), and *Chiefs of State and Cabinet Members of Foreign Governments* (monthly). Publications lists are available from the CIA Office of Public Affairs or from NTIS (see entry Q13). Maryland University, American University, and George Mason University subscribe to all CIA documents.

K7 Civil Aeronautics Board (CAB)

1 a. *1825 Connecticut Avenue, NW*
   Washington, D.C. 20428
   (202) 673-5990 (Information)

b. Open to the public.

c. C. Dan McKinnon, Chairperson

2. CAB promotes and regulates the civil air transport industry within the United States and between the United States and foreign countries.

BUREAU OF INTERNATIONAL AVIATION
(202) 673-5417

Daniel M. Kaspar, Director

Air transportation between the U.S. and foreign countries is conducted pursuant to international agreements. The bureau, on behalf of CAB, advises and assists the State Department in the negotiations of these agreements and participates in the formulation of U.S. positions for international civil aviation conferences. Ronald Miller (202/673-5414) is the desk officer for Eastern Europe and the USSR.

3. Not a major source for the Russianist, the CAB Library contains approximately 2,000 volumes, including some information on international agreements and treaties. Mary Louise Ransom (202/673-5101) heads the library.

K8 Commerce Department

1 a. *Fourteenth Street between Constitution Avenue and E Street, NW*
Washington, D.C. 20230
(202) 377-2000 (Information)

NOTE: Branches are scattered throughout the city and suburbs.

b. Open to the public.

2. Some divisions of the department engage in research on the USSR, examining the commercial and business climate in, and U.S. trade possibilities with, the Soviet Union. Research is conducted primarily in-house, although on occasion contract research opportunities do materialize. The department's main objective is to facilitate trade and promote U.S. economic and technological development.

3. The main library and those of various branches are described in entries A11–14, 44, 51, and 54.

4. Current internal records are stored in the records management facilities of each major subunit of the Commerce Department until they are transferred to the National Archives and Records Service (entry B6). Inventories of retired office files are maintained by the department. Ivy Parr (202/377-3630), chief of the Records Management Division, can direct researchers to appropriate records-management offices and provide assistance in obtaining retired documents.

The head of the Central Reference and Records Inspection Facility, Geraldine LeBoo (202/377-4217), is the department's principal Freedom of Information officer. She can direct researchers to the appropriate Freedom of Information officers in other departmental subunits as required.

5. The department's annual *Commerce Publications Catalog and Index* is available from the Office of Publications (202/377-3721). Descriptions and acquisition information for other Commerce Department publications are provided below under their originating offices. See entry Q13 for the Commerce Department's National Technical Information Service (NTIS), the main distributor for public sale of research reports prepared and sponsored by U.S. Government agencies.

After the State Department, the Commerce Department appears to be the government agency with the most diverse and extensive resources and activities of interest to the Russian/Soviet-area specialist. Relevant sections are described below.

INTERNATIONAL TRADE ADMINISTRATION (ITA)
Main Commerce Building
(202) 377-2867

Lionel H. Olmer, Under Secretary

ITA's objective is to promote progressive business practices and world trade, strengthen the international trade and investment position of the United States, actively support the private economic sector, and assist the economy in adapting to changes within the U.S. economic system. The administration's principal publication is the biweekly *Business Review,* which contains reports on foreign and domestic business conditions and is available from GPO, Washington, D.C. 20402.

Assistant Secretary for International Economic Policy
(202) 377-1461

Deputy Assistant Secretary for Europe
USSR Affairs Division
(202) 377-4505

Hertha W. Heiss, Director

At present almost all ITA activities involving the USSR are channeled through the Office of the Assistant Secretary. Staff members compile, maintain, and disseminate most of the Commerce Department's information about Soviet trade and related economic subjects. It is responsible for trade and export promotion as well as for export control.

Of major importance to researchers is the vast statistical data base maintained by the branch. It has perhaps the most extensive computerized trade information available in the Washington, D.C., area. Trade figures are available for all foreign countries, and the staff is willing to assist scholars; call for information.

The office also coordinates Commerce Department contacts with international trade organizations and other U.S. Government-affiliated agencies. For example, the division has worked closely with the U.S. Commercial Office in Moscow as well as with Soviet trade representatives in the United States.

The USSR Affairs Division distributes, without charge, a large number of publications and information sheets, both its own and those of other government agencies. Researchers should request a list of publications. Also available are information sheets and lists of Soviet commercial representatives in the U.S., U.S. companies in the USSR, and trade intermediaries for U.S. companies.

BUREAU OF ECONOMIC ANALYSIS (BEA)
Tower Building
Fourteenth and K streets, NW
Washington, D.C. 20230
(202) 523-0793 (Information)

BEA prepares, develops, and interprets the economic accounts of the U.S., including its international transactions (financial and trade flows). The BEA monthly *Survey of Current Business* on occasion carries economic data on the USSR. The Reference Room (202/523-0595) of the bureau, located in room B-7, maintains a collection of BEA periodicals and staff papers.

International Investment Division
(202) 523-0657

This division receives confidential statistical reports from U.S. corporations with foreign investments and uses this information to prepare statistical aggregates on U.S. direct investment abroad and analyze the economic impact of multinational corporations.

Balance of Payments Division
(202) 523-0620

This division estimates balance of payments transactions between the United States and the rest of the world. Some estimates are made for transactions between the United States and individual countries, but the Soviet bloc, including Eastern Europe, is considered as a whole. Estimates of certain types of transactions between the United States and individual countries are less useful than the aggregates.

Estimates for recent quarters and years are published in the March, June, September, and December issues of the *Survey of Current Business,* a monthly publication of the BEA. In the June issue, quarterly and annual estimates of U.S. transactions with certain countries and areas are published for the previous three years. Other relevant publications include *U.S. Direct Investment Abroad, 1977* (1981) and *Selected Data on U.S. Direct Investment Abroad, 1950–76* (1982).

Data on U.S. private investments in the USSR can be provided to researchers by the staff, but confidential information on the investments of individual companies cannot be released. Portions of the investment data go as far back as 1929. Some computer tapes of the division's raw data are available from NTIS (entry Q13).

BUREAU OF THE CENSUS
Location:
Suitland at Silver Hill roads
Suitland, Maryland

Mail:
Department of Commerce
Washington, D.C. 20233
(301) 763-4040 (Public Information)

Although the primary focus of the Census Bureau is domestic, useful foreign data are collected by one of its divisions. The Census Bureau Library is described in entry A11.

Foreign Demographic Analysis Division (FDAD)
Scuderi Building
4235 Twenty-eighth Avenue
Marlow Heights, Maryland 20031
(301) 763-2870

Samuel Baum, Chief

FDAD studies demographic, education, manpower, and population questions. Staff members also do input/output studies and work on research and development. Some of the unit's research is computerized, namely, population projections, input/output studies, and related work. Within the division there are two branches that can assist the Russianist: the USSR Population, Employment, Research and Development Branch (Stephen Rapawy, Chief, 301/763-4020) and the USSR Input-Output Branch (Dmitri M. Gallik, Chief, 301/763-4022). The FDAD library, and the division's elaborate, non-computerized system of card files, is described in entry A14.

It should be noted that at the time this edition of the *Guide* was being prepared, the Census Bureau was contemplating reorganization. Although the scope of the work will remain the same, branch and bureau names may change.

NATIONAL TELECOMMUNICATIONS AND INFORMATION ADMINISTRATION
Main Commerce Building
Washington, D.C. 20230
(202) 377-1866

This branch offers little substantive information for the Russianist. There are, however, some contacts with Soviet specialists, mostly through the International Telecommunications Union, of which both the U.S. and USSR are members.

PATENT AND TRADEMARK OFFICE
Location:
Crystal Plaza 3
2021 Jefferson Davis Highway
Arlington, Virginia

Mail:
Washington, D.C. 20231

Office of Legislation and International Affairs
(703) 557-3065

Patent and trademark material and information from around the world are maintained here. The office also has manufacturing, technical, and scientific information. For the Soviet Union, as for many other nations, the staff exchanges communications, documents, and delegations as part of its work. The unit's vertical files, consisting largely of working papers, contain one drawer of Soviet material, mostly on industrial properties. The office's own small library has a few holdings concerned with the USSR, but the distinct Patent Office Scientific Library is the major resource for scholars in this part of the Commerce Department and is described in entry A54.

NATIONAL BUREAU OF STANDARDS (NBS)
Location:
Gaithersburg, Maryland

Mail:
Washington, D.C. 20234
(301) 921-1000

Edward L. Brady, Associate Director, International Affairs (301/921-3641)
Kurt F. J. Heinrich, Chief, Office of International Relations (301/921-2463)

NBS has occasional contacts with USSR scientists and scientific institutions within the framework of various bilateral agreements. The Office of the Associate Director for International Affairs can direct researchers to appropriate points of inquiry within the bureau or provide necessary information directly. All major components of NBS exchange information and materials with their Soviet counterparts. The three major operating units of the bureau are the National Measurement Laboratory, National Engineering Laboratory, and Institute for Computer Sciences and Technology. The staff of these three units have participated in six of the cooperative agreements with the USSR: science and technology, transportation, oceanography, environment, energy, and housing (see Appendix I).

NBS has published several bibliographies, translations, and reports that might be useful to Soviet area scholars. (For Library Services see entry A44.)

NATIONAL OCEANIC AND ATMOSPHERIC ADMINISTRATION (NOAA)
Washington Science Center
6010 Executive Boulevard
Rockville, Maryland 20852
(301) 443-8910 (Information)

NOAA has a number of divisions in the D.C. area that work on one or more of the U.S.-USSR bilateral agreements. Individual NOAA scientists may also have professional contact with their counterparts in the Soviet Union. The following are some of the more important branches of NOAA for Russianists. (For library services see entry A51.)

Office of International Affairs
Page Building 2
3300 Whitchaven Street, NW
Washington, D.C. 20235
(202) 632-5111

Coordinating NOAA work with that of international organizations like the UN, this office can provide general information about NOAA activities that relate to the USSR.

Office of Oceanic and Atmospheric Research
Washington Science Center, Building 5
6010 Executive Boulevard
Rockville, Maryland 20852
(301) 443-8845

This office conducts research programs on all aspects of NOAA activity other than fishing. It is responsible for administration of the U.S.-USSR agreement on ocean science and for certain aspects of the U.S.-USSR agreement on the environment.

National Environmental Satellite, Data, and Information Service
Federal Building 4.
Suitland and Silver Hill roads
Suitland, Maryland 20233
(301) 763-5904

This service collects, compiles, and distributes data on the world environment, with particular reference to atmosphere, climate, oceans, and weather, and regularly exchanges such data with the USSR.

National Weather Service
Gramax Building
8060 Thirteenth Street
Silver Spring, Maryland 20910
(301) 427-7645

The service observes current weather conditions, distributes data, forecasts weather conditions, and conducts meteorological and hydrological research.

National Marine Fisheries Service
Page Building 2
3300 Whitehaven Street, NW
Washington, D.C. 20235
(202) 634-7514

This service administers bilateral agreements with respect to foreign fishing in the U.S. Fishing Conservation Zone. It also supports U.S. delegations at multilateral conferences dealing with Antarctica, living marine resources, and marine mammals.

K9   Commission on Security and Cooperation in Europe (CSCE)

1 a. *House Annex II, Room 3257*
     Washington, D.C. 20515
     (202) 225-1901

   b. Open to researchers by appointment.

c. Dante B. Fascell, Chairperson
Robert Dole, Cochairperson
R. Spencer Oliver, Staff Director

2. Established in 1976, CSCE monitors signatories' compliance with the Helsinki agreement of 1975, the thirty-five-nation Accord on Security and Cooperation in Europe. In particular, the staff is interested in humanitarian rights in the USSR and Eastern Europe and the "freer flow of information, ideas, and people" across national borders (so-called "Basket III" matters). The independent commission set up by Congress consists of fifteen members, twelve from the Senate and House and three from the executive branch.

4. Records, trip reports, and other materials relating to the commission's duties are collected and maintained and are available to researchers. The vertical-file collection consists of information produced by European and American organizations interested in questions of defense, human rights, and other matters related to the Helsinki accords, plus an extensive collection of post-1975 *samizdat* materials.

5. Researchers should inquire about publications of proceedings of members' appearances at congressional committee hearings.

K10 Congress—Standing Committees

1 a. *The Capitol*
Washington, D.C. 20510
(202) 224-3121 (Information)

b. The Senate and House of Representatives galleries and most committee hearings are open to the public.

2. Sessions of Congress run in two-year cycles, concurrent with the elected term of the House. At the beginning of each two-year session, Congress "reorganizes" itself, making alterations in the committee structure as deemed necessary, electing its officers, and assigning its members to various committees and subcommittees. Congress does most of its legislative work in committees. Although committee schedules are subject to frequent alterations, legislative calendars are available, and announcements of forthcoming committee activities, including locations and subject matter, appear in the "Daily Digest" section of the *Congressional Record*. The *Washington Post* newspaper also publishes the schedule of congressional activities each day. Many congressional activities are followed by the *Washington Monitor* (entry Q23) and *Congressional Quarterly Weekly Report* (entry Q4).
    The Congressional Research Service (CRS) serves as the principal research arm of the Congress and is described in entry K11.

3. Described elsewhere are the Library of Congress (entry A37), Senate Library (entry A56), and House of Representatives Library (entry A28).

5. The daily *Congressional Record* is the official published version of the proceedings on the floors of the Senate and House of Representatives. Transcripts of hearings, special reports, and other documents produced by the various committees and subcommittees of Congress are available from the committees themselves. Some of these publications may also be purchased from the GPO (entry Q9). Several—although not all—committees maintain mailing lists, and researchers may request to have their names included on these lists. GPO also occasionally prepares subject-bibliographies

of congressional publications on foreign affairs, U.S. intelligence activities, and other topics. Lists of these bibliographies, and the bibliographies themselves, are available without charge.

The committees listed below have the jurisdictions and functional responsibilities indicated. This is a selective list of only the more important committees, from the viewpoint of Soviet area specialists. No attempt has been made to name the various subcommittees with more specific spheres of responsibility. A variety of activities of these committees are worth the researcher's attention. Many publish documents relating to their work; they hold regular meetings, at least once a month, which are generally open to the public; and they convene hearings annually that are open to the public in most cases. Hearings especially produce a wealth of oral (and written) testimony that can be of considerable value to Russianists. Experts from the academic community and other specialists usually testify at these hearings, and the proceedings are then published.

STANDING COMMITTEES OF THE SENATE

COMMERCE, SCIENCE, AND TRANSPORTATION
Russell Senate Office Building, Room 237
(202) 224-1251

Of special interest is this committee's concern with foreign commerce, science, transportation, communications, and the transfer of technology among nations.

AGRICULTURE, NUTRITION, AND FORESTRY
Russell Senate Office Building, Room 322
(202) 224-2035

The committee considers agriculture and forestry questions in general; commodities exchanges; the production, marketing, and price stabilization of agricultural products and commodities; and school nutrition programs.

APPROPRIATIONS
Capitol Building, Room S-130
(202) 224-7200

This committee reviews appropriations for support of all government agencies.

ARMED SERVICES
Russell Senate Office Building, Room 212
(202) 224-3871

The Armed Services Committee concerns itself with national defense in general; the Defense, Army, Navy, and Air Force departments; military matters; and some aeronautical and space questions of military significance.

FINANCE
Dirksen Senate Office Building, Room 2227
(202) 224-4515

The Finance Committee reviews matters of reciprocal trade agreements, tariffs, import quotas, customs, and ports of entry and delivery.

FOREIGN RELATIONS
Dirksen Senate Office Building, Room 4229
(202) 224-3943

This is one of the most important committees for the Russianist. It looks after questions of U.S. relations with foreign countries, treaties, protection of American citizens abroad, expatriation, international conferences and congresses, the American National Red Cross, foreign intervention and declarations of war, the diplomatic service, the UN and other international organizations, foreign loans, some aspects of U.S. foreign trade, and American business interests abroad.

JUDICIARY
Dirksen Senate Office Building, Room 2226
(202) 224-5225

This committee's concerns include protection of trade and commerce, immigration and naturalization, espionage, the Patent Office, questions of patents, copyrights, and trademarks, and claims against the U.S.

LABOR AND HUMAN RESOURCES
Dirksen Senate Office Building, Room 4230
(202) 224-5375

This committee studies measures relating to education, labor, or public welfare in general; labor statistics and standards; and public health.

ENERGY AND NATURAL RESOURCES
Dirksen Senate Office Building, Room 3104
(202) 224-4971

This committee is concerned with issues surrounding U.S. energy policy; regulation, conservation, research and development, and distribution of natural resources; and domestic and foreign considerations pertaining to petroleum production and exportation.

STANDING COMMITTEES OF THE HOUSE OF REPRESENTATIVES

(No description is included for committees whose interests coincide with Senate committees of the same or similar name.)

AGRICULTURE
Longworth House Office Building, Room 1301
(202) 225-2171

APPROPRIATIONS
The Capitol, Room H-218
(202) 225-2771

ARMED SERVICES
Rayburn House Office Building, Room 2120
(202) 225-4151

BANKING, FINANCE, AND URBAN AFFAIRS
Rayburn House Office Building, Room 2129
(202) 225-4247

This committee considers banking and currency generally; public and private housing; matters of dollar valuation and devaluation; defense production; economic stabilization; international finance; and international financial and monetary organizations.

EDUCATION AND LABOR
Rayburn House Office Builidng, Room 2181
(202) 225-4527

FOREIGN AFFAIRS
Rayburn House Office Building, Room 2170
(202) 225-5021

ENERGY AND COMMERCE
Rayburn House Office Building, Room 2125
(202) 225-2927

The committee's jurisdiction includes matters of interstate and foreign commerce generally; foreign communications; travel and tourism; public health; and U.S. energy policy.

JUDICIARY
Rayburn House Office Building, Room 2137
(202) 225-8088

SCIENCE AND TECHNOLOGY
Rayburn House Office Building, Room 2321
(202) 225-6371

Matters relating to astronautical research and development, the Bureau of Standards, the National Aeronautics and Space Administration, the National Science Foundation, outer space (including its exploration and control), scientific research and development in general, environmental and energy research and development (except atomic energy), and the National Weather Service are some of the responsibilities of this committee.

WAYS AND MEANS
Longworth House Office Building, Room 1102
(202) 225-3628

The Ways and Means Committee is concerned with reciprocal trade agreements, customs, ports of entry and delivery, and revenue measures generally.

JOINT COMMITTEES OF THE CONGRESS

ECONOMIC
Dirksen Senate Office Building, Room G-207
(202) 224-0384

This very important committee looks into matters relating to economic growth and progress, energy, fiscal policy, and international economics.

LIBRARY
House Annex 1, Room 415
(202) 225-0392

This committee oversees the Library of Congress.

COMMISSION ON SECURITY AND COOPERATION IN EUROPE
House Annex 2, Room 3257
(202) 225-1901

This committee considers political, economic, and military affairs in Europe as they relate to U.S. security interests (see entry K9).

NOTE: Other less permanent committees of Congress, called select or special committees, would often be of great interest to Soviet-area specialists. For example, in recent years the Senate has had a Select Committee to Study Governmental Operations with Respect to Intelligence Activities and a Special Committee on National Emergencies and Delegated Emergency Powers, while the House has had its own Select Committee on Intelligence. For current information about these committees, researchers should consult the *Congressional Staff Directory*, ed. Charles B. Brownson (Mount Vernon, Va.: Congressional Staff Directory, Ltd.), an annual; or the Washington Monitor's *Congressional Yellow Book* (entry Q23).

K11 Congressional Research Service (CRS)

1 a. *Library of Congress*
James Madison Memorial Building
First Street and Independence Avenue, SE
Washington, D.C. 20540
(202) 287-5775

b. Closed to the public.

c. Gilbert Gude, Director

2.   CRS works exclusively for the Congress, conducting research, analyzing legislation, and providing information at the request of members, committees, and their staffs. Soviet-area specialists (including John T. Hardt, Chief, 202/287-8889) in the Foreign Affairs and National Defense Division (Stanley Heginbotham, Chief, 202/287-5064), upon request and without partisan bias, prepare studies, reports, compilations, digests, and background briefings on USSR-related issues of current concern to the Congress. These research and reference services are not available to the public.

3.   The Library of Congress is described in entry A37.

5.   All CRS research is restricted to the use of the Congress and is not for general distribution. Individual researchers may, however, often obtain copies from Congress, either through the office of a member or from a committee. Also, from time to time CRS studies are read into the *Congressional Record* or are published in congressional committee reports. CRS *Issue Briefs,* which are distributed only to members of Congress, review major policy topics, summarize pertinent legislative history, and provide reference lists for further reading. In addition, *Congressional Research Service Review, UPDATE from CRS,* and the cumulative *Subject Catalog of CRS Reports in Print* (1980) are all exclusive publications for the members of Congress. Researchers may note that CRS indexes current periodical articles on public policy issues—including foreign affairs by country—from some 3,000 U.S. and foreign journals and magazines. The "Bibliographic Citation" file is accessible to researchers in machine-readable format in the LC's SCORPIO automated data base (see entry A37).

K12 Defense Department (DOD)

1 a. *The Pentagon*
Washington, D.C. 20301
(202) 545-6700 (Information)
(202) 697-1160 (Public Affairs)

b. Closed to those without security clearance or appointments made in advance.

2. DOD has divisions that support some in-house research. Most research conducted for DOD is on a contract basis. (A good estimate would be that as much or more government funding goes to research for this and the other military departments than goes to any other agency's work.) DOD, however, gives out very few research grants.

3. See the Defense Technical Information Center (entry G4), Defense Mapping Agency Hydrographic/Topographic Center (entries A16 and E1); and Defense Audiovisual Agency (entry F1).

4. Each major subunit of DOD controls its own internal records until they are retired to the jurisdiction of the National Archives and Records Service (entry B6). DOD's Records Management Branch (202/695-0970) can refer researchers to individual records-control offices within the department. Requests under the Freedom of Information Act for the records of the Office of the Secretary of Defense and of the Joint Chiefs of Staff are processed by the Directorate for Freedom of Information and Security Review (202/697-4325) in the Office of the Assistant Secretary of Defense for Public Affairs. Other DOD branches also have Freedom of Information officers; the Directorate for Freedom of Information can refer researchers to the appropriate offices.

5. The Defense Technical Information Center (entry G4), closed to the public, is the repository for both classified and unclassified research reports produced under DOD contracts. The unclassified research reports are also available from the National Technical Information Service (entry Q13). There are many more offices, divisions, and task forces of interest to Russianists in this department and its sister agencies (the Army, Navy, and Air Force departments are described in entries K4, K29, and K2 respectively) than can be described fully in these pages. Although the work of the various sections may be quite different, it all comes down basically to the fields of military and defense affairs. The best guide a researcher can have to the labyrinths of the four military/defense agencies is to obtain and study the most recent edition of the DOD Telephone Directory, available from GPO and its numerous bookstores. This book also contains an organizational directory for the four departments. A second very useful aid for this, as for other government agencies, is the *Federal Yellow Book*, published and constantly updated by the Washington Monitor, Inc. (entry Q23).

The more important divisions of DOD are described in more detail hereafter. At this point it may be useful to list, but not discuss, some of the other sections or offices that either seem less substantial as resources or would prove difficult to gain access to: Defense Nuclear Agency (202/325-7004); Assistant Secretary for Program Analysis and Evaluation (202/695-0971); Defense Advisor for NATO (202/697-4196); Deputy Assistant Secretaries for European and NATO Affairs (202/697-8101); East Asian and Pacific Affairs (202/697-2307); International Economic Affairs (202/697-3248); and Policy Plans and NSC Affairs (202/697-0268).

OFFICE OF THE SECRETARY OF DEFENSE (OSD)—Public Affairs
Philip A. Farris, Staff Assistant for Public Correspondence
(202/697-1160)

Because of the sensitive nature of DOD work, it is sometimes difficult to obtain information about the department, its staff, and that work. For this reason, Mr. Farris should be of considerable interest to researchers. He can assist in locating the divisions and personnel most appropriate for making further inquiries. He can provide general information about DOD also. (For more specific inquiries, based on the Freedom of Information Act, Russianists should contact Lee Taylor at 202/697-1171.)

OFFICE OF THE SECRETARY OF DEFENSE (OSD)—Policy
(202) 697-6301

This office supports a diverse research program relating in part to foreign policy, military, and security affairs of the Soviet Union. A small number of staff specialists produces research that appears in policy papers, largely unpublished and classified. Most published research, however, is conducted by independent scholars and analysts on contract. DOD Policy Staff coordinates U.S. Government funding of the National Council for Soviet and East European Research (entry H24), and sponsors numerous classified and unclassified U.S.-Soviet force balance assessments.

OSD Policy makes no comprehensive bibliography of its published Soviet-area studies available to the public. Nonsensitive studies sponsored by the office are generally available through the Defense Technical Information Center (entry G4). Researchers may contact the director of Policy Research (202-697-6301/1385) for a description of work on their subject and for help in gaining access to this material. Examples of the published work sponsored by OSD Policy: *A Pilot Study: Soviet Perceptions of Arms Control and Correlation of Forces,* by W. Scott Payne et al. (Arlington, Va.: System Planning Corporation, 1980); *The Soviet Threat in the Middle East,* by T. N. Dupuy et al. (Dunn Loring, Va.: Historical Evaluation and Research Organization, 1980).

DEFENSE ADVANCED RESEARCH PROJECTS AGENCY (DARPA)
1400 Wilson Boulevard
Arlington, Virginia 22209
(202) 694-3032

Undertaking no research of its own, DARPA functions as a corporate research division in a private industry. Its programs focus on proof-of-concept demonstrations of revolutionary approaches for improved conventional, rapid deployment, sea power, and strategic forces and on scientific investigation into advanced basic technologies of the future. DARPA also undertakes studies, directly relating to the DOD research and development program, that address potential U.S. adversaries' military capabilities. DARPA accepts unsolicited proposals from private individuals, educational institutions, commercial and industrial research organizations, DOD or other government laboratories, and other private and public organizations.

DEFENSE INTELLIGENCE AGENCY (DIA)
(202) 695-7353

DIA produces some research on the USSR. Its work is classified, and no bibliographies of its research are available. Similarly lacking are details on its publications. Most agency research is done in-house. Occasionally, outside researchers are employed on contract to perform studies of Soviet economics, foreign policy, military policy, and many other subjects.

Nonagency researchers are prohibited access to the DIA library.

NATIONAL SECURITY AGENCY (NSA)
Fort George G. Meade, Maryland 20755
(301) 688-6524 (Information and Freedom of Information)

The NSA is one of the "big three" of the U.S. intelligence community (along with the CIA and DIA) and perhaps the most secretive. The agency conducts highly technical communications intelligence-gathering activities worldwide. Its organizational structure remains classified.

ORGANIZATION OF THE JOINT CHIEFS OF STAFF (JCS)
(202) 695-7678 (Public Affairs)
(202) 697-4325 (Freedom of Information)

Plans and Policy Directorate
    European Division
    (202) 697-4911

The European Division prepares policy papers and estimates for the Joint Chiefs of Staff relating to U.S. security interests and the Soviet Union. All products are classified.

Office of the Secretary of the Joint Chiefs of Staff
    Historical Division
    (202) 697-3088

The Historical Division prepares histories and special background studies on the JCS. Although most of this division's products are classified, several volumes dealing with the JCS during the 1940s have been declassified and released to the National Archives and Records Service (entry B6). Chief Historian Robert J. Watson and his staff provide reference assistance and can help researchers identify and locate JCS documents.

    Documents Division
    (202) 695-5363

The Documents Division is the JCS "archive." This division reviews internal records for release through the National Archives and processes Freedom of Information Act requests for JCS documents. Declassification usually follows a twenty-year waiting period.

K13 Education Department

1 a. *400 Maryland Avenue, SW*
    Washington, D.C. 20202
    (202) 245-2424

  b. Open to the public.

2. The Education Department (inaugurated May 4, 1980) administers more than 160 programs drawn principally from the former Health, Education and Welfare Department's Office of Education. Certain education-related activities of the Defense, Justice, Housing and Urban Development, and Labor departments, and the National Science Foundation have also been shifted to the new Education Department. The department is charged with ensuring equal educational opportunity for all; promoting improvement in the quality of education through research, evaluation, and management; and monitoring the accountability of federal educational programs.

    Although a broad range of research activities are conducted in-house, on occasion outside consultant and contract research projects are available.

3. The National Institute of Education—Educational Research Library is described in entry A47.

4–5. Internal records and publications are described with their respective agencies, below.

PUBLIC INFORMATION SERVICE (ASSISTANT SECRETARY FOR LEGISLATION AND PUBLIC AFFAIRS)
(202) 245-8564

This office should be contacted for general information about the Education Department. The staff can help the researcher locate the appropriate divisions relating to his or her needs. The office also handles Freedom of Information requests (Jack Billings, 202/472-3338).

INTERNATIONAL EDUCATION PROGRAMS (IEP)
Regional Office Building 3, Room 3919
Seventh and D streets, SW
Washington, D.C. 20202
(202) 245-9691

Kenneth Whitehead, Director

The Education Department, through its Office of International Education Programs (IEP) is responsible for expanding the international and global dimensions of American education and for promoting awareness of other cultures. IEP activities include foreign language and area training, curriculum development, research, exchange, and a wide range of services in the international education field. Details about each of these activities, which are briefly described below and usually include Russian/Soviet studies, may be obtained from the office.

Five programs for individuals and institutions are conducted primarily within the United States. The first four are authorized by Title VI of the Higher Education Act of 1965, as amended, and the last by the Mutual Educational and Cultural Exchange (Fulbright) Act of 1961:

The National Resource Centers program provides grants to higher education institutions to establish, strengthen and operate centers focusing on one world region or on general worldwide topics.

The Foreign Language and Area Studies Fellowship program offers academic-year and summer awards for graduate students in foreign language and area studies. The grants made to selected U.S. higher education institutions must include study of the language(s) of the geographic area of specialization.

The Research program provides grants to institutions of higher education, organizations, and individuals to support surveys and studies to determine the need for increased or improved instruction in modern foreign language, area, and international studies.

The Undergraduate International Studies and Foreign Language program awards grants to higher education institutions and public and private nonprofit organizations to plan, develop, and carry out a comprehensive program to strengthen and improve undergraduate instruction in international studies and foreign languages. Projects designed to integrate undergraduate studies with M.A. degree programs are also eligible for support.

The Foreign Curriculum Consultant program brings experts from other countries to the United States for an academic year to assist selected American educational institutions in planning and developing their curricula in foreign languages and area studies.

Six programs for individuals, groups, institutions, and nonprofit educational organizations are conducted primarily overseas. The first five are authorized by the Fulbright Act and the last by Memoranda of Understanding between this department and individual foreign governments:

The Faculty Research Abroad program is designed to assist higher education institutions in strengthening their international studies programs by providing awards to key faculty members to maintain expertise, update curricula, and improve teaching methods and materials in foreign language and area studies.

The Doctoral Dissertation Research Abroad program provides assistance for graduate students to engage in full-time dissertation research abroad in modern foreign language and area studies. This program is designed to aid prospective higher education teachers and scholars improve their research knowledge and capability in world areas not widely included in American curricula and enhance understanding of these areas, cultures, and languages.

The Group Projects Abroad program provides grants to U.S. educational institutions or nonprofit educational organizations for training, research, advanced foreign language training, curriculum development, and/or instructional materials acquisition in international and intercultural studies. Participants may include college and university faculty members, experienced elementary and secondary school teachers, curriculum supervisors and administrators, and selected higher education students specializing in foreign language and area studies.

The Seminars Abroad program provides opportunities for teachers at the elementary, secondary, and college levels to participate in a variety of short-term seminars abroad on teaching methods.

The Teacher Exchange program provides opportunities for elementary and secondary school teachers and, in some cases, college instructors and assistant professors to teach outside the United States. Various arrangements are made by the U.S. Government with other countries to provide for a direct exchange of teachers.

Special Bilateral Projects with other nations support short-term institutes, research seminars, and exchanges focusing on the study of foreign languages and cultures. Eligible applicants include scholars, language teachers, curriculum developers, vocational and technical specialists, and educational administrators.

In addition to grant programs, IEP provides a number of services in the field of international education:

The Comparative Education staff prepares and publishes studies on educational systems of other countries. It also provides consultative and technical assistance on education systems abroad to U.S. educational institutions, agencies, organizations, and individuals.

The UNESCO Recruitment staff works with UNESCO in recruiting American educators for field positions abroad.

The International Visitors staff plans itineraries and provides educational counseling for visiting foreign educators who are not on U.S. Government grants. The staff also arranges appointments for individual foreign educators who wish to consult with education specialists working for the Education Department.

The Educational Development staff arranges educational training programs for teachers and administrators from other countries. Training includes regular courses, special seminars, and site visits to demonstration and research centers.

CLEARINGHOUSE
Gertha Bass (202/245-7804)

The Clearinghouse staff prepares and distributes brochures, pamphlets, and other reference materials on the programs and services of the IEP and also answers inquiries about similar programs operated outside the IEP. Scholars might want to request the free *Selected International Education Publications of the U.S. Department of Education to Further International Education* (1982) for an informative list of publications relating to international education. Other useful titles available include: *International Education Programs and Services* (1980), *Study and Teaching Opportunities Abroad* (1980), and *Foreign Students' Guide to Study in the United States* (1981).

NATIONAL INSTITUTE FOR HANDICAPPED RESEARCH (NIHR)
Office of International Activities
Switzer Building, Room 3042
330 C Street, SW
Washington, D.C. 20201

Martin McCavitt, Special Assistant for International Activities (202/245-0027)

NIHR, previously called the Rehabilitation Service Administration, was shifted from the former Health, Education, and Welfare Department to the Education Department in 1980. The office conducts research programs designed to explore the physical, social, psychological, and vocational needs of handicapped persons. Although there is at present no direct research relating to the USSR, the office on occasion participates with other government agencies in professional exchanges with counterpart Soviet organizations.

NATIONAL CENTER FOR EDUCATION STATISTICS (NCES)
Presidential Building, Room 205,
6525 Bellcress Road
Hyattsville, Maryland 20782
(301) 436-7881

Marie D. Eldridge, Administrator

NCES collects analyses and disseminates U.S. and foreign education statistics. For data related to the USSR contact Larry Suter (301/436-6684) of the Educational Indicators and Foreign Statistics Branch. The major activities of NCES are described in its annual report, *The Condition of Education.*

K14 Energy Department (DOE)

1 a. *James Forrestal Building*
1000 Independence Avenue, SW
Washington, D.C. 20585
(202) 252-5575 (Information)

b. Open to the public, but appointments are recommended. Some DOE files and documents are classified. Inquiries should be directed to the Freedom of Information and Privacy Activities Division (Milton Jordan, 202/252-6020).

2. DOE was established in 1977 to provide the framework for a comprehensive and balanced national energy plan through the coordination and administration of the energy functions of the federal government. DOE's responsibilities include research, development and demonstration of energy technology; energy conservation; nuclear weapons programs; regulation of energy production and use; and a central energy data collection and analysis program. Many departmental activities are international in dimension. Research is conducted by in-house researchers and by outside contract.

3. The DOE library is described in entry A18.

5. Some publications of interest include: *Guide for the Submission of Unsolicited Proposals* (1980); *The DOE Program Guide for Universities and Other Research Groups* (1980); *Energy Abstracts for Policy Analysis* (monthly), containing worldwide abstracts of journal articles and books on energy analysis; *Annual Report to Congress,* with international statistical charts and tables; *Energy Meetings,* a listing of conferences, symposia, workshops, congresses and other formal meetings pertaining to DOE's programmatic interests; and *First Annual Report on Nuclear Non-Proliferation* (1979). Most of these publications are available free from the Office of Public Affairs (James Forrestal Building, Room GA 343, 202/252-6827). Below are described those subdivisions of the department of potential interest to Russianists.

OFFICE OF INTERNATIONAL AFFAIRS (IA)
1000 Independence Avenue, SW
Washington, D.C. 20585
(202) 252-5800

Henry E. Thomas, Assistant Secretary

This office is responsible for developing, managing, and directing programs and activities that support U.S. energy and foreign policies. The office assesses world price and supply trends, as well as technological developments, and it studies the effects of international actions on U.S. energy supplies. IA also coordinates cooperative international energy programs and maintains relationships with foreign governments and international organizations. This office prepares the periodically updated unclassified report, *International Bilateral and Multilateral Arrangements in Energy Technology.*

The Office of Intelligence (John B. K. Labarre, Director, 202/252-5174) coordinates DOE participation in the intelligence community; analyzes economic, political, and technical intelligence as it relates to energy production and consumption in foreign countries; and provides other intelligence services for DOE.

It should be noted that at the time this edition of the *Guide* was being prepared, there was substantial evidence that the IA was being phased out of existence. Congress had budgeted little money for the organization, and many bureau and branch chief slots were vacant.

ASSISTANT SECRETARY FOR DEFENSE PROGRAMS
1000 Independence Avenue, SW
Washington, D.C. 20585
(202) 252-2177

Office of International Security Affairs (202) 252-2100

Julio L. Torres, Director

>Division of Politico-Military Security Affairs
>(202) 252-2127

>John A. Griffin, Director

Although this office primarily handles issues related to nuclear energy and nonproliferation, it also works on international policy matters—including security of foreign oil production and its availability to the U.S.—with the State Department, Defense Department, and CIA. Files are classified; the staff, however, will meet with visiting scholars by appointment.

ENERGY INFORMATION ADMINISTRATION (EIA)
James Forrestal Building, Room IF048
1000 Independence Avenue, SW
Washington, D.C. 20585
(202) 252-6411

J. Erich Evered, Administrator

EIA, the primary data analysis arm of the Energy Department, is responsible for the collection, processing, and publication of data on energy reserves; the financial status of energy-producing companies; production, demand, and consumption; and analysis of long-term energy trends in the U.S. and abroad.

National Energy Information Center (NEIC)
(202) 252-2363
(202) 252-8800 (Information)

John E. Daniels, Director

NEIC might be a good first point of contact with the Energy Information Administration. The center serves as an inquiry, referral, and reference service for the EIA and DOE. NEIC distributes a number of publications of potential interest to researchers, including *Energy Information Administration Annual Report to Congress,* which contains international energy forecasts and oil price information; *International Energy Annual*; and *Monthly Energy Review.* Also available are *EIA Monthly Publications: New Releases* and *EIA Publications Directory.* These latter publications can also be found at GPO (entry Q9) outlets and through NTIS (entry Q13).

K15 Environmental Protection Agency (EPA)

1 a. *401 M Street, SW*
  Washington, D.C. 20460
  (202) 382-7550 (Public Information)

  b. Open to the public, appointments are recommended.

  c. William D. Ruckelshaus, Administrator (202/382-4700)

2. EPA supports both in-house and contract research and participates in cooperative environmental research on an international level. Most programs and projects are coordinated through a single office.

OFFICE OF INTERNATIONAL ACTIVITIES
(202) 382-4870

Richard Funkhouser

The international activities of EPA administered by this office are designed to encourage worldwide cooperation in studying and overcoming long-range environmental problems. In pursuing this goal, EPA maintains contacts with scientists and policymakers from other countries and multilateral organizations. Researchers should check first with this office at EPA as it can direct them to appropriate divisions of the agency with USSR-related activities.

U.S./USSR and U.S./PRC (People's Republic of China) Environmental Programs
(202) 382-4890

Linwood Starbird, Executive Secretary

The environmental agreement accounts for most of the contact EPA has with the
Soviet Union. Currently forty-two projects are maintained under the agreement, of
which EPA is involved in fifteen of them.

EPA also participates, along with the USSR, in many international programs concerned with environmental matters, such as the UN Environmental Program and
international oil spill cleanup activities.

For more information about EPA programs, contact Gary Waxmonsky, executive
secretary of the bilateral agreement (202/382-4878).

3. The EPA headquarters library (202/382-5926) contains approximately 7,000 books,
1,000 periodical subscriptions, a collection of 25,000 bound reports and documents,
and 145,000 microfilm items. The facility is open to the public for on-site use from
8:00 A.M. to 5:00 P.M., Monday through Friday. Interlibrary loan and photocopying
services are available. The collection is primarily technical in nature and includes the
limited number of reports generated by EPA on its activities relating to the USSR.

5. *Monthly Accession List* is circulated within EPA. *Annual Journal Holdings Report*;
EPA Publications Bibliography Quarterly Abstract Bulletin, which is based on the
library's bibliographic activities; the two-volume *EPA Cumulative Bibliography, 1970–
1976*; and *EPA Reports* are available through the NTIS Service (entry Q13). For
general news about EPA activities the bimonthly *EPA Journal* is useful and is available
through GPO (entry Q9) on a subscription basis.

NOTE: As this guide went to press a shake-up at the EPA resulted in numerous
personnel changes.

K16 Export-Import Bank of the United States (Eximbank)

1 a. *811 Vermont Avenue, NW*
Washington, D.C. 20571
(202) 566-8990 (Information)

b. Open to the public. Internal records are restricted.

2. The Eximbank is an independent agency of the U.S. Government providing loans,
guarantees, and insurance to facilitate the financing of U.S. exports. Working with
both the State and Commerce departments, the bank's staff assesses the ability of
foreign buyers to pay for U.S. imports. Individual country loan records are confidential, but staff officers will discuss general questions with researchers.

OFFICE OF POLICY ANALYSIS
(202) 566-8861

Jane C. Cruse, Vice President

The policy analysis staff prepares research studies on international economic developments that affect the bank and its programs. These studies occasionally consider
issues related to the USSR. Research topics include methodologies for economic
analysis and reviews of bank programs; export financing patterns in the U.S. and

abroad; trends in individual industries and commodities worldwide; domestic and international capital-market developments; and fluctuations in interest rates, prices, and other economic indicators. Most research products are confidential.

OFFICE OF DIRECT CREDITS AND FINANCIAL GUARANTEES
Europe and Canada Division
(202) 566-8813

Raymond J. Albright, Vice President

International economists and loan officers maintain loan-project files and prepare country and regional studies on the economic conditions and "credit worthiness" for all parts of the globe. Since 1974 Eximbank has been precluded by law to extend credits to the USSR. If and when the bank's activities with the Soviet Union resume, researchers should find much to interest them here.

3. The Eximbank library is described in entry A20.

4. Virtually all the bank's loan-project files, research reports, and other internal records are considered confidential. Access may only be pursued through Freedom of Information Act procedures, which have not been very successful in the past. Most of Eximbank's internal records (since 1934) are under the custody of the Office of Administration's Records and Central Files Manager, Helene H. Wall (202/566-8815). Records for 1937–67 are being microfiched and the originals transferred to the National Archives and Records Service (entry B6). A computerized index is being developed for records pertaining to the bank's active loan projects.

5. The Public Affairs Office makes available the annual *Report to the U.S. Congress on Export Credit Competition and the Export-Import Bank of the United States* as well as press releases and a number of frequently updated brochures and booklets on Eximbank programs. These publications are available without charge.

K17 Federal Reserve System

1 a. *Twentieth Street and Constitution Avenue, NW*
   Washington, D.C. 20551
   (202) 452-3204 (Information)

 b. Open to the public, appointments are recommended.

 c. Paul A. Volcker, Chairman

2. The Federal Reserve System serves as the central bank of the United States. Foreign-related activities of interest to researchers fall within the responsibilities of the International Finance Division.

INTERNATIONAL FINANCE DIVISION
(202) 452-3614

Edwin M. Truman, Director

This division monitors U.S. balance of payments, movements in exchange rates and transactions in foreign exchange markets, capital flows between the U.S. and foreign financial centers, and other economic and financial developments abroad that affect

U.S. monetary policy. In addition, the division assists the Federal Reserve in its advisory and consultative role within the U.S. Government in discussions of international financial matters; in directing U.S. participation in various international financial and monetary organizations; and in maintaining informational contacts with the central banks of other countries. The division also collects and analyzes information and data relating to the activities of U.S. banks abroad and foreign banks in the U.S.

Within this division, the World Payment and Economic Activities Section is specifically responsible for monitoring the financial situation of world governments, including that of the USSR.

Russianists should contact Keith Savard (202/452-2337) for help with Soviet-related questions.

3.   The Research Library of the Board of Governors (Ann Roane Clary, chief librarian, 202/452-3398) is open to the public from 9:00 A.M. to 5:00 P.M., Thursdays, and to researchers by special arrangement. Interlibrary loan service and limited photocopying facilities are available. The collection consists of some 85,000 monographic volumes and 2,300 current periodical subscriptions. The subject strengths in the collection are in the areas of banking, economic conditions, and monetary policy in the United States and abroad. Researchers may note that the library's holdings contain a large number of foreign monetary and banking laws, from 1915 to 1960, publications of foreign central banks, and official statistical releases of more than 100 foreign countries, including the Soviet Union. A biweekly *Research Library Recent Acquisitions* and a computer-generated printout of the library's periodicals are available.

4.   All requests for access to classified records and documents should be directed to Rose Arnold (202/452-3684), the system's Freedom of Information officer.

5.   *Federal Reserve Board Publications* lists selected publications and staff studies of the Federal Reserve Board. *Federal Reserve System Purposes and Functions* (1979) is a handbook presenting a concise account of the responsibilities and operating techniques of the system in the areas of monetary policy, banking, and financial regulations. Statistical releases and staff studies are published from time to time in the monthly *Federal Reserve Bulletin*. The system's *Annual Report* provides useful summaries of its activities.

K18   General Accounting Office (GAO)

1 a.   *441 G Street, NW*
Washington, D.C. 20548
(202) 275-2812 (Information)

b.   Open to the public; appointments are recommended.

c.   Charles A. Browsher, Comptroller General

2.   An independent, nonpolitical agency in the legislative branch of the government, GAO assists Congress, its committees, and its members in carrying out their legislative and supervisory responsibilities. Most GAO research is conducted in-house; limited consulting opportunities, however, are also available.

The International Division (202/275-5518) evaluates the effectiveness of U.S. foreign aid programs, the utility of establishing military installations in foreign areas, and the impact of U.S. policy on U.S. trade and international financial status. The division also reviews government bilateral and multilateral programs and agreements to determine whether or not they are fulfilling their intended purposes. In recent years this division has examined such issues as U.S. assistance in resettling Soviet refugees, progress on the bilateral agreements, and wheat sales to the USSR.

3. The GAO Library consists of two components, the Technical Library (202/275-5180) and the Law Library (202/275-2585), and is open to the public for on-site use from 8:00 A.M. to 4:45 P.M., Monday through Friday. Interlibrary loan service and photocopying facilities are available. The collection consists primarily of materials in the areas of program evaluation, policy analysis, energy, accounting, law, and civilian and military regulatory materials. The library maintains current and retrospective files of most GAO special reports and annual reports. The library is only of general interest to Russianists.

4. GAO's Freedom of Information officer is Nola Casieri (202/275-6172). For information concerning retired and inactive files, contact Edmond Sawyer, technical information specialist (202/275-5042), in the Information Management Office. Microfilm copies of some of the documents transferred to the National Archives are available in the library. Researchers should be aware, however, that Congress is exempt from the provisions of the Freedom of Information Act and that as an agency of Congress GAO is also exempt. Nevertheless, GAO attempts to abide by the intent of this law whenever possible.

5. GAO's principal publication is its annual *Report to the Congress*, which includes comments on the financial administration of U.S. programs for developing countries. Also available without charge is the semiannual *Publication List*, which contains information about other special country reports and program target evaluations.

K19 Health and Human Services Department (HHS)

1 a. *200 Independence Avenue, SW*
Washington, D.C. 20201
(202) 245-6343 (Information)

b. Open to the public.

2. Formerly part of the Department of Health, Education and Welfare, HHS administers more than 300 programs designed to protect and advance the health and quality of life for Americans. Some programs are international in scope and include USSR-related components. The department conducts in-house research and sponsors a number of outside research, consulting, and exchange programs.

3. The National Library of Medicine is described in entry A48 and the HHS Library in A26.

4–5. Internal records and publications are described below with their respective offices. Additional printed information available to the public is listed in the annually updated *Publications Catalog of the Department of Health and Human Resources*. Although most documents and records are open to the public, occasional reference to the department's Freedom of Information Officer, Russell M. Roberts (301/427-7453), may be required.

With the State and Commerce departments, HHS may be the government agency of most value and potential interest to Soviet-area scholars.

OFFICE OF THE ASSISTANT SECRETARY FOR HEALTH AND SURGEON GENERAL

Office of International Health (OIH)
Parklawn Building
5600 Fishers Lane
Rockville, Maryland 20857
(301) 443-1774

Overall policy-level administrative responsibility for the planning, budgeting, and coordinating of international health activities is handled by OIH. The Division of Multilateral Affairs (301/443-6278) is the official liaison office with such international health organizations as the World Health Organization; UN Children's Fund; UN Development Program; Commission on Narcotic Drugs; UN Fund for Drug Abuse Control; UN Economic and Social Council; UN Fund for Population Activities; UN Environment Program; UN Food and Agricultural Organization; and UN Educational, Scientific, and Cultural Organization. The office cooperates with the Agency for International Development in providing technical assistance for health and nutrition program analysis and planning, preparing country background papers and *Syncrisis Studies* of particular countries' health conditions within the context of overall socioeconomic development, and planning and conducting health sector studies and policy studies. Of particular interest is the Divison for Bilateral Programs, where functional and geographical duties are assigned to individual staff members. Linda Bogel (202/443-1776) and Peter Henry (202/443-4540) oversee the Soviet Union.

A descriptive brochure on the OIH and its various divisions is available.

PUBLIC HEALTH SERVICE (PHS)

PHS, which traces its origins back to a 1798 act of Congress authorizing the establishment of marine hospitals to care for American merchant seamen, has vastly broadened its scope and is now charged with promoting and assuring the highest level of health attainable for all Americans and with developing cooperation in health projects with other nations. Its major components include the Alcohol, Drug Abuse and Mental Health Administration; Center for Disease Control; Food and Drug Administration; Health Resources Administration; Health Services Administration; National Center for Health Services Research; National Center for Health Statistics; and National Institutes of Health. Cooperative bilateral and multilateral research and other health projects may be administered by subunits of many of these agencies.

Health Service Administration
5600 Fishers Lane
Rockville, Maryland 20857
(301) 443-2216

John H. Kelso, Acting Administrator

Contact William R. Gemma (301/443-6152) for information on the administration's international activities. There are at present no programs relating to the USSR.

Health Resources Administration
3700 East-West Highway
Hyattsville, Maryland 20782
(301) 436-7200

Robert Graham, Acting Administrator

Office of International Affairs
(301) 436-7179

James Mahoney, Acting Director

This office coordinates programs in health, manpower planning, and health information assistance. There are at present no programs relating to the USSR.

ALCOHOL, DRUG ABUSE, AND MENTAL HEALTH ADMINISTRATION (ADAMHA)

International Activities Office
5600 Fishers Lane
Rockville, Maryland 20857
(301) 443-2600

Berkley C. Hathorne, International Activities Officer

The work of this administration is divided among three institutes: the National Institute of Mental Health (301/443-3673), the National Institute on Drug Abuse (301/443-6480), and National Institute on Alcohol Abuse and Alcoholism (301/443-3885). Through these institutes ADAMHA conducts research programs and funds individual studies in many foreign countries, including the USSR. Research grants, whether domestic or foreign, are enumerated in the annual *Alcohol, Drug Abuse, Mental Health, Research Grant Awards* catalog, complete with basic details such as the investigators, project titles, and amounts awarded. General areas of research span the biological, epidemiological, behavioral, and psychological sciences, and include a number of anthropological and sociological studies. The International Activities Office maintains contract-research project files, and staff members can refer researchers to pertinent sources of information within each institute.

Each institute maintains an information clearinghouse with a bibliographic data base containing translated abstracts of English and foreign-language books (including Russian), periodical literature, and research reports. Computer searches can be conducted without charge for qualified researchers, and staff members will assist in obtaining copies of the full texts of items cited and/or abstracted in the data bases.

NATIONAL INSTITUTES OF HEALTH
9000 Rockville Pike
Bethesda, Maryland 20205

Fogarty International Center
Building 38A
(301) 496-1415

Claude Lenfant, Director

International Coordination and Liaison Branch
(202) 496-5903

Philip Schambra, Chief

This branch of the Fogarty International Center coordinates the work done under the U.S.-USSR Agreement for Cooperation in the Fields of Medical Science and Public Health, a bilateral program dating from 1972. The USSR Ministry of Health administers the Soviet aspects of the agreement.

There are currently many independent projects within the program of health cooperation. The U.S. National Institutes of Health collaborate with counterpart Soviet ministries on studies of health problems that are of mutual interest and importance to the two countries. Among the participating U.S. institutes are the National Eye Institute, National Institute of Mental Health, Center for Disease Control, National Institute of Environmental Health Sciences, and National Cancer Institute.

An exchange program for health professionals is also part of the agreement. Since 1972 several hundred U.S. and USSR scientists and specialists have participated in the exchange. The visits normally last from one to twelve months.

The Fogarty Center is also responsible for a number of publications relating to Soviet health, some of which are the direct result of the accord. Among them are: *A Bibliography of Soviet Sources on Medicine and Public Health in the U.S.S.R.*, by Lee Perkins (1975); *Fundamental Principles of Health Legislation of the U.S.S.R.* (January 1971); *Medical Care in the U.S.S.R.*, by Dr. Patrick B. Storey et al. (1971); *Public Health Planning in the U.S.S.R.* (1976); *Soviet Biomedical Institutions: A Directory* (1974); *Soviet Medicine: A Bibliography of Bibliographies* (1973); *Soviet Medical Research Priorities for the Seventies*, comp. by Dr. Joseph R. Quinn (reprinted November 1973); *Surgical Management of Cardiovascular Emergencies*, by B. V. Petrovsky and M. DeBahey; and *USA-USSR Preclinical Antitumor Chemotherapy Test Data and Their Clinical Correlation*, by a team of Soviet and American authors. Many titles are available from GPO or, in single copies, available without charge from this branch.

SOCIAL SECURITY ADMINISTRATION

Office of International Policy

Comparative Studies Staff
Universal North Building, Suite 940
1875 Connecticut Avenue, NW
Washington, D.C. 20009
(202) 673-5719

The Comparative Studies Staff maintains professional ties with social welfare and health administrators worldwide. There has been intermittent contact with the Soviet Union. The staff collects data directly from individual countries and indirectly through the assistance of the Geneva-based International Social Security Association; the data include country-specific statistics and information on old age and survivor disability insurance, health-care systems, unemployment insurance, worker's compensation, and family allowances. This information is used in the preparation of the biannual comparative statistical handbook *Social Security Programs throughout the World,* available from the GPO (entry Q9). Staff members on occasion contribute articles to the Office of Research and Statistics monthly *Social Security Bulletin* and to other publications. In addition, in-house and contract research studies prepared under the auspices of this staff provide in-depth analyses of various aspects of the social security systems of particular foreign countries. A bibliography listing these studies by country and subject, *International Studies by the Social Security Administration,* is available. This office is also a good source for information concerning research being done on health-related issues both inside and outside HHS.

The Comparative Studies Staff Research Room, headed by Ilene Zeitzer (202/673-5713) is open to the public and maintains a collection of books, periodicals, and vertical files on all countries of the world, including the Soviet Union.

K20 Housing and Urban Development Department (HUD)

1 a. *451 Seventh Street, NW*
Washington, D.C. 20410
(202) 755-5111 (Information)

b. Open to the public.

2. OFFICE OF INTERNATIONAL AFFAIRS (OFFICE OF THE SECRETARY)

Ambassador Theodore R. Britton, Jr., Assistant to the Secretary for International Affairs (202/755-7058)

HUD is involved in cooperative activities with many foreign countries and organizations. The Office of International Affairs assists in formulating HUD policy relating to bilateral and multilateral agreements and projects in housing and urban affairs. This office also manages the foreign visitors program of the department. Technical assistance programs and support for research and educational activities have been scaled down in the past several years. Nevertheless, the staff can provide documentation and responses to written requests and can assist in planning procedures and project evaluations.

The information and documentation services of the International Affairs Office may be of greatest interest to researchers. Through various organizations and formal and informal arrangements with foreign governments, this office has amassed an extensive collection of documents, reports, periodicals, and monographs on housing, urban affairs, and related topics. Bibliographic references to this information, indexed by subject, country, and author, are incorporated in HUD's Foreign Information Retrieval System. The staff will run searches on this data base for researchers without charge. *Foreign Accessions List* is published bimonthly by this office, and interested persons will be placed on a mailing list upon request. For further information about these documentation services, contact Information Specialist Susan Judd (202/755-5770).

A primary responsibility of this office is to administer HUD's bilateral agreements, including the U.S.-USSR Agreement on Cooperation in the Field of Housing and Other Construction. HUD cooperates directly with its counterpart agency, the USSR State Committee for Construction Affairs (GOSSTROY). A Joint Committee was established in 1975 to oversee agreement activities. At the first Joint Committee meeting, six Working Groups were established to develop and implement substantive programs in areas considered to be of interest and benefit to both countries. HUD is the lead agency for three Working Groups: Utility Systems, Building Materials and Components, and New Towns. The other three Working Groups are: Building Design and Construction Management (lead agency—the General Services Administration), Construction in Seismic Areas (lead agency—National Science Foundation), and Building for Extreme Climates and Unusual Geological Conditions (lead agency—Corps of Engineers). At present, the six Working Groups are responsible for twenty-seven different projects. Project activities include joint meetings for technical discussions; formal seminars; joint or complementary research and publication of significant results; field visits to construction plants and other sites; exchange of documents; and longer-term (one-two months) exchanges of individual specialists. On the American side, activities are carried out by representatives of several federal agencies as well as the private sector.

3. The HUD library is described in entry A29.

5.   The technical information obtained through cooperation under the U.S.-USSR Housing Agreement is disseminated both through joint publications and through HUD materials. Work products that have thus far been completed or are underway include: *Bibliographies,* catalogs documents received from the Soviets, each document is reviewed and evaluated for its potential value to American users and then listed in a bibliography issued for each Working Group collection; *Building Electrical, Plumbing, and Heating/Ventilating/Air Conditioning Systems* (1981); *Building Under Cold Climates and on Permafrost,* a collection of twenty-one papers (1981); *The Management of New Towns in the U.S. and U.S.S.R.* (forthcoming); *Planning New Towns* (1981); *Soviet-American Glossary,* a concise English-Russian glossary of specialized design and construction terms (1979); *Soviet Housing and Urban Design,* a compendium of eleven papers written by American technicians and scholars for presentation at a December 1979 conference sponsored by HUD's Office of International Affairs and the Kennan Institute for Advanced Russian Studies (entry H23).

HUD's Office of International Affairs assumes responsibility for distribution of all reports to American specialists. The office draws upon its mailing lists and also "advertises" through *HUD International Bulletin.* Distributed to approximately 5,000 institutions, universities, and professionals in the construction and urban affairs fields, the *Bulletin* is available without charge.

K21 Interior Department

1 a.   *C Street between Eighteenth and Nineteenth streets, NW*
       Washington, D.C. 20204
       (202) 343-3171 (Information)

   b.   Most offices are open to the public; appointments are recommended.

2.   The principal responsibility of the Interior Department is the administration of nationally owned public lands and natural resources. Several agencies of the department, however, also conduct in-house research on, collect data about, and promote information and visitor exchanges with the USSR, as described below. Occasionally outside scholars are hired as consultants.

3.   The Interior Department Natural Resources Library and Geological Survey Library are described in entries A31 and A22, respectively.

4–5.   Internal records and publications are described with their respective offices below.

TERRITORIAL AND INTERNATIONAL AFFAIRS

Office of the Assistant Secretary
(202) 343-4736

Robert Sturgill, International Programs Officer (202/436-7912)

The International Programs officer serves as a coordinator of, and policy overseer for, the various Interior Department activities that are international in scope. He should be the first contact point for researchers interested in the USSR-related activities of the department.

BUREAU OF MINES (ASSISTANT SECRETARY FOR ENERGY AND MIN-
ERALS)
Columbia Plaza
2401 E Street, NW
Washington, D.C. 20241
(202) 634-1300

Robert C. Horton, Director

The bureau has little personal contact with its counterpart in the Soviet Union. Both
sides, however, exchange information and publications. The office also studies and
reports on minerals, mines, and metallurgy of the USSR.

Two publications that may be of interest to Russianists are the *Minerals Yearbook*
(1980) and *Mineral Facts and Problems* (1980). The former is designed to be an annual
publication, but there is about a three-year lag in its appearance; the latter is a
quinquennial publication. Both publications contain international reports and other
information and are available from the bureau's Publication Division (301/436-7912).

U.S. GEOLOGICAL SURVEY (USGS) (ASSISTANT SECRETARY FOR ENERGY
AND MINERALS)
National Center
12201 Sunrise Valley Drive
Reston, Virginia 22092
(703) 860-6167 (Public Inquiries)

The USGS maintains a significant number of reciprocal contacts with Soviet specialists
and arranges for participation by both countries in a variety of conferences and meetings.

Publications of the survey of interest to Soviet-area scholars include *USGS Yearbook*
and *Bibliography of Reports Resulting from USGS Technical Cooperation with Other
Countries.*

International Activities Committee (IAC)
(703) 860-6418

John A. Reinemund, Chairperson

IAC consists of representatives of the divisions of USGS. Its purpose is to oversee
and coordinate the branches of the survey that study international issues. This committee can direct researchers to appropriate contacts within USGS divisions.

Geologic Division

Office of International Geology
(703) 860-6418

John A. Reinemund, Chief

This office works with other offices within the Geologic Division on questions relating
to the USSR. Among the relevant units are:

Office of Earthquake Studies (703/860-6471)

The office studies earthquakes worldwide and issues a quarterly progress report to
the State Department. Although the main branches of the office are in Colorado and
California, the staff here can inform Soviet area scholars of current news in their field.

Office of Regional Geology (703/860-6411)

Douglas M. Morton, chief, is the person Russianists should contact here.

Office of Mineral Resources (703/860-6561)
Office of Resource Analysis (703/860-6446)

This office may be able to provide researchers with information on Soviet mineral resources.

Water Resources Division

Office of International Hydrology
(703) 860-6548

Della Laura, Chief

The division has some contact with the Soviet Union, as it has sponsored trips to the USSR by division personnel and has coordinated visits to the U.S. by Soviet hydrologists. There is also some exchange of information between the two countries through the office. In its role as a water resource management agency, the division works closely with UNESCO and similar international organizations.

National Mapping Division

Office of International Activities
(703) 860-6241

Clifton J. Fry, Jr., Chief

The National Mapping Division has little contact with the Soviet Union. There may be some information regarding USSR activities in Antarctica. An important function of the division is to provide training assistance to staff members of foreign government agencies responsible for publishing geologic maps and cartographic illustrations in government reports. The USSR, however, does not participate in this program.

FISH AND WILDLIFE SERVICE (FWS) (ASSISTANT SECRETARY FOR FISH AND WILDLIFE AND PARKS)
(202) 343-4717
International Affairs Staff
(202) 343-5188

Lawrence N. Mason, Chief

FWS participates in the environmental protection bilateral agreement between the U.S. and USSR. American and Soviet scientists research such areas as aquaculture, arctic ecosystems, endangered plants and animals, and land reclamation. There are about twenty scientific exchanges between the countries annually.

NATIONAL PARK SERVICE (ASSISTANT SECRETARY FOR FISH AND WILDLIFE AND PARKS)

International Park Affairs
1100 L Street, NW
Washington, D.C. 20240
(202) 343-4621

Rob Milne, Chief (202/523-5260)

Together with the Environmental Protection Agency, the Park Service also participates in the U.S.-USSR bilateral agreement on environmental protection. To be more precise, one of the twelve areas of concern under this agreement is the urban environment, and the joint working group for this topic included a project on environmental improvements to sites of historical monuments. A researcher may want to obtain a copy of *A Report by the U.S. Historic Preservation Team of the U.S.-USSR Joint Working Group on the Enhancement of the Urban Environment* (1975) for further information.

BUREAU OF LAND MANAGEMENT (ASSISTANT SECRETARY FOR LAND AND WATER RESOURCES)

International Activities
(202) 343-3189

Jordan Pope

The staff is actively engaged in work on the environmental protection bilateral agreement. Current joint projects include range management of arid land and research on land reclamation problems associated with surface mining.

K22 International Trade Commission (ITC) (formerly, Tariff Commission)

1 a. *701 E Street, NW*
Washington, D.C. 20436
(202) 523-0161 (Information)

   b. Open to the public.

2. OFFICE OF ECONOMICS

East-West Trade Statistics Monitoring System
(202) 523-1539

Tom Jennings, International Economist

This unit monitors East-West trade. A similar unit in the Commerce Department concentrates more upon and promotes exports, whereas this system looks at both imports and exports. It produces monthly and quarterly computer runs on U.S. trade with nonmarket economies. The data for these runs come from the Commerce Department's Census Bureau, but the Statistics Monitoring System analyzes the material differently, so that its information is distinct and unique. These computer runs are available to outside researchers. The system also collects a wide variety of information and materials of potential interest to Russianists.

   In accordance with the 1974 trade bill, under which this unit operates, the Statistics Monitoring System publishes a *Quarterly Report to the Congress and the Trade Policy Committee on Trade between the United States and the Non-Market Economies*. This report is available through the Office of the Secretary (202/523-5178). On occasion the office also issues special reports relating to the USSR.

   The ITC Office of Trade and Industry does some commodity analysis and other work that might involve the Soviet Union, but inquiries should be made to the Office of Economics.

3. The ITC library is described in entry A33.

4. The Office of the Secretary (202/523-0161) maintains control of retired internal records. Researchers should direct inquiries to the Freedom of Information Office (202/523-0471).

5. ITC publications include *Annual Report to Congress* and *Quarterly Report on East-West Trade*. The latter is an invaluable, up-to-date compilation of trade-related statistics, organized by country or region. The Soviet Union is included.

K23 Justice Department

1 a. *Constitution Avenue and Tenth Street, NW*
Washington, D.C. 20530
(202) 633-2007 (Information)

b. Some departmental agencies, such as the Federal Bureau of Investigation (FBI) are closed to the public. Researchers should contact each office for its respective policy on accessibility.

2. Justice Department divisions with activities relating to the USSR are described following point 5, below.

3. The Justice Department Library (Ms. Terry Appenzellar, library director, 202/633-2133), open from 9:00 A.M. to 5:30 P.M., Monday through Friday, contains approximately 150,000 volumes of legal and general reference works. The collection is accessible by special permission. Interlibrary loan service is available. The library cannot be considered a major resource for Russianists.

4. Questions related to the department's restricted internal records are answered by the Freedom of Information Office (202/633-3452).

5. Publications are described with the appropriate issuing agency below.

CRIMINAL DIVISION

FOREIGN AGENTS REGISTRATION UNIT
(202) 724-6922

Political or quasipolitical agents of foreign governments (including lobbyists but excluding diplomats and commercial representatives) and representatives of foreign political parties are required to register with this unit and provide it with a detailed description of their activities and sources of support. In addition, they must file a copy of any material they disseminate in this country. These records are accessible to researchers at the Public Office, Federal Triangle Building, 315 Ninth Street, NW, Washington, D.C. 20530; call (202) 724-6926 for information. The Public Office charges a fee for photocopying these records for researchers. *Annual Report* of the attorney general lists the foreign agents registered by this office. Soviet foreign agents are included.

Other branches of the Criminal Division with international responsibilities include the International Affairs Office (202/724-7600), which handles judicial assistance and extradition matters, and the General Litigation and Legal Advice Section (202/724-6943), which deals with criminal matters related to immigration.

FEDERAL BUREAU OF INVESTIGATION (FBI)
J. Edgar Hoover Building
Pennsylvania Avenue between Ninth and Tenth streets, NW
Washington, D.C. 20535
(202) 324-3000

As the principal investigative arm of the Justice Department, the FBI has a wide range of responsibilities in the criminal, civil, and security fields, including espionage, sabotage, and other domestic security matters. FBI internal records are classified; through Freedom of Information procedures, however, past official FBI investigations information may be made available. Requests should be sent to the director of the FBI; the Public Affairs Office (202/324-3691) can provide basic information and assistance. A guide to what information the bureau might have on Soviet activities is the book *KGB: The Secret Work of Soviet Secret Agents,* by John Barron (New York: Reader's Digest Press, 1974).

IMMIGRATION AND NATURALIZATION SERVICE (INS)
425 Eye Street, NW
Washington, D.C. 20536
(202) 633-4330 (Information)

The Statistical Analysis Branch (202/633-3053) of INS monitors immigration and non-immigrant visits to the U.S. A detailed set of figures for immigrants and nonimmigrants is prepared quarterly and includes such data as country of origin, age, sex, and occupation. The branch library contains useful historical literature and statistical data. Cumulative statistical tables with information on past and present immigration and nonimmigrant visitors to the U.S. are reproduced in the INS *Annual Report* and *Statistical Yearbook.* Copies are available from the Statistical Branch.

In the spring 1976 issue of the *I and N Reporter* is a short article on Russian Orthodox Old Believers in Alaska who have become U.S. citizens.

FOREIGN CLAIMS SETTLEMENT COMMISSION OF THE UNITED STATES
1111 Twentieth Street, NW
Washington, D.C. 20578
(202) 653-6166 (Information)

The Foreign Claims Settlement Commission of the United States administers claims by U.S. nationals against foreign governments in cases involving numerous U.S. claimants. (Claims involving a single U.S. claimant remain under the jurisdiction of the State department.) The claims files include individual claims, supporting documents, and the commission's rulings on the legitimacy of the claimants' evidence. Stored in the Washington National Records Center in Suitland, Maryland, they can be retrieved for researchers to examine in the commission's library. There appear to be records of several claims against the USSR; many claims stem from Soviet participation in World War II.

The library (202/653-5883) contains bound volumes of the commission's claims decisions since 1950.

The commission publishes an *Annual Report* to Congress as well as brochures describing current programs.

K24 Labor Department

1 a. *200 Constitution Avenue, NW*
Washington, D.C. 20210
(202) 523-7316 (Information)

b. Open to the public.

2. Labor Department divisions with activities relating to the USSR are described following point 5, below.

3. The Labor Department Library is described in entry A36.

4. For access to classified documents researchers must contact the Labor Department's Freedom of Information Privacy Act Office (202/523-6807).

5. Publications are described with the appropriate issuing agency, below.

This department is one of the great disappointments for Russian-area scholars. It used to do much substantive work but now does little or none.

BUREAU OF LABOR STATISTICS
(202) 523-1102

The Division of Foreign Labor Conditions, which was quite active in studying the USSR and other nations, was liquidated in 1972. Its monthly publication *Labor Developments Abroad* ceased with the January 1972 issue. The current Foreign Labor Statistics and Trade Division (202/523-9291) compiles international labor statistics, mostly of the developing countries. Although their resources are limited, the staff is willing to help researchers with USSR-related questions.

BUREAU OF INTERNATIONAL LABOR AFFAIRS
(202) 523-6043

Here again the current situation is discouraging. The Office of Foreign Labor Affairs (202/523-7571), despite having no direct contacts with Soviet labor ministries, attempts to monitor labor developments in the USSR. This office is also responsible for organizing infrequent visits to the U.S. by Soviet labor officials.
    The Office of International Organizations and Technical Assistance (202/523-6241) monitors Soviet compliance with labor standards negotiated at international labor conventions.

NOTE: As this edition of the *Guide* went to press (late-1982), the Labor Department was facing major reorganization. Although the functions will remain substantially the same, office names and telephone numbers may change.

K25 National Aeronautics and Space Administration (NASA)

1 a. *400 Maryland Avenue, SW*
Washington, D.C. 20546
(202) 755-2320

b. Open to the public; appointments are recommended.

2. NASA supports very little outside research on subjects other than aeronautical and space research and development. It has contracted a few studies concerning such subjects as U.S.-Soviet cooperation in space. In-house research is limited to subjects not in the social sciences. NASA interaction with other nations is conducted by the International Affairs Division.

INTERNATIONAL AFFAIRS DIVISION
(202) 755-3868

Kenneth Pederson, Director

This division is a good first point of contact in NASA. The office coordinates and directs NASA's activities in connection with a variety of international cooperative agreements on space, including research on satellites and other space-related projects.

Most of the work has come under the umbrella of the now-expired 1972 bilateral agreement between the U.S. and USSR calling for cooperation in the exploration and use of outer space for peaceful purposes. Although the scientific cooperation may diminish somewhat in the future, individual projects and programs are continuing. NASA and counterpart Soviet agencies have conducted joint studies, exchanges of scientific-technical information and specialists, and, in 1975, the Apollo-Soiuz joint space flight. Specific fields in which the two countries work together include space meteorology; the exploration of near-earth space, the moon, and the planets; the natural environment; and space biology and medicine. Currently, there is intensive work on the space applications of a satellite search and rescue system.

NASA HEADQUARTERS HISTORY OFFICE
Reporter Building, Room 706
Seventh and D streets, SW
Washington, D.C. 20546
(202) 755-3612

Thomas Chappelle, Acting Director
Lee Saegesser, Archivist (202/755-3610)

The office holds materials on aeronautics and astronautics, with greatest emphasis on recent American civilian activities, especially those connected with NASA or its predecessor agency, the National Advisory Committee on Aeronautics (NACA).

Also, Mr. Saegesser has more than two file cabinets full of information on Russian/ Soviet astronautics and related subjects. Much of this material is on Soviet space programs. The subject matter of the files ranges from Soviet aeronautics and astronautics (late 1800s-present) to Soviet satellites (arranged alphabetically by name of spacecraft) to the Apollo-Soiuz project. This vertical-file collection should be a major resource for Russianists. A list of holdings is available.

3. The NASA Headquarters Library (600 Independence Avenue, SW, Washington, D.C. 20546) has two major bibliographic resources of value to historians of Soviet science and technology. The first is the computerized RECON system, to which the library has access through its terminals. Since 1961 comprehensive bibliographic citations for reports and other publications on all aspects of aeronautics and astronautics have been put into the system. Since 1972 citations include abstracts as well. Published Soviet literature is included in the RECON data base, making it of great use to Russianists. RECON citations are also part of the NTIS retrieval system. Because the RECON system is primarily for the use of NASA employees, outside researchers

would probably have difficulty in gaining access to RECON unless they are under contract to NASA or some other government agency.

The second bibliographic tool is a card file maintained by NASA and its predecessor, NACA, from 1915 to 1962. The materials are again on astronautics and aeronautics, and citations to Soviet-related aspects are included. The file itself is now in Langley, Virginia, but the headquarters library has a complete microfilm of the cards.

The library's bound volumes and periodicals are also a resource for Russianists in many respects. Virtually complete information on the national space program, including cooperative efforts in space with the USSR, plus most NASA publications and those of its predecessor are here—an important resource for these fields.

The librarian is Mary E. Anderson (202/755-2210); the library, in room A-39, is open from 8:00 A.M. to 4:30 P.M., Monday through Friday.

NASA's Audiovisual Section (Austin L. Gaver, head, 202/-755-8366), located at 400 Maryland Avenue, SW, Washington, D.C. 20546, maintains a photolibrary of more than half a million items, including a selection of Landsat photos organized on a geographical basis. Two helpful catalogs, *NASA 1981 Photography Index* and *NASA Films*, are available.

The NASA Goddard Space Flight Center Library is described in entry A25.

5. NASA has an extensive publications program. It publishes in-house or by contract many titles of interest to scholars in the Soviet field. Of most value for Russianists, however, will probably be NASA's Technical Translations (TTF). More than 10,000 titles have been published, and a very large proportion has been translated from Russian. Among the works to appear so far are a multivolume edition of the writings of N. A. Rynin and several books by Konstantin Tsiolkovskii. The series is available through NTIS. Bibliographic references to these and other NASA publications are a regular feature of the semimonthly, GPO-issued *Scientific and Technical Aerospace Reports* (STAR). This publication has an annual cumulative index.

The division of NASA that produces the translation series and other valuable works is the Scientific and Technical Information Branch. Russianists should contact Myron Nagurney, foreign-literature specialist (202/755-3582), for more information.

K26 National Endowment for the Humanities (NEH)

1 a. *Pennsylvania Avenue and Twelfth Street, NW*
Washington, D.C. 20004
(202) 724-0386

b. Open to the public.

c. Dr. William Bennett, Chairperson

2. NEH makes grants to individuals, groups or institutions (schools, colleges, universities, museums, public television stations, libraries, public agencies, and private nonprofit groups) to increase understanding of the humanities. The disciplines include, but are not limited to, archaeology; comparative religion; history; the history, criticism, and theory of the arts; languages; linguistics; literature; jurisprudence; philosophy; and "those aspects of the social sciences which have humanistic content and employ humanistic methods." The major divisions of NEH of potential interest to Russianists are listed below.

RESEARCH PROGRAMS DIVISION
(202) 724-0226

This division provides grants for long-term collaborative research programs that promote intercultural study, publications, and conferences. The division also funds projects through such organizations as the International Research and Exchange Board (IREX).

FELLOWSHIPS AND SEMINARS DIVISION
(202) 724-0238

This division grants fellowships and stipend awards to support individuals in their work as scholars, teachers, and interpreters of the humanities.

EDUCATION PROGRAMS DIVISION
(202) 724-0351

The Education Programs Division provides grants to strengthen institutional educational programs from the elementary school to university levels.

5. The booklet *Overview of Endowment Programs*, issued annually, would probably be most useful to scholars. It lists and describes the activities of four basic divisions of NEH (Education Programs, Fellowships and Seminars, Research Programs, and Public Programs) and provides information about application procedures and deadlines. More detailed informational publications on each of the divisions are also available.

Annual Report contains particulars about the endowment and its programs and lists all grant recipients and the amounts awarded for each year.

The bimonthly journal *Humanities* has articles on NEH-funded projects, bibliographies, and other features of potential interest to scholars.

All of the above and other miscellaneous publications of NEH are available without charge with the exception of *Humanities*, which is available for sale from GPO (entry Q9).

K27 National Science Foundation (NSF)

1 a. *1800 G Street, NW*
Washington, D.C. 20550
(202) 632-5728 (Public Information)

b. Open to the public, from 8:30 A.M. to 5:00 P.M., Monday through Friday.

2. NSF initiates and supports fundamental and applied research in all scientific disciplines. For fiscal year 1981 more than $967 million was budgeted for research and related activities. This support is made through grants, contracts, and similar agreements awarded to universities and other research organizations. Most research focuses on scientific questions concerning fundamental life processes, natural laws and phenomena, fundamental processes influencing the environment, human behavior, and selected societal questions. Research with international implications and particularly with Soviet-related components could be supported by any one of the five major scientific directorates of the NSF: Directorate for Astronomical, Atmospheric, Earth, and Ocean Sciences (202/357-9714); Directorate for Biological, Behavioral, and Social Sciences (202/357-9854); Directorate for Engineering (202/357-9832); Directorate for Mathematical and Physical Sciences (202/357-9742); Directorate for Scientific, Technological, and International Affairs (202/357-7631).

The Division of Information Systems (202/357-9760) prepares for the Division of International Programs the quarterly *International Implications Report,* which lists all NSF grants and contracts by international implication and by country. This in-house document is the most convenient source for discovering what research is being conducted in or about a particular country. It may be made available for on-site examination to researchers by the Division of International Programs. Another, less convenient source for this information is *National Science Foundation Annual Report,* which lists in its second volume all NSF grants and awards. This publication may be obtained from the Division of Grants and Contracts (202/357-7880) or from the Office of Public Information (202/357-9498).

Major programs relating to the Soviet Union are described below.

DIRECTORATE FOR ASTRONOMICAL, ATMOSPHERIC, EARTH, AND OCEAN SCIENCES
Division of Polar Programs
(202) 357-7766

Edward P. Todd, Director
Joseph E. Bennett, Head, Polar Coordination and Information Section
(202) 357-7819

NSF conducts extensive research in the polar regions of the world. For twenty years there has been an exchange of scientists and information on the questions involved in this work. None of the records or information generated by this research is classified; it is all accessible to researchers. Inquiries should be directed to Mr. Bennett.

Other branches of this directorate that have or have had contacts with the USSR include: Astronomical Sciences Division (202/357-9488), Atmospheric Sciences Division (202/357-9874), Earth Sciences Division (202/357-7958), and Ocean Sciences Division (202/357-9639).

DIRECTORATE FOR SCIENTIFIC, TECHNOLOGICAL, AND INTERNATIONAL AFFAIRS

The directorate has five divisions under it, each of which might have programs of some relevance for Russianists. The most important is:

Division of International Programs
(202) 357-9552

Dr. Bodo Bartocha, Director

> Special Programs Section
> U.S.-USSR Cooperative Research
> (202) 357-7494

> Gerson S. Sher, Head

Since the expiration of the science and technology agreement in 1982, the activities of this office have been significantly reduced; Fiscal Year 1983 calls for no Soviet-related programs. The section is, however, a good information source for Russianists, as it can supply data on past joint U.S.-USSR projects and indicate present plans for future programs in the event budgetary constraints ease. The staff is also willing to direct scholars to other divisions within NSF conducting Soviet-related research.

Division of Science Resource Studies
(202) 634-4634

Charles E. Falk, Director

This division collects data and sponsors studies on the scientific (human and capital) resources of foreign countries. It has a library of reference materials on this subject.

The other three divisions of the directorate that may be contacted for information about Soviet-related activities are: Industrial Science and Technological Innovation Division (202/357-9666), Intergovernmental and Public Service Science and Technology Divison (202/357-7552), and Policy Research and Analysis Division (202/357-9689).

DIRECTORATE FOR BIOLOGICAL, BEHAVIORAL, AND SOCIAL SCIENCES

This directorate has many programs in the biological, behavioral, and neural sciences, including ones in anthropology, linguistics, and psychology. The Division of Social and Economic Sciences (202/357-7966) has programs in economics, geography and regional science, law, political science, sociology, and some history (mostly history of science). For Russianists seeking funding for a research project, this division would probably be the best first point of contact in NSF.

5. A number of publications, in addition to those already described, will help scholars learn more about NSF programs and procedures for making grant applications. *Grants for Scientific Research* provides general information about the NSF grant procedure for research projects. *NSF Grant Policy Manual* contains comprehensive statements of NSF policy and explains the terms and conditions under which awards will be made. The annual *NSF Guide to Programs* summarizes NSF programs for each fiscal year. *NSF Bulletin* publishes a list of deadlines and target dates for NSF proposals in its October issue. The annual *Division of Social Sciences Grant List* lists all awards, renewals, and supplemental funding by program and contains project titles. *NSF Grants and Awards,* also an annual, lists all awards granted by the NSF. See also the *NSF List of Publications, NSF Organizational Directory,* and brochures from each division describing the procedures for grant applications for their programs.

Under the Special Foreign Currency Science Information (SFCSI) Program, translations of foreign languages are made available to scientists within individual NSF agencies. Since 1959, more than one million pages of material have been translated in this program. NSF neither announces nor distributes the translations; the Commerce Department's NTIS (entry Q13), however, does both.

Provided that the material has been deposited in NTIS by the agency, the translations from the SFCSI Program are reported in the NTIS *Government Reports Announcements/Index* and *Weekly Government Abstracts.* NTIS has also published four volumes of an annotated bibliography, covering the years 1960–79, entitled *Translations from the Scientific Literature.* Among other NSF publications of particular interest to Soviet-area scholars are *Soviet Research and Development: Its Organization, Personnel, and Funds,* by Alexander G. Korol (Cambridge, Mass., 1965) and two earlier books by Nicholas De Witt—*Education and Professional Employment in the USSR* (1961) and *Soviet Professional Manpower: Its Education, Training, and Supply* (1955).

K28 National Security Council (NSC)

1 a. *Old Executive Office Building*
Seventeenth Street and Pennsylvania Avenue, NW
Washington, D.C. 20506
(202) 395-3044

b. Closed to the public.

2.   The NSC staff members, including its Soviet specialists, are not normally accessible to outside scholars. Individual exceptions have been made in the past. On occasion the NSC employs academic specialists as consultants.

4.   Most NSC internal documents are restricted to authorized government officials. Researchers interested in pursuing Freedom of Information Act procedures should contact the NSC Freedom of Information Act officer (202/395-3103). Periodically NSC provides the Military Archives Division—Modern Military Branch of the National Archives and Records Service (entry B6) with an updated computer printout list of documents wholly or partially declassified. Some NSC records are transferred to the presidential library system of the National Archives.

K29   Navy Department (and the Marine Corps)

1 a.   *The Pentagon*
Washington, D.C. 20.30
(202) 545-6700 (Information)

   b.   Access to the Pentagon is limited to persons with a security clearance or by invitation.

2.   Most research on the USSR is conducted in-house.

3.   See the Libraries section for the Naval Observatory Library (entry A52) and Navy Department Library (entry A53); the Archives section for the Marine Corps History and Museums Division (entry B5) and Naval Historical Center Operational Archives Branch (entry B7); and the Film section for the Naval Historical Center's Curator Branch, Photo section (entry F11).

4.   Internal records procedures are described in the Defense Department entry (K12).

5.   Publications are described under relevant divisions.

NOTE: Readers are referred to the statements made at the beginning of the Defense Department entry (K12); they pertain to this agency also and should assist scholars who wish to know what resources exist for them in the Navy Department.

OFFICE OF INFORMATION (OFFICE OF THE SECRETARY)
(202) 697-7391

Commodore Jack A. Garrow, Chief

This office provides assistance to researchers in locating appropriate offices and personnel. It should be the researcher's initial contact point with the Navy Department.

OFFICE OF NAVAL RESEARCH (ONR) (OFFICE OF THE SECRETARY)
Ballston Center Tower One
800 North Quincy Street
Arlington, Virginia 22217
(202) 696-4258
Rear Admiral Leland S. Kollmorgen, Chief

ONR is engaged in a wide variety of naval research, much of which is international in dimension, including branches of the biological, mathematical, physical, and psychological sciences. No index to the research projects or completed reports are available, but the staff will assist in locating materials. Most research is done through external research contracts. For specific information regarding ongoing projects of ONR, the researcher should contact the heads of the four science divisions: Engineering Sciences (A. M. Diness, 202/696-4407), Environmental Sciences (Gordon Hamilton, 202/696-4530), Life Sciences (G. L. Bryan, 202/696-4425), Mathematics and Physical Sciences (T. G. Berlincourt, 202/696-4212).

NAVAL RECORDS AND INFORMATION MANAGEMENT DIVISION (OFFICE OF THE CHIEF)
Commander K. B. Patton, Director (202/697-2330)

This division is responsible for management, disposal, and access to all records of the department. Two useful offices are: Freedom of Information and Privacy Act (Gwen Aitken, 202/694-2817) and Records Disposal (Cindy Wendberg, 202/695-1921).

OFFICE OF NAVAL INTELLIGENCE (OFFICE OF THE CHIEF)
Rear Admiral Sumner Shapiro, Director (202/695-3944)

Soviet science, technology, and naval programs are followed closely by this office. Most work is classified because of the nature of the sources used. Researchers who desire information should write a letter of inquiry directly to the office, explaining precisely what is wanted and requesting advice on how to get it. The researcher should cite the Freedom of Information Act as it pertains to his or her case.

The distinct Naval Intelligence Command (Building 1, 4600 Silver Hill Road, Suitland, Maryland 20389, 202/695-2988) answers to the Office of Naval Intelligence. The Office of the Inspector General (Anthony V. Krochalis, 202/763-3558) can assist researchers with Freedom of Information Act requests and with other general information as well. A valuable information pamphlet entitled *Naval Intelligence Command* and an intelligence organizational chart are available without charge. The annual command history (including both classified and unclassified material) and *Command Newsletter,* published yearly, might be of interest to the researcher. In 1979, *History of the Office of Naval Intelligence, 1865–1918,* by Jeffrey Dorwart, appeared. This is the first volume of a projected naval intelligence history and may be of interest to Russianists.

DEPUTY CHIEF OF NAVAL OPERATIONS (Plans, Policy, and Operations)

Politico-Military Policy and Current Plans Division
(202) 695-2453

Ronald J. Kurth, Director

The division's Europe and NATO Plans and Policy Branch monitors political and military developments as they relate to the USSR. The branch is responsible for preparing policy papers on issues of special interest to the U.S. Navy.

NAVAL HISTORICAL CENTER (OFFICE OF THE CHIEF)
Washington Navy Yard, Building 220
M at Eighth streets, SE
Washington, D.C. 20374

Rear Admiral J. D. H. Kane, Jr., Director (202/433-2210)

William S. Dudley, Head, Historical Research Branch (202/433-2364)
Henry Vadnais, Head, Curator Branch (202/433-2318)
Commander T. A. Damon, Director, Navy Memorial Museum (202/433-3519)
Dean C. Allard, Director, Operational Archives Branch (202/433-3224)
Richard T. Speer, Head, Ships Histories Branch (202/433-3643)
Stanley Kalkus, Director, Navy Library (202/433-2386)

The Naval Historical Center conducts research, writing, and publications programs on U.S. naval history. In addition to its library (entry A53), archives (entry B7), and photo section (F11), the center is a valuable resource for the Russianist. The Ships Histories Branch, for example, has published the informative eight-volume *Dictionary of American Naval Fighting Ships.* The center also houses a collection of 500 photos relating to pre- and post-revolutionary Russia, mostly of ships. Naval historical material is also located in the National Archives (entry B6).

The center—and its predecessor, the Naval History Division—has published two books of value to researchers:

United States Naval History: A Bibliography, comp. W. Bart Greenwood et al., 6th ed. (1972), lists works (books and articles) chronologically as well as by war and subject. Several Russian/Soviet-related citations can be found in its pages.

U.S. Naval History Sources in the Washington Area and Suggested Research Subjects, comp. Dean C. Allard and Betty Bern, 3d rev. ed. (1970), is especially good in describing the more important archival holdings in the area.

U.S. MARINE CORPS

History and Museums Division
Washington Navy Yard, Building 58
M at Eighth streets, SE
Washington, D.C. 20374
(202) 453-2273

Many important historical sources from this division and the department as a whole have already gone to the National Archives. Russianists can find there material on naval involvement in north Russia in 1918, the lend-lease program of World War II, and hundreds of other subjects. Some important items, however, remain in the division, including personal papers and oral history collections. See the entry for this division in the Archives section (B5). The staff can also provide assistance to researchers in trying to locate other relevant Marine Corps materials.

K30 Senate Historical Office

1 a. *Office of the Secretary*
Senate Historical Office
U.S. Senate
Washington, D.C. 20510
(202) 224-6900

b. Open to the public from 9:00 A.M. to 5:00 P.M., Monday through Friday.

c. Richard A. Baker, Senate Historian

2. The office serves as a clearinghouse for information related to research about the U.S. Senate and its 1,700 current and former members. Although it does not fund

research, it does seek to facilitate research in the Senate's official records at the National Archives and in collections of members' papers in repositories across the nation.

3. No library as such now exists. The office maintains a collection of 30,000 photographs of former senators and Senate-related activities.

5. In 1983 the office published a comprehensive guide to the locations and extent of former senators' research collections. This includes information on personal papers, office files, oral histories, photographs, and portraits. The office is also preparing a catalog of unprinted Senate committee hearing transcripts for the period 1947–69 and maintains a computer data base of citations to senatorial memoirs and autobiographies. The office conducts a series of oral history interviews with senior Senate staff, including those from the Foreign Relations Committee; a consolidated index to all interview transcripts is maintained. Finally, it edits for the Foreign Relations Committee transcripts of closed committee meetings. That series is currently available for the years 1947–59.

The semiannual newsletter *Senate History* is available without charge to researchers.

K31 Smithsonian Institution

1 a. *Headquarters:*
1000 Jefferson Drive, SW
Washington, D.C. 20560
(202) 357-2700

b. The headquarters building, and all the many bureaus (museums and galleries), are open to the public (excluding administrative offices). For visitors to the area, scholars included, the Smithsonian offers an instant reference service for events and exhibits of current interest: Dial-a-Museum (202/357-2020).

c. S. Dillon Ripley, Secretary

2. The Smithsonian supports research of all kinds, in and out of house, through numerous programs and divisions. Created by an act of Congress in 1846, it is one of the world's great scientific, cultural, and educational bodies. It is, in the words of the will of James Smithson, "an establishment for the increase and diffusion of knowledge among men." To fulfill this purpose the Smithsonian administers a large number of national collections, museums, and art galleries; conducts scientific and scholarly research; maintains laboratories, archives, and the National Zoo; and runs several educational, public service programs. Most activities and institutions related to Russian/Soviet studies are described in the appropriate sections of this *Guide*: B2, C4, C7, C9, C10, C11, C12, and F10. Only a few other divisions of this massive enterprise are detailed here.

DWIGHT D. EISENHOWER INSTITUTE FOR HISTORICAL RESEARCH

National Museum of American History
Twelfth Street and Constitution Avenue, NW
Washington, D.C. 20560
(202) 357-2183

Forrest Pogue, Director

The institute (established in 1975) has a small staff and three full-time researchers. The field of study is military history, but more specifically, the meaning of war and its effects on civilization. Wars and their consequences—of all countries and time periods—come under the scrutiny of the researchers. The military history of Russia and the Soviet Union, directly or as part of larger conflicts, is naturally of concern in the institute's work.

The American Military Institute has given its specialized and valuable library of some four to five thousand books to the Eisenhower Institute. The holdings cover a broad range of military history topics and should prove to be a valuable resource for scholars in this field.

OFFICE OF FELLOWSHIPS AND GRANTS
(202) 287-3271

Gretchen G. Ellsworth, Director

The Office of Fellowships and Grants administers Smithsonian predoctoral and postdoctoral fellowship programs that enable scholars and students to work with Smithsonian staff experts, research collections, and laboratories. Awards range in length from a few weeks up to a year. Disciplines emphasized in these programs may be of interest to Russian-area specialists; they include several of the Smithsonian's traditional interests: anthropology, archaeology, art and cultural history, and museum management. The brochure *Smithsonian Opportunities for Research and Study in History, Art, Science* is available without charge.

SMITHSONIAN ASSOCIATES PROGRAMS
(202) 357-2696

The Associates offer various categories of membership, including Resident Associate, National Associate, and Contributing Member. Members are entitled to participate in numerous special Smithsonian educational and cultural programs, including occasional lectures on Soviet- and Russian-related topics. Smithsonian Associates may also take advantage of special culturally oriented educational tours of foreign countries (202/357-2477). Members and associates receive the monthly *Smithsonian* magazine; Resident Associates also receive the monthly *Associate* newsletter.

SPECIAL COLLECTIONS BRANCH (SMITHSONIAN INSTITUTION LIBRARIES)
(202) 357-1568

Ellen Wells, Head
(202) 357-1568

This newly created branch includes the Dibner Room Library, which contains some rare and unique items relating to Russia. In particular there are some first editions of scientific and mathematical works, with titles by Nikolai Ivanovich Lobachevskii and Dmitrii Ivanovich Mendeleyev. Some twelve volumes from 1728–50 contain commentaries on the Saint Petersburg Academy of Sciences. Most of these works are in Latin, German, or English. The Dibner Library is located in the National Museum of American History, first floor.

3. The Smithsonian Institution Libraries (Robert M. Maloy, director, 202/357-2240) are headquartered in the National Museum of Natural History, room 22. Component libraries of interest to Russianists are described in entries A41, A49, A50, B2, and B3.

4. The Smithsonian Institution Archives is described in entry B11.

5. The monthly *Smithsonian* magazine contains news of the institution and its activities, plus many fascinating articles on subjects of general interest; on occasion, pieces on Russia and the USSR are included.

K32 State Department

1 a. *2201 C Street, NW*
Washington, D.C. 20520
(202) 632-6575 (Information)
(202) 632-9606 (Bureau of Public Affairs)
(202) 632-5170 (Freedom of Information staff)

b. Open by appointment only.

2. The many State Department offices that monitor, research, and prepare policy papers on Soviet affairs are described following point 5 below. Unless otherwise noted, all offices are housed in the State Department Building. Within the limits of security restrictions and time constraints, personnel are usually willing to talk with researchers. Several divisions of the department engage consultants and contract for outside research on USSR issues.

3. The State Department library is described in the Libraries section, entry A57.

4. The internal classified records of the State Department (dispatches, telegrams and other cables, and messages between Washington and U.S. overseas diplomatic posts; inter- and intra-office memoranda; policy papers; and research studies) are filed with the Foreign Affairs Information Management (FAIM) of the Bureau of Administration. When these documents are retired from the department's files they are transferred to the Civil Archives Division, Diplomatic Branch, of the National Archives and Records Service (entry B6). A computerized index exists for all documents processed by FAIM since 1973.

Documents are usually declassified approximately twenty-five to thirty years after issuance, which often coincides with the publication of the department's latest official published record, *Foreign Relations of the United States.* Researchers with requests for more recent internal State Department records should contact the Freedom of Information staff. Documents released to researchers may be examined in the unit's reading room.

5 a. State Department publications include the monthly *Department of State Bulletin* (which contains official statements, addresses, congressional testimony, and news conference statements by the president, the secretary of state, and other officials, plus texts of selected treaties and international agreements and lists of Congressional documents on foreign affairs); Background Notes, a series of fact sheets on foreign countries; *Gist,* one-page reference aids on international issues; the monthly *State Magazine* ; and *Digest of International Law,* which covers all sources of international law including materials from treaties, executive agreements, legislation, statements before congressional and international bodies, and diplomatic notes.

Useful State Department directories include *Biographic Register of State Department Officials* (classified since 1974); *Diplomatic List* and *Employees of Diplomatic Missions* (quarterly lists of names and addresses of foreign diplomatic personnel in Washington); and the annual *Foreign Consular Officers in the United States.*

In addition, the department publishes a number of useful pamphlets, including *Key Officers of Foreign Service Posts: Guide for Business Representatives,* a quarterly directory prepared to aid Americans with business interests abroad; *Memorandum to U.S. Business Community from Department of State, Subject: Assistance in International Trade* (1975), another directory to assist U.S. businessmen; the periodically revised *Lists of Visits of Presidents of the United States to Foreign Countries; Lists of Visits of Foreign Chiefs of State and Heads of Government;* and *United States Chiefs of Mission, 1778–1973.*

Other publications, issued in several series, include: *General Foreign Policy Series; Commercial Policy Series; International Information and Cultural Series; International Organization Series;* and *Treaties and Other International Act Series.* The department also prepares the *Report Required by Section 657 Foreign Assistance Act,* which is submitted to the U.S. Congress and contains a myriad of information on U.S. foreign assistance and other transactions; and the annual *Country Reports on Human Rights,* which is also submitted to the U.S. Congress. *Foreign Policy and the State Department* is a useful but outdated pamphlet on the organization of the department and its overseas posts.

Special news releases, reports, discussion papers, information pamphlets, policy statements, speeches, addresses, news conference transcripts, and other special documents are frequently issued by the department. Scholars interested in being placed on the department's mailing list for these and other items should contact the Office of Opinion Analysis and Plans of the Bureau of Public Affairs (202/632-6575).

A special mailing list for Soviet-related materials is also available.

5 b.   For bibliographic access to the department's publications, scholars may consult: *Major Publications of the Department of State: An Annotated Bibliography,* rev. ed. (1977); issues of *Publications of the Department of State* 1929–52, 1953–57, and 1958–60; *Selected Publications and Audiovisual Materials of the Department of State;* and *Pocket Guide to Foreign Policy Information Materials and Services of the Department of State.* Other useful reference guides are *Government Publications Review,* by Frederic O'Hara (1976) and *U.S. Federal Official Publications,* by J. A. Downey (1978). All publications of the department are also listed in the *Monthly Catalog of U.S. Government Publications.* The quarterly *Selected State Department Publications* is available on request.

BUREAU OF EUROPEAN AFFAIRS
(202) 632-1752

Office of Soviet Union Affairs (often, "The Soviet Desk")
(202) 632-3738

Thomas W. Simons, Director

Perhaps the most important point of contact within the State Department, this staff serves the secretary on matters concerning the USSR. A front office coordinates and supervises four main branches:

Exchanges
(202) 632-2248

Current bilateral agreements between the U.S. and USSR are overseen by this branch. Here, information about U.S. delegation members on the joint committee for each agreement is available to researchers. The office also prepares the *Quarterly Status*

Report on the Implementation of U.S.-USSR Specialized Agreements for the president and the National Security Council. (See Appendix I.)

The branch also monitors and coordinates privately sponsored agreements and invitations between the two countries.

Economic Affairs
(202) 632-9370

This office monitors U.S.-USSR contacts and visits in economic matters. Although not extensively involved in research, the branch does produce economic analyses on Soviet affairs.

Bilateral Affairs
(202) 632-8671

The Bilateral Affairs office considers questions relating to consular and protocol questions, nationality issues and dissent in the Soviet Union, humanitarian aspects of the Helsinki accord, and U.S. congressional visits to the USSR or Soviet visits here. The branch also maintains the U.S. Representation List—a record of divided families with members in each country—and works with such organizations as the U.S. Information Agency (entry K35) and Radio Liberty (entry Q17).

Multilateral Affairs
(202) 632-0821

This branch deals with issues concerning USSR relations with other countries, monitoring Soviet actions and policies that affect the world geopolitical balance. Soviet-related UN affairs and U.S.-USSR military questions (arms control, for example) come under the scrutiny of this office.

BUREAU OF INTELLIGENCE AND RESEARCH (INR)
(202) 632-0342

Office of Research and Analysis for the Soviet Union and Eastern Europe
(202) 632-9194

Robert H. Baraz, Director (202) 632-9194

The office conducts both self-initiated and directed research for the State Department and the National Security Council on economic, political, and politico-military affairs of actual or potential U.S. policy concern. It should be the researcher's first contact within INR. The office has three divisions:

Soviet Foreign Political Division
(202) 632-2488

Isabel Kulski, Chief

Soviet Internal Affairs Division
(202) 632-9204

Donald Graves, Chief

Eastern Europe Division
(202) 632-2877

Ivan V. Matusek, Chief

Office of Long-Range Assessments and Research (LAR)
(202) 632-1342

E. Raymond Platig, Director

This office seeks to maintain a steady exchange of information and ideas between government personnel and private scholars. It does not conduct research itself but is a servicing staff for such work. With the advice of policy and research offices, LAR arranges for nongovernmental scholars to advise the department as contract researchers or consultants; sponsors and organizes symposia, conferences, roundtables, and seminars for researchers in and out of the government; and publishes contract studies, bibliographies, directories, and other reports. LAR also provides staff services for the State Department Foreign Affairs Research Council. This departmentwide body represents all bureaus in planning major research projects and reviews all contract research proposals to insure that department research needs are met.

>Europe and Global Research Group
>(202) 632-2225

>Erik Willenz, Chairman

In consultation with relevant policy and research offices, the staff initiates and receives research proposals. Mr. Willenz has a thorough knowledge of world communist parties and may be of considerable help to researchers.

Office of Economic Analysis
(202) 632-2186

>Communist Economic Relations Unit
>(202) 632-9128

>John T. Danylyk, Chief

Activities of this unit include the preparation of reports and analyses on the economic situations of all communist countries except Cuba. Most of the work is classified.

Office of Politico-Military Analysis (PMA)
(202) 632-2043

Robert A. Martin, Director

This office studies such matters as Soviet military deployment, international arms sales, national military production and capabilities, international security issues, and potential global confrontations. The work, almost entirely classified, also includes arms negotiations and other matters. Information comes largely from the Defense Department and the CIA. The office often works closely with the Bureau of Politico-Military Affairs in this same department. The activities of the former Office of Strategic Research have been incorporated into this office.

Office of the Geographer
(202) 632-1428

Lewis M. Alexander, Director

This office does studies on international boundaries, most of which is classified, and the law of the sea (laws and practice), some of which is unclassified. Publications that may interest researchers include: *International Boundary Studies*, which concerns changes in land boundaries; *Limits in the Sea*, concerning maritime boundary changes; and *Geographic Notes*, an intermittent publication that reports on significant changes of sovereignty. The office also publishes other geography-related miscellanea, including maps.

BUREAU OF POLITICAL-MILITARY AFFAIRS
(202) 632-9022

The Bureau of Political-Military Affairs develops policy guidelines and provides general direction within the department on issues that affect U.S. security policies, military assistance, nuclear policy, and arms control and disarmament matters. In addition, the bureau maintains liaison with the Defense Department and other federal agencies on a wide range of political and military matters. Most records and documents of the bureau are classified. The bureau is divided into four main divisions, each headed by a deputy director:

Deputy Director for Regional and Policy Analysis
(202) 632-3302

Deputy Director for Nuclear and Theater Affairs
(202) 632-4370

Deputy Director for Security Assistance
(202) 632-8698

Deputy Director for Strategic and Theater Affairs
(202) 632-1791

The Office of the Senior Adviser for Soviet Affairs (Jeremy R. Azrael, 202/632-2478) advises the director of the bureau on issues specifically related to the USSR.

BUREAU OF PUBLIC AFFAIRS
(202) 632-6575 (Public Information)

Office of Public Programs
(202) 632-1433

Thomas Bleha, Director

This office organizes the State Department's Scholar-Diplomat Seminars, which bring scholars (usually recent Ph.D.s) into the department for a week of discussion sessions and participation in the work of either a geographic or functional bureau. There are also seminars related to many of the functional interests of the department, such as economic and business affairs, politico-military affairs, legal affairs, international organizations, population, educational and cultural affairs, and science and technology. Media-Diplomat and Executive-Diplomat Seminars are also offered. In addition, this unit organizes conferences and special briefings on U.S. foreign policy and handles requests from universities, businesses, and civic organizations for department speakers. Pamphlets describing these and other public programs are available.

Office of the Historian
515 Twenty-second Street, NW
Washington, D.C. 20520
(202) 632-8888

William Z. Slany, Historian

General and European Division
(202) 632-8978

Charles S. Sampson, Chief

The primary activity of the Office of the Historian is to prepare the State Department's documentary series Foreign Relations of the United States (since 1861), a compendium of declassified telegrams, diplomatic notes, memoranda, and other materials. The staff maintains close contacts with the department's Foreign Affairs Information Management (FAIM), described below, the Diplomatic Branch of the National Archives and Records Service (entry B6), and the presidential libraries throughout the country. Staff members can provide information about past and present records-filing systems of the department and the location, content, and accessibility of U.S. diplomatic records and source materials. They are also available for consultation and research guidance.

In addition to Foreign Relations of the United States, this office publishes on occasion historical studies on various topics of U.S. diplomatic history. Other publications of interest include the documentary collections *American Foreign Policy, 1950–55*; *Basic Documents*; and *American Foreign Policy: Current Documents*, 12 vols. (1956–67). The office also issues *Selected State Department Publications,* a quarterly.

BUREAU OF ADMINISTRATION

Foreign Affairs Information Management Center (FAIM)
(202) 632-0394

William H. Price, Director

Freedom of Information Staff (202/632-1267)

The central file of internal State Department documents and records (airgrams, cables, memoranda, papers, reports, etc.) are administered by FAIM until they are shipped to the National Archives. Records received by FAIM since July 1973 have been indexed by computer. The FAIM files and computer index are not accessible to outside researchers. To attempt to gain access, individuals must use Freedom of Information procedures. (For more information about records management, see point 4 of this entry.)

This center publishes an unclassified series Country Fact Sheets, a regularly updated compendium of data from the State Department, Defense Department, Agency for International Development, U.S. Information Agency, and the Arms Control and Disarmament Agency. Country Fact Sheets are distributed to the libraries of several U.S. Government agencies and cover basic facts, treaties, international agreements, military forces, the status of foreign military purchases and military assistance programs, economic indicators, trade, principal foreign-aid donors and external aid obtained, U.S. assistance commitments, AID projects, cultural information programs being carried out by foreign countries in the U.S., foreign investment (by investor country), U.S. private investment levels, an evaluation of the domestic climate for foreign investment, major governmental officials, U.S. citizen presence, UN participation, and an annotated bibliography of the State Department Library's holdings on the country in question.

FAIM also prepares *Monthly Highlights Report,* a selection of major items from incoming State Department message traffic, organized by geographic region of the world and subdivided by type of reporting (economic, military, political, sociological, and technological). This publication is classified and for internal use only.

BUREAU OF ECONOMIC AND BUSINESS AFFAIRS
(202) 632-0296

The Bureau of Economic and Business Affairs is organized on a functional basis, with many of its offices involved in Soviet economic issues. This bureau has the primary responsibility in the State Department for formulating and implementing U.S. foreign economic policy. It monitors economic policies of foreign countries, coordinates U.S. economic policies for the USSR with the Bureau of European Affairs and other government agencies, conducts bilateral and multilateral negotiations on economic issues, and represents the U.S. at international conferences. Its five major divisions are briefly described below.

International Finance and Development
Deputy Assistant Secretary (202/632-9496)

The responsibilities for international finance and development are divided between four offices. The Office of Business Practices (202/632-1486) is concerned with the legal aspects of technology transfer, copyright laws, and antitrust matters. The Office of Monetary Affairs (202/632-1114) has the primary responsibility for maintaining State Department relations with the International Monetary Fund and liaison with the Treasury Department and for following global, regional, and individual country monetary conditions. The Office of Development Finance (202/632-9426) represents the State Department in interagency discussions on U.S. loan policies and contributions to international financial institutions and the department's ties to the World Bank. The Office of Investment Affairs (202/632-1128) is responsible for investment policy, investment disputes, expropriation cases, and problems involving multilateral corporations around the world. This office monitors U.S. corporate interests with respect to the Soviet Union.

Trade and Commercial Affairs
Deputy Assistant Secretary (202/632-2532)

International trade policy questions are managed by the Office of International Trade (202/632-9458), which drafts commercial policy, conducts bilateral and multilateral trade negotiations, and monitors Soviet participation in various international economic forums. The Office of East-West Trade (202/632-0964) is responsible for specific export control policies; and the Office of Commercial Affairs (202/632-0354) works with the Commerce Department on U.S. trade promotion activities.

International Resources and Food Policy
Deputy Assistant Secretary (202/632-1625)

The Office of International Commodities (202/632-7952) is involved in negotiating multilateral commodities agreements while the Office of Food Policy and Programs (202/632-3090) coordinates U.S. food-aid programs with the Agriculture Department.

Transportation and Telecommunications
Deputy Assistant Secretary (202/632-4045)

Bilateral commercial aviation negotiations are conducted through the Office of Aviation (202/632-0316), while the Office of Maritime Affairs (202/632-0704) monitors shipping regulations and cargo preference laws in the USSR and worldwide in its efforts to discourage discrimination against U.S. commercial shipping. The Office of International Communications Policy (202/632-3405) is concerned with radios, telegraphs, telephones, undersea cables, and international agreements and regulations governing satellite/space systems.

International Energy Policy
Deputy Assistant Secretary (202/632-1498)

The Offices of Energy Consumer Country Affairs (202/632-8097) and of Energy Producer Country Affairs (202/632-0641) formulate energy policy, represent the U.S. at international conferences, and participate in negotiations with foreign energy producers.

BUREAU OF INTERNATIONAL ORGANIZATION AFFAIRS
(202) 632-9600

Nicholas Platt, Acting Assistant Secretary

This bureau coordinates and develops policy guidance and support for U.S. participation in the activities of the UN, its specialized agencies, and other international organizations. The bureau's staff in the various functional offices monitors the activities of Soviet representatives to the UN and the repercussions of these activities on U.S. policy positions. Various functional offices of the bureau include: UN Political and Multilateral Affairs (Philip C. Wilcox, acting director, 202/632-2392); Human Rights Affairs (Warren E. Hewett, director, 202/632-0520); UNESCO Agency (David Rowe, agency director, 202/632-0917); International Women's Programs (Julia Jacobson, deputy director, 202/632-1120); and Office of International Conferences (John W. Kimball, director, 202/632-0384).

A useful publication is the annual *U.S. Participation in the UN: Report by the President to the Congress.* Researchers may examine the bureau's collection of UN documents through its UN Documents and Reference Staff (Mary Rita Jones, chief, 202/632-7992).

BUREAU OF HUMAN RIGHTS AND HUMANITARIAN AFFAIRS
Melvyn Levitsky, Assistant Secretary (202/632-0334)
Office of Human Rights (202/632-0798)

This office monitors and assesses human rights conditions around the world and makes policy recommendations concerning U.S. economic and military assistance programs. This office also coordinates the preparation of the State Department's annual series of 155 unclassified Country Reports on Human Rights Practices, which cover many countries, including the Soviet Union.

BUREAU OF OCEANS AND INTERNATIONAL ENVIRONMENTAL AND SCIENTIFIC AFFAIRS (OES)
James L. Malone, Assistant Secretary (202/632-1554)

This bureau manages U.S. representation in international negotiations and conferences; it also assists in formulating U.S. policy in the areas of environment, health, and natural resources (202/632-7964); nuclear energy and energy technology (202/632-3310); oceans and fisheries (202/632-2396); science and technology (202/632-3004); and population (202/632-3472). USSR-related matters handled by OES include maritime boundaries, law of the sea issues, marine pollution, and fishing disputes. OES also serves as liaison for U.S. fisheries and science attaches in the USSR. The staff is willing to assist legitimate scholarly research efforts.

OFFICE OF THE LEGAL ADVISER
Ted A. Borck, Assistant Legal Adviser for European Affairs (202/632-9500)

The staff of the assistant legal adviser for European affairs can provide researchers with information on Soviet legal issues, including the status of treaties and other international agreements. The legal adviser's assistants for various functional issues, such as human rights (202/632-3044); economics and business (202/632-0242); politico-military affairs (202/632-7838); ocean, environment, and scientific affairs (202/632-1700); and international claims (202/632-1367) on occasion handle specific questions relating to the USSR. Researchers may make arrangements to use the law library of the legal adviser (202/632-2628).

Publications of the legal adviser include the annual *Digest of United States Practice in International Law*, containing policy statements of the official U.S. position on every major question of international law, including human rights and the law of the sea; *Treaties in Force*, an annual list of all U.S. international agreements in force on January 1 of each publication year; the annual *United States Treaties and Other International Agreements* (since 1950); and *Treaties and Other International Agreements of the United States of America, 1776–1949*, 13 vols.

POLICY PLANNING STAFF
(202) 632-2372

Paul Wolfowitz, Director

The Policy Planning Staff serves in an advisory capacity to the Office of the Secretary of State, providing broad global policy recommendations and perspectives independent from the policy viewpoints of the geographic bureaus. The staff includes functional and area specialists who are accessible to scholars. The Policy Planning Staff sponsors a regular series of Open Forum luncheon discussions for department personnel to facilitate internal departmental debate on policy issues. A product of these discussions is the classified magazine *Open Forum*.

BUREAU FOR REFUGEE PROGRAMS
(202) 632-5230

Richard D. Vine, Director

The Bureau for Refugee Programs is primarily responsible for implementing U.S. refugee policies. U.S. contributions for refugee assistance and relief to the UN High Commissioner for Refugees are also administered by this office. The bureau deals with issues surrounding the admission and placement of refugees in this country. Refugee officer Indy Chavchavadze (202/632-4698) of the Office of Refugee Assistance, Relief, and Protection can provide additional information. There have been several Soviet-related refugee programs.

FOREIGN SERVICE INSTITUTE
1400 Key Boulevard SA-3
Arlington, Virginia 22209
(703) 235-8750

Stephen Low, Director

School of Professional Studies and Office of Academic Affairs
(703) 235-8779

J. Brian Atwood, Dean

School of Area Studies
(703) 235-8839

Dwight R. Ambach, Dean

East Europe and USSR Studies
(703) 235-8841

Walter D. Connor, Chairperson

This unit runs training programs on the Soviet Union and Eastern Europe. The language and area training is only for U.S. Government personnel. Scholars are sometimes employed not so much as consultants but as lecturers.

The office publishes selected bibliographies by country and has issued *A Study Guide and Syllabus for Eastern Europe and the Soviet Union.*

Other divisions of the institute of interest to the scholar include the Executive Seminar in National and International Affairs (Jack Perry, coordinator, 703/235-8766); School of Language Studies (Pierre Shostal, dean, 703/235-8816); and Department of North and East European Languages (Ronald Goodison, chairperson, 703/235-1523).

The Foreign Service Institute also maintains an Overseas Briefing Center with post reports, general information, and audiovisual materials on foreign cities with U.S. diplomatic missions.

___

K33 Transportation Department (DOT)

1 a. *400 Seventh Street, SW*
Washington, D.C. 20590
(202) 426-4321 (Information)

b. Open to the public; appointments are recommended.

2. DOT international activities related to the USSR are described below. The agency supports a small amount of research that involves the Soviet Union.

3. The DOT Library is described in entry A59.

4–5. Internal records and publications are described with their respective offices, below.

___

RESEARCH AND SPECIAL PROGRAMS ADMINISTRATION
(202) 426-4461

Information Resources Management
(202) 426-0975

James Duda, Chief

The activities of the Office of Resources Management include DOT management responsibilities for the Transportation Research Information Services Network (TRIS-NET). TRISNET is an informal cooperative information exchange system designed to serve the information needs of the transportation segment of the general public. Libraries and institutions nationwide participating in TRISNET include the Transportation Research Board, National Academy of Sciences' National Research Council; Transportation Department Library, Northwestern University; University of California; and any subscribers to the Lockheed Dialogue System. TRISNET provides information on the location of sources of information on transportation (including data bases and transportation-related information centers) and maintains TRIS-ONLINE, a computerized bibliographic card file of important periodical, monograph, and current research literature in the field (complete with abstracts of the information and source references for obtaining copies of cited items). The TRIS-ONLINE system contains a small but growing collection of /data in its International Transportation Research Information System (IN-TRIS), which includes references to international literature on transportation issues. A small number of entries on transportation problems are related to the Soviet Union.

Although somewhat dated, two useful booklets describing TRISNET, *TRISNET: A Network of Transportation Information Services and Activities* (1978) and *TRISNET: Directory to Transportation Research Information Service* (1976), are still available. DOT also publishes an informative brochure entitled *Users of Transportation Research Now Have Online Access to the TRIS Data Base,* available without charge.

ASSISTANT SECRETARY FOR POLICY AND INTERNATIONAL AFFAIRS
(202) 426-4544

Office of International Policy and Programs
(202) 426-4368

> International Cooperation Division
> (202) 426-4398
>
> Dr. Bernard Ramundo, Chief

This division coordinates U.S. efforts on the bilateral agreement with the USSR on transportation. The chairperson of the U.S. delegation of the joint committee is the assistant secretary for policy and international affairs. The executive secretary for the U.S. side is the head of this division, Dr. Ramundo. The agreement and the work of this division cover almost all aspects of land, water, and air transportation. Thus, the International Cooperation Division is the most important unit to contact at DOT for information about other administrations within the agency involved with the Soviet Union. Mildred Allen, an international transportation specialist, is the staff member currently concerned with Soviet affairs.

> International Trade Division
> (202) 755-7684
>
> Arnold Levine, Chief

The International Trade Division works closely with the Treasury, State, and Commerce departments on issues related to trade policy. The staff also collects and maintains information, mostly secondary sources in English, on questions of international transportation. The material is then filed by geographic location.

FEDERAL AVIATION ADMINISTRATION (FAA)
800 Independence Avenue, SW, Washington, D.C. 20591
(202) 426-8058 (Public Information)

Office of International Aviation
(202) 426-3213

> International Analysis and Coordination Division
> Analysis and Evaluation Branch
> (202) 426-3230

The Analysis and Evaluation Branch of the Office of International Aviation Affairs maintains filebooks known as Country Profiles, which contain general and statistical information on current aviation activities in various foreign countries, including the USSR. This branch also maintains internal document files of memos, correspondence, and in-house research papers for many foreign countries. Researchers interested in using these files should contact Jane Stolar, international aviation analyst. The office has also been involved in the aviation agreement between the U.S. and USSR. Researchers should contact Frank McCabe at (202) 426-3217.

Interagency Group on International Aviation (IGIA)
(202) 426-3180

Housed within the FAA, IGIA is the administrative group within the Office of International Aviation that monitors and coordinates the international aviation activities of all U.S. Government agencies. This office, which serves as the U.S. depository for all International Civil Aviation Organization documents, maintains a complete set of those documents as well as a small reference library. These materials are primarily for the use of the staff but may be made available to outside researchers.

MARITIME ADMINISTRATION
400 Seventh Street, SW
(202) 426-5823

Harold E. Shear, Administrator

Office of International Activities
(202) 426-5772

Reginald A. Bourdon, Director

The Maritime Adminstration was transferred to the Transportation Department from the Commerce Department in 1981. The Office of International Activities should be the first point of contact for information on administration participation in international programs. The staff can discuss with Russianists the administration's work that relates to the USSR, such as shipment of grains and other commodities to the Soviet Union, trade studies, and international cooperation.
    The office has in the past been involved in the bilateral maritime and transportation agreements. Currently, however, very little work is being done in this area.

Office of Trade Studies and Statistics
(202) 382-0374

William B. Ebersold, Director

This office compiles statistical data on U.S. waterborne trade with foreign countries and foreign merchant shipping with the U.S. Data are available in hard copy or on computer printout. Publications of the office include: *New Ship Construction, Merchant Fleets of the World, A Statistical Analysis of the World's Merchant Fleets,* and *Essential U.S. Trade Routes.*

U.S. COAST GUARD
2100 Second Street, SW
Washington, D.C. 20593

Admiral John B. Hayes, Commandant (202/426-2390)

Some branches of this administration, which should be considered as a minor resource for Russianists, occasionally deal with questions that relate, directly or indirectly, to the USSR. Among these divisions, and the affairs involved, are:

Commandant's International Affairs Staff
(202) 426-2281

International maritime and UN matters, security assistance.

Office of Operations—Operational Law Enforcement Division
(202) 426-1894

International laws and treaties, enforcement.

Office of Marine Environment and Systems
(202) 426-2007

Environmental questions.

FEDERAL HIGHWAY ADMINISTRATION (FHWA)
400 Seventh Street, SW
Washington, D.C. 20590
(202) 426-0650

Ray A. Barnhart, Administrator

A component of DOT since 1966, FHWA carries out the highway transportation programs of the department and has some limited international activities. The Foreign Project Division (Joseph DeMarco, chief, 202/426-0380) provides technical assistance advisers for AID sponsored projects and maintains contacts with individual foreign countries. In 1982 there were no activities relating to the USSR.

K34 Treasury Department

1 a. *Fifteenth Street and Pennsylvania Avenue, NW*
Washington, D.C. 20220
(202) 566-5252

b. Open by appointment.

2. Research is primarily, although not exclusively, conducted in-house. Most Treasury Department international activity of interest to Russian specialists is administered by the Office of the Assistant Secretary for International Affairs.

OFFICE OF THE ASSISTANT SECRETARY FOR INTERNATIONAL AFFAIRS (OASIA)
Assistant Secretary (202/566-5363)

OASIA monitors international financial and monetary conditions on both a functional and a geographical basis. USSR-related issues may by considered from a global or topical perspective by various offices within the office, including the Office of the Deputy Assistant Secretary (DAS) for Trade and Investment Policy (202/566-2748), DAS for Commodities and Natural Resources (202/566-5881), and DAS for International Monetary Affairs (202/566-5232).

Office of Trade and Investment Policy
(202) 566-2748

> Office of East-West Economic Policy
> (202) 566-2611

> Stephen J. Canner, Director

There is no independent section of this division to study just the USSR. Several staff members, however, are designated to oversee the USSR. Any one of these would no doubt be the best point of contact for Russian-area specialists.

The office does little original research of its own but does keep track of the current economic (especially financial) situation in the USSR. Most of this work is classified and based almost entirely on governmental sources. Staff economists help the department formulate international economic policy.

Other divisions of the Office of Trade and Investment Policy appear to be of negligible interest for Russianists. Similarly, other branches of the Office of International Affairs would have few resources for Soviet-area scholars.

OFFICE OF THE ASSISTANT SECRETARY FOR ECONOMIC POLICY
(202) 566-2551

Manuel H. Johnson, Acting Assistant Secretary

Within this office, the deputy assistant secretary for international economic analysis is responsible for developing forecasts of U.S. trade and current account balances for use by the officials of the department in formulating international economic policy; conducting research and analysis of major policy issues in the international trade, monetary, and energy areas; producing information on flows of banking and corporate capital into and out of the U.S.; and monitoring the extent of portfolio investment by foreigners in the U.S. and U.S. residents abroad. This unit also maintains the Developing Countries Data Bank, which contains information from 1960 to the present, on national income, balance of payments, and foreign debts of developing nations. This data bank, however, is not accessible to the public.

3. The Treasury Department Library, located in room 5030, is open from 9:00 A.M. to 5:30 P.M., Monday through Friday. The library receives, on a reciprocal basis, official statistical bulletins and central bank annual reports from many foreign governments. Holdings related to the USSR are not substantial enough for the library to be considered a scholarly resource. It might be noted, though, that it does have one of the largest collections of legislative histories outside of the Library of Congress.

The library's monthly bibliographic acquisitions list, *Treasury Notes,* contains citations to books received by the library, a selection of article titles that may be of interest to department employees, and occasional abstracts on specific topics.

Librarian Elizabeth Knauff and her reference staff (202/566-2777) can provide assistance to researchers. Interlibrary loan services and photocopying facilities are available.

4. Retired Treasury Department internal records are controlled by the Office of Administration's Information Resources Management Branch (202/376-1569). Access to most documents is only through Freedom of Information procedures, which are handled by Judith M. Sorrentino (202/376-1577).

5. *A Select List of Treasury Publications* is available from the Office of Public Affairs (202/566-2041). Useful items include the *Annual Report of the National Advisory Council on International Monetary Policies, Report on Developing Countries External*

Debt and Debt Relief Provided by the United States, and Foreign Credits by the United States Government—Status of Active Foreign Credits of the United States Government. The monthly Treasury Bulletin also carries international financial statistics.

K35 U.S. Information Agency (USIA)

1 a. 1750 Pennsylvania Avenue, NW
Washington, D.C. 20547
(202) 724-9578 (Information)

b. Open to the public; appointments are recommended.

c. Charles Z. Wick, Director

2. As a result of a 1977 reorganization, the U.S. International Communications Agency (ICA) was established in April 1978, consolidating the old U.S. Information Agency and Bureau of Educational and Cultural Affairs of the State Department. In September 1982 ICA was renamed U.S. Information Agency. USIA disseminates information about the U.S. abroad and conducts educational and cultural exchange programs between the U.S. and other countries. Research is conducted both in-house and on a contract basis and focuses primarily on international public opinion and media affairs.

NOTE: USIA divisions with activities relating to the USSR are described following point 5, below.

3. The USIA library is described in entry A61.

5. The agency issues a wide variety of publications, research reports, films, and tapes. Much of the material is unclassified and listed in catalogs. For information about these catalogs and access to specific items in them, contact the respective offices. Two publications of direct interest to Russianists are Problems of Communism and America Illustrated (in Russian); details about the first are in the Publications and Media section (entry Q14). Information about the staffs of both, however, follows.

OFFICE OF EUROPEAN AFFAIRS
(202) 724-9085
North Central, Eastern and Southern Europe
(202) 724-9037

Soviet Union
(202) 724-9295

Mark Dillon, Country Affairs Officer

Concerned with policy and coordination, this office provides broad managerial oversight of the post and programs in the USSR and relays area and post needs and perspectives to the appropriate management and functional offices of USIA. A scholar might use this office as a first point of contact in the agency, as the staff is knowledgeable about all USIA activities relating to the USSR.

ASSOCIATE DIRECTOR FOR PROGRAMS
(202) 724-9349

Office of Research
(202) 724-9545

Gerald Hursh-Cesar, Director

Europe Research Branch
Soviet and Eastern European Research Unit
(202) 724-9269

Will Brooks, Unit Chief

This unit studies and maintains information about Soviet audiences, attitudes, media habits, public opinion, and other demographic and sociological topics. Besides its own in-house work, the branch contracts for research from outside scholars and sometimes employs consultants.

The office also conducts a series of seminars, cosponsored with the International Research and Exchange Board, on various Soviet-related topics. Designed primarily for government personnel, outside scholars may attend with special permission.

The staff publishes a number of short papers and research reports yearly, most of which are intended for internal government use. The material, however, is unclassified and accessible to scholars.

This unit is pleased to discuss its work with scholars who telephone first to make arrangements.

PRESS AND PUBLICATIONS SERVICE
1776 Pennsylvania Avenue, NW
Washington, D.C. 20547
(202) 724-9712

James A. McGinley, Director

Publications Division
(202) 724-9718

Problems of Communism Branch
(202) 724-9651

Paul A. Smith, Editor/Chief

The publication *Problems of Communism* is described in the Publications and Media section (entry Q14) The office itself, however, offers the Russian specialist some interesting resources. The bibliographic features of the branch are very useful. There is a small reference collection here of worldwide sources, and it may well be the most current collection of material in the field of communist affairs. The branch receives up to 200 books a year for review; some of these books are held in the office for two to three years, and then discarded. The books themselves and the review files are of potential value to researchers.

Equally important is the expertise of the editors and other staff workers. Their contacts with the academic world are extensive, as they are closely associated with government and private specialists in Soviet and communist affairs. The nature of their work (which does not involve classified sources) permits staff members to be much more accessible than similar Soviet experts in the State Department or CIA. Scholars who wish to keep abreast of developments in communist studies may want to be in touch with this office.

America Illustrated Magazine Branch
(202) 724-9706

Robert Poteete, Editor/Chief

The publication itself, in Russian, is distributed only in the USSR; its contents may be of interest to Soviet-area specialists who want to examine some of the information that the U.S. sends to the Soviet Union. In addition, the staff of translators and editors represents a resource of excellent linguistic skills and expertise on Soviet culture and audience attitudes.

ASSOCIATE DIRECTOR FOR BROADCASTING
HHS North Building
330 Independence Avenue, SW
Washington, D.C. 20547
(202) 755-4180

John Hughes, Associate Director

Office of Programs
(202) 755-4557

> USSR Division
> (202) 755-4422

This is the home of the famous Voice of America (VOA) broadcasts to the Soviet Union. (It should be noted that the Europe Division, 202/755-4210, handles broadcasts to Estonia, Latvia, and Lithuania.) Details about the broadcasting activities of the division(s) may be found under VOA in the Media and Publications section of the guide (entry Q22).

The greatest resource for scholars at VOA, however, might well be the staff itself. Many members are native speakers of the languages in which they broadcast. There are thus linguistic skills here matched only by a few other agencies or facilities in the area.

Staff members also stay current on events of importance in the areas and regions of their specialty. Furthermore, many both engage in and are knowledgeable about scholarly work in their fields. These activities, together with frequent VOA contacts with Soviet personnel, make the staff a major resource for Russianists.

K36 The White House

1 a. *1600 Pennsylvania Avenue, NW*
Washington, D.C. 20500
(202) 456-1414

b. Open by appointment only.

2–5. OFFICE OF PUBLIC LIAISON

Special Assistant to the President for Public Liaison
(202) 456-7140

The office provides a liaison between the Executive Office and major ethnic organizations (fraternal, religious, business, etc.) in the U.S. It receives and offers advice on foreign and domestic policy as it relates to ethnic groups. On occasion, the office sponsors conferences on specific subjects to which all ethnic groups are invited to send representatives for meetings with government officials. These irregular symposia are attended by invitation only.

Of interest to scholars is the office's card file, which lists all major ethnic organizations and their publications. Although perhaps not as comprehensive as other published lists of such groups, this file would at least be more current than most sources.

L Government Agencies (Soviet, International, and Other)

Government Agency (Soviet, International, and Other) Entry Format (L)

1. General Information
   a. *address; telephone number(s)*
   b. conditions of access
   c. name/title of director and heads of relevant divisions

2. Organization Functions, Programs, and Research Activities (including in-house research, contract research, research grants, and employment of outside consultants)

3. Libraries and Reference Facilities

4. Internal Records (including unpublished research products)

5. Publications
   a. published reports, periodicals, and series
   b. bibliographies

In the case of large, structurally complex organizations, a detailed description of relevant divisions follows the description of the organization as a whole; included is information on the above-numbered points.

Introductory Note

As the nation's capital, Washington, D.C., is affected by the presence of a wide range of foreign and diplomatic personnel. Of particular interest to the Russianist is the Soviet embassy (entry L7) and its support agencies. The Soviet embassy may be an important resource for the scholar, especially if research work involves official contact with individuals or institutions within the USSR. Although often subject to severe time constraints, Soviet embassy staff members are willing to give assistance to the visiting scholar. Advance appointments are strongly recommended. The names listed below are current as of August 1982 and are therefore subject to change. The scholar should consult the latest *Diplomatic List* (entry K32) for up-to-date personnel listings.

In addition to the embassy and legations discussed below, other international organizations, such as the World Bank (entry L1), also make their home in Washington. Despite limited Soviet participation in such organizations, they can often be valuable resources for statistical and other raw data on the USSR.

L1   International Bank for Reconstruction and Development (World Bank)

1 a. *1818 H Street, NW*
       Washington, D.C. 20433
       (202) 477-1234

   b. Not open to the public; visitors are received by appointment.

   c. A. W. Clausen, President

2.   The World Bank has only tangential contacts with the Soviet Union. As an international organization, the bank provides capital and technical assistance for long-term economic development projects to stimulate economic growth in less-developed countries. The World Bank has traditionally financed the development of all kinds of capital infrastructure, such as roads and railways, telecommunications, ports, and energy. Emphasis is placed on investments designed to directly affect the well-being of the masses of poor people in developing countries by making them more productive and integrating them into the development process. This new priority is reflected in the increasing number of projects in agriculture, rural development, education, family planning, nutrition, water and sewerage facilities, and low-cost housing.
   The World Bank is also involved in a growing program of economic and social research to improve its understanding of the processes of social and economic change and the impact of bank policies on those processes. Research is conducted by the bank's staff, occasionally in collaboration with outside specialists. The bank also utilizes individual professional and academic consultants (technical specialists, notably engineers, agronomists, and fiscal experts) and supports research projects in academic and research institutes in several countries. The pamphlets *World Bank Research Program: Abstracts of Current Studies* (1981) and *Use of Consultants by the World Bank and Its Borrowers* (1977) provide details about these research activities and are available without charge from the Publications Unit (see point 5, below).

3.   The Joint Bank-Fund Library is described in entry A34.

4.   Some bank research reports and other internal working papers are filed in the Records Center, which maintains the indexed "Documentation Available to the Staff." The bank and the International Monetary Fund (entry L2) share a Joint Computer Center, mostly for internal support (programs are separate). Generally, access to the computer is restricted to the staff of the two organizations.

5 a.   Although many of its studies and reports are restricted, the World Bank does issue a wide variety of publicly available publications that frequently contain information of interest to a researcher. The annual *World Bank Atlas* includes figures of gross national product, population, and growth rate for many countries, including the Soviet Union. The *Atlas* might interest Soviet-area specialists because it may contain the most unbiased comparison of U.S.-USSR gross national products available.
   The publication *World Tables* appears in both book and computerized form. Communist countries are included in several editions covering the years 1950, 1955, and 1960–77.

5 b.   Many of the bank's publications are available without charge. *The World Bank Catalog of Publications* lists both free publications and those for sale. It is available from the Publications Unit (202/477-2403). Scholars interested in being placed on the World Bank mailing list should call (202) 477-2058.

L2   International Monetary Fund (IMF)

1 a.   *700 Nineteenth Street, NW*
Washington, D.C. 20431
(202) 477-7000

b.   Open by appointment.

c.   J. de Larosiere, Managing Director

2.   IMF works to promote international monetary stability by eliminating restrictive exchange practices among member nations and by allocating the fund's monetary reserves to assist members in meeting temporary balance-of-payments problems. The fund's departments compile and analyze statistics on international financial and economic conditions. Little contract work is funded, but IMF maintains a pool of private international fiscal and central banking specialists to act as advisers to foreign governments.

The Bureau of Statistics of IMF does no original research on the USSR, which is not a member nation of the fund. It publishes data acquired from other countries in useful form. The monthly *Direction of Trade* (*DOT*) includes figures for the Soviet Union in some tables; they are derived from data for all other countries. *DOT* has an annual cumulation and review issue.

3.   The Joint Bank-Fund Library is described in entry A34.

5.   *International Financial Statistics* (*IFS*), with information for individual countries, area and world aggregates, and *Balance of Payments Yearbook* (*BOP*) do not carry data for the USSR but still may be of value for students of international economics. Both are monthlies; some issues of the *IFS* have twenty-five-year reviews of data.

The bureau has a computer system, called Data Fund, which makes the above titles (*DOT, IFS,* and *BOP*) available in machine-readable form. In each case, the version on computer tapes is more detailed than the bound volume.

IMF has many other publications, but none of substantial interest to Russianists. Scholars may write for a free brochure listing and describing all publications.

L3   Latvian Legation

1 a.   *4325 Seventeenth Street, NW*
Washington, D.C. 20011
(202) 726-8213

b.   Inquiries are answered by the staff as time permits.

c.   Anatol Dinbergs, Charge d'Affaires
Valdemars Kreicbergs, Counselor

2.   The Latvian Legation has no connection with the USSR; it is the last accredited

diplomatic delegation to the U.S. from the Latvian Government in power before the Soviet occupation of the country. Its records and activities all reflect this situation.

5. *Latvian Information Bulletin* is a quarterly newsletter distributed to most members of the U.S. Congress and to many libraries. The legation has also produced a general handbook on Latvian history, geography, and culture. Both publications are available without charge.

L4 Lithuanian Legation

1 a. *2622 Sixteenth Street, NW*
Washington, D.C. 20009
(202) 234-5860

b. Open by appointment. Inquiries are answered by the staff as time permits.

c. Dr. Stasys A. Backis, Charge d'Affaires

2. The Lithuanian Legation has no connection with the Soviet Union; it is the last accredited diplomatic delegation to the U.S. from the Lithuanian government in power before the Soviet occupation of the country.

5. The legation distributes pamphlets and information sheets published by a Lithuanian information center in New York. The staff can also provide an extensive bibliography of Lithuanian-related publications.

L5 Soviet Radio and Television Bureau in Washington

1 a. *Mail:*
USSR Embassy
1125 Sixteenth Street, NW
Washington, D.C. 20036
(301) 587-8769
(301) 588-2782

b. Open by appointment.

c. Alexander N. Druzhinin, Bureau Chief
Vladimir V. Gusev, camera operator

2. The bureau retains few, if any, films of the stories it files. All films are sent to Moscow for developing and editing, to be used on Soviet television. Some materials— mostly scripts and notes for news stories and analysis—are maintained in Washington and are accessible to researchers.

In addition, the bureau can provide some bibliographic help and can aid in locating or contacting sources in the USSR for scholars interested in Soviet broadcasting and news operations.

As time permits, the bureau staff is available for discussions and meetings with researchers.

L6 TASS News Agency—Washington Bureau

1 a. *National Press Building, Room 883*
Fourteenth and F streets, NW
Washington, D.C. 20045
(202) 628-7858

b. Open by appointment.

c. E. Egorov, Chief

2. TASS is an international news reporting agency like United Press International, Associated Press, or Reuters. The Washington bureau is most interested in Washington affairs—the business of the White House, Congress, State, and other departments.

Reports are sent from the bureau to headquarters in Moscow for use on Soviet radio and television and in newspapers, especially papers outside Moscow and Leningrad. Most foreign news reported in the USSR comes from TASS offices worldwide.

L7 USSR Embassy

1 a. *1125 Sixteenth Street, NW*
Washington, D.C. 20036
(202) 628-7551/7554

b. Open by appointment. In general, the embassy staff is very busy and has limited time for discussions or consultations with researchers.

c. His Excellency Anatolii F. Dobrynin, Ambassador

2. There are several important divisions of the embassy with which researchers should be acquainted. Because personnel changes fairly frequently, it is highly recommended that researchers obtain the most recent copy of the State Department publication entitled *Diplomatic List* ("The Blue List"), which provides names and addresses of the current embassy staff. This list comes out three times a year and is up to date. The names and addresses given here are for the summer of 1982. (One should note that the USSR has begun contruction of a new embassy; these new quarters may house some of the divisions that at present are in the Sixteenth Street building.)

3. The embassy film library is described in entry F3.

INFORMATION DEPARTMENT
1706 Eighteenth Street, NW
Washington, D.C. 20009
(202) 232-3756

Georgy Isachenko, Director

This is one of the most important branches; it handles press releases, called "News and Views from the USSR," which are issued as circumstances warrant. The office also distributes governmental statements by Soviet leaders, including Communist Party officials. Members of the academic community would find this department an appropriate point of contact, whereas reporters and journalists should usually work with the Press Department. Materials are available without charge at the embassy.

The monthly publication *Soviet Life,* comes under the Information Department. Feliks V. Alekseyev is the editor of *Soviet Life* in Washington; the telephone number for *Soviet Life* is (202) 232-7768.

Another division located at this Eighteenth Street address is the Office of Public Cultural Exchanges, which handles exchanges of public and private organizations.

PRESS DEPARTMENT
1125 Sixteenth Street
Washington, D.C.
(202) 347-1347

The department staff is responsible for answering the questions of the American press; thus, journalists and reporters should find this division of more value than the Information Department.

MILITARY, AIR, AND NAVAL ATTACHÉS OFFICE
2552 Belmont Road, NW
Washington, D.C. 20008
(202) 332-3741

Researchers studying questions of Soviet military and defense, strategic arms and their limitations, force reductions, and related matters may wish to contact this office. Written or telephone requests for information or to schedule a meeting should be made well in advance and be as specific as feasible on the subject of inquiry. There are many restrictions on access to the staff.

CONSULAR AND VISA OFFICE
1825 Phelps Place, NW
Washington, D.C. 20008
(202) 332-1513

Those who intend to visit the Soviet Union as individuals, not with a group or on a scholarly exchange, will have to come to this office. The staff here can provide limited travel information on the USSR.

Several of the offices listed below might be of interest to the Russianist; all are located at the Sixteenth Street address and can be reached on the embassy telephone numbers: Office of the Cultural Counselor, Anatoly M. Dyuzhnev (the cultural counselor oversees most cultural, academic, and sports exchanges, e.g., visits of musical and dance groups, gymnastics teams, and individual Soviet scholars and students); Office of the Scientific Counselor, Igor M. Makarov; Office of the Agricultural Counselor, Logvin A. Overchuk; Office of the Counselor for Medicine, Mikhail V. Borisov.

L8 USSR Trade Representation in the U.S.A.

1 a. *2001 Connecticut Avenue, NW*
Washington, D.C. 20008
(202) 234-7170
(202) 232-5988

b. Open by appointment only. Staff members have a limited amount of time to meet with visitors.

c. Yuri Kalashnikov, Trade Representative of the USSR in the U.S.A. and Commercial Minister

2.   The principal efforts of this office are aimed at increasing trade between the U.S. and the USSR. Its work involves American businessmen (rather than scholars) and cannot be considered a major resource. Nevertheless, the staff has available information of a basic and general nature about USSR trade, U.S.-USSR trade, and other statistics.

5.   The office has a wide variety of pamphlets, brochures, and other publications on trade matters.

L9   U.S.-USSR Fisheries Claims Board—Office of the Soviet Part

1 a.   *Mail:*
USSR Embassy
1125 Sixteenth Street, NW
Washington, D.C. 20036
(202) 628-7551

b.   Open by appointment only.

c.   Gennadii M. Chursin

2.   Established by a bilateral agreement in 1973, the board began operations here in early 1974. (Another board sits in Moscow.) Both countries have two representatives on the four-member board, which provides an informal process for working out settlements of claims arising from damage to fishing vessels or gear. The board provides an effective means of averting conflict between fishermen of both countries who fish in the same areas.

The Washington board works with the U.S. State Department and the USSR Ministry of Fisheries. As their time permits, the Soviet delegates should be able to discuss their work with Russianists and to supply useful information and materials to researchers.

5.   The board issues an annual report that is submitted to the U.S. secretary of state and to the Soviet minister of fisheries. Copies are available.

NOTE: The Estonian Legation is located in New York and is therefore not included in this *Guide*. For convenience, however, the address is listed here: Legation of Estonia, Office of Consulate General, 9 Rockefeller Plaza, New York, New York 10020. Telephone: (212) 247-1450.

M Associations (Academic, Professional, Cultural)

Association (Academic, Professional, Cultural) Entry Format (M)

1. *Address; Telephone Number(s)*

2. Founding Date

3. Chief Official and Title

4. Staff

5. Number of Members

6. Program or Description

7. Sections or Divisions

8. Library

9. Conventions/Meetings

10. Publications

11. Affiliated Organizations

Introductory Note

Academic, professional, and cultural associations related to the field of Russian/Soviet studies are listed in this section of the *Guide*. These organizations provide the Washington metropolitan area with a broad range of activities, functions, and services, which promote ethnicity and diversity in the United States.

It should be noted that association members can often put scholars in contact with other scholars and professionals having research or other relevant expertise in Russian- and Soviet-related areas. Indeed, the members themselves may be of considerable value to the researcher. Often they possess unrivaled language skills or other professional experience. Additionally, the associations typically serve as clearinghouses for information in their field of interest.

Finally, the researcher should keep in mind that many of the groups (particularly the ethnic-cultural ones) are ephemeral, and the contact addresses—which are often residences—may change as new officials are selected.

M1 American Association for the Advancement of Slavic Studies (AAASS)—Washington Chapter

1. *c/o Stephen Rapawy*
    12004 Old Bridge Road
    Rockville, Maryland 20852
    (301) 763-4020 or (301) 770-6911

2. In the late 1940s, local Soviet specialists met regularly in an "unclassified forum." When AAASS became a membership group a decade later, this body became the Washington chapter in 1960.

3. Stephen Rapawy, President

4. The chapter has an executive committee of about nine.

5. There are approximately 450 dues-paying members, but the number of those attending functions occasionally is higher.

6. This AAASS local chapter is a rather informal organization, yet it is probably the largest and most active of all chapters. The explanation for this success lies in the large concentration of people in the Washington area—in the academic community, government service, and private business—with an interest and expertise in Russian/Soviet affairs.

Nationally, AAASS is a scholarly association of people in all fields of Slavic studies: history, language, literature, political science, sociology, culture, geography, and so on. Washington-chapter members reflect these same interests, especially as they relate to military, defense, and foreign policy questions involving the Soviet Union. Through AAASS a large part of the Washington community of Russian/Soviet-area specialists is able to come together and discuss, or listen to speakers discuss, matters of mutual and current interest.

Any Russianist coming to the D.C. area for a sojourn or a longer stay should get in touch with chapter officials to learn of activities and events in which he or she would like to take part. Perhaps more important, the chapter can serve as the means of putting the Russianist in contact with others who share the same or similar interests.

9. During the academic year the Washington chapter meets monthly to hear well-known speakers discuss such topics as Soviet foreign policy; Soviet domestic, political, economic, and social conditions; and dissent. In May each year the group holds a two-day symposium devoted to major questions relating to the USSR. These meetings are open to the public, although regular attendance should lead to (dues-paying) membership. Many meetings are cosponsored by local institutions (see point 11). The national organization holds annual conventions in different cities in the fall. The presentation of research papers on many subjects is the major feature of the convention. Regional affiliates of AAASS also hold annual conferences, usually in conjunction with other Slavic associations.

10. The proceedings of the chapter's annual symposia since 1972 have been or are being published. The volumes appear irregularly.

AAASS publishes the quarterly *Slavic Review, Current Digest of the Soviet Press,* and *Index to Pravda.* The weekly *Current Digest,* contains translations or abstracts materials from the Soviet press. *Index,* also in English, appears monthly with an annual cumulation; it contains both a subject and a personal name index (more than 15,000 headings) with extensive cross references.

AAASS Newsletter, issued eight times a year, has professional news; announcements; information about grants, fellowships, and jobs; a schedule of meetings, conferences, and other events; and much more. An annual *AAASS Directory of Members* is also available.

In addition, the organization publishes the important *American Bibliography of Slavic and East European Studies,* which lists books and articles; the bibliography is compiled annually by the staff of the Library of Congress's European Division. Finally, AAASS publishes and distributes other worthwhile titles, generally reference works, such as *Sources of Support for Research in Russian and Soviet Studies* (cosponsored by the Kennan Institute [entry H23])

11. The Washington Chapter, one of ten regional affiliates, works and often cosponsors events with such institutions as the Sino-Soviet Institute of George Washington University (entry H15) and the Kennan Institute for Advanced Russian Studies (entry H23) of the Woodrow Wilson International Center for Scholars (entry H31).

M2 American Association of Museums (AAM)

1. *1055 Thomas Jefferson Street, NW*
   Washington, D.C. 20007
   (202) 338-5300

2. 1906

3. Lawrence L. Reger, Director
   Maria I. Papageorge, Coordinator, International Council of Museums
   Committee of AAM

4. The staff consists of about thirty individuals.

5. Membership includes both museums and individuals; the latter number approximately 7,000.

6. AAM is an information clearinghouse that gathers and disseminates statistics and other data on museums. AAM's institutional and individual members combine to provide considerable expertise on museums in general and museum occupations.

AAM's International Council of Museums (ICOM) conducts tours of American museums for foreign—including Soviet—museum professionals. This, together with other programs, has resulted in some contacts between the AAM and the USSR.

10. AAM publications include the bimonthly *Museum News* and the monthly newsletter *Aviso.* ICOM also publishes a quarterly newsletter that lists current international exhibitions in the U.S.

11. AAM serves as an "umbrella" organization for many museum associations in the United States. Also, the association frequently works on projects funded by such government agencies as the U.S. Information Agency (entry K35).

M3   American Bar Association (ABA)—Governmental Affairs Group (formerly Governmental Relations Office)

1.   *1800 M Street, NW*
     Washington, D.C. 20036
     (202) 331-2200

2.   1878 ABA

3.   Robert D. Evans, Director, Governmental Affairs Group

4.   The group includes about twenty-five lawyers and secretaries.

5.   Nationwide ABA membership is almost 300,000—more than half of all U.S. attorneys.

6.   ABA is a professional organization committed to legal research and an improved legal system.

7.   ABA national headquarters are located in Chicago, yet the International Law Section is based in Washington. The section has under it committees on Soviet law, international human rights, and international trade.

Also in the International Law Section is the International Legal Exchange Program (Edison W. Dick, executive director) that arranges individual placements of both U.S. attorneys in foreign countries and foreign attorneys here. The program additionally hosts visiting legal scholars and generally promotes the study of law on an international level.

ABA has, further, a Standing Committee on Law and National Security and a Standing Committee on World Order under Law. Researchers should call the Washington office for more information about these committees.

9.   The International Law Section holds its annual meeting in Washington each spring, simultaneously with the American Society of International Law (entry M18). ABA's annual meeting is held in August in different cities; it features educational programs by various sections, some of which might interest the Russian/Soviet area specialist. Irregular symposia, called National Institutes, occasionally deal with topics on the USSR or East-West relations.

10.   ABA has published *Current Legal Aspects of Doing Business with Sino-Soviet Nations* (1973), *Business Transactions with the USSR* (1975), *A Contrast between the Legal Systems in the U.S. and the Soviet Union* (1968), *Confrontation in the American-Soviet Relationship: Can It be Managed?* (1980); *Freedom of Expression and Dissent in the Soviet Union* (1982); and *Soviet Perception of Western Realities* (1977).

M4   American Committee on East-West Accord

1.   *227 Massachusetts Avenue, NE, Suite 300*
     Washington, D.C. 20002
     (202) 546-1700

2.   Formerly known as the American Committee on U.S.-Soviet Relations, the committee was founded in 1974.

3.   Robert D. Schmidt, President
Carl Marcy, Codirector
Jeanne Vaughn Mattison, Codirector

4.   The staff consists of five professionals.

5.   Committee membership of about 300–400 includes individuals from business, academia, the government, and other prominent Americans.

6.   The committee is both a political lobby and an educational and cultural organization. Its purpose is to improve relations and communications between the U.S. and the USSR. To do this it seeks to educate Congress and the public on issues relating to educational, cultural, and commercial exchanges with the Soviet Union. Members speak and write on these questions, raise funds to further the committee's aims, and hold occasional forums to discuss other matters of concern.

9.   The conferences and other meetings that the committee convenes to discuss issues are sporadic, and information about them would have to come from the staff. An annual meeting of the membership is held in Washington; outside scholars may attend by invitation.

10.   A bimonthly newsletter, *East-West Outlook,* contains articles on topical U.S.-USSR issues and information about current committee events and projects. Researchers may also receive a descriptive brochure by calling the office.
The committee has produced a twenty-four-minute documentary film entitled *Survival . . . or Suicide,* which has been aired over more than 800 television stations. It has published two books, *Common Sense in U.S.-Soviet Relations* and *Common Sense in U.S.-Soviet Trade.* Other books are in preparation.

M5   American Council On Education (ACE)

1.   *1 Dupont Circle, NW*
Washington, D.C. 20036
(202) 833-4950

2.   1918

3.   Jack W. Peltason, President

4.   Cassandra A. Pyle, Director, Division of International Education and Council for International Exchange of Scholars

6–7.   The ACE administers the Council for International Exchange of Scholars (CIES), composed of thirteen scholars nominated by the American Council on Education, American Council of Learned Societies, the National Academy of Sciences (entry M47), and Social Science Research Council. CIES is a private organization that assists the United States Information Agency (entry K35) administer the Fulbright Program (Mutual Educational and Cultural Exchange Act of 1961). The council publicizes the program, reviews applications, and nominates candidates for grants to U.S. citizens to teach or conduct research abroad. It also assists foreign nationals with their Fulbright Programs of research and lecturing in the U.S. Information and applications may be obtained from: Council for International Exchange of Scholars (CIES), 11 Dupont Circle, NW, Suite 300, Washington, D.C. 20036.
The Division of International Education of ACE has broad functional responsibilities. Its three main objectives are to identify national issues of importance to higher

education, and help shape international education policies at the federal level and coordinate new policy initiatives on behalf of higher education. The division also fosters knowledge and awareness about international issues within higher education in the United States and shares information with overseas institutions and associations.

10. CIES announces the annual Fulbright Competition in the spring with a brochure entitled *Fulbright Senior Scholars: Awards Abroad*, available without charge from the address given under points 6–7.

M6 American Film Institute (AFI)

1. *John F. Kennedy Center for the Performing Arts*
   Washington, D.C. 20566
   (202) 828-4000

2. 1967

3. George Stevens, Jr., Chairperson
   Jean Firstenberg, Director

6. The AFI gathers and maintains information about the cinema past and present; it obtains, stores, and shows motion pictures as well as promotes the art of film and filmmaking. The institute shows Soviet films, at times in conjunction with the Kennan Institute (entry H23). In 1975–76, and again in 1982, it has sponsored series of early and recent Soviet features.

AFI staff also maintains a file on books, clippings, and magazines on Soviet-related film studies.

7. The Education Services unit, now located in Los Angeles (Dr. Peter Bulkowski, director), may be of interest to Russianists. For example, its clippings file contains reviews of many Russian films released in America, especially since 1967. The film festival file has entries for the Moscow Film Festivals and the branch has, in addition, the publications of CILECT (Centre International de Liaison des Ecoles de Cinema et de Television in Brussels) that concern film education in various countries, including the Soviet Union. The Theater Programming Section (Michael Clark, manager) has files with information about movies that the AFI has shown, including Soviet films. This unit also maintains loose contacts with many other countries, including the USSR.

10. With UNESCO the AFI published *The Education of the Film-Maker: An International View* (Paris: UNESCO, 1975), for which AFI is the sole American distributor. The book contains a chapter on Russia.

Currently the institute is engaged in a major publishing venture, the multivolume *American Film Institute Catalog of Feature Films in the U.S., 1893–1970*. So far the volumes on the 1920s and the 1960s have appeared. Each volume contains information about Soviet films shown in this country.

American Film Magazine, a subscription periodical sent to members ten times a year, might occasionally carry pieces that relate to Russia/USSR.

M7 American Friends Service Committee (AFSC)

1. *1822 R Street, NW*
   Washington, D.C. 20009
   (202) 483-3341

2.   1952 locally; 1917 nationally, in Philadelphia

3.   James Hauser, Acting Director, Washington Office

4.   The Washington Office consists of five staff members.

6.   AFSC is a nonprofit Quaker organization that maintains a variety of service, development, reconciliation, and social change programs at home and abroad.

AFSC sponsors a series of ongoing professional exchanges with Soviet counterpart institutes. Topics of study include disarmament, strengthening international organization, and security in Europe. Researchers should contact the office for more information on the programs.

9.   AFSC conducts seminars for government officials on a regular basis.

11.   Locally, the committee works with other Quaker groups, such as the Friends Committee of National Legislation. AFSC headquarters, 1501 Cherry Street, Philadelphia, Pennsylvania 19102, may be contacted for further description of committee activities and for information about AFSC publications.

M8   American Gas Association (AGA)

1.   *1515 Wilson Boulevard*
       Arlington, Virginia 22209
       (703) 841-8000

2.   1919

3.   George H. Lawrence, President

6.   The association has worked with the State Department and the Energy Information Agency of the Energy Department on the exchange of technical information with the USSR, mostly under the bilateral agreement on energy (which has expired). Representatives from the Soviet Union visited the U.S. in 1975 and an AGA delegation went to the USSR in 1976. An association staff member to contact about these trips is Richard Schollhammer.

8.   The AGA library contains 21,800 volumes and currently receives 675 periodicals. It focuses on the American gas industry. Its large vertical-file collection includes three to four folders on the gas industry in the USSR. Files contain clippings from trade journals and newspapers.

The library also has copies of the reports made on the reciprocal trip to the Soviet Union by association members and of the Soviet delegation's visit here.

The library is open by appointment from 9:00 A.M. to 5:15 P.M., Monday through Friday. Interlibrary loan services and photocopying facilities are available. Steven Dorner is the manager of the library.

11.   The association is a member of the International Gas Union (IGU) and provides industry personnel to serve on technical committees covering all phases of gas industry operations. The USSR is also a member of IGU and likewise provides members to serve on the technical committees. For more information about these contacts, contact Leonard Fish.

M9 American Historical Association (AHA)

1. *400 A Street, SE*
   Washington, D.C. 20003
   (202) 544-2422

2. 1884; incorporated by Congress 1889

3. Samuel R. Gammon, Executive Director

4. The staff consists of about twenty individuals.

5. At present AHA has about 13,000 members.

6. The AHA is a nonprofit, professional organization that seeks to encourage and improve the study and teaching of history and promote general interest in history. It also awards prizes for history writing.

The biennial Soviet-American Historical Colloquia are of particular significance for Russianists. The Fourth Colloquium, held in April 1981, considered the topic of U.S. and USSR socioeconomic developments and trends between the two world wars. The Fifth Colloqium is to be held in Kiev in the fall of 1983.

7. The AHA Committee on Quantitative Research in History, reconstituted as a standing committee under the Research Division in October 1975, has implemented an exchange program with the Soviet Academy of Sciences. Joint work is planned in the area of quantitative methods applied to historical research. Exchanges took place in 1979 and 1981.

The association's Standing Committee on International Historical Activities also has contact with Soviet historians, often through work on the quinquennial congresses of the International Committee of Historical Sciences.

9. AHA holds an annual convention in December; the site varies.

10. *American Historical Review* appears five times a year. One or more articles on Russian/Soviet topics can be expected annually. In addition, reviews of books on pertinent subjects are included in every issue. Since 1976 the association has published a valuable index to periodical literature on individual countries and regions; *Recently Published Articles* comes out three times per year. (Before 1976, this feature appeared in the *American Historical Review.*)

11. At least seventy societies, associations, and groups are affiliated with AHA. These societies generally are for the study of special historical topics or geographic areas. Some two dozen of these affiliates usually meet with AHA at its annual convention.

M10 American Historical Society of Germans from Russia—The Nation's Capital Area Chapter

1. *3705 South George Mason Drive, 212 South*
   Falls Church, Virginia 22041
   (703) 931-8953

2. 1975 locally; 1968 nationally

3. Mrs. Olinda Brown, President (elected annually)

4.   The local chapter has an executive board of six.

5.   Washington-area membership is twenty-nine individuals and families; nationwide there are more than 6,000 members, totaling more than 10,000 individuals.

6.   This is a nonsectarian historical society devoted to the discovery, collection, and preservation of all kinds of information about Germans who have emigrated from Russia/USSR. It disseminates this information in various ways (publications, meetings), has established repositories to maintain it, and promotes research on this subject.

8.   The society has no library of its own in the D.C. area, but it has established its national library and archives at the Greeley (Colo.) Public Library. Washington researchers can obtain this material through interlibrary loan. A bibliography of holdings exists (see point 10). In addition, one local member, Ms. Emma S. Haynes, has a substantial personal collection.

9.   The group has an annual national convention, held in different cities. Of more interest are the quarterly meetings of the local chapter. These are open to the public and scholarly in nature. Any researchers concerned with Germans in and from Russia will certainly want to contact the society for information about these activities.

10. The local chapter publishes a newsletter. National headquarters (1139 South Seventh Street, Lincoln, Nebraska 68502) publishes a newsletter three times per year; *The Journal of the American Historical Society of Germans from Russia,* four times a year; and a semiannual genealogical magazine entitled *Clues.* In addition, headquarters publishes the bibliography for the Greeley, Colorado, collection, which includes biographic and genealogical data, documents, photographs, maps, material objects, and other items.

M11 American Latvian Association in the United States, Inc. (ALA)

1.   *P.O. Box 432*
     Rockville, Maryland 20850
     (301) 340-1914

2.   1951

3.   Janis Riekstins, President (elected annually)
     Anita Terauds, Secretary General (permanent)

4.   There are two full- and one part-time employees.

5.   The association nationwide has more than 5,000 dues-paying members, most of whom are also members of local affiliated groups. Local members number perhaps 200. About 200 American Latvian organizations belong to the association.

6.   ALA is a private, nonprofit organization of persons of Latvian descent living in the U.S. Its purpose is to unite and represent all American Latvians in an effort to preserve the Latvian ethnic identity, promote cultural cooperation between American Latvians and other Americans, and inform the public about the Soviet occupation of Latvia and its consequences.

7.   The association has bureaus for the following activities: cultural, educational, informational, athletic, and community welfare.

8.   ALA maintains twenty-five file-drawer cabinets of annual reports, correspond-

ence, organization records, photographs, and other materials pertaining to conditions in Latvia, Latvian organizations throughout the world, Soviet dissidents, and the Helsinki conference. Also included are the records (twenty boxes) of the Committee for a Free Latvia. Much of the material is in the process of being cataloged and organized. Researchers should write or call to make an appointment to examine the material.

9. The annual national convention is held in May; the site varies. Board members of the national organization meet for business about every two months.

10. *Latvian News Digest* appears five times per year; *ALA Vestis* appears quarterly.

11. Local affiliates include the Latvian Evangelical Lutheran Church (entry P5); Washington Latvian Society (entry M75); and Latvian Welfare Association (Daugavas Vanagi) (entry M41). The association is also affiliated with the World Federation of Free Latvians.

M12 American Latvian Theatre—Washington Ensemble

1. *9106 Shad Lane*
   Potomac, Maryland 20854
   (301) 299-8543

2. 1960 locally; 1949 New York

3. Anda Ursteins Juberts, Director
   Karlis Kuzulis, Administrator

4. The ensemble consists of fifteen actors and actresses. (Guest actors from the New York Ensemble participate in most performances.) In addition, there are two scene painters, two lighting engineers, and two permanent stage technicians.

6. The American Latvian Theatre group performs plays in Latvian. A traveling ensemble, it has given performances in many U.S. and Canadian cities with large Latvian communities. The ensemble has also been invited to Cologne, West Germany, and recently to Gotland, Sweden, where it gave special festival performances.

The current director, Anda Ursteins Juberts, is the daughter of the late director, Osvalds Ursteins, who was the director of the National Theatre of Latvia in Riga. The actors do not make their living from the theater, but many are professionals from theaters in Latvia. Younger actors have been schooled in special courses and through training performances.

8. Although it has no library as such, the ensemble does have some video and audio recordings of performances and of intervews with actors.

9. A schedule of performances may be obtained from the above address.

11. The Washington Ensemble is one of three groups of the American Latvian Theatre; others are in Boston and New York.

M13 American Political Science Association

1. *1527 New Hampshire Avenue, NW*
   Washington, D.C. 20036
   (202) 483-2512

2.   1903

3.   Thomas E. Mann, Executive Director

4.   The staff consists of about twenty individuals.

5.   Of the 9,000 members, a majority come from the academic community; the rest are government workers, journalists, and other interested persons.

6.   The association is a professional and scholarly organization devoted to the promotion, improvement, and furtherance of the political science discipline. The work of individual members is often in the sphere of international politics and affairs, Soviet domestic politics and government, and similar fields of paramount importance to Russianists. Specialists should also note that the organization maintains contacts with Soviet scholars and academic institutions.

9.   Both the U.S. and USSR are members of the International Political Science Association, which holds its international conventions every few years. The 1979 meeting was held in Moscow; the 1982, in Rio de Janeiro. These meetings bring together political scientists of both countries for discussions.

The association has annual conventions, at which there are always sessions on different aspects of Soviet government and politics as well as on international affairs and other topics relating to the Soviet Union. The convention also serves as a professional meeting place for those seeking positions and potential employers.

10.   *American Political Science Review,* a quarterly, publishes articles and reviews of books in the field of Soviet studies.

M14 American Psychiatric Association (APA) and Washington Psychiatric Society (WPS)

1.   *1700 Eighteenth Street, NW*
Washington, D.C. 20009
(202) 797-4900

2.   1844 APA; 1949 WPS

3.   Melvin Sabshin, M.D., Medical Director, APA
Daniel X. Freeman, M.D., President, APA (Chicago, Illinois)

6–7.   A professional organization of practicing psychiatrists, APA engages in a wide variety of activities, for which it has established a number of councils. The branch of particular interest is the Council of International Affairs. Two of the council's components are the Task Force on Cross-Cultural Perspectives of Psychiatric Practice (since 1975) and Task Force on Liaison with International and Foreign Psychiatric Organizations (since 1973). The council serves as the association's link with the World Psychiatric Association, composed of forty to fifty national societies, including that of the USSR. APA thus may have occasional direct and indirect contact with its Soviet counterpart and individual Soviet psychiatrists. The World Psychiatric Association holds a World Congress of Psychiatry every five years. This congress discusses questions raised by its members. The use and abuse of psychiatry in the Soviet Union is a topic of interest to some members and may be a subject for discussion. Ellen Mercer (202/797-4881) is the staff member assigned as liaison with the Council on International Affairs. At present a few other consultants for the council are also in the D.C. area.

Individual members of the association are often involved in activities related to the

USSR. For example, Dr. Sabshin, APA medical director, has made personal trips to the Soviet Union. Other members are participating in work designed to draw up an international code of ethics for psychiatrists throughout the world.

Finally, WPS, a D.C. branch of APA, maintains a list of Washington-area psychiatrists that is broken down in many ways, including by language. The latest list included the following number of physicians available to examine and treat patients in the given language: Armenian—two; Russian—four; Turkish—five; and Ukrainian—one. (Other members can treat the deaf and individuals who speak Hebrew and Yiddish.)

8. The library holds some 15,000 works on psychiatry and the history of psychiatry. A small number deal directly with the Soviet Union. The collection of vertical-file material contains a folder (three-quarters inch thick at present) with clippings, references, and bibliographies on Soviet psychiatry plus a report by the president of APA on his trip to the USSR. This library generally provides basic research material on the subjects of psychiatry, psychology, and mental health in the USSR.

The library is open to non-APA members by permission of the staff only. The librarian is Zing Jung (202/797-4957). Hours are 9:00 A.M. to 5:00 P.M., Monday through Friday. Interlibrary loan service and photocopying facilities are available.

10. The APA *Roster of Organizational Components,* an annual compilation of members' names and lists of committees, councils, and task forces, should be of interest to scholars. *Directory of Members of the Washington Psychiatric Society and Clinical Psychiatric Facilities in the Washington Area* has, among other useful pieces of information, the list of foreign-language physicians noted earlier.

11. APA has representatives to some seventeen other organizations and bodies that are not, strictly speaking, affiliates. The association has district branches throughout the U.S.; the Washington Psychiatric Society is the branch of the APA in the D.C. area.

M15 American Psychological Association (APA)

1. *1200 Seventeenth Street, NW*
   Washington, D.C. 20036
   (202) 833-7600

2. 1892

3. Dr. Michael Pallak, Executive Director

4. A staff of approximately 260 carries out the functions of the APA.

5. Membership consists of 55,000 professionals nationwide as well as a number of foreign affiliates.

6–7. A national professional association of psychologists, APA strives to advance psychology as a science and profession and as a means of promoting human welfare.

The association's Committee on International Relations in Psychology maintains some contact with national psychological societies abroad, including the USSR, through the International Union of Psychological Science and other channels. The Washington office has an International Affairs Department (202/833-3560) that responds to inquiries concerning international activities and organizations.

8. A small library, mostly for in-house use, is headed by Betty Lawton (202/833-7589). APA also maintains the Psychological Information Services ("PsychINFO"),

a computerized data base that contains unpublished theses, monographs, periodicals, and more. The service receives approximately ten Soviet psychological publications. Abstracts are entered into PsychINFO and published in the journal *Psychological Abstracts*. Scholars should contact (202) 833-5907 for data-base information.

9. APA holds an annual convention, usually in late August, in various North American cities. Occasional sessions during the convention focus on foreign and international psychology.

10. The association's extensive publications program includes monthly: *American Psychologist, Contemporary Psychology, Journal of Personality and Social Psychology, Psychological Abstracts, Psychological Bulletin*; bi-monthly: *Developmental Psychology, Journal of Abnormal Psychology, Journal of Applied Psychology, Journal of Consulting and Clinical Psychology, Journal of Counseling Psychology, Journal of Educational Psychology, Psychological Review*; quarterly: *Journal of Experimental Psychology, Professional Psychology*. Many of these publications occasionally carry articles of interest to the Russianist. A descriptive brochure is available.

M16 American Red Cross

1. *Seventeenth and D streets, NW*
    Washington, D.C. 20006
    (202) 737-8300

2. 1881

3. Jerome H. Holland, Chairperson

6. The Red Cross is largely a volunteer organization that attempts to prevent and/or lessen human suffering caused by natural or manmade disasters in this country and abroad. The American Red Cross, along with another 128 national Red Cross and Red Crescent societies, supports the League of Red Cross Societies, a worldwide federation, and International Committee of the Red Cross. The Alliance of Red Cross and Red Crescent Societies of the Soviet Union is also a member of these international bodies and thus occasionally has contact with the American society. In particular, the American Red Cross receives and acts upon requests for information about estranged relatives of U.S. citizens in the Soviet Union. The Red Cross has sometimes been able to reunite these families. Questions involving the USSR and refugees, war victims, and Soviet Jews might also come to the attention of the Red Cross.

7. The Office of International Services, Joseph P. Carniglia, director (202/857-3591), handles and coordinates work concerning the above matters.

8. The National Headquarters Library has a number of resources of interest to Russian/Soviet-area specialists. For its significant archival and vertical-file material, see the entry in the Archives and Manuscript Depositories section (B1). The library holds several Red Cross publications that may contain pieces about Russia. Among these are the *Red Cross Courier* (title varies), 1922–51; *The American Red Cross Magazine* (title varies), 1912–20; and *International Review of the Red Cross*, of the International Committee of the Red Cross. More importantly, the library has *The Red Cross Bulletin*, 1920–21, published in Riga by the American Red Cross Commission to Western Russia and the Baltic States, and an incomplete run of *Sovetskii krasnyi krest* magazine since 1970. The card file index to *The American Red Cross Magazine* includes several entries under "Russia."

The library also has a small number of books on Russia/USSR in general and a handful of titles concerned with Red Cross activity during and after World War I in European Russia, the Ukraine, the Baltic area, and Siberia.

The library is open to researchers from 8:30 A.M. to 4:45 P.M., Monday through Friday. Staff members to consult include: Roberta Biles, library director (202/857-3491); and Rudy Clemen (202/857-3647) and Leon Gilbert (202-857-3459) in international affairs. Interlibrary loan service and photocopying facilities are available.

9.   The International Conference of the Red Cross meets every four years. It is at these meetings that the American members contact their Soviet counterparts and discuss mutual concerns.

10.   Other than occasional press releases that deal with questions involving the USSR, the publication that might most interest Russianists is the League of Red Cross Societies' *Panorama*. Appearing six times per year, *Panorama* carries news and information about the Red Cross societies of individual nations, including the Soviet Union.

11.   While the American Red Cross has no affiliates (in the strict sense of the word) other than the members of the world federation, it does have written agreements for cooperation with virtually every voluntary public service organization in this country.

___

M17 American Russian Aid Association—Washington Branch

1.   *4123 Harrison Street, NW*
Washington, D.C. 20015

2.   Circa 1960 locally

3.   Selene Obolensky, President (202/244-4728)
Serge Martinoff, Treasurer (202/362-3039)

4.   The branch has four officers.

5.   About forty people belong to the local group.

6.   As a charitable organization, the association helps to support elderly Russian Americans through contributions, fundraising concerts, charity balls, and other cultural events.

___

M18 American Society of International Law

1.   *2223 Massachusetts Avenue, NW*
Washington, D.C. 20008
(202) 265-4313

2.   1906

3.   Seymour J. Rubin, Executive Director

4.   The office staff consists of about twenty individuals.

5.   The membership numbers approximately 5,000, including lawyers, educators, diplomats, government officials, businessmen, students, clergymen, and others interested in international law and relations.

6. The society promotes the study of international law and seeks to encourage the role of law in international relations. Its work includes the organization of study groups on such topics as the law of treaties, the role of international law in civil wars, international telecommunications, nuclear energy and world order, science and international law, oceanic resources, the self-determination of nations, and economic and trade matters.

8. The society library is of minor interest to Russianists at present, but it does contain a number of Soviet periodicals.

9. The society's annual meeting is held in April, in Washington.

10. The society publishes a bimonthly newsletter, the bimonthly *International Legal Materials,* the quartlery *American Journal of International Law,* the annual *Proceedings,* and a series of monographs called Studies in Transnational Legal Policy.

M19 American Sociological Association (ASA)

1. *1722 N Street, NW*
   Washington, D.C. 20036
   (202) 833-3410

2. 1905

3. William D'Antonio, Executive Officer

4. The staff consists of seventeen individuals.

5. The membership numbers approximately 13,000.

6. The association's purpose is to further research and teaching in sociology. Scholars, professional social workers, and others belong to this membership organization. Distinguished experts on Soviet society and social institutions are among these ranks.

7. The Committee on World Sociology, chaired by Professor D. Wiley of Michigan State University, has under it various liaison groups for different regions of the world. The Soviet Union and Eastern Europe have such a liaison within the committee. Although no member of this liason is currently in the Washington area, the association can put researchers in touch with committee members around the country.

9. ASA has annual conventions. At these meetings, a session or two usually relate to the Soviet field. The convention is also of value for keeping Russianists aware of each other's work and with available positions.

10. *Contemporary Sociology* is published six times a year by ASA. One can expect to find in the journal a few pieces on the USSR each year as well as reviews of relevant books.

11. ASA is a member of the International Sociological Association (ISA), of which the USSR is also a member. ISA has an executive committee and various research committees; American and Soviet sociologists often serve together on ISA and conduct professional work. The international body has congresses every four years.

ASA also has an Official Representative to the American Association for the Advancement of Slavic Studies (entry M1).

M20 Amnesty International, USA—Washington Office

1. *705 G Street, SE*
   Washington, D.C. 20003
   (202) 544-0200

2. 1976 locally; 1961 internationally in London

3. Patricia L. Rengel, Director

4. This office has six paid staff workers as well as unpaid interns and volunteers.

5. The organization numbers more than 80,000 individual members/contributors nationwide.

6. Amnesty International is a worldwide movement of people working for the release of prisoners of conscience, fair trials for political prisoners, and an end to torture and the death penalty. (Prisoners of conscience are persons imprisoned for ethnic, religious, or political beliefs and not for violent action.) The group writes letters to the prisoners' countries, visits these countries' local embassies, and in every way possible attempts to secure the release—and, if desired, the emigration—of these prisoners. The family of the prisoner is also sustained and/or assisted in emigrating. Members of the association disseminate information about their work through a variety of media, including frequent public talks and discussions.

9. The organization's working groups hold meetings often. Interested researchers should contact the local office to ascertain which group(s) might be dealing with prisoners in the USSR. The U.S. section of Amnesty International holds an annual general meeting for its membership.

10. The International Secretariat in London publishes detailed reports on the conditions in countries around the world. An annual report presents a comprehensive overview of worldwide Amnesty International concerns and activities. In addition, external documents are released periodically by the International Secretariat. The U.S. section publishes the monthly newsletter *Amnesty Action*; the triannual bulletin *Matchbox*; and the quarterly bulletin *Labor News*. These reports and newsletters are available from regional offices.

11. Amnesty International has consultative status with the UN (ECOSOC), UNESCO, and the Council of Europe and has cooperative relations with the Organization of African Unity (Bureau for the Placement and Education of African Refugees).

M21 Armenian Assembly Charitable Trust—National Headquarters

1. *1420 N Street, NW, Suite 101*
   Washington, D.C. 20005
   (202) 332-3434

2. 1972

3. Nubar Dorian, Cochairperson (in New York)
   Robert A. Kaloosdian, Cochairperson (in Boston)
   Mihran Agbabian, Cochairperson (in Los Angeles)

4. A small staff, normally about six persons, manages the Washington office. Ross Vartian is the director.

6. Despite its rather unusual name, the assembly is a research-oriented organization with interests in all aspects of Armenian life in the U.S. Soviet-area scholars can obtain from the staff information about Armenian culture, history, and so on, here. More importantly, the Armenian Assembly serves as a referral center, directing researchers who inquire about specific topics to individuals and organizations throughout the U.S. with information on the subject. This service could be invaluable to specialists on Soviet Armenia.

8. A small but valuable library collection is located at the assembly. There are perhaps 150 books, mostly in English. There is also a research file here, with clippings, reports, publications, and other materials relating to Armenia and Armenians. Some items may be of value to Soviet-area scholars.

9. The Armenian Assembly has published the second edition of the *Directory of Armenian Scholars in United States and Canadian Institutions* (1976), which should be of great interest to researchers. On occasion the staff also issues research papers.

M22 Armenian National Committee—Washington Representative

1. *Location:*
212 Stuart Street
Boston, Massachusetts 02117

Mail:
P.O. Box 91 BB Annex
Boston, Massachusetts 02117

Toll-free from D.C.:
Ask operator for ENterprise 1-9842

There is no institutional address in Washington.

2. In the 1920s the Armenian National Committee grew out of an earlier group working for Armenian independence.

3. Colonel Harry A. Sachaklian, Washington Representative (703/356-8114)

6. The committee is a political organization seeking the independence of the Armenian homeland. Its goal is a free, independent, and united Armenia. In pursuit of this purpose it holds public demonstrations and attempts to educate the American public about the situation of Armenia and Armenians. The committee pays close attention to Soviet Armenia.

10. Boston headquarters issues in English *The Armenian Weekly* and *The Armenian Review,* a quarterly. It also publishes a daily newspaper in Armenian.

11. The Armenian National Committee is an affiliate of the international Armenian Revolutionary Federation (Dashnak Party, founded in 1890). The local representative is affiliated with the Armenian Assembly Charitable Trust here in Washington (entry M21).

M23 Arms Control Association (ACA)

1. *11 Dupont Circle, NW*
    Washington, D.C. 20036
    (202) 797-6450

2. 1971

3. William H. Kincade, Executive Director

4. There are six full-time staff workers, one full- and two to four part-time interns.

5. The organization numbers 1,400 individual U.S. citizens.

6. ACA is a private, nonprofit, nonpartisan membership organization whose goal is to educate the public by means of effective programs in arms control and disarmament. Members include many persons with extensive experience in the fields of arms control and national security.

8. The association library maintains a vertical-file collection.

9. In the past ACA has sponsored special conferences and meetings on specific topics. For example, in September 1981, the association held an unofficial international meeting in Brussels, Belgium, to examine the issues connected with nuclear weapons in Europe.

10. ACA publishes the monthly bulletin *Arms Control Today,* which features several short articles, a calendar, other news, and extensive bibliographic listings.
In 1978 ACA and the Carnegie Endowment issued the book *Negotiating Security: An Arms Control Reader,* ed. William H. Kincade and Jeffrey Porro. The association has sponsored other such books as well.

11. Under a cooperative agreement, ACA participates in a number of joint ventures with the Carnegie Endowment (entry M28).

M24 Association of American Geographers (AAG)

1. *1710 Sixteenth Street, NW*
    Washington, D.C. 20009
    (202) 234-1450

2. 1904

3. Patricia J. McWethy, Executive Director

4. The staff consists of six individuals.

5. The organization has a nationwide membership numbering 6,000 professional educators, scientists, and others in the field of geography.

6. AAG is a professional association that promotes members' interests, furthers the discipline, sponsors geographic investigations, and encourages applications of geographic research in government, education, and business.
The association has just completed a study of Soviet natural resources in the world economy. An assessment was made of the production potential of various Soviet

resources and the impact each would have on world commodity markets. The results of the study will be published by the University of Chicago Press.

7.   AAG has many sections, committees, and commissions. A Committee on International Projects is responsible for developing conferences and collaborative research projects with foreign scholars. There is also a USSR/Eastern Europe Specialty Group for members.

9.   The association holds annual meetings in April at different sites. Its nine divisions hold their own annual meetings each fall.

10.   AAG has a number of publications, some of which may carry pertinent (to Russianists) information on occasion: *AAG Newsletter,* ten times per year; *Annals of the AAG,* a quarterly; the *Professional Geographer,* also a quarterly; and a quadrennial directory of membership. In addition, AAG issues monographs, maps, and other materials.

M25 Association of Former Intelligence Officers (AFIO)

1.   *6723 Whittier Avenue, Suite 303A*
McLean, Virginia 22101
(703) 790-0320

2.   1975

3.   John M. Maury, President
John K. Greaney, Executive Director

4.   The staff consists of an executive director, assistant director, and a clerical worker.

5.   There are 3,200 members in eighteen chapters, ninety-five percent of whom are former government intelligence professionals (from the military services, the State Department, CIA, and other intelligence or security agencies).

6.   This private, nonpartisan, dues-paying organization has an educational purpose: to promote a full understanding of the role of intelligence in America.

7.   To carry out its program the association has two major sections: a roster of speakers and an academic program. The association's experts on Soviet operations are available for speaking engagements nationwide. The office also serves as a clearinghouse of information to the media and provides a liaison with the academic community.

9.   The association's annual convention is held in October. Speakers at the 1981 convention included Richard Allen and Ambassador Helms.

10.   The quarterly *Periscope* contains intelligence news.

M26 Bandurist Ensemble of Washington

1.   *8614 Hidden Hill Lane*
Potomac, Maryland 20854
(301) 299-4397

2.   Circa 1965

3.   Ihor Masnyk, Director

4.   There is an assistant director as well as the director, Mr. Masnyk.

5.   Twenty-four amateur musicians currently participate in this youth ensemble, but the group is growing.

6.   This amateur musical group performs on the bandura, an old Ukrainian stringed instrument. The ensemble has about six to eight engagements a year, playing at ethnic affairs, at local institutions, and for such events as the presidential inauguration. In addition to directing the group's performances, Mr. Masnyk also gives without charge bandura lessons to children. All instruments, it might be noted, come directly from the Ukraine.

8.   Mr. Masnyk has a collection of some fifty books and record albums relating to Ukrainian music and many more individual music scores. He also notes that the summer 1970 issue of *Guitar Review* (no. 33) has an article about bandura history and music.

M27 B'nai B'rith—International Headquarters

1.   *1640 Rhode Island Avenue, NW*
      Washington, D.C. 20036
      (202) 857-6600

2.   1930s locally; 1843 internationally

3.   Jack J. Spitzer, President

4.   In the U.S., B'nai B'rith and its various agencies (Hillel, Anti-Defamation League) have about 1,000 executive personnel and specialists in Washington, New York, and other field offices.

5.   Current membership numbers approximately half a million people of all ages, most of them in the U.S.

6.   B'nai B'rith is a Jewish community service and public affairs organization. Its work is also educational, as the association tries to sensitize the U.S. public, government figures, and Jews themselves to Jewish problems. This effort involves the USSR directly, for B'nai B'rith and its supporters actively work to encourage the Soviet Union to relax its emigration laws and grant its citizens full religious, civil, and human rights. The Washington headquarters also maintains the B'nai B'rith Klutznick Museum (Anna Cohn, director, 202/857-6583), which holds one of the largest collections of Jewish art in North America, including items from Eastern Europe and Russia.

7.   The most important section of the organization for Russianists is the B'nai B'rith International Council. Its director is Warren Eisenberg. William Korey, an authority and published scholar on the question of Soviet Jewry, is the director of International Research Policy. George Spectre is the associate director of the council, which is located in Washington. The telephone number for the International Council is (202) 857-6545. From this branch, scholars should be able to get current information on the situation of Soviet Jews, details on individual cases, and much more valuable data.

8.   B'nai B'rith has a limited collection of books on Soviet Jewry.

9. The world group sponsors occasional meetings and symposia on topics of interest to Soviet area scholars. In addition, there is a biennial convention at which at least one session would concern Soviet Jews. For more details about these events, one should contact B'nai B'rith directly. The International Council holds annual meetings; unfortunately, these are normally closed to outsiders.

10. B'nai B'rith has published a number of works relating to Soviet Jewry. They include: *Jewishness Rediscovered,* by A. Voronel and V. Yakhat (1974); *Jews as Non-Persons,* by William Korey (1972); *Why They Left: A Survey of Soviet Jewish Emigrants,* by Maurice Friedberg (1972).

The organization also prepares reports and papers on topical issues which may touch upon the Soviet Union. A descriptive brochure is available to scholars.

11. B'nai B'rith has no affiliates as such; it does, however, sponsor the important Academic Committee on Soviet Jewry in New York.

M28 Carnegie Endowment for International Peace—Washington Office

1. *11 Dupont Circle, NW*
   Washington, D.C. 20036
   (202) 797-6400

2. 1910

3. Thomas L. Hughes, President

4. Some twenty-five to thirty senior and resident associates work in the endowment's offices in Washington and in New York (30 Rockefeller Plaza).

5. The endowment is not a membership organization.

6. As an operating (not a grantmaking) foundation, the Carnegie Endowment conducts its own programs of research, discussion, education, and publication in international affairs and U.S. foreign policy. Program areas change periodically; recently, they have included: national security and arms control, executive-congressional relations in foreign policy, South Africa, the Middle East, South and Southwest Asia, the Horn of Africa, Latin America, international economic issues, and U.S.-Soviet relations.

10. Of particular interest to Soviet scholars are a recent study *In Afghanistan's Shadow: Baluch Nationalism and Soviet Temptations,* by Selig S. Harrison (1981), and a four-part report *Challenges for U.S. National Security,* by the Carnegie Panel on U.S. Security and the Future of Arms Control (1981). Information on current activities and a list of publications are available without charge. The endowment is also the publisher of the quarterly journal *Foreign Policy* (entry Q8).

M29 Carpathian Alliance Washington Branch

1. *2615 Thirtieth Street, NW*
   Washington, D.C. 20008
   (202) 234-2330

2. 1970s locally, 1949 nationally

3.   Julius Hutnyk, Local Coordinator

5.   Nationwide the alliance has nearly 300 members. Members are Ruthenians and Ukrainians who lived or were associated with the area of the Carpatho-Ukraine (currently the Transcarpathian region of the Ukrainian SSR).

6.   The goals of the organization are to render all possible aid to the Old Country and to immigrants from there; develop fraternal relations between the two waves of Ruthenian immigrants (pre- and post-World War II) in this country; inform the American public about the history and people of Carpatho-Ukraine; and foster Ruthenian national traditions and consciousness and religious ways, thereby enriching American culture.

9.   The alliance's executive board, elected every two years, meets frequently during the year to take care of business and arrange its activities. In the past it has helped organize cultural affairs, such as presenting plays, holding literary evenings, and sponsoring lectures. The group also celebrates important holidays, often with other organizations.

10.   The alliance has published two periodicals. *Karpatska Zoria* is now defunct, but appeared regularly in the 1950s. Currently, the newletter *Visnyk* appears irregularly. In addition, the organization publishes or republishes numerous works of history, poetry, and memoirs relating to Ruthenia and Carpatho-Ukraine.

11.   The Carpathian Alliance cooperates and works with many other organizations, especially other Ukrainian bodies, such as the Ukrainian Congress Committee of America (entry M64), Ukrainian Youth League, and Carpatho-Russian Orthodox Church.

M30 Congress of Russian Americans—Greater Washington Branch

1.   *8811 Colesville Road, Apartment 618*
      Silver Spring, Maryland 20910

2.   1974 (reorganized 1975) locally, 1973 nationally

3.   Victor Petrov, President (301/780-2071)
      George Meyer, Secretary (301/585-4006)

4.   An executive board of ten is supplemented by volunteer staff workers.

5.   About fifty dues-paying members reside in the Washington area. Nationwide there are approximately 1,800 members in some twenty-five branches.

6.   This national organization promotes Russian ethnic interests and culture in the U.S., and particularly seeks the support of elected government officals for its work. It has established a modest scholarship fund and is trying to establish a nursing home for elderly Americans of Russian descent.

9.   The local branch holds monthly business meetings and an annual election meeting; a national convention is held every three years.

10.   The bilingual newsletter *A Russian American,* put out by the main office in New York, averages four issues per year. Contents include reports on congressional activities relating to ethnic groups.

Mr. Petrov is also the editor of a local monthly newsletter, *Stolichnij Listok* (Capital news).

11. The group maintains permanent contact and cooperates with the Tolstoy Foundation; Russian Center in San Francisco; Homeland (Rodina) in Lakewood, New Jersey; Russian Academic Group in New York; Association of Russian Engineers in New York; and other U.S. Russian organizations.

M31 Council for a Livable World—Washington Office

1. *100 Maryland Avenue, NE*
   Washington, D.C. 20002
   (202) 543-4100

2. 1962 (by Leo Szilard)

3. Jerome Grossman, President
   George Kistiakowsky, Chairperson
   John Isaacs, Legislative Director (in Washington)

4. The office has five staff members.

5. There are twenty-four persons on the council's board; nationwide the council has some 60,000 supporters.

6. The council works against the proliferation of nuclear weapons with the aim of averting nuclear war. The USSR, being one of the major nuclear powers, is of direct and active concern to the organization.

7. The political and legislative arms of the council attempt to draft laws, influence congressional action, and promote the cause of arms control.

9. At monthly meetings legislative proposals and actions are discussed.

10. The council is developing a newsletter, which will probably come out six times a year (in a nonelection year). Members and supporters also receive mailings and other information put out by the staff.

Council for International Exchange of Scholars See entry M5

Daugavis Vanagi See entry M41

M32 Diplomatic and Consular Officers, Retired (DACOR, Inc.)

1. *1718 H Street, NW*
   Washington, D.C. 20006
   (202) 298-7848

2. 1952

3. Allen B. Moreland, Executive Director

4. There are five full-time, paid staff members; many volunteers serve on the organization's various committees.

5. There are about 2,000 members.

6. DACOR, Inc., is an association of active and retired United States foreign service officers, ambassadors, and other public officials involved in foreign affairs. The organization can be a useful source of information for scholars interested in contacting former U.S. diplomats involved in Soviet affairs.

7. Most of the association's work is done by such committees as the library, fellowship, and legislative committees.

8. The small DACOR library contains volumes written by foreign service officers or generally about the foreign service. There are also biographic registers. Researchers may use the library with permission of the executive director.

9. An annual meeting is held in Washington, D.C., in April.

10. The association publishes the monthly *DACOR Bulletin*.

Dobro Slovo   See entry M52

M33 Estonian American National Council—Washington Representatives

1. *19102 Stedwick Drive*
   Gaithersburg, Maryland 20879
   (301) 340-1954

3. Maido Kari, Director for Washington
   Juhan Simonson, President of the National Council (see point 11)

4. There are a few volunteer staff workers in Washington.

5. The local affiliate of the council, the Washington Estonian Society (entry M73), has about 200 members. Nationwide the council claims as members a majority of the 25,000 Estonians in the U.S.

6. The main purpose of the council, a political lobby, is to promote Estonian and Baltic independence. It further supports schools and a variety of cultural activities.

9. Every three years national elections of representatives take place. The fifty elected representatives meet annually to choose a board of directors, which meets monthly.

11. Besides the local affiliate noted in point 5, the council, whose national headquarters is the Estonian House, 243 East Thirty-fourth Street, New York, New York 10016, is affiliated with: Estonian Educational Society, Inc., Estonian Film Center, Estonian Learned Society in America, Estonian Music Center, Estonian Relief Committee, Estonian School Fund in U.S.A., Inc., Estonian World Council, Henryk Visnapuu Literary Foundation, Society of Estonian Journalists, Union of Estonian Student Corporations.
   These organizations are based at the New York Estonian House. There is also an important Estonian Archive in Lakewood, New Jersey.

M34 Ethnic Foundation

1. *1341 G Street, NW*
    Washington, D.C. 20005
    (202) 628-9439

2. 1959

3. Colonel J. Jaroslav Sustar, Executive Vice Chairperson

6. The foundation is a nonprofit, nonpolitical, private organization that works with a number of national minorities in this country on education, research, and social service. Some ethnic groups represented in the foundation are of the USSR.

10. The foundation publishes the bimonthly *Ethnic Newsletter.*

11. The organization is an affiliate of the National Confederation of American Ethnic Groups.

M35 Foreign Policy Discussion Group

1. *815 Connecticut Avenue, NW*
    Washington, D.C. 20006
    (202) 298-8290

2. 1968

3. Charles T. Mayer, President

5. Approximately seventy-five to eighty individuals belong to the group; membership is by invitation only.

6. The group is designed to improve the understanding and knowledge of foreign policy problems among its members.

9. Ten times per year (monthly except in the summer) the group holds meetings at which important foreign policy figures address the members. Two recent speakers, for example, have been columnist Robert Evans and French Ambassador M. De Laboulaye. These gatherings are absolutely closed to nonmembers.

M36 Fund for the Relief of Russian Writers and Scientists in Exile (The Litfund)—Washington Branch

1. *c/o Professor Helen B. Yakobson*
    Department of Slavic Languages and Literatures
    George Washington University
    Washington, D.C. 20052
    (202) 676-6336

2. 1918 nationally

3. Professor Helen B. Yakobson, President

4. There is a staff of two: the president and a secretary. There is also an advisory board of eight people.

5. No precise membership figures are available for the Washington group. Perhaps thirty to sixty people attend Washington-area functions regularly. Nationwide there are about 275 individual members.

6. The fund is a charitable organization designed to help Russian cultural figures (and their widows and children) in the U.S. and elsewhere outside the Soviet Union. It sponsors literary evenings, lectures, and concerts.

7. The Washington Branch has no sections or divisions. The national organization is divided into local groups, the Washington Branch being one of three.

9. Several meetings are held each year in Washington for literary, musical, or lecture evenings.

M37 International Dostoevsky Society

1. *c/o Professor Nadine Natov*
    Department of Slavic Languages and Literatures
    George Washington University
    Washington, D.C. 20052
    (202) 676-7084

2. 1971

3. Professor Nadine Natov, Executive Secretary

5. There are 150 members, including university or research institute personnel and private scholars from twenty-two countries, studying the life and works of the Russian writer Fedor Dostoevskii; many have published articles or books on the subject.

6. The society aims to further Dostoevskii studies and to develop contacts between Dostoevskii scholars in different countries.

7. There is a North American Dostoevsky Society (NADS) in the U.S., organized in 1970 for U.S. and Canadian Dostoevskii scholars.

9. At the local level, Professor Natov, together with other Washington-area Russianists, organizes forums, meetings, and seminars on Dostoevskii. NADS holds annual meetings in December. On an international scale, the society organizes major triennial symposia in different countries; the next scheduled (fifth) symposium is to be held in 1983 in France.

10. Publications include the *Newsletter,* issued once or twice a year; the proceedings of the international symposia; and the annual *Dostoevsky Studies,* a scholarly journal that includes an extremely valuable bibliography of works on Dostoevskii.

M38 International Religious Liberty Association and North American Religious Liberty Association

1. *Department of Public Affairs and Religious Liberty*
    General Conference of Seventh-Day Adventists
    6840 Eastern Avenue, NW
    Washington, D.C. 20012
    (202) 722-6681

2.   1888

3.   B. B. Beach, Director (of the department)

4.   The Washington office has a staff of about five.

5.   At present the national group has a membership of several tens of thousands, divided into some fifty local groups.

6.   The association works with various world governments and their officials in an attempt to secure freedom of religious belief and practice for individuals and peoples. Thus, among its concerns is the question of the religious freedom of groups in the USSR.

10.   Currently the bimonthly magazine *Liberty* is published; its editor, Roland Hegstad, lives in the Washington area. A closely associated European organization (see point 11) publishes the semiannual *Conscience and Liberty*.

11.   The association is affiliated with a similar organization based in Europe: the International Association for the Defense of Religious Liberty.

M39 Jewish Community Council of Greater Washington

1.   *1522 K Street, NW, Suite 920*
     Washington, D.C. 20005
     (202) 347-4628

2.   1945

3.   Michael Berenbaum, Executive Director
     Marlene Gorin, Associate Executive Director
     Marilyn Kalusin, Assistant Director of Domestic Affairs
     Samuel H. Sislen, Director of International Affairs

5.   Membership includes 211 constituent synagogues and Jewish organizations in the greater Washington area.

6.   The Jewish Community Council of Greater Washington conducts information and advocacy programs concerning Soviet Jewry within and on behalf of the Washington Jewish community.

7.   The Soviet Jewry Committee coordinates USSR-related activities.

8.   Reference materials, including selected articles and periodicals on Soviet Jewry, are available.

9.   Meetings, briefings, and other events are scheduled on an ongoing basis. Researchers should contact the office for more information.

10.   Two council publications of interest to researchers are the topical newsletter, *Yachad/Solidarity*, and the weekly newsletter *Reports*.

M40 Joint Baltic-American Committee

1.   *P.O. Box 432*
     Rockville, Maryland 20850
     (301) 340-1954

2. 1961

3. Guners Meirovics, Chairperson

4. The staff consists of a paid public relations director and an administrative assistant.

5. The committee members are representatives of the Lithuanian American Council (entry M45), American Latvian Association in the U.S. (entry M11), and Estonian American National Council (entry M33), who in turn represent the bulk of Baltic Americans.

6. The committee concerns itself with U.S. policy toward the Baltic nationalities. It seeks congressional and public support for the Baltic American viewpoint on issues involving these peoples.

Because it represents all three nationalities, the committee is the most important organization for Baltic-area specialists to contact in this region. The member representatives can answer inquiries about local resources, activities, and organizations related to the Estonian, Latvian, and Lithuanian communities.

9. The committee holds weekly meetings.

M41 Latvian Welfare Association (Daugavas Vanagi)—Washington Chapter

1. *10309 Duvawn Place*
    Silver Spring, Maryland 20902
    (301) 649-5683

2. 1950 (national organization founded in Washington)

3. Karlis Kuzulis, Chairperson

4. Approximately ten persons serve on the executive board.

5. The chapter has about 100 members; more than 3,000 persons nationally and 10,000 internationally belong to Daugavas Vanagi.

6. The association is primarily a welfare organization, as its name indicates. It helps the needy, poor, and ill of Latvian descent, in this country and abroad. Daugavas Vanagi is also a cultural group, sponsoring art exhibits, lectures, and theatrical performances related to Latvian culture. Members also demonstrate their support for Latvian independence in many ways.

9. More information about the events noted in point 6 may be obtained from the association. The executive board has regularly scheduled business meetings; the chapter has annual elections for officers.

10. The international organization publishes the bimonthly *Daugavas Vanagi,* which contains news of the association, literary pieces, and reports on Latvian affairs. The local chapter's newsletter appears five to six times a year. Both are in Latvian.

11. Branches of the international association are in Canada, Europe, and Australia; the U.S. national headquarters is in Minneapolis. The local chapter is an affiliate of the American Latvian Association in the U.S. (entry M11).

M42 Latvian Women's Club in Washington, D.C.

1. *9714 Hedin Drive*
    Silver Spring, Maryland 20903
    (301) 439-8197

2. 1952 Washington

3. Anna Udris, President

4. Eight to twelve people serve on the club's executive board.

5. About fifty-five members belong to the organization.

6. The Latvian Women's Club is an educational, charitable, and social group. It sponsors lectures, slide talks, art exhibits, and shows of ceramics and national costumes—all activities designed to preserve and promote Latvian culture in the U.S. Latvian is spoken at most of the meetings.

8. The club has no library or formal research facilities, although individual members may have valuable archival materials in their possession.

9. Information about the club's calendar of activities may be obtained from the president.

11. The Latvian Women's Club is an affiliate of the General Federation of Women's Clubs in Washington. In addition, it associates closely with other Latvian groups in the area.

M43 Legion of Estonian Liberation, Inc.—Washington Branch

1. *117 Julian Court*
    Greenbelt, Maryland 20770
    (301) 474-7786

2. 1953 nationally, somewhat later locally

3. Lieutenant Colonel Juri Raus, Local Commander
    Colonel Ylo Anson, National Commander

5. Local membership numbers about fifteen to twenty individuals; nationwide membership is between 700 and 800. There are fourteen regional chapters.

6. The legion, composed of Estonian veterans, is a political and social organization. Its most important work centers on educating the U.S. Congress and public about Estonian culture and about the Soviet occupation of Estonia. Members also gather available information and records of Estonian military participation in World Wars I and II or other engagements as well as information relating to Soviet intelligence penetration into the U.S. Estonian community. (Records are kept in the Estonian Archive in Lakewood, New Jersey.)

9. On occasion the association sponsors lectures.

10. Most members subscribe to the West German monthly newspaper *Voitleja* (The fighter), although it is not published by the legion. The organization has also published

Estonian War of Independence: 1918–20; scholars should contact Mr. Raus for information about the volume.

11. The legion cooperates closely with the Estonian American National Council (entry M33).

M44 Lithuanian American Community (LAC) of the United States, Inc.— Greater Washington Chapter

1. *7210 Abbington Drive*
    Oxon Hill, Maryland 20705
    (301) 839-3376

2. About 1960 locally; 1951 nationally, with headquarters in Philadelphia

3. Ms. Virginia Gureckas, President (elected annually or biannually)

4. The Washington chapter has a small executive board.

5. Approximately 200 adults are active members in the D.C. area; nationwide membership is about 25,000.

6. LAC is primarily a cultural and educational organization. Its purpose is to organize and unite persons of Lithuanian descent in the U.S., support the U.S. Constitution, perpetuate Lithuanian customs in this country, help Lithuanians outside the U.S., and offer moral support for the Lithuanian homeland and for those who seek its independence. In the U.S. the LAC works with other social and political institutions or associations to disseminate information about Lithuania and Lithuanians and promote, develop, and represent Lithuanian culture in American activities.

9. The local chapter holds an annual election meeting; the LAC national executive committee meets three times a year.

10. The Lithuanian World Community, Inc., of which the LAC is an affiliate, publishes in Lithuanian the monthly *Pasaulio Lietuvis* (The world Lithuanian) at its headquarters in Chicago.

11. As noted above, the Washington chapter is an affiliate of the national association (with headquarters in Philadelphia) and of the Lithuanian World Community, Inc., in Chicago.

M45 Lithuanian American Council, Inc.—Washington Representative

1. *14 High Street*
    Frostburg, Maryland 21532
    (301) 689-1725 (evenings)
    (301) 689-3115 (days)

2. About 1945 nationally

3. Dr. John Genys, Washington Representative
    Dr. Casimir Sidlauskas, National President

5. The national council is a federation of some twenty Lithuanian organizations.

6.   The council's objective is to use all legal means to restore independence to Lithuania. It is frequently consulted by the State Department and other U.S. Government agencies on matters relating to Lithuania.

9.   Council meetings are held annually and a Lithuanian Congress quadrennially.

10.   The national office regularly issues brief news releases concerning Lithuania. These releases, which appear every week or two, provide information to about twenty Lithuanian-language newspapers in the U.S.

11.   Dr. Genys is the council representative to the Joint Baltic-American Committee (entry M40). A list of member organizations may be obtained by contacting the National Council at 2606 West Sixty-third Street, Chicago, Illinois 60629 (312/778-6900).

M46   Namysto (The Necklace) Singing Ensemble

1.   *1003 La Grande Road*
     Silver Spring, Maryland 20903
     (301) 434-6075

2.   1971

3.   Peter Krul, Musical Director

5.   The group has six female vocalists and three instrumentalists (bass guitar, lead guitar, and electric organ).

6.   The ensemble performs five to six concerts a year in the Washington, D.C., area and other major cities, including New York. Namysto sings mostly festive, modern Ukrainian songs.

8.   Peter Krul has a collection of musical arrangements, about twenty books, and thirty to forty records of Ukrainian songs and music.

10.   The group has recorded two albums on Namysto's own label; they are available at the address given above. In the future Mr. Krul hopes to publish some of the songs and music he has arranged.

M47   National Academy of Sciences (NAS)

1.   *2101 Constitution Avenue, NW*
     Washington, D.C. 20418
     (202) 334-2000

2.   1863

3.   Frank Press, President

4.   NAS has a staff of approximately 1,200.

5.   Membership totals more than 1,300.

6.   A private and nonprofit organization, NAS promotes science and its use for human benefit. The academy is supported by government and private funds and the voluntary services of U.S. scientists.

The major thrust of the academy's work is to report to and advise the government, without fee and when requested, on matters relating to science and technology. It also administers grants and fellowships to individual private scholars.

7.   The principal operating agency of the academy is the National Research Council (NRC). An organizational directory is available from the Office of Information. Following is a brief description of the units with a special interest in international work:

Within the Office of International Affairs is the Section on USSR and Eastern Europe that conducts exchange programs with the academies of sciences of the USSR, Bulgaria, Czechoslovakia, the German Democratic Republic, Hungary, Poland, Romania and Yugoslavia. Its activities are overseen by the Advisory Committee on USSR and Eastern Europe. Staff director of the Advisory Committee is Lawrence C. Mitchell (202/334-2644). The section maintains a collection of unpublished reports of U.S. scientists about their exchange visits in the USSR and Eastern Europe. These reports are available to researchers; permission must be obtained from the authors to quote or cite the reports publicly.

The Fellowship Office of the Office of Scientific and Engineering Personnel (202/ 334-2861) administers several NSF fellowship grant programs. Perhaps more importantly, it issues a valuable and informative booklet entitled *A Selected List of Major Fellowship Opportunities and Aids to Advanced Education.* The most recent issue is dated spring 1979. Copies are available without charge.

The commission's Associateship Office (202/334-2760), which offers laboratory positions for U.S. citizens, is only a minor resource for Russianists.

9.   Scholars should contact the individual bodies of interest to inquire about meetings and access to them.

10.   Every study project set up to advise the government issues a formal report which is publicly available.

11.   The National Academy of Engineering and the Institute of Medicine were organized under the NAS charter in 1964 and 1970, respectively.

M48 National Captive Nations Action Committee

1.   *1330 Massachusetts Avenue, NW*
Washington, D.C. 20036
(202) 393-1923

2.   1959

3.   Lev E. Dobriansky, Chairperson

5.   Members include leaders in government, churches, the academic world, labor, and business and civic, women's fraternal, and other groups.

6.   The committee conducts research and disseminates information about the "captive nations" of the USSR and Eastern Europe and coordinates the activities of many state and local groups. It distributes books about the captive nations and sponsors the annual National Captive Nations Week (third week in July). The committee also presents the Freedom Foundation Washington Award.

8.   The organization houses its archives and library in the Syracuse (N.Y.) University library and the Hoover Institution, Stanford University, Palo Alto, California.

9.   The committee cosponsors various symposia and seminars devoted to Soviet-related matters. Information concerning these activities may be obtained from the address given in point 1.

10.   Congressional publications, such as the hearings of appropriate committees, carry statements of committee members and other relevant information. The association also sponsors monographs published by university and commercial presses.

11.   The committee cooperates with a large number of ethnic groups in the U.S., including the American Latvian Association (entry M11) and Ukrainian Congress Committee of America (entry M64).

M49   National Conference on Soviet Jewry

1.   *2027 Massachusetts Avenue, NW*
     Washington, D.C. 20036
     (202) 265-8114

2.   1973 locally; 1971 nationally (Member organizations were cooperating in the early 1960s.)

3.   David A. Harris, Director, Washington Office

4.   The Washington Office has a staff of three.

5.   There are thirty-nine nationwide members of the conference.

6.   The National Conference on Soviet Jewry works to make known to the government and the public the situation of Soviet Jews. In addition, the association tries to assist those Jews who want to emigrate from the USSR. The Washington Office in particular serves as a liaison with the government; it maintains files with information on U.S. legislation about emigration and immigration. Many case histories of individual Soviet Jews are also kept here.

9.   Each spring the conference holds a leadership assembly in Washington, with discussions and other activities of potential interest to scholars. Sessions are open to the public; a registration fee is charged.

10.   New York headquarters publishes a weekly *Press Service* with information on specific cases and trends plus news of conference activities. Send subscriptions for the bulletin to the New York Office. The conference issues a number of pamphlets and a bibliography on the subject of Soviet Jewry; researchers can obtain a list of available materials from the Washington Office.

11.   The national conference is an umbrella organization for its constituent groups and has no other affiliates.

M50   National Education Association (NEA)

1.   *1201 Sixteenth Street, NW*
     Washington, D.C. 20036
     (202) 833-4000

2.   1857

3.   Terry Herndon, Executive Secretary

4.   Administrative and support staff totals 600.

5.   Active membership of NEA comprises more than 1.7 million teachers throughout the country.

6–7.   The association has an Office of International Relations and Peace Programs (202/822-7488). This division has an informal exchange program with the Soviet Teachers' Union. Members of NEA staff visit the USSR and members of the Soviet teachers union come to this country. Visits have been irregular and have involved small groups only.

11.   NEA has an affiliate in each state of the U.S.

M51 National Geographic Society

1.   *Seventeenth and M streets, NW*
      Washington, D.C. 20036
      (202) 857-7000

2.   1888

3.   Gilbert M. Grovsvenor, President

4.   The Washington Office has a staff of nearly 2,000.

5.   A total of 10.7 million persons belong to the society.

6.   The society sponsors expeditions and research in geography, natural history, archaeology, astronomy, ethnology, and oceanography. It sends writers and photographers to all parts of the world and disseminates the information gathered in magazines, maps, books, monographs, lectures, filmstrips, and media services. It gives awards for outstanding achievement in or service to geography.
      In Explorers Hall at the society's headquarters, visitors may view displays and weekly movies on a variety of subjects. There is no admission charge.

7.   The still-photo collections of the society are, unfortunately, closed to outsiders. They represent a tremendous research resource for Russianists. It is a great loss to researchers that some accommodation cannot be worked out by the society to permit them—without making inordinate demands on the time, facilities, and staff of the National Geographic—to examine the thousands upon thousands of items in these collections. See entry E7 in the Map Collections section for more information.

8.   The society library is described in entry A46.

9.   Weekly travelog lectures, held from October to March with brief intermissions, are open to members only. For information and a schedule call (202) 857-7700.

10.   The society publishes the famous monthly *National Geographic* and the monthly *National Geographic World*. Among dozens of other National Geographic publications are nature, history, and science books; an atlas of the world; "books for young explorers"; twelve-inch and sixteen-inch physical globes; and a mural map of the world. Special interest and general reference maps include one entitled "Peoples of the Soviet Union" (1976) and, on the back, the Soviet Union (1976). A publication order list is available without charge.

M52 National Slavic Honor Society (Dobro Slovo)—Washington-Area Chapters

1. At least four universities in the Washington area have chapters of this society: Georgetown (entry J6), George Washington (entry J5), Howard (entry J9), and Maryland (entry J10). Contact the Russian or Slavic languages and literatures departments at each school to contact the individual chapters.

2. 1961 nationally; local chapters originated soon thereafter.

5. Nationwide membership includes universities with an interest in Slavic studies.

6. Dobro Slovo is an honorary recognition society for those involved in Slavic studies. Undergraduates, graduate students, and faculty members participate. The American Association of Teachers of Slavic and East European Languages (AATSEEL) originally started the society as a means of encouraging Slavic studies and stimulating teacher-student contacts.

   The activities of different local chapters vary widely. Among the types of activities sponsored by the chapters are lectures or talks by distinguished speakers in the Russian/Soviet field, films, concerts, literary evenings, and social events.

9. Information about all meetings and other scheduled events of individual local chapters may be obtained from the groups themselves.

   The annual convention of Dobro Slovo is held in December in conjunction with the AATSEEL meeting.

11. The National Slavic Honor Society is an affiliate of the AATSEEL.

M53 National Strategy Information Center (NSIC), Inc.—Washington Office

1. *1730 Rhode Island Avenue, NW, Suite 601*
   Washington, D.C. 20036
   (202) 296-6404

2. 1962

3. Frank R. Barnett, President

4. Washington operations are run by a small staff headed by Dr. Roy Godson, director. The New York Office has a full-time staff of about ten. In addition, some 200 scholars assist NSIC as part-time lecturers, tutors, and speakers. They also write monographs for the center's publication series.

6. A nonpartisan, tax-exempt organization, NSIC conducts educational programs in national and international security affairs and national defense. Advocating no political causes, with officers and directors drawn from various political persuasions, NSIC seeks to bring civilian and military people together in a cooperative effort to educate the public. A major concern is the Soviet military and strategic program. NSIC works with colleges, universities, and high schools and business, professional, and labor groups in the U.S. and abroad.

9. Most of the center's programs, including seminars, conferences, and talks, are designed for and open to members of the organizations and institutions sponsoring

the events. Registration fees are charged by the sponsoring bodies. For information about the NSIC schedule of events, contact the office at the address above.

10. NSIC publishes two important series: Agenda Papers and Strategy Papers. Agenda papers are about thirty pages long geared to stimulate discussion of urgent U.S. domestic and foreign policy problems. Strategy Papers are monographs on the same subjects. Recent titles of interest include: *Conventional War and Escalation: The Soviet View*, by Joe Douglass and Amoretta Hoeber. Strategy Paper No. 37 (1981); *Soviet Perceptions of Military Power: The Interaction of Theory and Practice*, by John Dziak. Strategy Paper No. 36 (1981); *How Little Is Enough: SALT and Security in the Long Run*, by Francis Hoeber. Strategy Paper No. 35 (1981); *NATO, Turkey and the Southern Flank: A Mideastern Perspective*, by Ihsian Gurkan. Agenda Paper No. 11 (1980).

Center associates also speak on local radio and television programs about defense and security issues.

11. Cooperative programs with a number of institutions have been developed by NSIC over the years. These include sponsoring workshops and publishing the scholarship of a joint effort with the National Security Education Program of New York University; organizing academic programs for the armed services; providing services for the American Bar Association's Standing Committee on Law and National Security (entry M3); cosponsoring leadership conferences with the Advanced International Studies Institute (entry H1); and, with Georgetown University, helping train young American labor leaders in matters of foreign and defense policy.

M54 Organization for the Defense of Four Freedoms for Ukraine (ODFFU)—Washington Branch (No. 17)

1. *414 Deerfield Avenue*
   Silver Spring, Maryland 20910
   (301) 588-7165

2. 1964 locally; 1947 nationally, in New York

3. Mykola Kormeluk, Branch President
   H. Bilinsky, chief national official (editor)

4. The branch has a staff of five.

5. Local membership totals thirty-five.

6. The stated aims of ODFFU are to work for the establishment of an independent, integrated Ukrainian state; defend for this state the four freedoms of the Atlantic Charter (freedom of speech, of conscience, from fear, and from want); inform Americans about the Ukraine and ODFFU's work; organize material and moral support for the efforts noted here; fight communism and imperialism and those opposed to a Ukrainian state based on the Atlantic Charter's freedoms; and cooperate with other organizations having similar aims.

9. The national organization holds a convention every three years; the local branch has annual meetings.

10. *Visnyk* (The herald) is a monthly publication of ODFFU (New York).

11. Branch No. 17 cooperates with the Ukrainian Congress Committee of America (entry M64).

M55 Overseas Writers

1. *National Press Building, Room 1029*
   Fourteenth and F streets, NW
   Washington, D.C. 20045
   (202) 737-2934

2. 1921

3. John Maclean, President (1982-83)

5. The association has about 200–250 members in the area.

6. Overseas Writers is an organization of American and foreign media correspondents who have worked abroad. Soviet-area specialists will be interested in those members who have served as correspondents in Moscow. The association should be able to put researchers in touch with such members who are currently in the Washington area. Many members, of course, spend a great deal of time covering the Soviet Union from the U.S. The association should also be able to put researchers in touch with these writers.

11. Although not affiliated in the strict sense, there is some overlap of membership and interest between this organization and the Department of State Correspondents Association, composed of media representatives who cover the State Department.

M56 Plast, Inc.—Branch 26 (Washington)

1. *900 La Grande Road*
   Silver Spring, Maryland 20903
   (301) 445-1456

2. 1955 locally; 1949 nationally; 1911 in the Ukraine

3. Orest Hawryluk, Branch 26 President

4. Twelve persons serve on the executive board of the Washington Branch 26.

5. There are some 250 Plast members in the Washington-area, ninety younger than eighteen years of age; and approximately 3,600 nationwide.

6. Plast is a Ukrainian youth organization for both boys and girls, similar to the scouting movement. Plast members go hiking and camping and learn to become U.S. citizens. The Ukrainian cultural heritage also is a part of the education that these young people receive.

7. Plast has four age divisions: six to eleven years; twelve to eighteen years; eighteen to twenty years; and over twenty-one years.

9. The two younger age groups meet for weekly activities; the older divisions get together irregularly.

10. The world council publishes three monthly magazines for participants in the movement; all are in the Ukrainian language: *Hotuys,* for those six to eleven; *Yunak,* for twelve to eighteen year-olds; and *Plastovy schlyakh,* for those over eighteen. Additionally, *Vohon' orlinoyi radi* and *V dorohu z yunatstvom* are published for counselors.

11.   Parents and friends of Plast members can join Plastpryat, an auxiliary local group of about sixty members. National headquarters of Plast is in New York. Each national council, in turn, belongs to a world council for the entire movement.

M57 Providence Association of Ukrainian Catholics in America, Inc.— Washington Branch

1.   *c/o Ukrainian Catholic National Shrine of the Holy Family*
     4250 Harewood Road, NE
     Washington, D.C. 20017
     (202) 526-3737

2.   1956 locally; 1912 nationally

3.   Maria Slota, Secretary

4.   An executive board of four manages the branch.

5.   About 125 families belong to the organization in the Washington area and some 19,000 individuals nationally.

6.   The main aims of the association are to support Catholic activities, promote Ukrainian cultural events, and provide its members with life insurance.

9.   The association sponsors a few concerts and lectures each year and holds occasional ad hoc meetings.

10.   The national organization, based in Philadelphia, publishes *America* five times per week. Four issues are in Ukrainian and one issue is in English. The association also publishes books and almanacs irregularly.

11.   The association is an affiliate of the Ukrainian Congress Committee of America (entry M64).

M58 Russian Children Welfare Society Abroad—Washington Branch

1.   *5437 Thirty-third Street, NW*
     Washington, D.C. 20015
     (202) 244-4728

2.   About 1956 locally; about 1923 nationally

3.   Selene Obolensky, President
     Sergei Martinoff, Vice President/Secretary

4.   There are three officers.

5.   Thirty-five members belong to the local branch.

6.   The society is a nonprofit charity organization that helps needy Russian children living outside the Soviet Union. Its fundraising activities include sponsoring a charity ball and a raffle each year. Currently it supports several children, mostly in Europe.

M59 Saint George Pathfinders of America (SGPA)—National Headquarters and National Capital Area Chapter (NCAC)

1. *742 Azalea Drive*
   Rockville, Maryland 20850
   (301) 340-7806

2. 1965 locally; 1949 nationally

3. Michael A. Daniels, National President/Chapter Director

4. Headquarters has a staff of five; nine members serve on the chapter staff.

5. Approximately fifty young people belong to the local group (excluding staff); nationally there are about 600 members.

6. Modeled on the scouting movement, the Pathfinders apply scouting principles to an ethnic-religious group. Members explore Russian culture, history, and religion while participating in a scouting program of hiking, camping, and so on. Most activities are carried on in the Russian language.

7. The four divisions of the chapter are organized according to age and sex groups that correspond to the Boy, Girl, and Cub Scouts and the Brownies.

8. The chapter has a very small library of about 100 books. These books, in both Russian and English, are for and about youth.

9. The Pathfinders have biweekly troop meetings and scheduled, although irregular, outings and camping trips. Staff meetings are held about once a month. Regional leadership conferences take place about three times a year, and every few years several chapters get together for a camporee.

10. The national organization publishes the quarterly newsletter *The Scout* and the monthly *Bulletin* for the leaders.

11. The Saint George Pathfinders currently has nine chapters nationwide. The local group coordinates its efforts closely with the Church of Saint John the Baptist in Washington (entry P6).

M60 School of Ukrainian Studies of Greater Washington

1. *925 Schindler Drive*
   Silver Spring, Maryland 20903
   (202) 593-8132 (evenings)
   (202) 287-6295 (days)

2. 1963

3. Bohdan Yasinsky, Director

4. The school employs seventeen teachers and two student-teachers.

5. Between 120 and 130 students, grades kindergarten to eleventh, attend the school.

6. The Maryland Board of Education recognizes and has accredited this Ukrainian-language school. Subjects taught include Ukrainian culture, history, and language. School is in session 4½ hours every Saturday, September through June.

8. A small library of about 350 books in Ukrainian is located at the school and is open during class time. The holdings include four children's periodicals.

9. Regular events at the school range from the monthly PTA meetings to frequent speaking engagements for outside experts to educational field trips once or twice a year. On occasion the children present plays and concerts, which are open to the public.

10. The school's annual report of four to five pages is available from the director.

11. The educational councils of the Ukrainian Congress Committee of America (entry M64) and World Congress of Free Ukrainians affiliate with this institution.

M61 Shevchenko Scientific Society—Washington Study Center

1. *1108 Dunoon Road*
   Silver Spring, Maryland 20903
   (301) 434-5097

2. About 1958 locally; 1873 in the Ukraine

3. Dr. George Starosolsky, Head, Washington Study Center

4. Four members serve on the voluntary executive board.

5. The fifteen area members come from the government, professional, academic, and religious communities.

6. The Shevchenko Society, named after the great Ukrainian poet and artist, promotes the study of Ukrainian culture, history, and science. It sponsors lectures on many different subjects by members and nonmembers. The organization helps publish scholarly monographs. In addition, the society holds a few commemorative gatherings during the year.

9. The lectures mentioned above take place once or twice a year at the society's ad hoc meetings.

10. The central organization, located in New York, issues the irregular *Zapysky* (Proceedings of the society). Currently the association focuses on support of monographs, as stated in point 6.

M62 Ukrainian Academy of Arts and Sciences in the United States, Inc.— Washington Branch

1. *7601 Wildwood Drive*
   Takoma Park, Maryland 20912
   (301) 439-7484

2. 1956 locally

3. Petro Odarchenko, President, Washington Branch

5. At present the local branch of the academy has twelve members.

6. The Ukrainian Academy is a learned society, devoted to scholarly research and the advancement of knowledge in all spheres but particularly those of Ukrainian history, culture, literature, and architecture.

9. During the past twenty-five years, the local branch has held several scientific meetings and conferences. About 160 papers on the above and other topics were read by members at these conferences.

10. The members of the branch have published articles and contributions in both English and Ukrainian in the following scientific and literary publications: *Almanac Slovo* (New York and Toronto); *Annals of the Ukrainian Academy of Arts and Sciences in the U.S.*; *Memoirs of the Shevchenko Scientific Society* (Munich, New York, Paris); *Novi Dni*; *Slavic Review*; *Suchasnist*; *Symbolae in Honorem Georgii Y. Shevelov* (Munich); *Ukrainian Encyclopaedia* (Paris and Toronto). The New York headquarters also published *Symposium of Science*, to which local members contributed.

M63 Ukrainian Association of the Washington Metropolitan Area

1. *P.O. Box 713*
   Washington, D.C. 20044

2. Formed 1951, incorporated 1955

3. Walter O. Demchuk, President (703/987-8798)

4. About ten members serve as the executive board.

5. There are some 150 dues-paying members.

6. This group organizes and coordinates cultural, charitable, scientific, and literary activities for the Ukrainian community in the Washington-area. It sponsors several lectures a year and a New Year's Ball in mid-January. The association also supports a local accredited Ukrainian school (entry M60) and a number of charities.

7. There is a women's auxiliary, which has, among other things, published an English-language booklet entitled *Ukraine*.

9. The executive board meets monthly, and the membership convenes annually for elections.

10. The Ukrainian Association publishes a bilingual monthly bulletin from September through June, which includes announcements of community events and articles.

M64 Ukrainian Congress Committee of America—Washington Branch

1. *810 Eighteenth Street, NW, Suite 501*
   Washington, D.C. 20006
   (202) 638-0988 (Ukrainian National Information Service)

2. 1964 locally; 1940 nationally

3. Katherine Chumachenko, Director, Information Service
   Lev E. Dobriansky, National President
   Theodore Caryk, Local President

4. A small, volunteer executive board runs the local branch.

5. The branch has some 130 dues-paying individual members, and six dues-paying organizations belong. Nationwide, approximately fifty to seventy thousand individuals and fifty-five organizations are members.

6. The committee coordinates the politically oriented affairs of its member organizations. It also promotes Ukrainian culture and history by sponsoring literary and "academic" evenings and occasional concerts. Much of the latter activity is centered around Ukrainian holidays in January and March. In 1977 the Washington branch opened the Ukrainian Information Service, which works primarily on public relations, often at the government level. This service is a valuable source of general information about the Ukrainian community in the Washington area.

7. The Information Service maintains committees for cultural affairs, contacts with other ethnic groups, and other matters.

9. The local board meets monthly; the branch meets yearly for elections; and the national organization meets every four years.

10. National headquarters in New York publishes in English the *Ukrainian Quarterly*. Ukrainian-language news notices appear monthly in *Svoboda* (New York) and *Amerika* (Philadelphia).

11. The six local affiliates are the Organization for the Defense of Four Freedoms for Ukraine (entry M54), Plast (entry M56), Providence Association of Ukrainian Catholics (entry M57), Ukrainian National Aid Association (entry M68), Ukrainian National Association (entry M69), and the Ukrainian National Women's League of America (entry M70).

M65 Ukrainian Engineers' Society of America—Washington Branch

1. *5304 Wakefield Road*
    Washington, D.C. 20016
    (202) 656-4359

2. About 1961 locally; about 1951 nationally

3. Dr. Basil Nakonechny, Chairperson

4. Four officers serve the society.

5. Some twenty-five individuals with engineering or scientific degrees belong to the society.

6. This professional society seeks to promote members' skills and interests as well as provide social contacts.

10. The national organization publishes the semiannual *Ukrainian Engineering News*, printed partly in Ukrainian and partly in English.

11. The society is closely tied with the Ukrainian Technical Society in Canada, which helps publish *Ukrainian Engineering News*.

M66 Ukrainian Fraternal Association—Branch 284 (Washington)

1. *11 Apple Grove Road*
Silver Spring, Maryland 20904
(301) 593-5105

2. 1955 locally; 1910 nationally

3. Dmytro Korbutiak, Secretary

4. The branch's executive board numbers four.

5. The Washington group has 130 members. Some 300 lodges nationwide have more than 22,000 members.

6. Founded in Pennsylvania among Ukrainian miners, the association today is a national fraternal insurance organization. Offering moral and monetary aid to members in case of death, illness, or other need, the group's U.S. assets total more than ten million dollars.

9. The local branch holds meetings from time to time and has social events as well.

10. Available by subscription from the national organization are the weekly *Narodna Volya* (six pages in Ukrainian, two in English) and the English-language *Forum*, a quarterly for youth. *Almanakh*, with a calendar, literary pieces, and other information, appears irregularly.

11. Affiliates include the World Congress of Free Ukrainians, American Fraternal Congress, and other organizations.

M67 Ukrainian Music Institute of America, Inc.—Washington Branch

1. *c/o Mrs. Taissa Bohdansky*
138 Eastern Parkway
Newark, New Jersey 07106

2. 1957 locally

3. Olha Sushko-Nakonechny, Branch Chairperson (and teacher)

5-6. The institute enrolls a small number of young people for music lessons (singing and piano). The children are encouraged to appreciate and understand all classical music as well as Ukrainian music. The group performs occasionally at concerts in the area.
   The national organization fosters the study and dissemination of Ukrainian music in various ways. Researchers should write to the above address for publications of Ukrainian music. That office can also provide the names of scholars and specialists in Ukrainian music in the U.S.

M68 Ukrainian National Aid Association of America—Branch 151 (Washington): Taras Shevchenko Branch

1. *5003 Laguna Road*
   College Park, Maryland 20740
   (301) 474-2897

2. 1965 locally; 1914 nationally

3. Stephen Slota, Acting President and Treasurer

4. There are two officers and two support staff members at present

5. The branch has twenty members.

6. The association is a fraternal insurance organization. National headquarters, in Chicago, awards a number of scholarships to young people of Ukrainian descent and also supports a variety of charities.

9. A convention every four years elects the national executive board.

10. The national organization issues a bilingual weekly newspaper, *Ukrainske Narodne Slovo*. In addition, it publishes one or two books a year.

11. The Aid Association is an affiliate of the Ukrainian Congress Committee of America (entry M64).

M69 Ukrainian National Association—Branch 15 (Washington)

1. *12523 Montclair Drive*
   Silver Spring, Maryland 20904
   (301) 622-0463

2. 1953 locally; 1894 nationally

3. Bohdan Yasinsky, President
   Ostap Zynjuk, Secretary

4. The branch has a small voluntary staff.

5. The local organization has 285 members.

6. The association is a fraternal and social organization. With 460 branches in the U.S. and Canada, the central body maintains a scholarship program for young people of Ukrainian descent and runs a vacation resort in the Catskill Mountains in southern New York State.

9. The branch has annual election meetings and irregular (but scheduled monthly) business meetings. The national group convenes every four years in different cities.

10. National headquarters in Jersey City, New Jersey, publishes the daily Ukrainian-language newspaper *Svoboda*; the English-language *Ukrainian Weekly*; and the monthly magazine for children *Veselka*.

11. The association is affiliated with the Ukrainian Congress Committee of America (entry M64).

M70 Ukrainian National Women's League of America, Inc.—Branch 78 (Washington)

1. *1413 South Twentieth Street*
    Arlington, Virginia 22202
    (703) 521-3048

2. 1965 locally; 1925 nationally

3. Marta Terleckyj, President

4. There is a voluntary staff of about seventeen.

5. Local membership numbers about sixty-five persons.

6. The league is a cultural and educational organization promoting Ukrainian culture and life in the U.S. It has a Saturday nursery school for three-to-five year-olds. The organization also runs a scholarship program for youths in South America. Among the charitable and philanthropic activities of the league are its efforts to help victims of war, natural disasters, and poverty. It also supports a program for elderly women in need of financial assistance.

    At its national headquarters in New York the league has established a folk art museum. The local branch, furthermore, sponsors Ukrainian art shows twice a year and participates in folk festivals held every two years by the Northern Virginia Folk Festival Association.

    The local branch also occasionally sponsors courses in traditional Ukrainian cooking and craftwork, such as *pysanki* (Easter eggs) and embroidery.

11. The group is an affiliate of the Ukrainian Congress Committee of America (entry M64), the World Federation of Ukrainian Women's Organization, and Northern Virginia Folk Festival Association.

M71 Ukrainian Philatelic and Numismatic Society—Washington Branch

1. *11017 Lombardy Road*
    Silver Spring, Maryland 20901
    (301) 593-5316

2. 1951

3. Val Zabijaka, Auctioneer (President Dr. B. M. J. Slusarczuk lives in Southfields, New York.)

5. There are some nine local members. Total membership of this international organization is approximately 300 persons, fifty percent in the U.S., forty percent in Canada, and ten percent in other countries.

6. The group's annual meeting is held in different cities each year.

8. The society's national library is in Philadelphia.

10. Three times a year the *Bulletin of the Ukrainian Philatelic and Numismatic Society* appears with its auction of stamps and bank notes. The journal *Ukrainian Philatelist*

is currently issued as an annual but should soon become semiannual. Plans are also underway for issuing a newsletter four to six times a year.

11. The American group has contacts with the Austrian, Canadian, and West German organizations.

M72 Washington Committee for Soviet Jewry

1. *8402 Freyman Drive*
   Chevy Chase, Maryland 20815
   (301) 587-4455

2. 1969

3. Joan Dodek, President

4. The executive board of eighteen is supplemented by many volunteer workers.

5. The committee has some 1,500 dues-paying members.

6. This voluntary, person-to-person organization maintains contact with Soviet Jews, sustains them, and tries to aid those who wish to emigrate. Members seek to publicize the situation of Soviet Jewry with leaflets, for example, and gain support for their work from private organizations and elected government officials. Committee activities focus as much as possible on individual cases.

7. Through the Adopt-a-Family and Right to Identity (RTI) programs, Washington Committee members send to Soviet Jews letters, packages, and cultural materials.

9. There are up to six open, public meetings each year, at which recent émigrés often speak.

10. The monthly newsletter *The Vigil* contains information about specific cases of Soviet Jews trying to emigrate and appeals for help as well as other information on the subject. The committee also publishes a large number of informational sheets and papers covering specific cases. Scholars may receive these items without charge by asking to be placed on the organization's mailing list. A list of publications is also available without charge.

11. The Washington Committee is an affiliate of the national Union of Councils for Soviet Jews, and works closely with the London 35's, Canadian 35's, Comité de Quinze (Paris), Medical Mobilization for Soviet Jewry, Student Struggle for Soviet Jewry, and the Soviet Jewry Legal Advocacy Center.

M73 Washington Estonian Society

1. *19102 Stedwick Drive*
   Gaithersburg, Maryland 20760
   (301) 869-3275

2. About 1962 (Two earlier local Estonian groups preceded this present one but have not survived.)

3. Maria Pedak-Kari, President (elected annually)

4. The society has an executive board of seven.

5. About 100–200 persons belong to and/or attend functions of the society.

6. A cultural and social organization, the Washington Estonian Society, sponsors a number of local events, such as concerts, lectures, and, usually with a Baltimore group, folk-dance demonstrations. Each February the members celebrate Estonian Independence Day with a major gathering. On occasion the society also shows motion pictures.
    A school for young children is operated by some members in private homes. Estonian language, history, and culture are the primary subjects taught.

9. The society meets once each month on a Sunday, by announcement.

11. The Washington Estonian Society is an informal affiliate of the Estonian American National Council (entry M33); some of its members belong to the National Council as well as to the Estonian World Council.
    The Reverend Mr. Troost is the pastor of Saint Mark's Lutheran Church for Estonians in the Washington area. Founded in 1949, the church rents facilities from the Cavalry Lutheran Church (9545 Georgia Avenue, Silver Spring, Maryland). Services are held every second Sunday. Many society members are also members of the congregation. The church runs confirmation classes and has, in the past, sponsored concerts and other events.

M74 Washington Institute of Foreign Affairs

1. *1775 Massachusetts Avenue, NW*
    Washington, D.C. 20036
    (301) 469-8466

2. 1961

3. Roy W. Henderson, Chairperson
    Lyman L. Lemnitzer, President

5. There are approximately 214 Washington-area resident members and another thirty-seven nonresident members. Membership is largely comprised of retired individuals from the academic, business, government, military, professional, and communities.

6. The institute's purpose is to "promote greater knowledge and understanding of international affairs and problems" among its members, other Americans, foreign officials and leaders temporarily in the U.S., and others concerned with international affairs.

9. The principal activity in this respect is the holding of regular meetings to hear prominent speakers discuss foreign affairs. The group seeks out highly qualified and experienced people to participate in these talks. The sessions are absolutely closed to nonmembers and are considered off the record. Members may not bring guests, although the speaker may.

10. The institute publishes a booklet that briefly states its purposes and activities and gives a list of members. Copies are available without charge.

M75 Washington Latvian Society

1. *2811 Crest Avenue*
   Cheverly, Maryland 20785
   (301) 772-6357

2. About 1950

3. Dr. Talivaldis Smits, Chairperson

4. The society has an executive board of six.

5. There are nearly 200 dues-paying members.

6. The Washington Latvian Society is primarily a cultural organization. It promotes and preserves Latvian customs, traditions, and ways in the U.S. The association also has a small scholarship program to aid needy youths of Latvian descent in obtaining an education. The society stands for and encourages the independence of the Latvian homeland as well.

9. Almost monthly the group sponsors lectures, literary evenings, concerts, or other cultural events. The proceedings are carried on in Latvian. Details about the calendar can be obtained from the chairperson.

11. This society is one of the many groups belonging to the American Latvian Association in the U.S., with headquarters in Rockville, Maryland (entry M11).

M76 World Federalists Association (WFA)

1. *1101 Arlington Boulevard, Suite S-119*
   Arlington, Virginia 22209
   (703) 524-2141

2. 1947

3. Norman Cousins, President

4. A staff of six works in the Washington office.

5. WFA has approximately 9,300 members.

6. A volunteer organization, WFA seeks to modify the world's present nation-state system of governments and the UN in order to establish a worldwide rule of law enforced by a new, voluntary world security system. The world authorities envisioned by the association would have limited but adequate power to handle certain global problems while safeguarding the rights of individuals.
   Among the problems studied by the World Federalists are the arms race and law of the sea.

7. WFA has a representative at the UN.

10. In 1976 the organization began publication of *World Federalist Newsletter*.

11. The national office in Washington has local affiliates throughout the U.S.

M77 World Peace through Law Center

1. *1000 Connecticut Avenue, NW, Suite 800*
    Washington, D.C. 20036
    (202) 466-5428

2. 1957 (begun as a committee of the American Bar Association)

3. Charles S. Rhyne, World President

4. A staff of twelve works in Washington. During the summer, the staff is supplemented by part-time help from law clerks.

5. Perhaps 15,000 worldwide members belong to the organization.

6. The center's primary purpose is to help strengthen the world's legal system—both its institutions, like the International Court of Justice, and its laws. It is nonpolitical and nonprofit and its participants speak as individuals rather than as representatives of a particular country or ideology. It sponsors research on a variety of topics.

7. The center comprises three associations that make up its professional membership: World Association of Judges, World Association of Lawyers, and World Association of Law Professors. For specific interests the center provides the following sections: Center Associates (nonlawyers), Criminal Law, Human Rights, Intellectual Property, Law, and Computer Technology. World Association of Lawyers has some thirty-four committees under it, each dealing with a different topic of international law or peace.

9. The center sponsors biennial world conferences, held throughout the world.

10. Publications include *World Legal Directory*; *World Law Review* (proceedings of the biennial conferences); *World Jurist*, a bimonthly newsletter; and a variety of special publications on current developments in international law.

11. The center has no affiliates except its three component associations noted in point 7.

NOTE: Human rights interest groups conduct research, seminars, meetings and other events that inevitably touch upon the USSR. In addition to the associations mentioned above, the following groups might be of interest to the scholar as they have or have had a role in advocating an international human rights policy:

American Association for the Advancement of Science (AAAS)
1776 Massachusetts Avenue, NW
Washington, D.C. 20036
(202) 467-4400

American Council for the Advancement of Human Rights
4801 Massachusetts Avenue, NW
Washington, D.C. 20016
(202) 364-8710

Coalition for a New Foreign and Military Policy
120 Maryland Avenue, NW
Washington, D.C. 20002
(202) 546-8400

Friends of *Kontinent*
c/o Yuri Olkhovsky
George Washington University
Washington, D.C. 20052

Human Rights Internet
1502 Ogden Street, NW
Washington, D.C. 20010
(202) 462-4320

International Association of Official Human Rights Agencies
706 Seventh Street, SE
Washington, D.C. 20003
(202) 547-8404

Sakharov International Committee
4201 Cathedral Avenue, NW
Washington, D.C. 20016
(202) 364-0200

United States Catholic Conference
1312 Massachusetts Avenue, NW
Washington, D.C. 20005
(202) 659-6600

Washington International Human Rights Law Group
1346 Connecticut Avenue, NW
Washington, D.C. 20036
(202) 659-5023

N Cultural-Exchange Organizations

Cultural-Exchange Organization Entry Format (N)

1. *Address; Telephone Number(s)*
2. Founding Date
3. Chief Official and Title
4. Staff
5. Program or Description
6. Budget and Its Source
7. Publications
8. Affiliated Organizations

Introductory Note

Complementing the many research centers and associations listed in other sections of this *Guide,* several organizations with cultural-exchange programs make their home in the Washington area. These organizations serve to connect diplomatic ties to actual social contact between the peoples of the United States and Soviet Union. As a result, the political relations between the two countries often affect the quantity and scope of the cultural-exchange programs. Among the programs listed in this section, some have curtailed their activities as a direct consequence of the cooling of political ties between the U.S. and USSR during 1979–81. These programs have nevertheless been included below and are discussed for their past records of exchanges and in anticipation of future activities. Other organizations, however, have been able to continue their programs, and they are considered accordingly.

N1 Academic Travel Abroad

1. *1346 Connecticut Avenue, NW, Suite 423*
   Washington, D.C. 20036
   (202) 785-3412

2. 1950

3. David T. Parry, Executive Director

4. Twenty-five full-time staff workers handle tour operations; there are also forty part-time workers, who are mostly tour directors.

5. Academic Travel Abroad organizes educational study and intellectual travel for groups only. Travel accommodations and educational programs are arranged for schools, colleges, museums, and professional organizations.

   Currently, thirty trips a year are organized to the Soviet Union and Eastern Europe.

6. Revenue comes from the various tours conducted by the association.

Agriculture Department   See entry K1

American Bar Association   See entry M3

N2   The American Council of Young Political Leaders (ACYPL)

1. *426 C Street, NE, Third Floor*
   Washington, D.C. 20002
   (202) 546-6010

2. 1966

3. Thomas R. Huston, Executive Director

4. The council has a staff of eight.

5. Before December 1979, ACYPL had an exchange program with the USSR. Every year, two delegations of young political leaders from this country went to the Soviet Union, and two Soviet delegations came to the U.S. Visitors spent from fourteen to eighteen days in the host country. Each delegation comprised about a dozen people. Scheduled activities for the exchange teams included visits with political leaders, trips to government organizations, and seminars with political figures and youth of the host country.

   Records and reports of these trips are on file at the ACYPL office and are accessible to scholars. Researchers should phone ahead to make inquiries and arrangements.

6. ACYPL is primarily funded by the U.S. Information Agency. ACYPL actively seeks the support of corporations, foundations, and other benefactors with an interest in promoting mutual understanding of political systems and institutions around the world.

8. The council is affiliated with the Atlantic Association of Young Political Leaders and the Atlantic Council of the U.S.

American Council on Education   See entry M5

N3   American Council on International Sports (ACIS)

1. *817 Twenty-third Street, NW*
    Washington, D.C. 20052
    (202) 676-7246/7247

2. 1976

3. Dr. Carl A. Troester, Director

4. The office has a small staff. Russianists may want to talk to Dr. Troester or his executive assistant, Gary Gepford. The executive board has ten members.

5. ACIS conducts a large number of programs on sports, physical education, and leisure studies. A major part of the work involves the exchange of people, information, and technical expertise. Exchange programs and contacts with Soviet sports and physical education specialists are planned for the near future. The council now has frequent contacts with the USSR, both directly and through international bodies.

    ACIS is, in addition, a referral and resource center. For example, it has developed a national and international data bank on physical education, sports, and recreational specialists.

6. The budget comes from grants from the State Department, UNESCO, OAS, IMF, and numerous other national government and private sector organizations.

7. An ACIS informational brochure is available.

8. The council cooperates with the State Department, U.S. Olympic Committee, and various international sports federations and organizations.

American Friends Service Committee   See entry M7

Commerce Department   See entry K8

Council for International Exchange of Scholars   See entry M5

Education Department   See entry K13

Environmental Protection Agency   See entry K15

N4   Experiment in International Living (EIL)—Washington Office

1. *1346 Connecticut Avenue, NW, Suite 820*
    Washington, D.C. 20036
    (202) 872-1330

2. 1932 nationally

3. Penny F. Linn, Director, Washington Office

4. This office has a small staff; at headquarters in Vermont and various regional offices the total staff numbers more than 120.

5. An independent, nonprofit, educational organization, EIL manages international home-stay exchange programs, travel abroad and to this country, and cross-cultural education programs. It operates the accredited School for International Training at its headquarters in Brattleboro, Vermont.

In the past, EIL has offered programs for students to visit the USSR; currently, however, there seems to be little Soviet-related activity. Russianists should contact the office for the latest information on this situation.

6. EIL derives its income from participants' fees, gifts, foundation and business grants, endowment revenue, and government contracts. Annual income and expenses total more than five million dollars each.

7. A number of informational brochures about summer programs and other activities are available without charge.

8. The EIL is a member of the U.S. National Commission for UNESCO, Society for International Development, American Council on Education, Association of World Colleges and Universities, Council for Advancement and Support of Education, Council on International Educational Exchange, 4-1-4 Conference, Japan Society, National Association for Foreign Student Affairs, National Council for Community Services to International Visitors, and Vermont Higher Education Council. In addition, EIL cooperates closely with the African-American Institute, AFS International Scholarships, American Friends of the Middle East, Educational Council for Foreign Medical Graduates, Girl Scouts of the U.S.A., Institute of International Education, International Christian Youth Exchange, International 4-H Youth Exchange, International Student Service, Latin-American Scholarship Program of American Universities, National Association of Teachers of Spanish and Portuguese, World University Service, Youth for Understanding, and other organizations.

Health and Human Services Department   See entry K19

Housing and Urban Development Department   See entry K20

Interior Department   See entry K21

Kennan Institute for Advanced Russian Studies   See entry H23

National Academy of Sciences   See entry M47

National Aeronautics and Space Administration   See entry K25

National Education Association   See entry M50

N5   National 4-H Council

1.   *7100 Connecticut Avenue*
Chevy Chase, Maryland 20815
(301) 656-9000

2. 1920

3. Grant A. Shrum, Executive Vice President
    Melvin J. Thompson, Coordinator, International Relations

4. The International Relations Division has three associates under its director; over-all, the Washington office has a professional staff of about forty, plus 150 secretarial and other support staff.

5. The 4-H has conducted programs of the International 4-H Youth Exchange (formerly, International Farm Youth Exchange) since 1948. Annually, approximately 1,500 4-H members and other youths in similar programs participate in exchange and training programs in more than thirty-five countries.
    From 1975 through 1979, 4-H conducted an exchange with the Soviet Union. In six-month programs, American youths studied Soviet farming while living and working on collective and state farms in the USSR. Simultaneously, Soviet counterparts came to the United States and participated in programs on American agriculture.

6. Sources of support for the international programs include business, industry, and foundation grants and participant fees.

7. Publications of potential interest to Russianists concerned with these youth exchanges are: *World Atlas of 4-H and Similar Youth Educational Programs,* 4th ed. (1983) and *International Intrigue,* program guides for people involved in these international activities.

8. The 4-H program is the youth branch of the Cooperative Extension Service of the Agriculture Department and the State Land-Grant Universities.
    The National 4-H Council is a nonprofit, educational organization in support of the 4-H program.

National Research Council   See entry M47

National Science Foundation   See entry K27

N6   Sister Cities International (SCI) (Town Affiliation Association [TAA] of the U.S., Inc.)

1. *1625 Eye Street, NW, Suite 424-26*
    Washington, D.C. 20006
    (202) 293-5504

2. 1956 organized as an arm of the National League of Cities; 1967 TAA incorporated with SCI as its principal program

3. Thomas W. Gittins, Executive Vice President, Washington, D.C., National Office

4. SCI Washington has a staff of nine, including directors of Member Services Youth Leadership Training Technical Assistance Programs.

5. The Sister City Program promotes international understanding and peace on a continuing long-term basis through affiliations between U.S. communities and cities

in other countries. Presently, some 720 U.S. cities have links with approximately 1,000 cities in seventy-eight other nations. Participating cities and their citizens exchange information, ideas, people, and things in the broad fields of education, government, culture, and economic and social relations.

Currently, five cities in the USSR have U.S. sister cities, one not far from Washington: Baku with Houston, Murmansk with Jacksonville, Nakhodka with Oakland, Odessa with Baltimore, and Tashkent with Seattle. Most of these affiliations began in 1975.

6. The organization receives annual dues from its member cities (according to a sliding scale based on population) and additional support from the U.S. Information Agency, U.S. Agency for International Development, and several private foundations.

7. SCI publishes an annual *Sister Cities by State and Country*; *Case Study Digest,* a quarterly with detailed reports on experiences of participating cities; the bimonthly *Sister Cities News* and *Washington Report,* each with news and advice on practical matters involved in the program; *Sister City Handbook,* an aid to establishing participation; *Youth and Education Program Kit; Research Reports*; and other brief pieces related to program implementation.

8. SCI maintains close relationships with the U.S. Information Agency, U.S Agency for International Development, National League of Cities, and International Union of Local Authorities in the Hague, Netherlands.

State Department   See entry K32

Transportation Department   See entry K33

U.S. Information Agency   See entry K35

Woodrow Wilson International Center for Scholars   See entry H31

P Religious Organizations

Religious Organization Entry Format (P)

1. *Address; Telephone Number(s)*
2. Chief Official and Title
3. Programs or Activities
4. Publications

Introductory Note

Several religious organizations with ties to the Soviet Union and/or its nationality components are represented in the Washington metropolitan area. Although many of the places of worship listed in this section are becoming increasingly "American" in flavor, they often serve as cultural centers for local religious/ethnic communities. The organizations typically provide for their parishoners a means to retain religious and ethnic heritages through parochial education and functions conducted in their respective native languages. They also extend to the Washington community a variety of interesting and culturally oriented events, such as bazaars, lectures, and concerts. Thus, the religious bodies are an important linguistic and cultural resource for the Russianist.

The researcher should also be aware that many of the academic, fraternal, and professional associations described in section M of this *Guide* have close ties with some of the religious organizations listed here.

P1   Armenian Apostolic Church of Saint Mary's

1. *4125 Fessenden Street, NW*
   Washington, D.C. 20015
   (202) 363-1923

2. Father Vertanes Kalayjian, Pastor

3.   The Holy See of the Armenian Church, the center of the Catholicos Patriarch of All Armenians, is located in Etchmiadzin, Soviet Armenia. Through the Diocesan Archbishop, headquartered in New York (630 Second Avenue, New York, New York 10016), Saint Mary's maintains a spiritual and moral allegience to the Holy See.

The church also serves as a cultural and community center for Armenians in the Washington metropolitan area.

P2   Armenian Church Legate

1.   *2801 Park Center Drive*
Alexandria, Virginia 22302
(703) 671-6196

2.   The Right Reverend Papken Varjabedian, Bishop. Bishop Varjabedian, former pastor of Saint Mary's, is the representative of the archbishop in the Washington area. He is spiritually under the church head in Soviet Armenia.

P3   Armenian Soorp Khatch (Holy Cross) Apostolic Church

1.   *4906 Flint Drive*
Chevy Chase, Maryland 20016
(301) 229-8742

2.   Father Sahog Vertanesian, Pastor

3.   In matters of faith there is no difference between the Soorp Khath and Saint Mary's churches, but the head of the Holy Cross Church is in Lebanon and has its own archbishop in New York. The Soorp Khatch Church is a community center for the local Armenian population.

Estonian Lutheran Church   See entry M73

P4   Holy Trinity Particular Ukrainian Catholic Church

1.   *Mail:*
P.O. Box 4214
Colesville Branch
Silver Spring, Maryland 20904

Services conducted at:
Ukrainian Catholic University
Washington Branch
2615 Thirtieth Street, NW
Washington, D.C. 20008

Future site of the new church:
16631 New Hampshire Avenue
Silver Spring, Maryland 20904

2.   Reverend Taras Lonchyna, Priest-administrator (301/681-9108)
Mykola Stawnychy, Chairperson (301/439-7319)

3.   Established in 1980, the church has three parish organizations: Sisterhood of the Pochaiv Theotokos, Saints Cyril and Methodius Brotherhood, and Saint Nicholas Youth Brotherhood.
The church grew out of the Holy Trinity Particular Ukrainian Catholic Church, Inc., a nonprofit Maryland religious corporation established in the 1970s to conduct the parish's financial matters.

P5   Latvian Evangelical Lutheran Church

1.   *400 Hurley Avenue (P.O. Box 18)*
Rockville, Maryland 20850

2.   Reverend Alexander Veinbergs, Pastor (301/966-9216)
Voldemars Sprogeris, President, Church Council (301/422-2461)

3.   Church activities include conducting school courses in religion and in Latvian culture (culture, geography, history) and sponsoring occasional talks relating to Latvia. Folk dancing and singing, concerts, arts and crafts shows, and other events are all a part of the community's life. These gatherings and the school classes are conducted in Latvian. The congregation numbers some 400 members.
A library of about 500 books is located in the church. Many volumes are on historical and religious subjects and are written in Latvian.

4.   *Baznicas Zinas* (Church news), a news bulletin, appears bimonthly.

League of Ukrainian Catholic Youth   See entry P11

Mariyska Druzyna   See entry P11

Providence Association of Ukrainian Catholics in America—Washington Branch   See entry M57

P6   Russian Orthodox Church of Saint John the Baptist

1.   *4001 Seventeenth Street, NW*
Washington, D.C. 20011
(202) 726-3000
(202) 726-4742 (parish hall)

2.   Father Victor S. Potapov, Pastor (301/589-6163)
Father Vladimir Danylevich, Assistant Pastor (301/589-8935)

3.   The Church of Saint John the Baptist is part of the Russian Orthodox Church abroad (i.e. outside the Soviet Union).
The parish, founded in 1949, is an active one, with at least 240 members. It sponsors a parish school that offers instruction in the Russian language, culture, religion, and

history. It also supports a scout troop (see the Saint George Pathfinders, entry M59). The sisterhood is in charge of a number of church functions, including the famous holiday bazaar featuring delicious food.

The parish library recently acquired a unique collection of early émigré books and other publications on Russian history, literature, theology, and culture.

Of particular interest will be the cultural and religious activities of the congregation. For example, the church holds meetings during which are held either general discussions or talks given by specialists on such subjects as Russian art, history, literature, and religion. More information about these meetings, which are always entirely in Russian and open to the public, may be obtained from the editor of the quarterly parish magazine, Professor Michael Zarechnak (202/829-7628).

4. The parish magazine *Prikhodskoi Listok* appears quarterly. *Prikhodskaya Zhizn'*, another parish publication, appears monthly and lists a schedule of services and church-related activities.

P7   Russian Orthodox Church of Saint Nicholas of the Orthodox Church in America (Saint Nicholas Cathedral, Russian War Memorial Shrine)

1. *3500 Massachusetts Avenue, NW*
   Washington, D.C. 20007
   (202) 333-5060

2. Reverend Arkady Moiseyev, Pastor (202/333-6491)
   Reverend Dmitry Grigorieff, Provost (301/320-4088)

3. The Orthodox Church in America (OCA), established in the second half of the eighteenth century, was under the Holy Synod until 1917. After the Bolshevik revolution, the church was, for practical purposes, self-governed. This situation was formally recognized by the Moscow patriarch in 1970. The Orthodox Church in America is thus autocephalous (self-governing) with Saint Nicholas as the primate's cathedral and with the chancery located in Syosset, Long Island.

For more information about parish activities, contact Father Moiseyev or Father Grigorieff, a professor in Georgetown University's Russian-area Studies Program (entry J8). For information on the diocese or the OCA in general, contact Ms. Mary Forbes, diocesan council secretary (202/362-2802).

P8   Saint Andrew's Ukrainian Orthodox Church

1. *4842 Sixteenth Street, NW*
   Washington, D.C. 20011
   (202) 291-8535

2. The Reverend Nicholas Czurak

3. The church's governing body *(uprava)* is the Saint Andrew Congregation (Sviat-Andriivska Parafiia) and is headed by Victor Cooley. Founded in 1949, the parish at present has about 200 members.

The Sisterhood of Saint Olha (United Orthodox Sisterhood of America), Washington Branch, is located at the church. Established in 1958, the sisterhood has its national headquarters in South Bound Brook, New Jersey. The local chapter, with some thirty-five members, is led by Sonya Krawetz. The group engages in religious, cultural, social, and welfare work; supports church activities; and raises funds through bazaars, suppers, and other events.

There is a small room at the church where various kinds of Ukrainian art work are sold, including *pysanky,* ceramics, and embroidery.

Saint Josaphat's Council of the Knights of Columbus   See entry P11

Saint Mark's Lutheran Church for Estonians   See entry M73

P9   Saint Sophia Religious Association of Ukrainian Catholics, Inc.— Washington Branch

1.   *2615 Thirtieth Street, NW*
     Washington, D.C. 20008
     (202) 234-2330

2.   Dr. George V. Starosolsky, Branch Director (301/434-5097)
     Mrs. Oksana Starosolsky, Assistant for Administration

3.   Established in 1974, the local branch is part of a national organization (with headquarters in Philadelphia) and an international association (with headquarters in Rome). It is also affiliated with the Ukrainian Catholic University in Rome. The association cooperates with and promotes the activities of the Ukrainian Catholic Church and conducts research on the religion of the church and the Ukrainian language, history, and culture. The Washington Branch is administered by a three-member executive board and has a membership of forty to fifty families.

Teaching and publishing activities of the association are the responsibilities of different members. A small museum has been established, containing about fifty items. The few icons there are mostly copies and reproductions mounted on wood. The ethnographic items—*pysanky,* ceramics, and embroidered articles—are of greater interest; some are twenty to forty years old, a few more than one hundred years old. Visitors should call first to make an appointment.

The small library has several hundred books on religion and Catholicism in general and on Ukrainian Catholicism in particular. There are also some periodicals. Researchers should make appointments to use the collection.

During the academic year, the association sponsors seminars, courses, and lectures on the Ukrainian Catholic Church and its work. A schedule of events is available without charge. In addition, unscheduled discussions and talks are held occasionally.

4.   The national organization has begun a publication program; its first book, *The Ukrainian Catholic Church, 1945–1975* (1976), is available at the Washington branch.

Seventh-Day Adventists'—General Conference—Archives   See entry B9

Sisterhood of Saint Olha   See entry P8

Sisters of Mercy of the Union—Office of Archives   See entry B10

P10 Ukrainian Catholic Association for the Patriarchal System— Washington Branch

1. *10407 Glenmore Drive*
   Adelphi, Maryland 20783
   (301) 434-1924

2. Pastor Procinski, Chairperson

3. The association has about fifty members locally and has been active for more than ten years. Its aim is to have the patriarchate recognized by the pope in Rome.
   On occasion the local branch invites speakers to talk on topics of interest to the membership.

4. The national headquarters in Philadelphia publishes a monthly bulletin *Patriarkhat* (The patriarchate), mostly in Ukrainian.

P11 Ukrainian Catholic National Shrine of the Holy Family (Holy Family Ukrainian Catholic Parish)

1. *4250 Harewood Road, NE*
   Washington, D.C. 20017
   (202) 526-3737

2. Father Stephen J. Shawel, C.SS.R., Pastor
   Father Joseph Denischuk, C.SS.R., Assistant Pastor

3. In 1975 Holy Family Ukrainian Catholic Parish acquired a three-acre site on Harewood Road in northeast Washington, planning to build there a Ukrainian Catholic National Shrine. The first phase of the project, construction of a parish shrine center, has been completed. The shrine itself (the second phase) is scheduled for completion by 1985. The third and final phase—a grotto of the Mother of God of Pochayiv, designed for outdoor services, and a commemorative cross—will be completed by 1988, in time for the celebration of the millennium of Christianity in the Ukraine.
   The parish has several religious organizations affiliated with it and engages in religious, cultural, educational, and social activities with many other groups. The more important bodies directly associated with the parish are:
   Mariyska Druzyna, Washington Branch. Founded in 1967, this branch of the international organization (headquarters in Philadelphia) has an executive board of four and about twenty members. The president is Stephanie Diachok (301/891-3660). The group helps the church in its social and welfare work and with educational, religious, and cultural activities. At its monthly meetings, members study religious questions with the pastor. Mariyska Druzyna is mainly for the Ukrainian-speaking women of the parish. The English-speaking Ladies Society of the Parish is headed by Jean Krasulski.
   League of Ukrainian Catholic Youth, Washington Branch. Organized in 1974, the branch now has about twenty-five members and is headed by Andrew Zabych (703/360-7489). There are five officers and four committees (organizational, spiritual, cultural-educational, and social). The purpose of the league is to unite parish youths

with those of other parishes and eparchies, encourage the faith, and help members retain their Ukrainian heritage.

Saint Josaphat's Council Knights of Columbus Branch. The purpose of this Catholic fraternal organization is to help in the religious, educational, and social activities of the parish. The branch, organized in 1980, presently has thirty-six members. The Grand Knight is Earl Martyn (202/727-3065).

A parish choir was also organized in 1980. Forty voices strong and under the direction of Professor Mykola Kormeluk, it performs during church services and at community functions. President of the choir committee is Mary Wuyek (301/422-8865).

The parish has a library of about 200 volumes, including religious and educational books, plus other literature, and is open to parishioners after Sunday services.

In 1981 the parish acquired the Ukrainian Memorial Cemetery, a six-acre section of the Cedar Hill Memorial Cemetery in Washington, D.C. Also in 1981 the church formed the Metropolitan Washington Ukrainian Self-Reliance Federal Credit Union (Dmytro Corbett, president, 301/593-5105).

4. In 1975 Father Joseph Denischuk published a 109-page book entitled *Ukrainian Catholic Shrine of the Holy Family* containing valuable histories of the parish and Ukrainian community in the Washington area. Copies are available without charge. A sequel will be published soon.

P12 Ukrainian Catholic Seminary of Saint Josaphat and Ukrainian Catholic Fraternity of Saint Josaphat

1. *201 Taylor Street, NE*
    Washington, D.C. 20017
    (202) 529-1177 (Seminary)
    (202) 529-0444 (Fraternity)

2. Father Walter Paska, Rector

3. The seminary offers courses in theology and religious studies, all taught in English. Father Paska may be contacted for discussions on Ukrainian history and culture generally and Ukrainian religious history and ideas particularly.

There is a small library (perhaps 2,000 volumes) at the seminary, covering theology, religion, history, and other subjects. Scholars might want to inquire about using books, many of which are in Ukrainian.

Seminarians in the fraternity take an active interest in current Ukrainian affairs, especially the issue of religious freedom and persecution in the Ukraine. Researchers may contact members for discussions on these and other matters.

P13 United States Catholic Conference (USCC)

1. *1312 Massachusetts Avenue, NW*
    Washington, D.C. 20005
    (202) 659-6812

2. J. Bryan Hehir, Associate Secretary, Office of International Justice and Peace
    Edward Doherty, Advisor, European Political and Military Affairs

3. The Catholic bishops of the United States have organized both the National

Conference of Catholic Bishops (NCCB), an episcopal conference responsible for the pastoral needs of the church, and the USCC, a nonprofit corporation designed "to unify, coordinate, promote and carry on all Catholic activities in the United States; to organize and conduct religious, charitable and social welfare work at home and abroad; to aid in education; to care for immigrants and generally to enter into and promote by education, publication, and direction the objects of its being." USCC is organized into three departments: communication, education, and social development and world peace. Additionally, the Office of International Justice and Peace considers human rights, economic concerns, and military and political affairs in various regions of the world, including the USSR. Staff members advise U.S. bishops on Soviet affairs, draft policy proposals, and conduct research.

USCC has little personal contact with the USSR. Mr. Doherty occasionally meets with Soviet diplomats to discuss arms control issues. USCC keeps files on all communist countries and on issues concerning the Helsinki Conference, which focus on human-rights abuses.

4. The USCC Office of International Justice and Peace has prepared a number of leaflets and pamphlets, some of which deal with the Soviet Union. A publications list is available. In 1977 USCC published the book *Religious Liberty in Eastern Europe: A Test Case for Human Rights*. A monthly newsletter, *NCCB/USCC Report*, and a descriptive brochure about the organization are also available.

Q Publications and Media

Publication and Media Entry Format (Q)

1. *Address; Telephone Number(s)*
2. Publisher, Chief Official, Editor, or Key Staff Members
3. Frequency of Issue and Content

Introductory Note

Publications and media often provide a valuable research tool for the researchers. The organizations listed here are intended to give an overview of the publications and media resources available in the Washington area. Some are devoted exclusively to coverage of the Soviet Union and/or its nationality components; others are general publications with some pertinence to the USSR. The researcher is advised that the publications listed here are largely in addition to other publications (which also contain information on the USSR) discussed throughout the rest of the organizations divisions (sections H–P) of this *Guide*.

Q1 *Air Force Magazine*

1. *1750 Pennsylvania Avenue, NW, Suite 400*
    Washington, D.C. 20006
    (202) 637-3300

2. Russell E. Dougherty, Publisher
    F. Clifton Berry, Jr., Editor-in-Chief
    Richard M. Skinner, Managing Editor

3. Established in 1918 (earlier: *Air Forces News Letter, Air Corps News Letter,* and *Air Services Weekly News Letter*), this monthly magazine reports on all aspects of aerospace, airpower, and related military matters. Recently this publication has begun an important annual feature: each spring it publishes a "Soviet Aerospace Almanac," which has extensive and detailed coverage of the "growth, organization, doctrine,

capabilities, and future trends of Soviet aerospace forces, and the military profession in the USSR." Many organizational charts and an aerospace weapons review are featured in this almanac.

Other special issues of the magazine include the "U.S. Air Force Almanac" and "Military Balance," both published annually. For these issues and the Soviet almanac, the magazine has permission to reprint materials from *The Military Balance,* published by the International Institute for Strategic Studies, London, and from *Jane's All the World Aircraft,* also a British publication.

Q2   American Journal of International Law

1.   *2223 Massachusetts Avenue, NW*
      Washington, D.C. 20008
      (202) 265-4313

2.   Louis Henkin and Oscar Schachter, Coeditors

3.   Established in 1907, *American Journal* is sponsored by the American Society of International Law (entry M18), which was founded in 1906.

      As a quarterly, the publication carries articles and documents on subjects such as Soviet foreign trade, foreign relations, and copyrignt law. General pieces on issues of international affairs and relations may also be of interest to Russianists. *American Journal* also frequently reviews recent Soviet publications.

Q3   Armed Forces Journal

1.   *414 Twenty-second Street, NW, Room 3603*
      Washington, D.C. 20037
      (202) 296-0450

2.   Army and Navy Journal, Inc., Publisher
      Benjamin F. Schemmer, Editor

3.   Founded in 1863 as the *Army and Navy Journal,* this monthly publication has also carried the following titles before its present one: *Army and Navy Journal and Register*; *Army, Navy, and Air Force Journal and Register*; and *Journal of the Armed Forces.*

      Armed Forces Journal often carries articles on various aspects of the Soviet military. In fact, virtually every issue has some piece of interest to Russian-area specialists. Subjects covered include the Soviet defense effort and buildup, the armed forces in the USSR, and U.S. responses to the Soviet military.

Carrollton Press, Inc.   See entry Q18

Q4   *Congressional Quarterly Weekly Report*

1.   *1414 Twenty-second Street, NW*
Washington, D.C. 20037
(202) 887-8500

2.   Peter Harkness, Executive Editor
Charles Hucker, Managing Editor

3.   This weekly publication was established in 1945. Issued by the Congressional Quarterly, Inc., it is almost indispensable for those researchers who wish to follow U.S. legislation—the content, status, and prospects thereof—and congressional action on defense and military issues, foreign trade questions, foreign policy and international affairs matters—almost anything related to the USSR.

NOTE: The Congressional Quarterly, Inc., Editorial Reports Library, an important resource for Russianists, is described in entry A15.

Q5   *Defense and Foreign Affairs*

1.   *1777 T Street, NW*
Washington, D.C. 20009
(202) 223-4934
International Telex: 64161

2.   Gregory R. Copley, Publisher and Editor-in-Chief
David S. Harvey, Editor

3.   Established in 1972, the monthly *Defense and Foreign Affairs* carries reports on NATO and Warsaw Pact armaments, military strategy, and political affairs. Of note are its data on arms transfers. The same publisher also issues *Defense and Foreign Affairs Daily* and the annual *Defense and Foreign Affairs Handbook*. Both contain useful information on Central and Eastern Europe and the USSR.

Q6   *East/West Technology Digest*

1.   *Welt Publishing Company*
1511 K Street, NW, Suite 316
Washington, D.C. 20005
(202) 737-8080

2.   Leo G. B. Welt, Publisher

3.   Established in 1976 (earlier entitled *Soviet Technology Digest*), *East West Technology Digest* is published monthly by the Welt Publishing Co., a division of the Welt International Corp., Washington, D.C. The Porter International Co. formerly owned the publication.
Digest reports on new technology in the Soviet Union and Eastern Europe, tech-

nology transfer, and science and technology matters of mutual East-West interest as well as patents, trademarks, models, and inventions.

The publication is available either by itself or, together with *Soviet Business and Trade* (entry Q19) and *China Business and Trade,* as part of the *East/West Business and Trade Package.*

Q7 Foreign Broadcast Information Service (FBIS)

1. *P.O. Box 2604*
   Washington, D.C. 20013
   (703) 351-3577

3. Associated with U.S. Government intelligence, FBIS publishes the series *Daily Reports* containing translations of significant foreign language material monitored from foreign radio and television broadcasts, press agency transmissions, newspapers, magazines, and journals. *Daily Reports* include translations of the speeches of foreign leaders; government statements; official communiqués and interviews; editorials, articles, and commentaries; and news reports on important political, economic, cultural, and scientific developments. *Daily Reports* are issued for several geographic areas, including the USSR. Edited versions of these reports are made available to the public on a subscription basis through the National Technical Information Service (NTIS) (entry Q13).

An index to FBIS publications on the USSR has not been prepared. Individual FBIS reports from 1945 to the present are available at the Library of Congress. *Daily Reports* are published in both hard copy and on microfiche. FBIS also runs the Joint Publications Research Service (entry Q10).

Q8 *Foreign Policy*

1. *11 Dupont Circle, NW*
   Washington, D.C. 20036
   (202) 797-6420

2. Charles W. Maynes, Editor
   Leigh H. Bruce, Assistant Editor

3. Established in 1970 and published by the Carnegie Endowment for International Peace (entry M28), this journal offers in-depth analyses of and provocative insights into the intricacies of international relations. It covers the whole range of political, economic, military, and human issues of concern to policymakers and laypersons alike. Of particular interest to Russianists, the publication carries at least one article per issue directly related to the USSR. The journal is indexed approximately every two years.

Q9 Government Printing Office (GPO)

1. *U.S. Government Printing Office*
   Superintendent of Documents
   Washington, D.C. 20402
   (202) 275-2051

2. Danford L. Sawyer, Jr., Public Printer

3. GPO executes orders for printing and binding placed by Congress and the departments and agencies of the U.S. Government. Through mail orders and government bookstores, GPO sells nearly 20,000 different publications originating in various government agencies.

The approximately 1,500 new titles that enter the sales inventory annually are listed in the *Monthly Catalog of Government Publications,* which has semiannual indexes. Orders for all titles listed in the *Monthly Catalog* may be placed by telephone (202/ 783-3238) or by writing to the Superintendent of Documents, GPO.

A sales catalog, *The GPO Sales Publications Reference File,* is issued bimonthly on microfiche. A useful set of about 300 Subject Bibliographies is also available for a wide range of topics, including agriculture; annual reports; armed forces; Background Notes; Country Studies (formerly known as Area Handbooks, prepared by the American University Foreign Area Studies Program, entry H3); directories and lists of foreign education; foreign investments; foreign languages; foreign relations of the U.S.; foreign trade; International Trade Commission publications; maps; military history; motion pictures, films, and audiovisual information; national defense and security; national and world economy; naval history; statistics; treaties; U.S. intelligence activities; and the USSR.

The quarterly *Price List 36,* available without charge, lists U.S. Government periodicals and subscription services sold by GPO. For further information, consult the GPO *New Catalogue,* a listing of approximately 1,000 recent and popular government publications.

GPO also administers the depository library programs, through which most government publications are made available in libraries throughout the country.

Q10 Joint Publications Research Service (JPRS)

1. *1000 North Glebe Road*
   Arlington, Virginia 22201
   (703) 841-1050

3. Sponsored by the Foreign Broadcast Information Service, JPRS provides translations and abstracts from foreign language political and technical media for U.S. Government agencies on a reimbursement basis. To provide this service, JPRS contracts with freelance translators with a variety of language backgrounds, including Russian. Interested skilled translators may send resumes to JPRS.

The JPRS reading room (open from 8:00 A.M. to 4:30 P.M., Monday through Friday) has microfiche copies of its reports since July 1975; a microfiche reader is available. Tables of contents of most JPRS publications since 1965 are on file in the reading room, arranged by series and geographic area. JPRS working files are accessible to researchers on a limited basis. JPRS publications are also available at the Library of Congress.

With the exception of copyrighted material, which only U.S. Government agencies receive, JPRS publications are sold by the National Technical Information Service (NTIS) (entry Q13). JPRS publications include translations of material on Soviet affairs, covering socioeconomic, government, political, and technical developments.

Lists of JPRS ad hoc publications can be found in the NTIS semimonthly publication *Government Reports Announcements and Index.* A monthly *TRANSDEX Index* to JPRS is available from the Micro-Photo Division of Bell and Howell, Old Mansfield Road, Wooster, Ohio 44691. The *Index* has keyword, name, and bibliographic listing sections.

Q11 *Journal of Social, Political, and Economic Studies*

1. *Council for Social and Economic Studies*
    1629 K Street, NW
    Washington, D.C. 20006
    (202) 789-0231

2. Roger Pearson, General Editor

3. The Council for Social and Economic Studies (formerly known as the Council on American Affairs) has published since 1976 the quarterly *Journal of Social, Political, and Economic Studies*, which deals with contemporary economic, social, and political issues on a worldwide basis. USSR-related articles appear from time to time. The council also publishes a series of monographs on similar topics. For instance, *Great Power Games: The Sino-Soviet-American Power Transition*, by Alan Sabrosky, appeared in 1982. A list of publications is available.

Q12 National Archives and Records Service (General Services Administration)—Office of the Federal Register

1. *Eighth Street and Pennsylvania Avenue, NW*
    Washington, D.C. 20408
    (202) 523-5240

2. John E. Byrne, Director

3. The Office of the Federal Register publishes a number of important publications concerned primarily with the operations of the United States Government: *Code of Federal Regulations* (annual), *Federal Register* (daily on weekdays), *Public Papers of the Presidents of the United States, United States Government Manual* (annual), and *Weekly Compilation of Presidential Documents*. These publications may be ordered from the Superintendent of Documents, GPO (entry Q9).

Q13 National Technical Information Service (NTIS)

1. *Operations Center:*
    5285 Port Royal Road
    Springfield, Virginia 22161
    (703) 377-0365 (Information)
    (703) 377-0366 (Bibliographic Search Service)

    7:45 A.M.–4:15 P.M., Monday-Friday

    NTIS Information Center and Bookstore:
    Main Commerce Department Building
    Fourteenth between Constitution and E streets, NW
    Washington, D.C. 20230
    (202) 724-3382 (Information)
    (202) 724-3383 (after-hours orders)

    9:00 A.M.–4:30 P.M., Monday-Friday

2. Joseph F. Caponio, Acting Director

3. The U.S. Commerce Department's NTIS is the main distributor for public sale of research reports and analyses prepared, sponsored, or funded by U.S. Government agencies. At present, it offers for sale more than one million titles. Most are scientific and technical, but there are also Commerce Department foreign market airgrams and international market-share reports, Foreign Broadcast Information Service (entry Q7) and Joint Publications Research Service (entry Q10) reports relating to the USSR, Environmental Protection Agency foreign environmental reports, and research on international energy matters and military sciences. In addition, NTIS includes in its collection State Department cables and airgrams on foreign political, economic, social, cultural, and military affairs (indexed by country and subject) as well as some unclassified Central Intelligence Agency research studies.

Items can be purchased in hard copy or microform. A computerized bibliographic search service (NTISearch) is available for a fee.

Finding aids include a biweekly *Government Reports Announcements and Index* (with annual cumulation), containing summaries of recently acquired research titles; and *Published Search Master Catalog*, a subject index to more than 1,000 published NTIS bibliographies produced by previous computer searches. The descriptive brochure *General Catalog of Information Services* is available without charge.

Q14 *Problems of Communism*

1. *1776 Pennsylvania Avenue, NW*
   Washington, D.C. 20547
   (202) 724-9651

2. Paul A. Smith, Jr., Editor

3. Established in 1951, this journal has a circulation of about 27,000 in more than ninety countries, including the U.S. (by special permission of Congress). It is a bimonthly publication of the U.S. Information Agency (entry K35).

This journal is a major resource, publishing information on current economic, political, and social affairs in the USSR, China, and other countries and on related aspects of the world communist movement. Its purpose is to provide a forum for communication among experts throughout the world regarding the pace and direction of change in the countries and movements covered by the journal, thus facilitating understanding and reducing the possibility of dangerous miscalculation in international affairs. *Problems of Communism* does not concern itself with policy and excludes all forms of advocacy for or against any political ideology or interest. Devoted to objective standards of evidence, and intellectually rigorous, the journal accepts only signed original contributions. Its worldwide contributorship includes academic scholars, government analysts, members of the banking and legal communities, and serious contemporary journalists.

Information about the journal's index can be found on the inside front cover of each issue. Information about reprints and the commercial availability of past issues on microform can be found on the inside back cover.

NOTE: Bibliographic and personnel resources of the journal are described in the U.S. Information Agency entry (K35).

Q15 Quarterly Journal of the Library of Congress

1. *Library of Congress Publishing Office*
    Washington, D.C. 20540
    (202) 287-5093

2. Frederick B. Mohr, Editor

3. *Quarterly Journal* provides information on the Library of Congress collections, new acquisitions, and programs. USSR-related articles are occasionally included. Subscriptions are handled through GPO (entry Q9).

Q16 Radio Free Europe (RFE)

1. *1201 Connecticut Avenue, NW*
    Washington, D.C. 20036
    (202) 457-6900

2. James Brown, Director, RFE Division

3. RFE research has been distributed to the public since about 1958. Weekly publications of this radio broadcasting organization include: *Situation Report,* one for each of the following countries: Bulgaria, Czechoslovakia, German Democratic Republic, Hungary, and Poland; *Background Report,* three to four times per week.
    These publications, issued by the Munich-based RFE/RL Inc., focus primarily on developments within Eastern Europe and on the world communist movement. They may be of value to Soviet-area specialists for the light they shed on Soviet relations within the communist bloc.
    The radio broadcasts and transcriptions themselves may also be of interest to Russianists. For more information about this resource, see the remarks under RFE's sister organization, Radio Liberty (entry Q17). Both radios are supervised in this country by the Board for International Broadcasting (entry K5).

Q17 Radio Liberty (RL)

1. *1201 Connecticut Avenue, NW*
    Washington, D.C. 20036
    (202) 457-6900

2. William Buell, Director

3. Circulation of RL materials outside the organization began in 1964.
    RFE/RL Inc., of Munich, West Germany, is the sponsoring organization. The director of RL Research is Keith Bush. In the U.S., the Board for International Broadcasting (entry K5) oversees RL and RFE (entry Q16).
    Radio Liberty Research Bulletins are issued weekly in English and on an ad hoc basis in Russian. Special supplements are issued periodically.
    The subjects covered in these publications are Soviet economics, culture, literature, politics, nationalities developments, and foreign affairs. Virtually all of the space in

RL publications is devoted directly to the USSR. These titles and the entire RL operation are major resources for Russianists.

Transcripts and other materials relating to the radio broadcasting operations of RL and RFE are primarily maintained in Munich; some records, transcripts, and tape recordings of broadcasts of the two operations, however, are available in Washington. Some items might prove invaluable to researchers in the Soviet field. Inquiries should be directed to Mr. Buell (202/457-6910).

The RL staff, in Munich, Washington, and New York, represents an important resource in the form of language skills, knowledge of Soviet audiences, and general expertise in Soviet-area studies.

Q18 Research Publications, Inc.

1. *12 Lunar Drive*
   Woodbridge, Connecticut 06525
   (203) 397-2600

   Washington Office (Declassified Documents):
   1911 North Fort Meyer Drive, Suite 905
   Arlington, Virginia 22209
   (703) 525-5940

2. Elizabeth Jones, Managing Editor

3. For Russianists interested in previously classified and restricted materials of the U.S. Government, there is the extremely valuable Declassified Documents Reference System. Beginning in 1975, Carrollton Press, which was acquired in 1981 by Research Publications, has issued quarterly catalogs of abstracts of documents from the Central Intelligence Agency, presidential libraries, Defense and State departments, National Security Council, and other agencies. These documents have been declassified in accordance with the Freedom of Information Act Amendments of 1974, executive order, and/or mandatory review procedures. Each annual collection contains a cumulative subject index. Excluded are materials that are automatically declassified or published elsewhere. The documents are also available from Research Publications on microfiche. At present, each annual collection contains some 1,500-2,000 documents. A retrospective collection consisting of more than 8,000 documents is not included in the annuals, bringing the total holdings of the collections to more than 20,000 items. Researchers should direct inquiries to Ms. Jones's office in Washington.

Q19 *Soviet Business and Trade*

1. *Welt Publishing Company*
   1511 K Street, NW, Suite 316
   Washington, D.C. 20005
   (202) 737-8080

2. Leo G. B. Welt, Publisher

3. *Soviet Business and Trade* is published by Welt Publishing Co., a part of the Welt International Corp. of Washington. Established in 1973 (earlier entitled *Soviet Business and Economic Report*), the journal was published until 1975 by the Porter In-

ternational Co. This biweekly (published only once in January) economic review covers most aspects of commerce and trade with the USSR and has information about a variety of Soviet industries and agriculture.

Soviet Business and Trade is available either by itself or, with the *East/West Technology Digest* (entry Q6) and *China Business and Trade,* as part of the *East/West Business and Trade Package.*

Soviet Life Magazine   See entry L7

Soviet Radio and Television Bureau   See entry L5

TASS News Agency   See entry L6

Q20   University Press of America

1. *4720 Boston Way, Suite K*
   Lanham, Maryland 20706
   (301) 459-3366

2. James Lyons, Managing Editor

3. University Press of America publishes books intended for the academic community, covering a wide range of topics, including economics, history, literature, philosophy, political science, religion, and sociology. The press uses a cost-efficient approach, employing a photoreproduction process to print typewritten and typeset manuscripts prepared by the authors.

An annual catalog lists recent titles by subject, with short summaries. Some recent titles include: *Calculus of Power: The Current Soviet-American Conventional Military Balance in Central Europe,* by Sherwood S. Cordier (1980); *Domestic Influences on Soviet Foreign Policy,* by Dina Rome Spechler (1978); *Soviet Views of the Cuban Missile Crises: Myth and Reality in Foreign Policy Analysis,* ed. Ronald R. Pope (1982).

Q21   *U.S. News and World Report*

1. *2300 N Street, NW*
   Washington, D.C. 20037
   (202) 861-2000

2. Marvin L. Stone, Editor

3. *U.S. News and World Report* is a weekly news magazine that monitors national and international affairs. Its bureau in Moscow contributes Soviet news and follows United States foreign policy—economic, military, and political—toward the USSR.

The semiannual *U.S. News and World Report Index* includes country and subject headings. A comprehensive index is available on microfiche.

Q22 Voice of America (VOA)

1. *Health and Human Services North Building*
    330 Independence Avenue, SW
    Washington, D.C. 20547
    (202) 755-4180

2. John Hughes, Associate Director for Broadcasting

3. Broadcasts in Russian began in 1947, others later.
    VOA broadcasts to the Soviet Union are a part of the U.S. Information Agency, Associate Director (Broadcasting)—Programs section. The USSR Division, headed by Christopher Squire (202/755-4422), handles almost all pertinent broadcasts. (The Europe Division, 202/755-4210, broadcasts to Estonia, Latvia, and Lithuania.)
    Currently VOA programs total sixteen hours a day in Russian (fourteen of original material, two of rebroadcasts), 4 1/2 hours in Ukrainian (3 1/2 original, one rebroadcast), and one hour each in Armenian, Georgian, and Uzbek. Broadcasts in each of the three Baltic languages also total one hour per day.
    Researchers may be interested both in details of programming and in tapes of the broadcasts themselves. Information about broadcast contents is published in the daily *Content Report,* which lists program titles and indicates in-house sources. See also the brief quarterly VOA *Broadcast Schedule,* one for each language service. Tapes of most broadcasts, unless of particular significance, are saved for only a short period— up to four months or six months at most. To look at content reports on the premises only (per government regulation) or to listen to the tapes (also on-site), make arrangements through the VOA Public Information Office at (202) 755-4744.
    More information about VOA and its staff may be found under the U.S. Information Agency (entry K35).

Q23 *The Washington Monitor, Inc.*

1. *301 Pennsylvania Avenue, NW*
    Washington, D.C. 20004
    (202) 347-7757

2. James Marsh, Publisher
    Deborah Drosnin, Editor, *Access Reports*
    Teri Calabrese, Editor, *Yellow Books*
    Melissa Cooperson-Yohe, Editor, *Weekly Regulatory Monitor*

3. The Washington Monitor publishes several serials that provide useful reference tools for researchers interested in utilizing personnel and other resources of the U.S. Government. *Federal Yellow Book* (bimonthly) and *Congressional Yellow Book* (quarterly) are telephone books for the top 27,000 federal and Capitol Hill employees, respectively. The Monitor also publishes *Weekly Regulatory Monitor,* a calendar of federal regulatory actions of general interest that is indexed monthly; and *Access Reports/Freedom of Information,* a biweekly newsletter reporting on the latest developments in the Freedom of Information field, including recent court decisions, pending legislation, and revisions in agency regulations. A companion service, *Reference File,* is updated throughout the year and contains full texts of federal agency Freedom of Information Agency regulations and relevant court opinions.

Q24 *Washington Post*

1. *1150 Fifteenth Street, NW*
   Washington, D.C. 20071
   (202) 334-6000 (Information)

2. Benjamin Bradlee, Executive Editor
   Howard Simons, Managing Editor

3. Established in 1877, this daily newspaper is published by the Washington Post Company.
   Correspondents in the USSR report on Soviet politics, economy, and foreign relations as well as other pertinent matters. The newspaper also covers all other national and international events that bear directly or indirectly on the Soviet Union.
   Washington Post Moscow correspondents are, in general, happy to speak with researchers about their experiences in the USSR. Stephen Rosenfeld spent some time there in 1959, 1962, and 1964–65; Robert Kaiser held the position in the early 1970s and wrote *Russia: The People and the Power* in 1976. Dusko Doder is currently in Moscow.
   The *Washington Post* library would be a major resource for scholars if they could gain access to it. It contains more than five million newspaper clippings, 600,000 photographs, and 20,000 books plus other materials of value. Items are arranged by name and subject. An index covers the period from 1940 to the present and has been microfilmed since 1972. The library is restricted to staff use, although it does have interlibrary loan services and photocopying facilities. Mr. Simons should be contacted by any outside researcher who seeks access to the collection. The facility is open from 10:30 A.M. to 7:00 P.M., Monday through Friday, and for a few hours on Saturday and Sunday.

Q25 *Washington Times*

1. *3600 New York Avenue NE*
   Washington, D.C. 20002
   (202) 636-3000 (Information)

2. James R. Whelan, Editor and Publisher

3. Financially underwritten by the Unification Church, the daily *Washington Times* began publication in 1982, in an attempt to fill the void created by the *Washington Star*'s failure in 1981.
   The *Times* covers national and international news relating to the USSR, relying primarily on wire services. Its library, only just established, is headed by Todd Lindsay.

Q26 *World Affairs*

1. *4000 Albemarle Street, NW*
   Washington, D.C. 20016
   (202) 362-6195

2.   Evron Kirkpatrick, Chairperson, Editorial Board
     Frank C. Turley, Managing Editor

3.   *World Affairs* is a quarterly publication of the American Peace Society. Established in 1834, it was called the *Advocate of Peace* until 1932.

The journal carries articles on foreign policy issues, international affairs, and related matters. It publishes articles on Soviet foreign policy, U.S.-Soviet relations, and other pertinent subjects during the course of a year. Often, a single issue is devoted to a particular question or problem.

APPENDIXES

I   U.S.-USSR Bilateral Agreements

As has been indicated throughout the body of this *Guide*, the future of the U.S.-USSR bilateral agreements hinges largely upon the status of the relations between the two countries. Beginning in 1972, eleven different agreements ranging from agriculture to energy to space were adopted; in the decade that followed, four of the eleven expired and were not renewed, namely: bilateral agreements in the areas of archival exchanges, energy, science and technology, and space.

Generally, the agreements bring together people, information and material for joint working projects, the fruits of which vary in quality and quantity. Below are listed the active agreements, together with the names and addresses of the executive secretaries. Researchers should contact these offices for information about current programs or projects underway. Many of the secretaries can also direct Russianists to appropriate people for information about expired U.S.-USSR agreements, should it be necessary. The active agreements include.

Agriculture Agreement
Mr. Doug Freeman
Office of International Cooperation and Development
Agriculture Department
Auditors Building, Room 4112
Washington, D.C. 20250
(202) 382-8021

Atomic Energy
Mr. John Metzler
Office of International Nuclear Cooperation
Energy Department
1000 Independence Avenue, SW, Room 7A 029
Washington, D.C. 20585
(202) 252-6777

Environmental Protection Agreement
Mr. Gary Waxmonsky
Environmental Protection Agency
West Tower, Room 811
401 M Street, SW
Washington, D.C. 20460
(202) 382-4878

Housing and Other Construction and Development Agreement
Ambassador Theodore Britton, Jr., Assistant to the Secretary for
International Affairs
Department of Housing and Urban Development
451 Seventh Street, NW, Room 2124
Washington, D.C. 20410
(202) 755-7058

*Medicine and Public Health and Artificial Heart Research and
Development Agreements*
Dr. Peter Henry
Office of International Health and Office of the Surgeon General
5600 Fishers Lane, Room 1875
Rockville, Maryland 20857
(301) 443-4010

Studies of the World Ocean Agreement
Mr. Ned Ostenso, Acting Assistant Administrator for Research and
Development for National Oceanic and Atmospheric Administration
6010 Executive Boulevard
Rockville, Maryland 20852
(301) 443-8344

Transportation Agreement
Dr. Bernard Ramundo
International Cooperation Division and Secretariat
Department of Transportation
400 Seventh Street, SW, Room 10302
Washington, D.C. 20590
(202) 426-4398

II Washington-area Meetings

Kennan Institute for Advanced Russian Studies (Woodrow Wilson International Center for Scholars). The institute sponsors regular discussions, talks, conferences, and film series of great interest to Russian/Soviet-area specialists (see entry H23).

Institute for Sino-Soviet Studies (George Washington University). The Soviet and East Europe Colloquium of the institute is held weekly during the academic year. Schedules are available; meetings are open by invitation (see entry H15).

American Association for the Advancement of Slavic Studies—Washington Chapter. Monthly meetings take place during the academic year, at which distinguished scholars give presentations (see entry M1).

State Department Meetings. The department's Bureau of Intelligence and Research periodically holds meetings on a variety of topics of current interest. Virtually all such events are open to researchers. The scholar should call (202) 632-0980 to inquire about attending (see entry K32).

Russian/Soviet Affairs Luncheons. These informal gatherings usually occur bimonthly. For access, contact the organizer, Donald Jameson, at Research Associates International, 1600 Wilson Boulevard, Arlington, Virginia 22209 (703/522-3253).

Fund for the Relief of Russian Writers and Scientists in Exile (The Litfund—Washington Branch). The Litfund holds several meetings per year; Russian is usually spoken (see entry M36).

NOTE: In addition to the meetings noted above, scholars would be wise to contact the appropriate departments of Washington-area universities. Often a researcher can obtain a monthly calendar and find information about events only recently scheduled.

III Library Collections: A Listing by Size of Russian/Soviet Holdings

NOTE: The size of Russian/Soviet holdings in the Washington, D.C., area library collections is difficult to determine. The following table provides estimates only.

More than 800,000 volumes:
Library of Congress (entry A37)

25,000–100,000 volumes:
Commerce Department—Foreign Demographic Analysis Library (entry A14)
Maryland University Libraries (entry A39)
National Library of Medicine (entry A48)
State Department Library (entry A57)

10,000–25,000 volumes:
Georgetown University Library (entry A23)
National Agricultural Library (entry A40)
U.S. Information Agency Library (entry A61)

5,000–10,000 volumes:
Air Force Intelligence Service (Air Force Department) (entry K2)
American University Library (entry A6)
Geological Survey (Interior Department)—Library (entry A22)
George Washington University Library (entry A24)
Interior Department—Natural Resources Library (entry A31)
Kennan Institute for Advanced Russian Studies (Woodrow Wilson International Center for Scholars)—Library (entry A35)
Naval Observatory (Navy Department)—Library (entry A52)
SRI International—Strategic Studies Center Library (entry H28)

IV Bookstores

The Victor Kamkin, Inc., Bookstore is the major resource in the Washington area for Soviet-area scholars. Located in Rockville, Maryland (12224 Parklawn Drive, 20852; 301/881-5973), Kamkin's is open from 9:00 A.M. to 5:00 P.M., Monday through Saturday. Current stock is nearly two million volumes, in all disciplines relating to Russia and the Soviet Union. The overwhelming majority of books come from the USSR, but the store also carries some émigré editions, including its own publications. Most works are in Russian and are new, but some of the stock is in English and some are used. All visitors to Washington should make a point of going to the bookstore at least once. Besides books, the store carries phonograph records, slides, art objects, toys and games, and other items from the Soviet Union. (Academics receive a ten percent discount.)

A second valuable outlet for Russianists is O. and A. Books, a small operation run by Professor Yuri Olkhovsky at his home (3319 Ardley Court, Falls Church, Virginia 22041; 703/998-5612). O. and A. sells *Kontinent* and other Russian-language publications from outside the USSR (i.e. non-Soviet).

A selective list of other bookstores, new and used, which might prove useful to Russian/Soviet specialists follows. Unless otherwise indicated, the stores carry mostly English-language trade and text books, with a good selection of cloth and paperbound volumes on Russian/Soviet current affairs, economics, foreign affairs, history, literature, and political science. Contact the individual stores to learn what days and hours they are open. Additionally, researchers would be wise to check the various student book stores at many of the area's colleges and universities (see section J of this *Guide*) as well as the Government Printing Office (entry Q9) and National Technical Information Service (entry Q13).

The Book Annex (202) 338-9544
1239 Wisconsin Avenue, NW
Washington, D.C. 20007
also: (202) 785-1133; 1342 Connecticut Avenue, NW
Washington, D.C. 20036

Common Concerns—Kramer Books, Inc. (202) 293-2072
1347 Connecticut Avenue, NW
Washington, D.C. 20036
The store has a limited selection continuously reviewed, of important and

fairly recent Western-language books on Russian/Soviet affairs, usually at tremendous savings—fun for browsing.

Estate Book Sales (202) 965-4274
2824 Pennsylvania Avenue, NW
Washington, D.C. 20007
Besides the English-language stock, there is a foreign-languages room downstairs with several shelves of used Russian books, most on languages and literature.

Globe Book Shop—Foreign Language Center (202) 393-1490
1700 Pennsylvania Avenue, NW
Washington, D.C. 20006

Horizon Bookshop (202) 965-8865
3131 M Street, NW
Washington, D.C. 20007
also: (703) 683-3081; 601 King Street
Alexandria, Virginia 22314

The Lantern—A Bryn Mawr Book Shop (202) 333-2803
2803 M Street, NW
Washington, D.C. 20007
The shop has several shelves of diverse used Russian books.

Maryland Book Exchange, Inc. (301) 927-2510
4500 College Avenue
College Park, Maryland 20740

Pentagon Bookstore (202) 521-3123
The Pentagon
Washington, D.C. 20330

Reiter's Students Book Co. (202) 223-3327
2120 Pennsylvania Avenue, NW
Washington, D.C. 20037
The store carries mostly technical books.

Rizzoli International Book Store (202) 337-7300
The Foundry
1055 Thomas Jefferson Street, NW
Washington, D.C. 20007

Second Story Books (202) 244-5550
3236 P Street, NW
Washington, D.C. 20007
also: (301) 656-0170; 7730 Old Georgetown Road
Bethesda, Maryland
also: (202) 659-8884; 2000 P Street, NW
Washington, D.C. 20036

Sidney Kramer Books, Inc. (202) 298-8010
1722 H Street, NW
Washington, D.C. 20006

NOTE: A most important resource for book lovers are several major book sales held each year in the Washington area. Probably the most significant of these sales for Russianists is that of the Association of American Foreign Service Wives, held annually in the fall at the State Department. Well more than 100,000 books are usually offered; there is a large foreign-language section, including books in Russian, Baltic, and other languages of the USSR. The Stone Ridge School sale also occurs in the fall; in 1981, more than 30,000 volumes were for sale. The Brandeis University and Vassar College book sales are held in the spring. All are advertised in the papers shortly before they occur; for example, notices of them appear in the book review section of the *Washington Post*. They generally last a few days.

V Housing, Transportation, and Other Services

This section is prepared to help outside scholars find suitable housing in Washington, D.C. It also contains data on local transportation facilities and information services. Prices quoted are current as of August 1982.

HOUSING INFORMATION AND REFERRAL SERVICE

For anyone interested in leasing an apartment or house, the *Apartment Shoppers' Guide* (ASGHD), updated every three months, is a valuable source of information. The directory, which quotes current rental prices, terms of leases and directions to each of the facilities listed, is available at People's Drug Stores and elsewhere in the Washington area. It is published by ASGHD (202/363-8016), located at 3301 New Mexico Avenue, NW, Suite 310, Washington, D.C. 20016. The staff provides a housing referral service, for a fee, from 9:00 A.M. to 5:00 P.M., Monday through Friday.

Help can also be obtained from the following local university housing offices:

George Washington University Off Campus Housing Resources Center (202) 676-6688
2121 I Street, NW (Rice Hall), Fourth Floor
Washington, D.C. 20052
Summer: 11:00 A.M.–7:00 P.M., Monday–Thursday; 1:00–5:00 P.M., Friday; 9:00 A.M.–1:00 P.M., Saturday
Winter: 9:00 A.M.–5:30 P.M., Monday–Friday

This office has listings of apartments and other housing in the Washington area. Open to the public, the office also distributes the *Apartment Shoppers' Guide* (see above), maps of Washington, D.C., and a *Guide to Off-Campus Housing* (annual) prepared by the office staff.

Georgetown University Off-Campus Housing Office (202) 625-3026
Healy Building Basement, Room GO8
Georgetown University
Thirty-seventh and O streets, NW
Washington, D.C. 20057
Summer: 10:00 A.M.–4:00 P.M., Monday–Friday
Winter: 1:00 P.M.–4:30 P.M., Monday–Friday

This office offers services similar to those at the George Washington University Housing Resources Center. During the summer months, use of the facility is restricted to Georgetown students, faculty, and staff.

Catholic University of America Off-Campus Housing Office (202) 635-5680
Saint Bonaventure Hall, Room 106
Catholic University of America
Washington, D.C. 20064
9:00 A.M.–5:00 P.M., Monday–Friday

Open to the educational public, this office provides services similar to those of George Washington University.

Northern Virginia Community College, Annandale Campus Housing Board (703) 323-3147
Student Activities Center
Godwin Building, Room 103
8333 Little River Turnpike
Annandale, Virginia 22003
8:30 A.M.–5:00 P.M., Monday–Friday

The board maintains a listing of rooms available in private homes.

NOTE: The off-campus housing offices of American University, Howard University, and the University of Maryland handle inquiries and requests from their own students and faculty members only.

Finally, the *Washington Post* classified section has extensive listings of apartment and house rentals.

SHORT-TERM HOUSING

For those who intend to stay for a short period of time (i.e. a few weeks to several months), the following facilities may be useful:

The Capitol Park (202) 479-6800
800 Fourth Street, SW
Washington, D.C. 20024

The Capitol Park is near the Library of Congress. Rates for a furnished one-bedroom apartment are by the week $49 per day, by the month starting at $75.

International Guest House (202) 726-5808
1441 Kennedy Street, NW
Washington, D.C.

Rates average $350 to $450 per month (minimum one semester stay), which includes two meals per day. Single and shared double or triple rooms are available. The house encourages a nationality quota policy that permits no more than ten Americans or three citizens from any one foreign country at any time.

The Woodner (202) 328-2800
3636 Sixteenth Street, NW
Washington, D.C. 20010

The Woodner has both unfurnished and furnished efficiency and one-bedroom apartments. Rates are $345 per month and up for an unfurnished efficiency, $445 and up for a one-bedroom apartment. Rates for furnished efficiencies and one-bedroom apartments are $575 and $690 respectively.

LONG-TERM HOUSING

Those wishing to rent an apartment or house for a year or more should consult not only the *Apartment Shoppers' Guide* and the local university housing offices but also the *Guide to Real Estate* in the yellow pages of the Washington-area's phone book.

Home and apartment rents vary greatly from one section to the other in the Washington area. Normally, rents are lower in suburban Virginia and Maryland than in Washington, D.C. One should also remember that it is difficult to find furnished apartments in the Washington area through regular real estate agents. People who need furnished quarters may have to take unfurnished apartments and rent furniture. Such an arrangement can be negotiated with real estate brokers. Even under such an arrangement, linen, blankets, dishes, silverware, and cooking utensils must be furnished by the tenant. Again, the *Post* classified advertisements should be checked.

TRANSPORTATION IN THE WASHINGTON AREA

Scholars should be advised that parking space in the nation's capital is limited, and that it is relatively expensive to park at commercial lots (e.g., $1.75 per hour). It may be preferable, therefore, to use either bus, Metro subway, or taxi to get around the downtown Washington area.

To National Airport

Metro buses 11A and 11E leave every ten minutes (more frequently in rush hour) from Tenth and Pennsylvania avenues, NW. There is also a Metro subway train that leaves every seven minutes from downtown stations for National Airport.

To Dulles International Airport

An airport bus leaves from the Capital Hilton Hotel, Sixteenth and K streets, NW, every hour on the hour, from 6:00 A.M. until 10:00 P.M. (fare: $7.75). Also, there is a limousine service daily to National Airport until 11:15 P.M. and to Dulles Airport until midnight. For further information call Airport Limo Inc. at (301) 532-1000.

To Baltimore-Washington (Friendship) International Airport

All buses leave from Sixteenth and K streets, NW, downtown Washington, making a stop at Greenbelt Station, Maryland. For further information call (301) 441-2345. The tickets are $7.50 for a single trip and $14.00 for a round trip.

Taxi

Fares in Washington, D.C., are based on a congressionally controlled zone system and are reasonable. Taxi fares crossing state lines into and out of Virginia and Maryland are, however, fairly expensive.

Metro Subway System

The subway system is an economical and efficient means of transportation in the Washington, D.C., area. Maps of the subway can be obtained at most subway stations. The system is rapidly expanding, with several new stops added yearly. For routes and schedule information, call (202) 637-2437.

Metro Buses

To get around town by metro bus, which links almost every major corner of metropolitan Washington, obtain a copy of *Getting about by Metro Bus*, available at Metro Headquarters, 600 Fifth Street, NW, Washington, D.C. 20001. For routes and schedule information, call (202) 637-2437.

Intercity Buses

Terminals are located at Twelfth Street and New York Avenue, NW, a short walk from a metro stop. Greyhound can be reached at (202) 565-2662 and Trailways at (202) 737-5800.

Trains

Union Station (50 Massachusetts Avenue, NE) is the terminal for all trains serving Washington, D.C. Located near the Capitol, it is within minutes of the downtown hotel area. For AMTRAK information, call (202) 484-7540.

INTERNATIONAL VISITORS INFORMATION SERVICE (IVIS)

A private, nonprofit community organization, IVIS offers a diversified program of services to international visitors to the Washington area. Its programs are operated with the support of more than 1,200 volunteers living in the Washington area. IVIS has two locations:

Main Information and Reception Center (202) 872-8747
801 Nineteenth Street, NW
Washington, D.C. 20006
and
Information Booth
Dulles International Airport

Multilingual staff and volunteers are available to help the visitor with sightseeing arrangements, hotel accommodations, and bilingual medical assistance. IVIS also provides tour brochures, maps, information, and telephone assistance in fifty-five languages, including Russian, while operating twenty-four hours a day, seven days a week. Persons in need of language assistance may call (202) 872-8747.

For the foreign student enrolled in U.S. institutions of higher education, it may be useful to contact the Foreign Student Service Council of Greater

Washington, 1623 Belmont Street, NW, Washington, D.C. 20009 (202) 232-4979. Its staff and volunteers provide home hospitality, sightseeing, and other services to the foreign students (local and transient).

OTHER SOURCES OF INFORMATION

Flashmaps! The Instant Guide to Washington (1981) is an inexpensive, useful, and quick reference book on the city and can be obtained at many area bookstores.

Free copies of the metropolitan Washington-area map are available from the District of Columbia Department of Transportation and from the Map Office, Presidential Building, Room 519, 415 Twelfth Street, NW, Washington, D.C. 20004. Mail orders must include a stamped, self-addressed, seven-by-ten-inch envelope. The office is open from 8:15 A.M. to 4:45 P.M., Monday through Friday (202/727-6562).

A FINAL WORD

In general, it costs more to live in Washington, D.C., than in neighboring Virginia or Maryland. For those intending to do research primarily in the city and especially along the Metro Blue Line, i.e. Foggy Bottom to Capitol Hill, however, the time lost commuting in and out of town and the transportation expense may well make up the difference in rental costs.

For those intending to have their family accompany them, it is worth noting that the D.C. public school system is presently undergoing an academic revival. Thus far, this program has reached the lower grades. There are very good public elementary school programs in new Southwest and Capitol Hill areas of the District.

One caution, the D.C. Department of Transportation is to be avoided at all costs. Pay to keep your out-of-District licensed car off the street. Permits are required for street parking and these can only be had with the local registration of your vehicle, which can be expensive.

VI Federal Government Holidays

Federal government offices are closed on the following holidays:

New Year's Day	January 1
Washington's Birthday	Third Monday in February
Memorial Day	Last Monday in May
Independence Day	July 4*
Labor Day	First Monday in September
Columbus Day	Second Monday in October
Veterans' Day	November 11*
Thanksgiving	Fourth Thursday in November
Christmas	December 25*

*If this date falls on a Saturday, the holiday is on Friday. If this date falls on a Sunday, the holiday is on Monday.

The public areas of the Smithsonian Institution and the General Reading Room of the Library of Congress are open on most holidays.

VII Standard Entry Formats

A. Entry Format for Libraries

1. General Information
    a. *address; telephone number(s)*
    b. hours of service
    c. conditions of access (including availability of interlibrary loan services and photocopying facilities)
    d. name/title of director and heads of relevant divisions

2. Size of Collection

3. Description and Evaluation of Collection
    a. narrative assessment of Russia/USSR holdings—subject and area strengths/weaknesses
    b. tabular evaluation of subject strength:

Subject Category	*Number of Titles*	*Rating (A–D)**
Philosophy and Religion		
History		
Geography and Ethnography		
Economics		
Sociology		
Politics and Government		
Foreign Relations		
Law		
Education		
Fine Arts		
Language		
Literature		
Military Affairs		
Bibliography and Reference		
Ukrainians		
Byelorussians		
Baltic Nationalities		
Caucasian Nationalities		
Central Asian Nationalities		
Siberian Nationalities		

*A—comprehensive collection of primary and secondary sources (Library of Congress collection to serve as a standard of evaluation)

B—substantial collection of primary and secondary sources; sufficient from some original research (holdings of roughly one-tenth those of the Library of Congress)

C—substantial collection of secondary and primary sources, many in Russian; sufficient to support graduate instruction (holdings of roughly one-half those of B collection)

D—collection of secondary and primary sources, some in Russian; sufficient to support undergraduate instruction (holdings of roughly one-half those of C collection)

---

4. Special Collections (periodicals, newspapers, government documents, maps, films, tapes)

5. Noteworthy Holdings

6. Bibliographic Aids Facilitating Use of Collection

B. Entry Format for Archives and Manuscripts Depositories

1. General Information
    a. *address; telephone number(s)*
    b. hours of service
    c. conditions of access
    d. photocopying facilities
    e. name/title of director and heads of relevant divisions

2. Size of Holdings Pertaining to Russia/USSR

3. Description of Holdings Pertaining to Russia/USSR

4. Bibliographic Aids Facilitating Use of Collection

C. Entry Format for Museums, Galleries, and Art Collections

1. General Information
    a. *address; telephone number(s)*
    b. hours of service
    c. conditions of access
    d. photocopying facilities
    e. name/title of director and heads of relevant divisions

2. Size of Holdings Pertaining to Russia/USSR

3. Description of Holdings Pertaining to Russia/USSR

4. Bibliographic Aids Facilitating Use of Collection

D. Entry Format for Collections of Music and Other Sound Recordings

1. General Information
   a. *address; telephone number(s)*
   b. hours of service
   c. conditions of access
   d. name/title of director and key staff members

2. Size of Holdings Pertaining to Russia/USSR

3. Description of Holdings Pertaining to Russia/USSR

4. Facilities for Study and Use
   a. availability of audiovisual equipment
   b. reservation requirements
   c. fees charged
   d. photocopying facilities

5. Bibliographic Aids Facilitating Use of Collection

E. Entry Format for Map Collections

1. General Information
   a. *address; telephone number(s)*
   b. hours of service
   c. conditions of access
   d. photocopying facilities
   e. name/title of director

2. Size of Holdings Pertaining to Russia/USSR

3. Description of Holdings Pertaining to Russia/USSR

4. Bibliographic Aids Facilitating Use of Collection

F. Entry Format for Film Collections (Still Photographs and Motion Pictures)

1. General Information
   a. *address; telephone number(s)*
   b. hours of service
   c. conditions of access
   d. name/title of director and key staff members

2. Size of Holdings Pertaining to Russia/USSR

3. Description of Holdings Pertaining to Russia/USSR

4. Facilities for Study and Use
   a. availability of audiovisual equipment
   b. reservation requirements
   c. fees charged
   d. photocopying facilities

5. Bibliographic Aids Facilitating Use of Collection

G. Entry Format for Data Banks

1.   General Information
   a.   *address; telephone number(s)*
   b.   hours of service
   c.   conditions of access (including fees charged for information retrieval)
   d.   name/title of director and key staff members
2.   Description of Data Files (hard-data and bibliographic-reference)
3.   Bibliographic Aids Facilitating Use of Storage Media

H. Entry Format for Research Centers and Information Offices

1.   *Address; Telephone Number(s)*
2.   Founding Date
3.   Chief Official and Title
4.   Staff, Research, and/or Teaching Personnel
5.   Parental Organizations
6.   Principal Fields of Research and Other Activities
7.   Library/Special Research Facilities (including specialized collections and unique equipment; availability to nonmembers)
8.   Recurring Meetings Sponsored by the Organization (open or closed)
9.   Publications or Other Media
10.   Affiliated Organizations

J. Entry Format for Academic Programs

1.   *Address; Telephone Number(s)*
2.   Chief Official and Title
3.   Degrees and Subjects Offered; Programs/Activities
4.   Library/Research Facilities
5.   Publications

K. Entry Format for U.S. Government Agencies

1.   General Information
   a.   *address; telephone number(s)*
   b.   conditions of access
   c.   name/title of director and heads of relevant divisions
2.   Agency Functions, Programs, and Research Activities (in-house research, con-

tract research, research grants, employment of outside consultants, and international exchange programs)

3. Agency Libraries and Reference Facilities

4. Internal Agency Records (unpublished materials and aids, indexes, vertical files, etc.)

5. Publications
   a. published research products
   b. research bibliographies

In the case of large, structurally complex agencies, each relevant division/bureau is described separately and cross-referenced in the text and indexes.

L. Entry Format for Government Agencies (Soviet, International, and Other)

1. General Information
   a. *address; telephone number(s)*
   b. conditions of access
   c. name/title of director and heads of relevant divisions

2. Organization Functions, Programs, and Research Activities (including in-house research, contract research, research grants, and employment of outside consultants)

3. Libraries and Reference Facilities

4. Internal Records (including unpublished research products)

5. Publications
   a. published reports, periodicals, and series
   b. bibliographies

In the case of large, structurally complex organizations, each relevant division or subunit is described separately and cross-references in the text and indexes.

M Entry Format for Associations (Academic, Professional, and Cultural)

1. *Address; Telephone Number(s)*

2. Founding Date

3. Chief Official and Title

4. Staff

5. Number of Members

6. Program or Description

7. Sections or Divisions

8. Library

9. Conventions/Meetings

10.   Publications

11.   Affiliated Organizations

N   Entry Format for Cultural-Exchange Organizations

1.   *Address; Telephone Number(s)*

2.   Founding Date

3.   Chief Official and Title

4.   Staff

5.   Program or Description

6.   Budget and Its Source

7.   Publications

8.   Affiliated Organizations

P.   Entry Format for Religious Organizations

1.   *Address; Telephone Number(s)*

2.   Chief Official and Title

3.   Program or Activities

4.   Publications

Q.   Entry Format for Publications and Media

1.   *Address; Telephone Number(s)*

2.   Publisher, Chief Official, Editor, or Key Staff Members

3.   Frequency of Issue and Content

BIBLIOGRAPHY

The union lists below are complemented for individual collections by bibliographic references at the end of entries (or of divisions within entries) in the appropriate sections of this book. The category "Other Guides and Directories," following the union lists, includes a number of works that provided the original basic lists of collections and organizations to investigate for this *Scholars' Guide*.

UNION LISTS—NATIONAL

National Union Catalog: A Cumulative Author List Representing Library of Congress Printed Cards and Titles Reported by Other American Libraries. Washington, D.C.: Library of Congress, 1953–. Monthly, with cumulations.

National Union Catalog, Pre-1956 Imprints: A Cumulative Author List Representing Library of Congress Printed Cards and Titles Reported by Other American Libraries. 754 vols. London: Mansell, 1968–81.

New Serial Titles: A Union List of Serials Commencing Publication after December 31, 1949. Washington, D.C.: Library of Congress, 1950–. Monthly, with cumulations.

Smits, R. *Half a Century of Soviet Serials, 1917–1968: A Bibliography and Union List of Serials Published in the U.S.S.R.* 2 vols. Washington, D.C.: Library of Congress, 1968.

Titus, E., ed. *Union List of Serials in Libraries of the United States and Canada.* 3d ed. 5 vols. New York: H. W. Wilson, 1965.

U.S. Library of Congress. *Cyrillic Union Catalog.* New York: Readex Micropring, 1963. 1,244 cards in 7 boxes.

U.S. Library of Congress. *Russian, Ukrainian, and Byelorussian Newspapers, 1917–1953: A Union List.* Comp. P. Horecky. Washington, D.C., 1953. 218 pp.

UNION LISTS—LOCAL

Art Serials: Union List of Art Periodicals and Serials in Research Libraries in the Washington, D.C., Metropolitan Area. Washington, D.C.: Washington Art Library Resources Committee, 1981.

Consortium Union List: Serials of Eight Colleges and Universities of the Washington, D.C., Metropolitan Area. 4th ed. Washington, D.C.: Metropolitan Washington Library Council, 1981.

Interlibrary Users Association. *Journal Holdings in the Washington-Baltimore Area.* 4th ed. Washington, D.C.: Library Council, Metropolitan Washington Council of Governments, 1981.

Law Librarians' Soviety, of Washington, D.C., Union List of Legal Periodicals Subcommittee, comp. *Union List of Legal Periodicals.* 4th ed. Washington, D.C., 1982.

Matthews, Donald N., ed. *Union List of Periodicals of the Members of the Washington Theological Consortium and Contributing Institutions.* 3d ed. Gettysburg, Pa., 1979.

OTHER GUIDES AND DIRECTORIES

American Library Directory. 34th ed. New York: Jacques Cattell Press, 1981.

Ayer Press. *'82 Ayer Directory of Publications.* Philadelphia, Pa.: Ayer Press, 1982.

Benton, Mildred. *A Study of Resources and Major Subject Holdings Available in U.S. Federal Libraries Maintaining Extensive or Unique Collections of Research Materials.* Washington, D.C.: Department of Health, Education, and Welfare, 1970.

Bhatt, Purnima M. *Scholars' Guide to Washington, D.C., for African Studies.* Washington, D.C.: Smithsonian Institution Press, 1980.

Calabrese, Teri, ed. *Federal Yellow Book.* Washington, D.C.: Washington Monitor, Inc., 1976–. Fully updated semiannually.

Congressional Staff Directory. Comp. Charles B. Brownson. Mount Vernon, Va.: Congressional Staff Directory, 1959–. Annual.

Dillon, Kenneth J. *Scholars' Guide to Washington, D.C., for Central and East European Studies.* Washington, D.C.: Smithsonian Institution Press, 1980.

Diplomatic List. Washington, D.C.: U.S. Department of State, 1982.

Dorr, Steven R. *Scholars' Guide to Washington, D.C., for Middle Eastern Studies*. Washington, D.C.: Smithsonian Institution Press, 1981.

Encyclopedia of Associations. Denise S. Akey, ed. 17th ed. 2 vols. in 3 pts. Detroit: Gale, 1982.

Grant, Steven A., and Brown, John H. *The Russian Empire and Soviet Union: A Guide to Manuscripts and Archival Materials in the United States*. Boston: G. K. Hall, 1981.

Green, Shirley L. *Pictoral Resources in the Washington, D.C., Area*. Washington, D.C.: Library of Congress, 1976.

Grow, Michael. *Scholars' Guide to Washington, D.C., for Latin American and Caribbean Studies*. Washington, D.C.: Smithsonian Institution Press, 1979.

Hamar, Philip M., ed. *A Guide to Archives and Manuscripts in the United States*. New Haven: Yale University Press, 1961.

Joyner, Nelson T., Jr. *Doing Business Abroad: Joyner's Guide to Official Washington*, 4th ed. Reston, Va.: Joyner and Associates, 1978.

Kim, Hong N. *Scholars' Guide to Washington, D.C., for East Asian Studies*. Washington, D.C.: Smithsonian Institution Press, 1979.

Library and Reference Facilities in the Area of the District of Columbia. Margaret S. Jennings, ed. 10th ed. Washington, D.C.: American Society for Information Science, 1979.

Mason, John Brown. *Research Resources: Annotated Guide to the Social Sciences*. 2 vols. Santa Barbara, Calif.: American Bibliographical Center, 1968–71.

Mayerchak, Patrick M. *Scholars' Guide to Washington, D.C., for Southeast Asian Studies*. Washington, D.C.: Smithsonian Institution Press, 1983.

Navon, Anita. *Research Materials for Slavists: U.S. Government Sources*. 2d rev. ed. Washington, D.C.: Association of Research Libraries, 1972.

Official Museum Directory. Washington, D.C.: American Association of Museums, 1982.

Rahim, Enayetur. *Scholars' Guide to Washington, D.C., for South Asian Studies*. Washington, D.C.: Smithsonian Institution Press, 1981.

Research Centers Directory. Robert C. Thomas and James A. Ruffner, 7th ed. Detroit: Gale, 1982.

Rowan, Bonnie G. *Scholars' Guide to Washington, D.C., for Film and Video Collections*. Washington, D.C.: Smithsonian Institution Press, 1980.

Schmeckebier, Laurence Frederick, and Roy B. Eastin. *Government Publications and Their Use*. Rev. ed. Washington, D.C.: Brookings Institution, 1969.

Sessions, Vivian S., ed. *Directory of Data Bases in the Social and Behavioral Sciences*. New York: Science Associates/International, 1974.

U.S. Congress. *Official Congressional Directory*. Washington, D.C.: Government Printing Office, 1809–. Annual.

U.S. Department of Health, Education, and Welfare. Office of Education. Institute of International Studies. *Inventory of Federal Programs Involving Educational Activities Concerned with Improving International Understanding and Cooperation*. Washington, D.C.: GPO, 1969.

U.S. Department of State. Office of External Research. *Foreign Affairs Research: A Directory of Governmental Resources*. Washington, D.C.: Government Printing Office, 1969.

U.S. Department of State. Office of Long-Range Assessments and Research. *Government-Sponsored Research on Foreign Affairs: Quarterly Report of Project Information*. Washington, D.C., 1981–.

U.S. International Communication Agency. *Foreign Correspondents in the United States*. Washington, D.C.: Foreign Press Center, 1981.

U.S. Library of Congress. National Referral Center for Science and Technology. *A Directory of Information Resources in the United States: Federal Government*. Washington, D.C., 1974.

_____. *A Directory of Information Resources in the United States: Social Sciences*. Rev. ed. Washington, D.C., 1973.

U.S. National Archives and Records Service. *United States Government Manual*. Washington, D.C., 1935–. Annual. (Title varies; sometimes with "Organization" before "Manual.")

U.S. National Historical Publications and Records Commission. *Directory of Archives and Manuscript Repositories*. Washington, D.C.: National Archives and Records Service, 1978.

Voluntary Transnational Cultural Exchange Organizations of the U.S.: A Selected List. Ed. David H. Smith. Washington, D.C.: Center for a Voluntary Society, 1974.

Washington Information Directory, 1982–1983. Washington, D.C.: Congressional Quarterly, 1982.

Washington V. Washington, D.C.: Potomac Books, 1979.

Wasserman, Paul, and Jean Morgan, eds. *Ethnic Information Sources of the United States*. Detroit: Gale, 1976.

Weber, Olga S. *North American Film and Video Directory*. New York: R. R. Bowker Co., 1976.

Williams, Martha, ed. *Computer-Readable Data Bases*. White Plains, N.Y.: Knowledge Industry Publications, 1982.

Wynar, Lubomyr R. *Encyclopedic Directory of Ethnic Newspapers and Periodicals in the United States*. 2d ed. Littleton, Colo.: Libraries Unlimited, 1976.

Wynar, Lubomyr R., with Lois Buttlar and Anna T. Wynar. *Encyclopedic Directory of Ethnic Organizations in the United States*. Littleton, Colo.: Libraries Unlimited, 1975.

Wynar, Lubomyr R., and Lois Buttlar. *Guide to Ethnic Museums, Libraries, and Archives in the United States*. Kent, Ohio: Center for Ethnic Publications, School of Library Science, Kent State University, 1978.

Zlotnik, Marc D. *A Scholars' Guide to Sources of Support for Research in Russian and Soviet Studies*. Washington, D.C.: Kennan Institute for Advanced Russian Studies, Woodrow Wilson International Center for Scholars, 1979.

INDEXES

I Personal Papers Index

II Library Subject-Strength Index

This index identifies the most useful library collections in the Washington, D.C., area by subject. The evaluations (A, B, and C/D) presented here are based on the criteria explained at the beginning of Section A and summarized below:

A—comprehensive collection of primary and secondary sources (Library of Congress collection to serve as a standard of evaluation)
B—substantial collection of primary and secondary sources; sufficient for some original research (holdings of roughly one-tenth those of the Library of Congress)
C/D—substantial collection of secondary and primary sources, many in Russian; sufficient to support graduate instruction (holdings of roughly one-half those of B collection) and collection of secondary and primary sources, some in Russian; sufficient to support undergraduate instruction (holdings of roughly one-quarter those of B collection)

The standard Library of Congress subject headings have been used for categorization. Some valuable specialized collections have been included here even though their rating is based on a subcategory of one of the major headings. The subject headings are listed below in the same order as they appear in Section A.

Philosophy and Religion
A collections: A37
B collections: A39, A61
C/D collections: A6, A10, A17, A23, A24, A49

History
A collections: A37, A57
B collections: A35, A39
C/D collections: A6, A8, A10, A14, A17, A23, A24, A30, A38

Geography and Ethnography
A collections: A37
B collections: A16, A46, A50, A57
C/D collections: A6, A10, A14, A23, A24, A39, A61

Economics
A collections: A14, A31, A33, A37, A40, A57
B collections: A12, A34, A39, A55, A59, A61
C/D collections: A6, A10, A12, A23, A24, A29, A30, A36

Sociology
A collections: A37, A48
B collections: A2, A14, A29, A61
C/D collections: A6, A10, A23, A24, A39, A57

Politics and Government
A collections: A18, A37, A57
B collections: A35, A39, A61
C/D collections: A6, A10, A14, A23, A24, A30

Foreign Relations
A collections: A37, A61
B collections: A14, A35, A39, A55, A56, A57
C/D collections: A6, A8, A10, A15, A23, A24, A28, A30

Law
A collections: A37
C/D collections: A14, A17, A23, A24, A39, A61

Education
A collections: A21, A37
B collections: A14, A39, A47, A57, A61
C/D collections: A6, A10, A23, A24, A30

Fine Arts
A collections: A37
B collections: A17, A27, A29, A39
C/D collections: A6, A10, A23, A24, A29, A58, A61

Language
A collections: A37, A39
B collections: A23, A24
C/D collections: A6, A10, A30, A38, A57, A58, A61

Literature
A collections: A37
B collections: A39
C/D collections: A6, A10, A23, A24, A30, A38, A57, A61

Military Affairs
A collections: A37
B collections: A14, A57, A61
C/D collections: A6, A8, A23, A24, A39

Bibliography, Reference, and General
A collections: A37
B collections: A35, A39
C/D collections: A14, A23, A24, A57, A61

Ukrainians
A collections: A37
B collections: A35
C/D collections: A6, A10, A17, A23, A24, A39, A40, A57, A61

Byelorussians
A collections: A37
B collections: A39
C/D collections: A23, A24, A40, A57, A61

Baltic Nationalities
A collections: A37
C/D collections: A6, A10, A23, A24, A39, A40, A48, A57, A61

Caucasian Nationalities
A collections: A37
B collections: A57
C/D collections: A6, A10, A17, A23, A24, A39, A40, A61

Central Asian Nationalities
A collections: A37
B collections: A57
C/D collections: A6, A10, A23, A24, A30, A39, A61

Siberian Nationalities
A collections: A37
B collections: A57
C/D collections: A6, A10, A23, A24, A30, A39, A61

III   Subject Index

Entry symbols correspond to the folowing sections of the text:

A—Libraries
B—Archives and Manuscript Depositories
C—Museums, Galleries, and Art Collections
D—Collections of Music and Other Sound Recordings
E—Map Collections
F—Film Collections (Still Photographs and Motion Pictures)
G—Data Banks
H—Research Center
J—Academic Programs
K—U.S. Government Agencies
L—Government Agencies (Soviet, International, and Other)
M—Associations (Academic, Professional, and Cultural)
N—Cultural-Exchange Organizations
P—Religious Organizations
Q—Publications and Media

Agriculture: A6, A10, A14, A24, A30, A31, A34, A36, A37, A39, A40, A57, A61, E6, F6, F7, K1, L7, N5, Q19
Alaska (Russian America): A6, A10, A23, A24, A30, A37, A39, A57, A61, B4, B6, B11
Anthropology: A6, A10, A23, A24, A37, A38, A39, A46, A50, A57, A61, B11, C10, C11, D3, E7, F10, K19, K27, K31, M2
Archaeology: A6, A10, A13, A23, A37, A39, A50, A57, A61, K26, K31
Architecture and Sculpture: A4, A6, A10, A17, A23, A24, A27, A29, A37, A39, A45, A61, B2, B4, C3, C4, F2, F7, M62, J11
Arctic and Antarctic: A6, A10, A23, A24, A30, A37, A39, A57, A61, B6, K27, K29, K31, M47
Armenians: A6, A10, A17, A23, A24, A37, A39, A40, A57, A58, A61, B3, C11, F2, H13, M21, M22, P1, P2, P3, Q22
Art. *See* Decorative Art; Music; Painting and Graphic Art; Sculpture; Theater and Dance; Ukrainians.
Astronomy: A37, A41, A52, K25

IV Name Index
(Organizations and Institutions)

Entry symbols correspond to the following sections of the text:

A—Libraries
B—Archives and Manuscript Depositories
C—Museums, Galleries, and Art Collections
D—Collections of Music and Other Sound Recordings
E—Map Collections
F—Film Collections (Still Photographs and Motions Pictures)
G—Data Banks
H—Research Centers
J—Academic Programs
K—U.S. Government Agencies
L—Government Agencies (Soviet, International, and Other)
M—Associations (Academic, Professional, and Cultural)
N—Cultural Exchange Organizations
P—Religious Organizations
Q—Publications and Media

The author, Steven A. Grant, was born in Portland, Oregon, in 1944. He attended Pomona College (B.A. 1966) and Harvard University (Ph.D. 1973). He has taught at George Washington University in Washington, D.C., and currently is senior Soviet analyst for the Office of Research, U.S. Information Agency. Among his publications are *The Russian Empire and Soviet Union: A Guide to Manuscripts and Archival Materials in the United States* (with John H. Brown, 1981), *Soviet Housing and Urban Design* (editor, 1980), and articles in *Slavic Review, Slavonic and East European Review*, and *Kritika*.

Mark H. Teeter, who revised the first half of this *Guide*, received his B.A. in Russian history from Stanford University in 1971 and his M.A. in Russian from San Francisco State University in 1975. He is presently writing his doctoral dissertation for the Russian Area Studies Program at Georgetown University. As a research associate at the Wilson Center's Kennan Institute for Advanced Russian Studies (1979–82), he coauthored the *Soviet Research Institutes Project. Volume III: The Humanities* (Washington: U.S.I.C.A., 1981).

Bradford P. Johnson, who revised the second half of this *Guide* and was responsible for final preparation of the entire manuscript, received his B.A. in Russian literature from Middlebury College in 1977 and his M.A. in Russian language and literature from University of Massachusetts at Amherst in 1981. He has taught the Russian language at both the secondary and university levels. Currently he is pursuing a law degree at Antioch School of Law in Washington, D.C., while continuing his association with the Wilson Center's Kennan Institute for Advanced Russian Studies.

Series editor Zdeněk V. David has been librarian of the Wilson Center since 1974. Previously, he taught history at Princeton University and the University of Michigan, Ann Arbor, and library science at Rutgers University. He served as Slavic bibliographer of the Princeton University Library from 1966 to 1974.